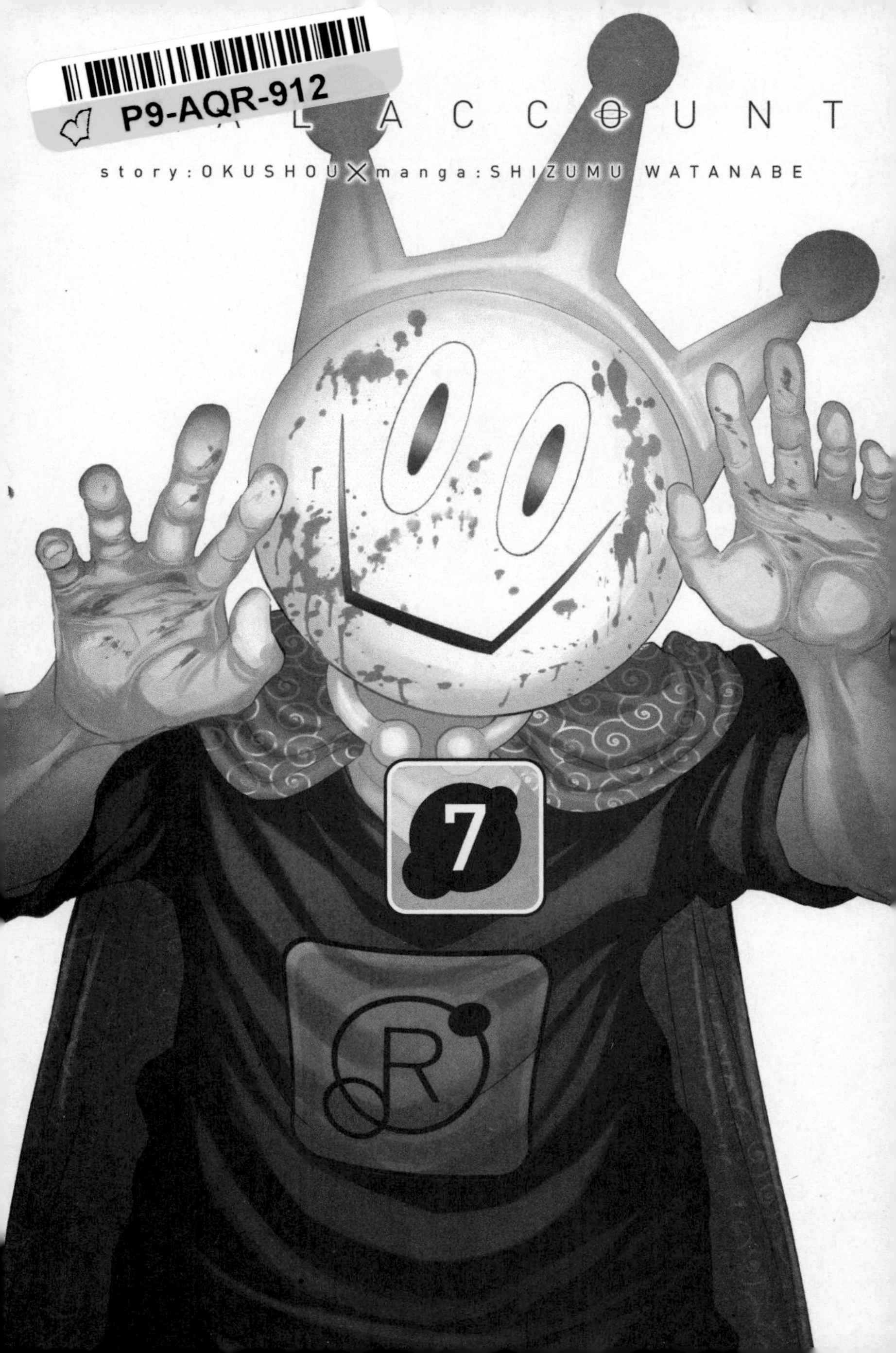
AL ACCOUNT
story: OKUSHOU × manga: SHIZUMU WATANABE
7

April 25, 20XX, just before 7:00 P.M.—Out of nowhere, 10,000 people were sucked into the world of Real Account! The victims soon found themselves participants in a series of mercilessly cruel games where they were forced to fight for their lives!

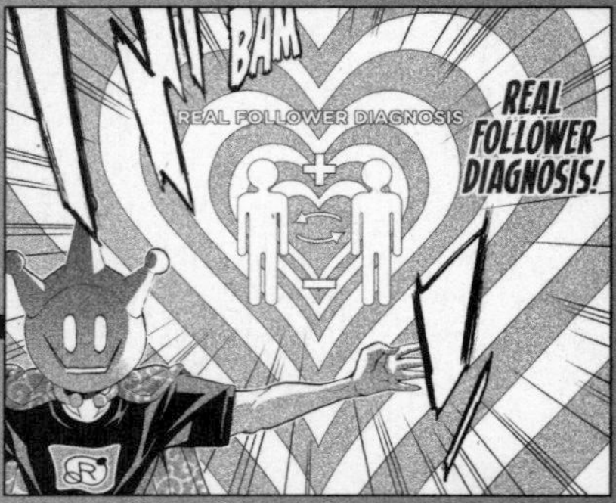
BAM
REAL FOLLOWER DIAGNOSIS
REAL FOLLOWER DIAGNOSIS!

▲ Players die if their follower count hits zero. Many unfollows ensued as people feared for their own lives. *[Time limit: 3 min.]*

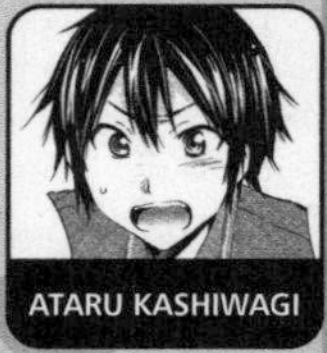
ATARU KASHIWAGI

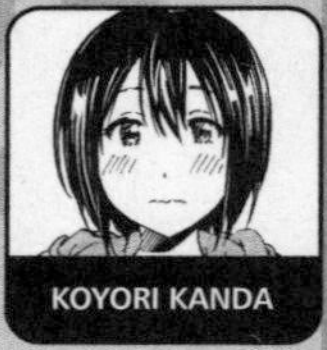
KOYORI KANDA

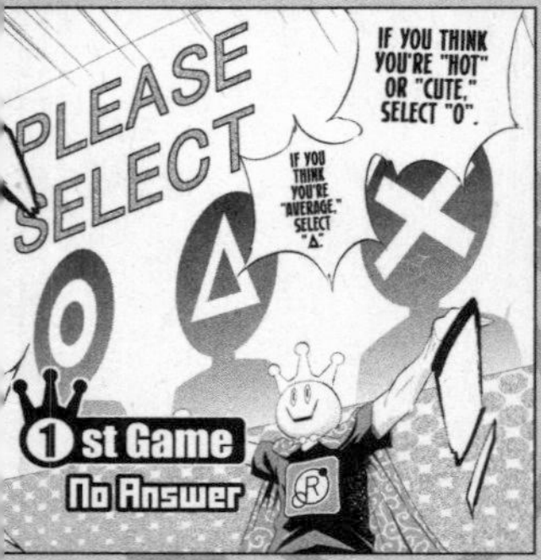
PLEASE SELECT
IF YOU THINK YOU'RE "HOT" OR "CUTE," SELECT "O".
IF YOU THINK YOU'RE "AVERAGE," SELECT "Δ".
1st Game
No Answer

▲ **Extra rule:** You can hide a single tweett. If someone guesses it, you die; if they get it wrong, they die. *[Time limit: 10 min.]*

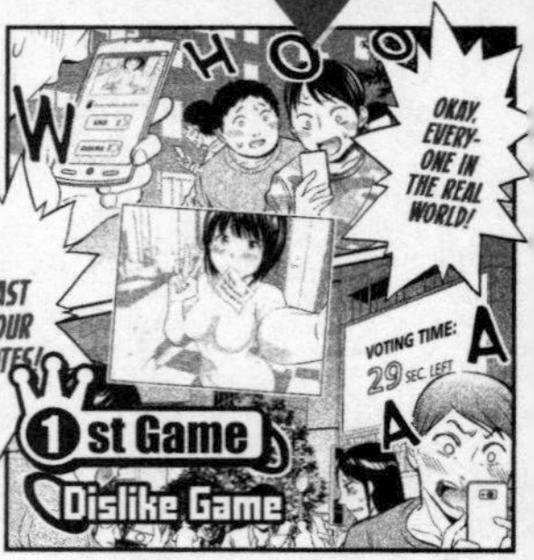
WHOOA
OKAY, EVERY-ONE IN THE REAL WORLD!
CAST YOUR VOTES!
VOTING TIME: 29 SEC. LEFT
A
A
1st Game
Dislike Game

▲ Real-world judges rate a picture randomly selected from players' smartphones.

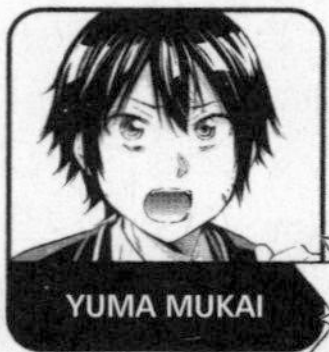
YUMA MUKAI

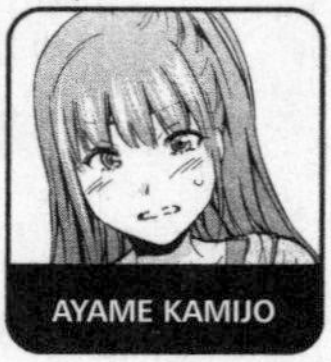
AYAME KAMIJO

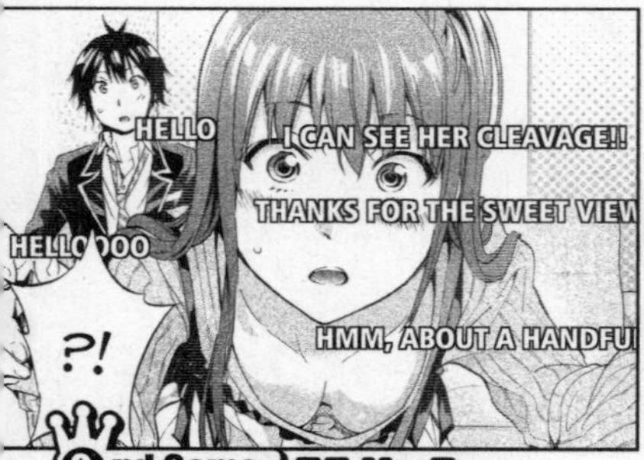
HELLO
I CAN SEE HER CLEAVAGE!!
THANKS FOR THE SWEET VIEW
HELLOOOO
?!
HMM, ABOUT A HANDFU

2nd Game R.A. Live Game

▲ Teams of two players stage a live broadcast, earning 100 yen in E-money for every viewer at the end. If you can't earn at least 100 viewers, you're dead. *[Time limit: 30 min.]*

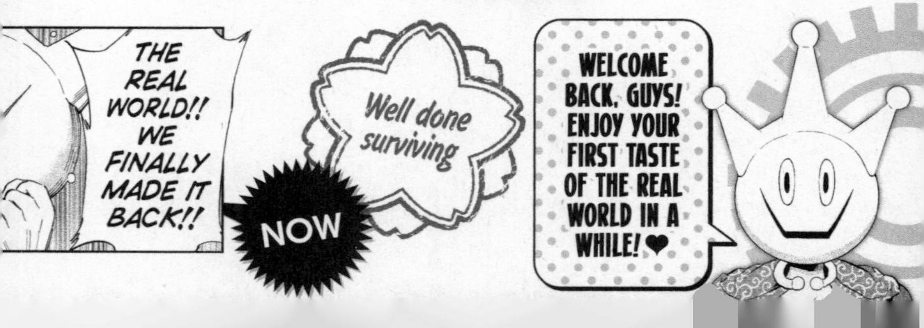
WELCOME BACK, GUYS! ENJOY YOUR FIRST TASTE OF THE REAL WORLD IN A WHILE! ❤
Well done surviving
NOW
THE REAL WORLD!! WE FINALLY MADE IT BACK!!

ATARU & YUMA'S

Deadly Road of Cruelty through REAL ACCOUNT

2nd Game
RT Game

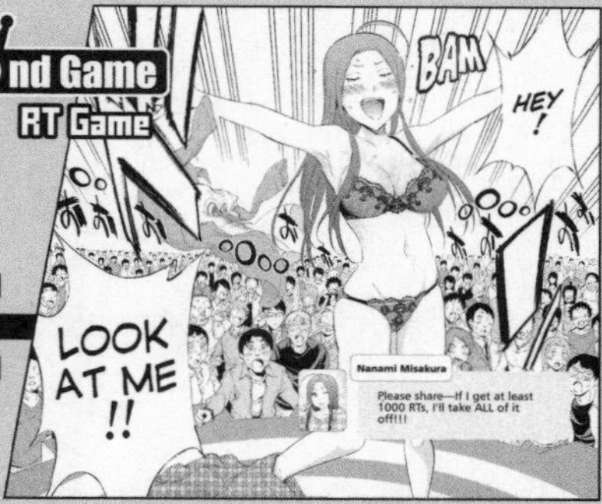
BAM
HEY!
LOOK AT ME!!
Nanami Misakura
Please share—If I get at least 1000 RTs, I'll take ALL of it off!!!

▲ An RT contest fought with a single tweett. Players earn 100 yen in E-money per RT; players with zero RTs are killed. *[Time limit: 10 min.]*

3rd Game
Dark History Trials

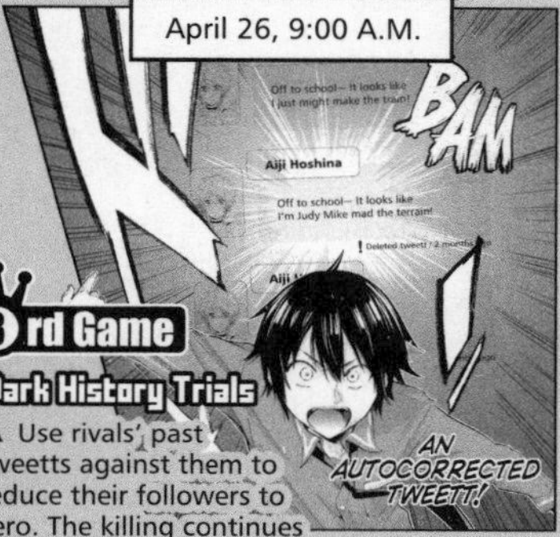
April 26, 9:00 A.M.
Off to school— It looks like I just might make the train!
BAM
Aiji Hoshina
Off to school— It looks like I'm Judy Mike mad the terrain!
Deleted tweett / 2 months
AN AUTOCORRECTED TWEETT!

▲ Use rivals' past tweetts against them to reduce their followers to zero. The killing continues until the original team of ten is cut down to three. *[Time limit: 30 min.]*

Extra rule:

You can hide a single tweett. If someone guesses it, you die; if they get it wrong, they die. *[Time limit: 10 min.]*

3rd Game
Appease the Attention Seeker

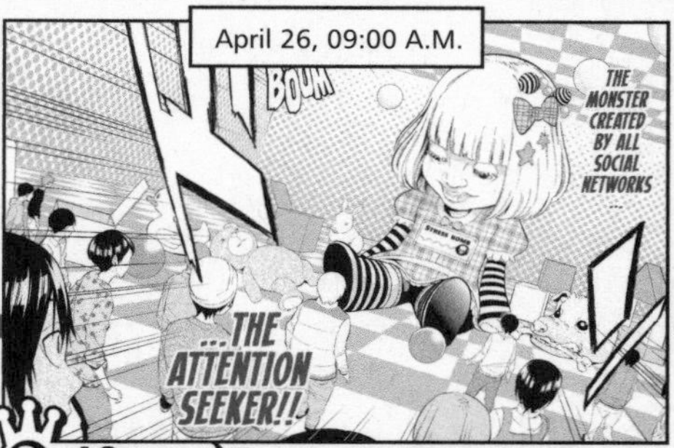
April 26, 09:00 A.M.
BOUM
THE MONSTER CREATED BY ALL SOCIAL NETWORKS...
...THE ATTENTION SEEKER!!

▲ "Appease" the monster and find the exit to escape the room, which explodes when time expires. *[Time limit: 30 min.]*

4th Game
Operation: Reply or Regret

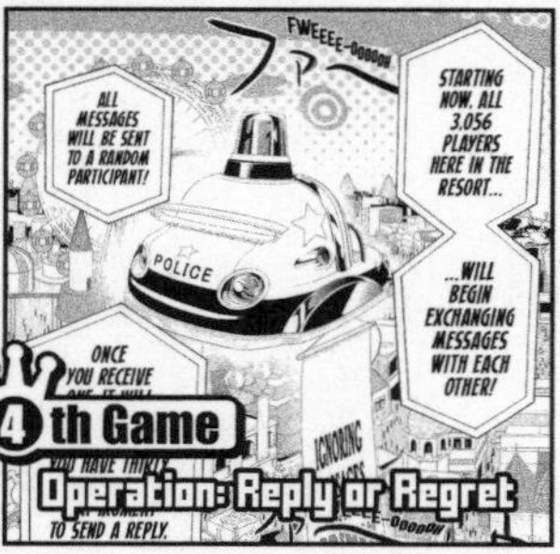
FWEEEE-OOOOOH
STARTING NOW, ALL 3,056 PLAYERS HERE IN THE RESORT...
ALL MESSAGES WILL BE SENT TO A RANDOM PARTICIPANT!
...WILL BEGIN EXCHANGING MESSAGES WITH EACH OTHER!
POLICE
ONCE YOU RECEIVE
TO SEND A REPLY.
IGNORING

▲ Receive a message, and you must reply within 30 seconds or die on the spot. The game ends if the player count's cut in half or someone sends the "Completed!" stamp.

5th Game
The Great Flamer Festival

► Players use the "fuel" in their phone to trigger net drama and burn down a festival tower. The crazier the content, the hotter the fire! *[Time limit: 60 min.]*

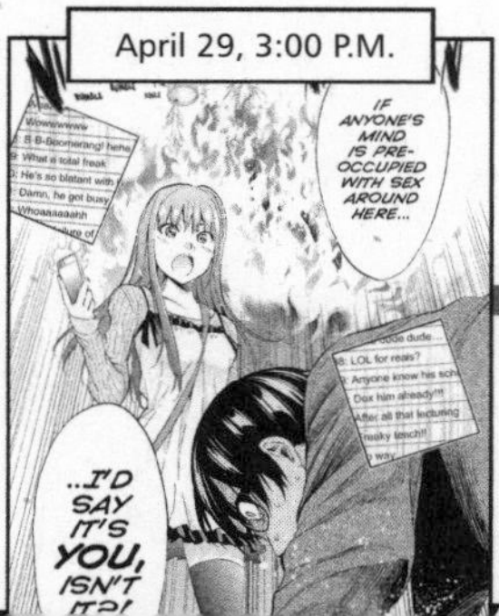
April 29, 3:00 P.M.
IF ANYONE'S MIND IS PRE-OCCUPIED WITH SEX AROUND HERE...
S: B-Boomerang! hehe
S: What a total freak
D: He's so blatant with
Damn, he got busy
B: LOL for reals?
D: Anyone know his sch
Dox him already!!!
After all that lecturing
freaky tench!!
...I'D SAY IT'S YOU, ISN'T

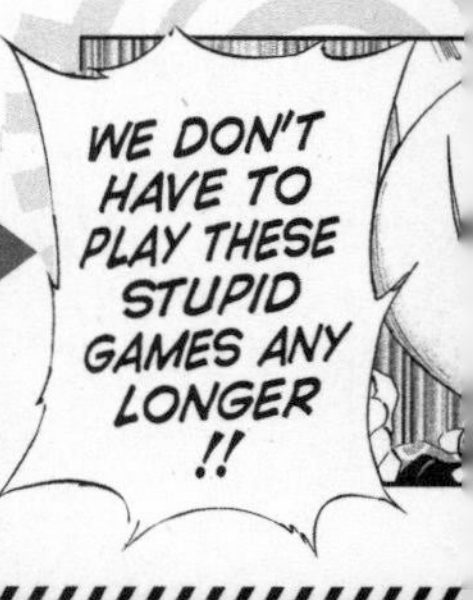
WE DON'T HAVE TO PLAY THESE STUPID GAMES ANY LONGER!!

CONTENTS

STORY

In the 5th game, "The Great Flamer Festival," Yuma initially refused to look into the smartphones of his competitors—only to have Mizuki Kurashina reveal that Yuma's goody-goody behavior was just a front for his hypocritical cynicism. This triggers momentous changes in Yuma's personality. He reveals Mizuki's trauma at the hands of his mother, cruelly pounding at his deepest emotional scars. Meanwhile, Nanako, investigating the drama with Imari, discovers a photo that links Yuma with the husband-and-wife team that operated a suspicious laboratory. The revelation is blogged about, allowing Yuma to survive the game—but right afterward, he falls unconscious. When he awakes, he finds himself and the other players back in the real world—all dressed as Marbles...

ACCOUNT 32
Social-Network Tag

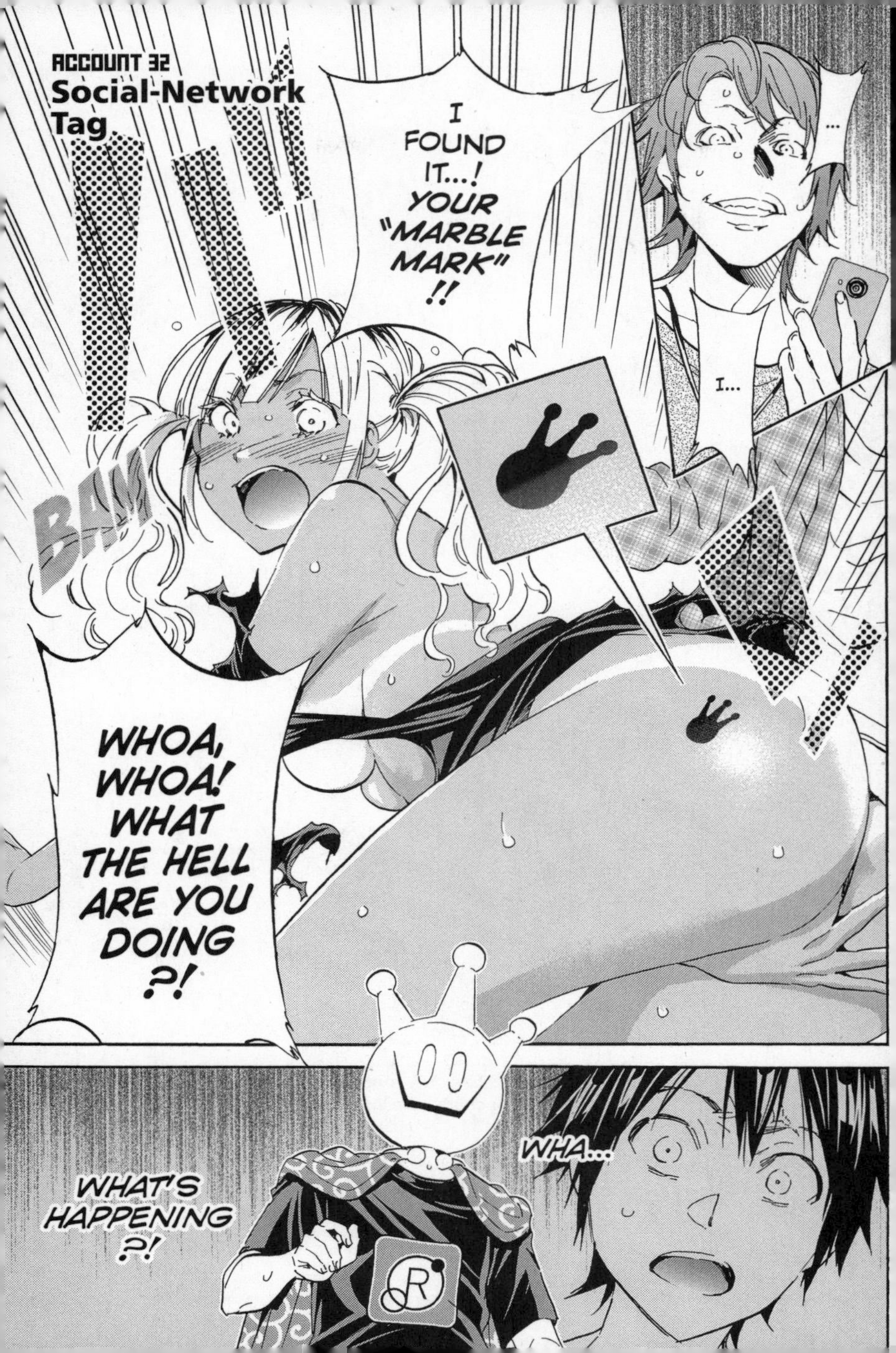
...
I...
I FOUND IT...! YOUR "MARBLE MARK" !!
BAM
WHOA, WHOA! WHAT THE HELL ARE YOU DOING ?!
WHA...
WHAT'S HAPPENING ?!

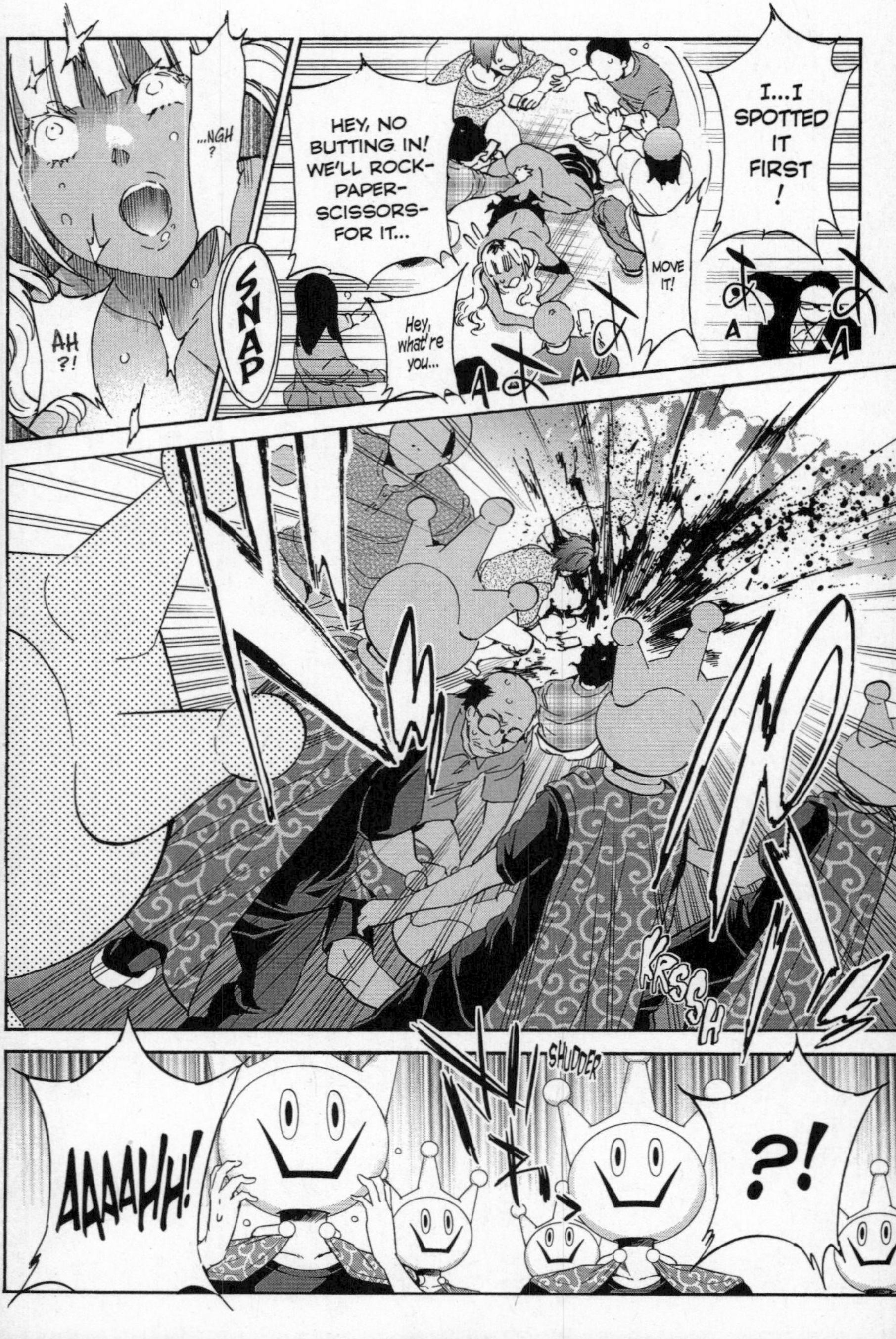
I...I SPOTTED IT FIRST!
A
A
MOVE IT!
A
A
Hey, what're you...
HEY, NO BUTTING IN! WE'LL ROCK-PAPER-SCISSORS-FOR IT...
SNAP
...NGH?
AH?!
KRSSH
?!
SHUDDER
AAAAHH!

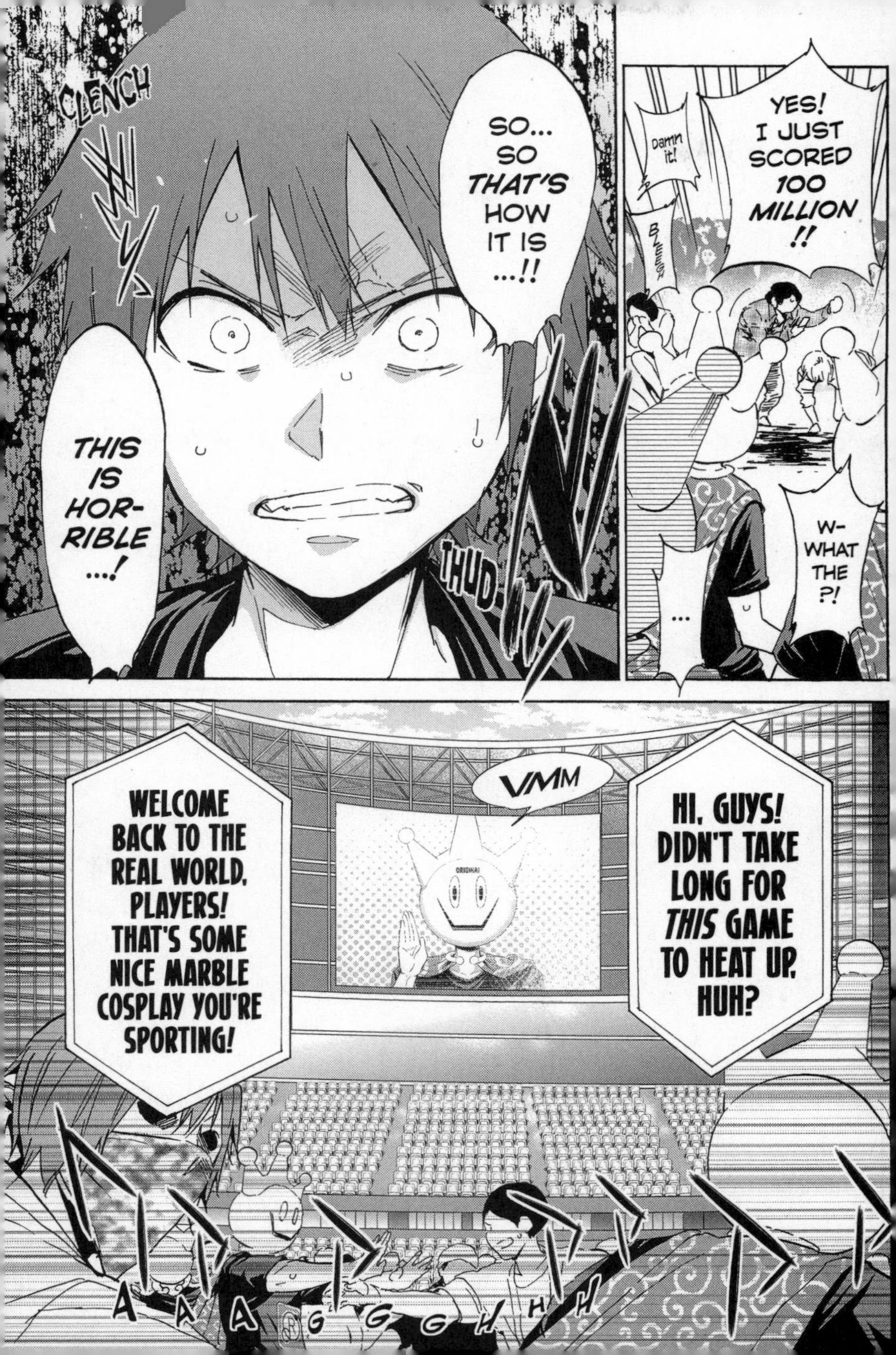
YES! I JUST SCORED 100 MILLION!!
Damn it!
BLEEGH
W-WHAT THE?!
...
CLENCH
SO... SO THAT'S HOW IT IS...!!
THIS IS HOR-RIBLE...!
THUD
VMM
HI, GUYS! DIDN'T TAKE LONG FOR THIS GAME TO HEAT UP, HUH?
WELCOME BACK TO THE REAL WORLD, PLAYERS! THAT'S SOME NICE MARBLE COSPLAY YOU'RE SPORTING!
AAAGGGHHH

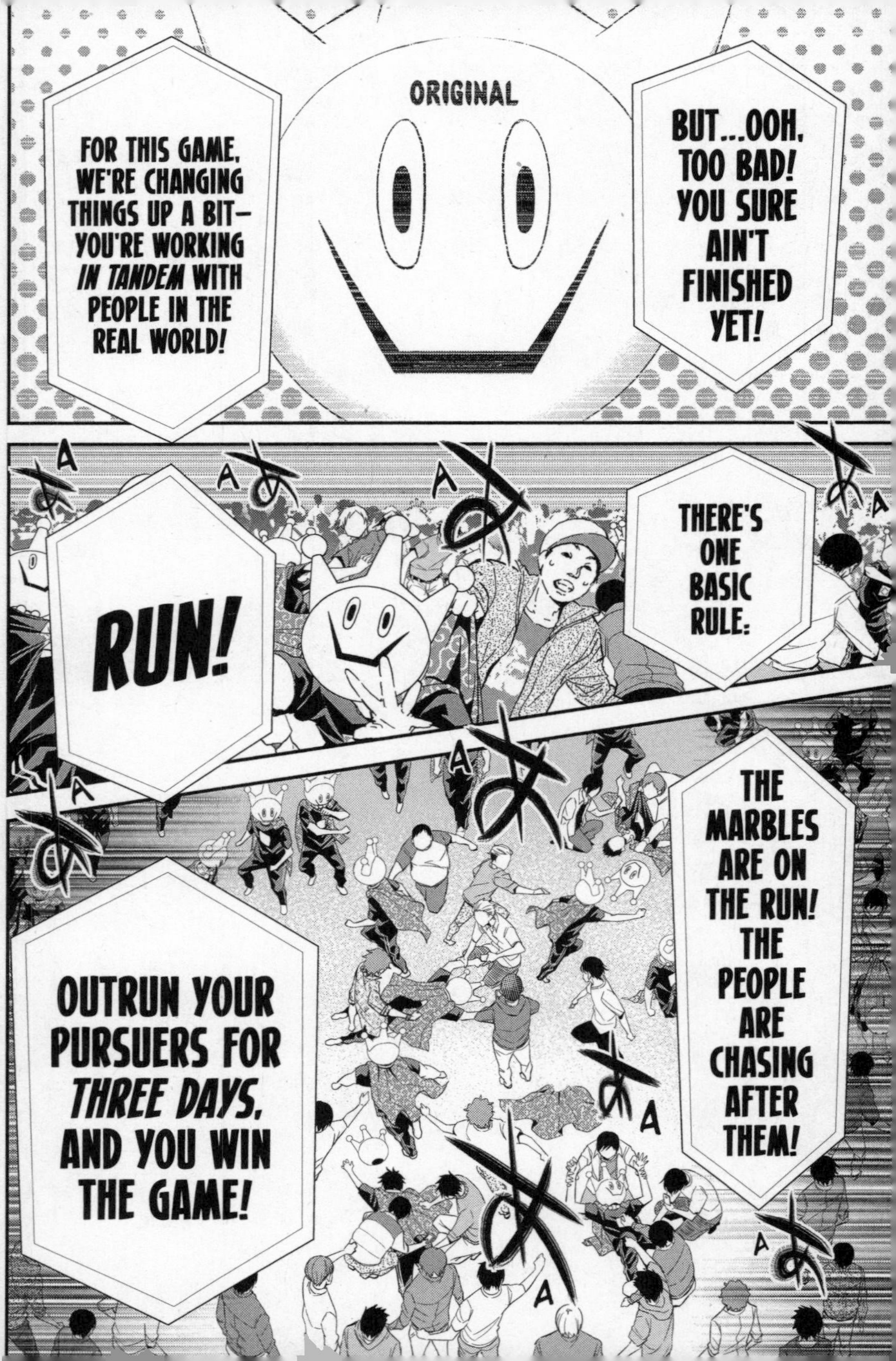
ORIGINAL
BUT...OOH, TOO BAD! YOU SURE AIN'T FINISHED YET!
FOR THIS GAME, WE'RE CHANGING THINGS UP A BIT—YOU'RE WORKING *IN TANDEM* WITH PEOPLE IN THE REAL WORLD!
THERE'S ONE BASIC RULE:
RUN!
THE MARBLES ARE ON THE RUN! THE PEOPLE ARE CHASING AFTER THEM!
OUTRUN YOUR PURSUERS FOR *THREE DAYS*, AND YOU WIN THE GAME!

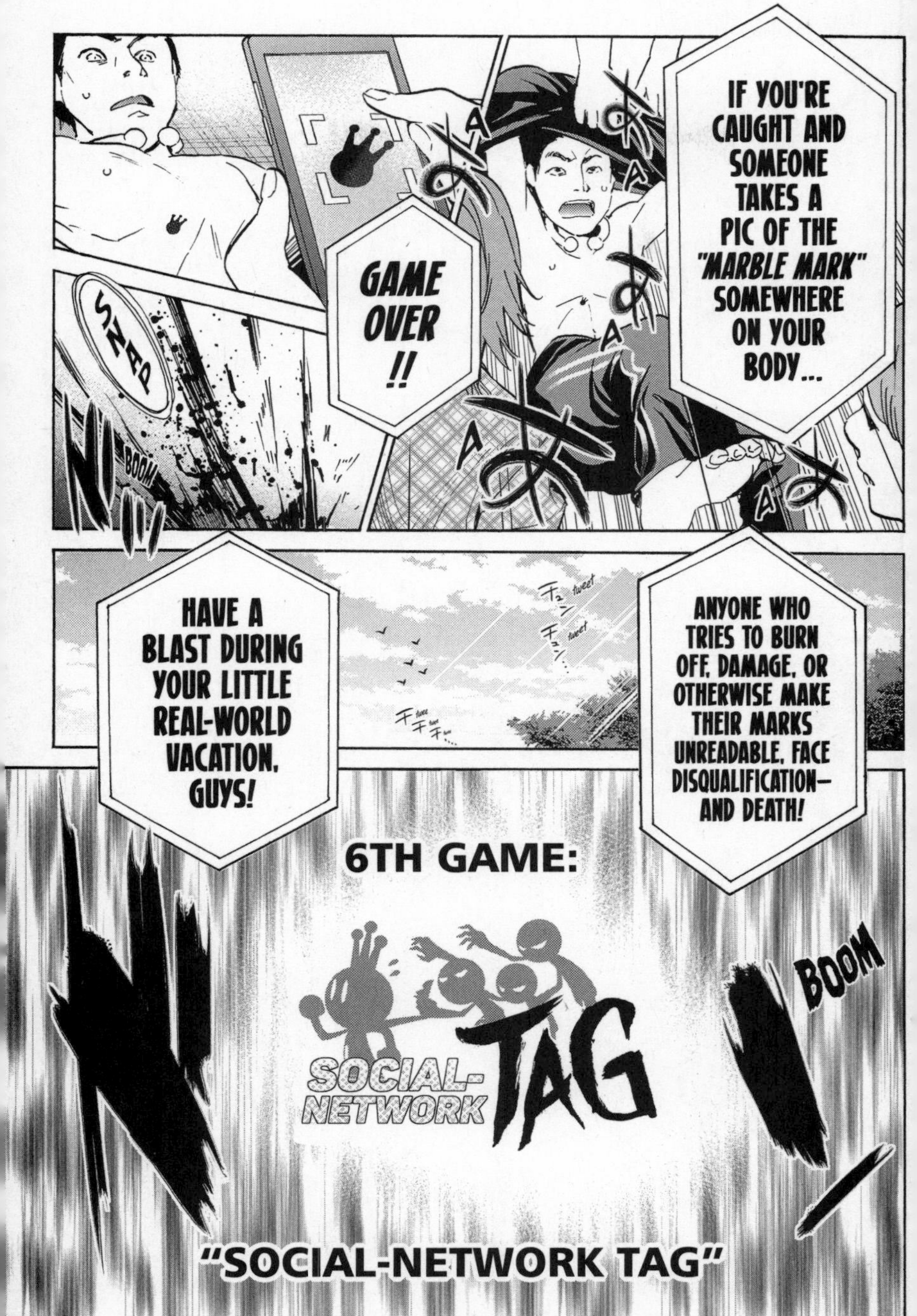
IF YOU'RE CAUGHT AND SOMEONE TAKES A PIC OF THE "MARBLE MARK" SOMEWHERE ON YOUR BODY...
A
A
A
A
A
GAME OVER!!
BOOM
ANYONE WHO TRIES TO BURN OFF, DAMAGE, OR OTHERWISE MAKE THEIR MARKS UNREADABLE, FACE DISQUALIFICATION—AND DEATH!
tweet
tweet
HAVE A BLAST DURING YOUR LITTLE REAL-WORLD VACATION, GUYS!
6TH GAME:
BOOM
SOCIAL-NETWORK TAG
"SOCIAL-NETWORK TAG"

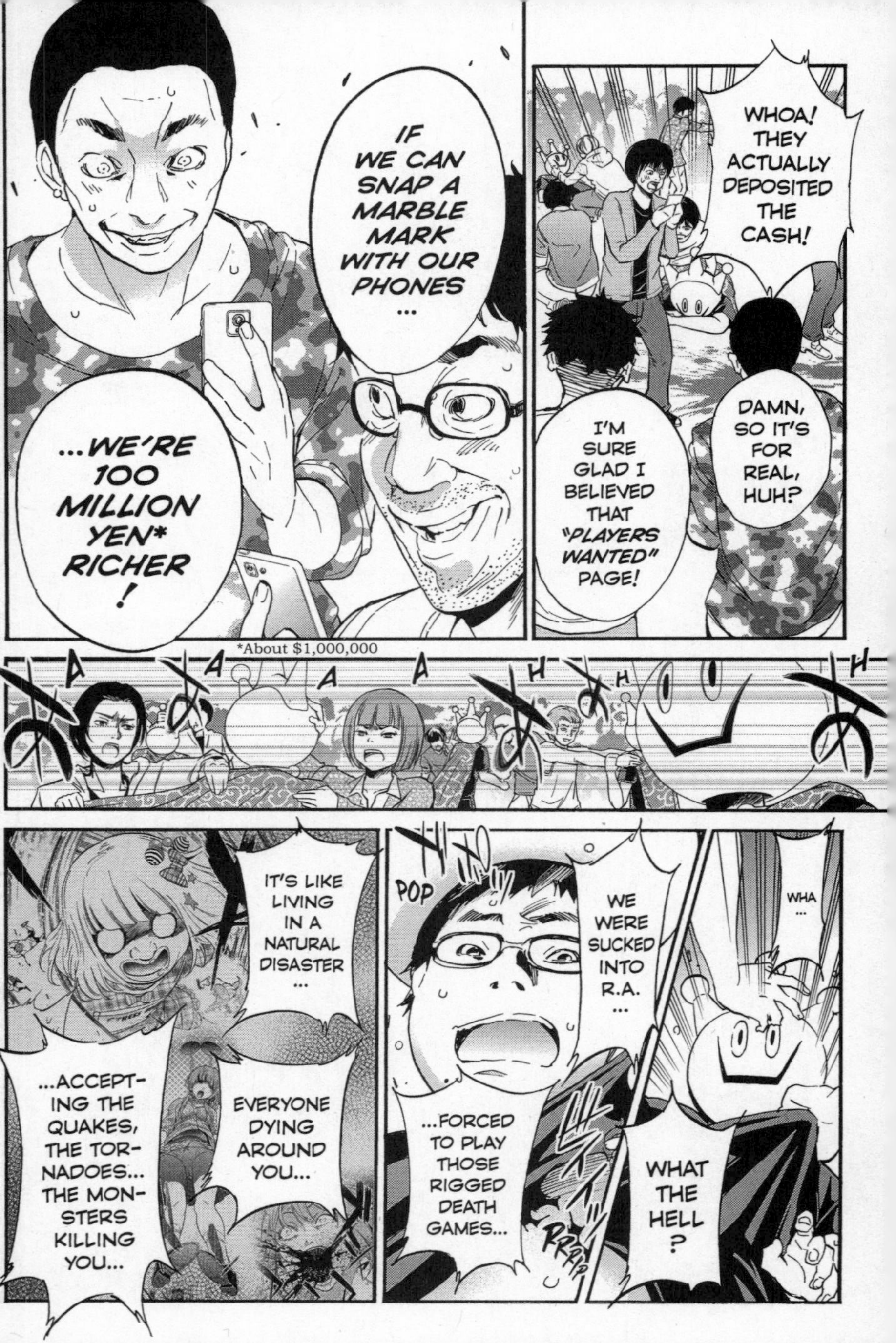
WHOA! THEY ACTUALLY DEPOSITED THE CASH!
DAMN, SO IT'S FOR REAL, HUH?
I'M SURE GLAD I BELIEVED THAT "PLAYERS WANTED" PAGE!
IF WE CAN SNAP A MARBLE MARK WITH OUR PHONES ...
...WE'RE 100 MILLION YEN* RICHER!
*About $1,000,000
WHA ...
POP
WE WERE SUCKED INTO R.A. ...
WHAT THE HELL ?
...FORCED TO PLAY THOSE RIGGED DEATH GAMES...
RRRIP
IT'S LIKE LIVING IN A NATURAL DISASTER ...
EVERYONE DYING AROUND YOU...
...ACCEPTING THE QUAKES, THE TORNADOES... THE MONSTERS KILLING YOU...

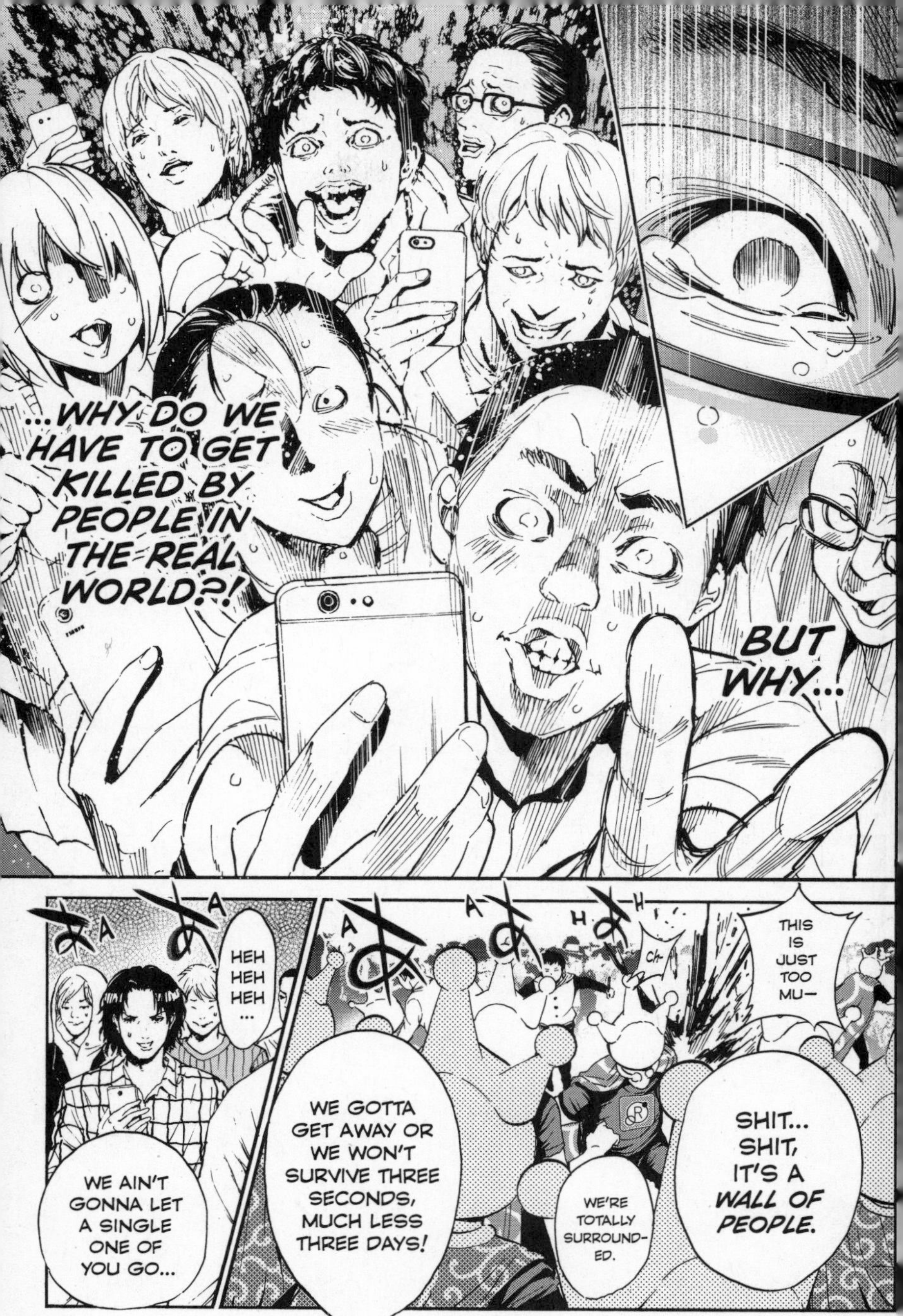
BUT WHY...
...WHY DO WE HAVE TO GET KILLED BY PEOPLE IN THE REAL WORLD?!
THIS IS JUST TOO MU—
Ch-
SHIT... SHIT, IT'S A *WALL OF PEOPLE.*
WE'RE TOTALLY SURROUND-ED.
WE GOTTA GET AWAY OR WE WON'T SURVIVE THREE SECONDS, MUCH LESS THREE DAYS!
HEH HEH HEH ...
WE AIN'T GONNA LET A SINGLE ONE OF YOU GO...

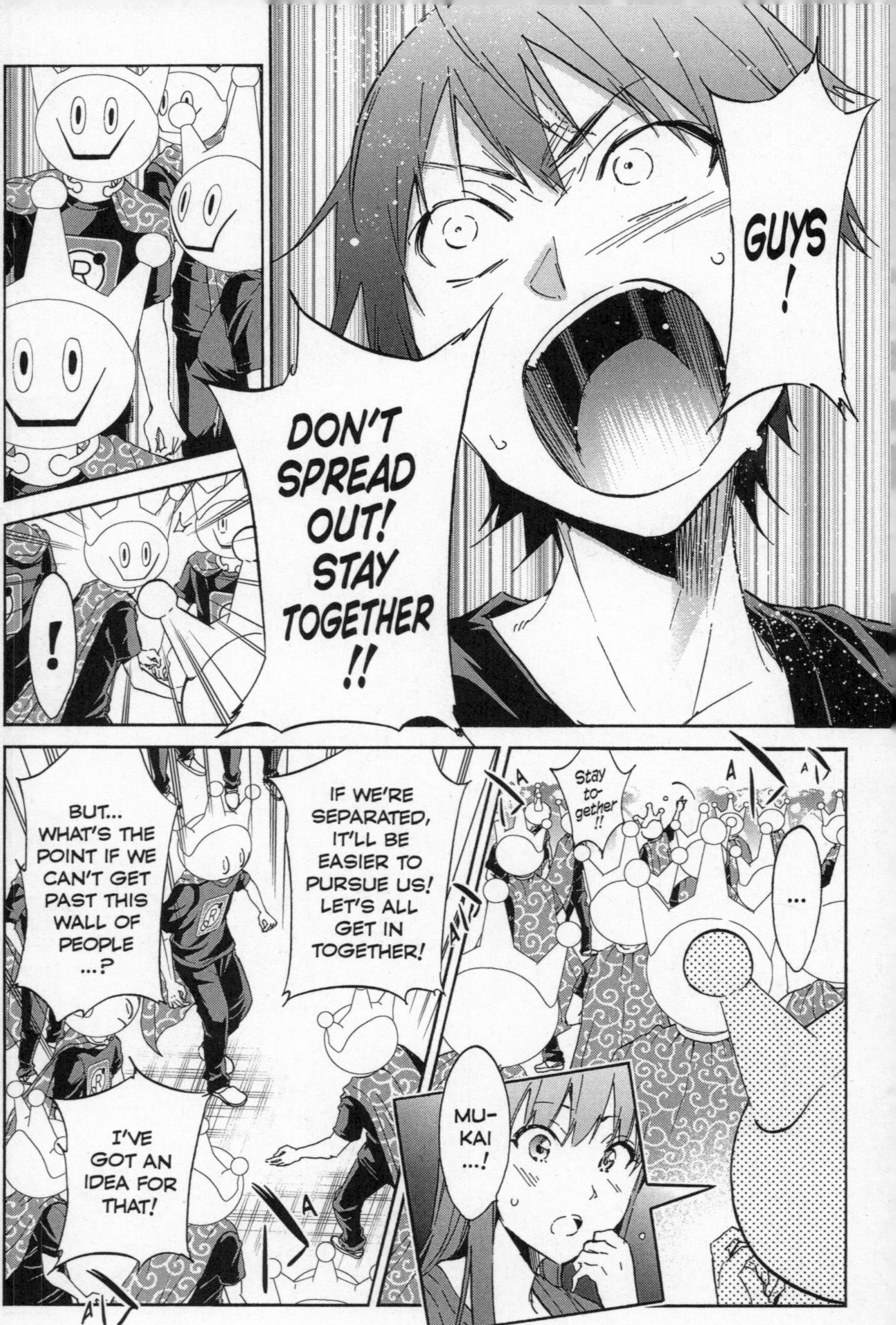
GUYS!
DON'T SPREAD OUT! STAY TOGETHER!!
!
Stay to-gether!!
...
MU-KAI...!
IF WE'RE SEPARATED, IT'LL BE EASIER TO PURSUE US! LET'S ALL GET IN TOGETHER!
BUT... WHAT'S THE POINT IF WE CAN'T GET PAST THIS WALL OF PEOPLE ...?
I'VE GOT AN IDEA FOR THAT!

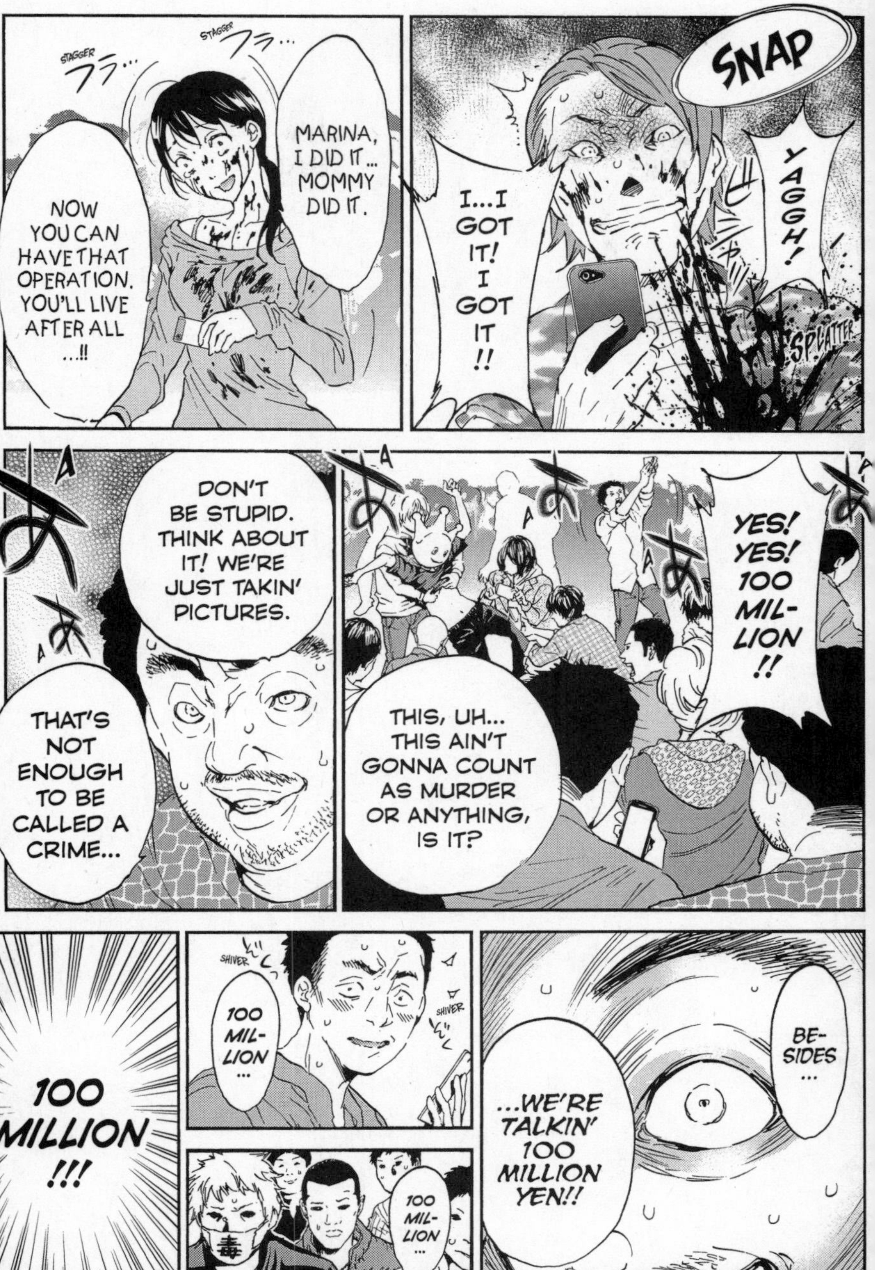
SNAP
YAGGH!
I...I GOT IT! I GOT IT!!
SPLATTER
STAGGER フラ...
MARINA, I DID IT... MOMMY DID IT.
STAGGER フラ...
NOW YOU CAN HAVE THAT OPERATION. YOU'LL LIVE AFTER ALL ...!!
YES! YES! 100 MIL-LION!!
A あ
THIS, UH... THIS AIN'T GONNA COUNT AS MURDER OR ANYTHING, IS IT?
A あ
DON'T BE STUPID. THINK ABOUT IT! WE'RE JUST TAKIN' PICTURES.
THAT'S NOT ENOUGH TO BE CALLED A CRIME...
BE-SIDES ...
...WE'RE TALKIN' 100 MILLION YEN!!
SHIVER
100 MIL-LION ...
SHIVER
100 MIL-LION ...
100 MILLION !!!
FACE MASK: Poison

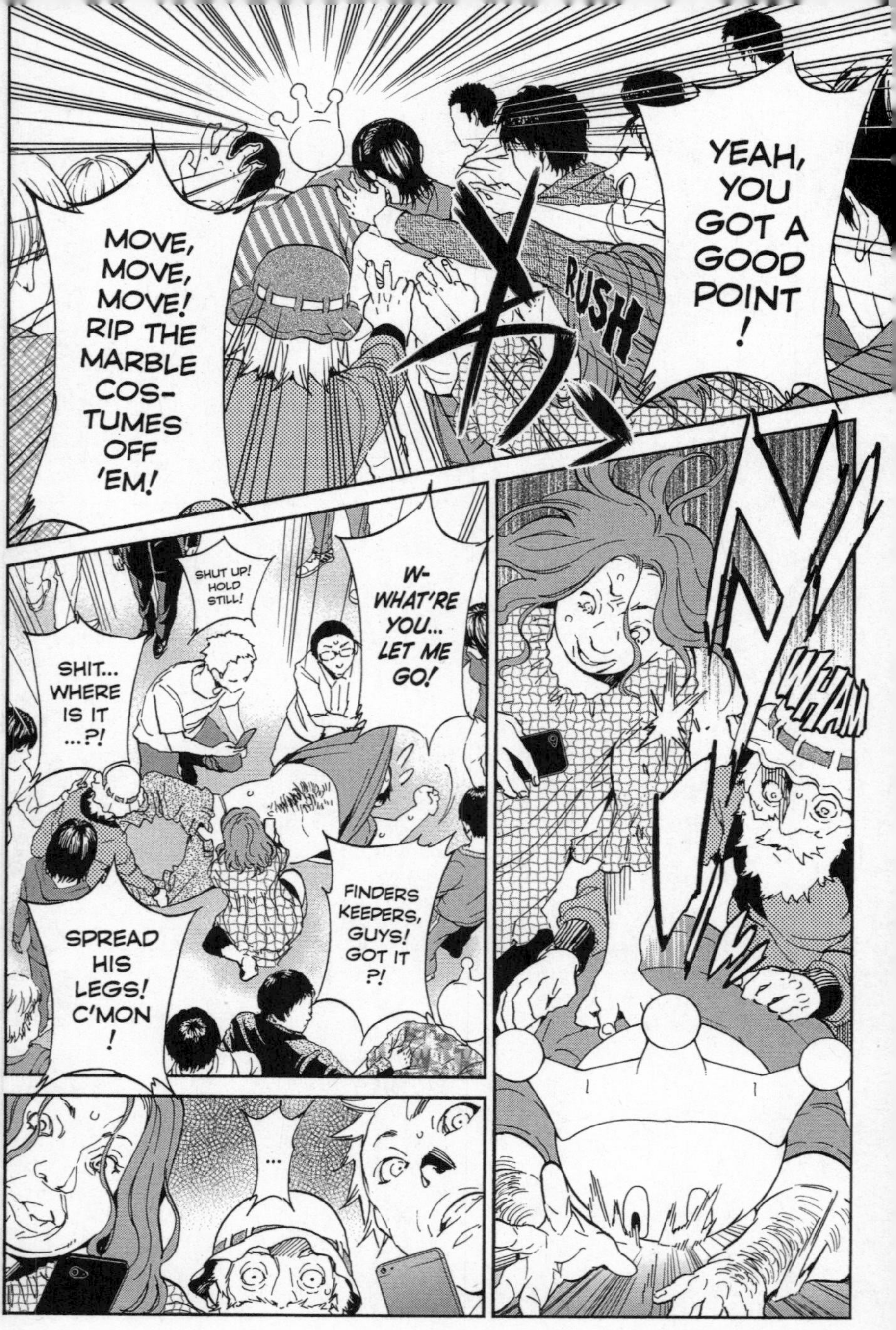
YEAH, YOU GOT A GOOD POINT!
RUSH
MOVE, MOVE, MOVE! RIP THE MARBLE COS-TUMES OFF 'EM!
WHAM
W-WHAT'RE YOU... LET ME GO!
SHUT UP! HOLD STILL!
SHIT... WHERE IS IT ...?!
FINDERS KEEPERS, GUYS! GOT IT ?!
SPREAD HIS LEGS! C'MON!
...

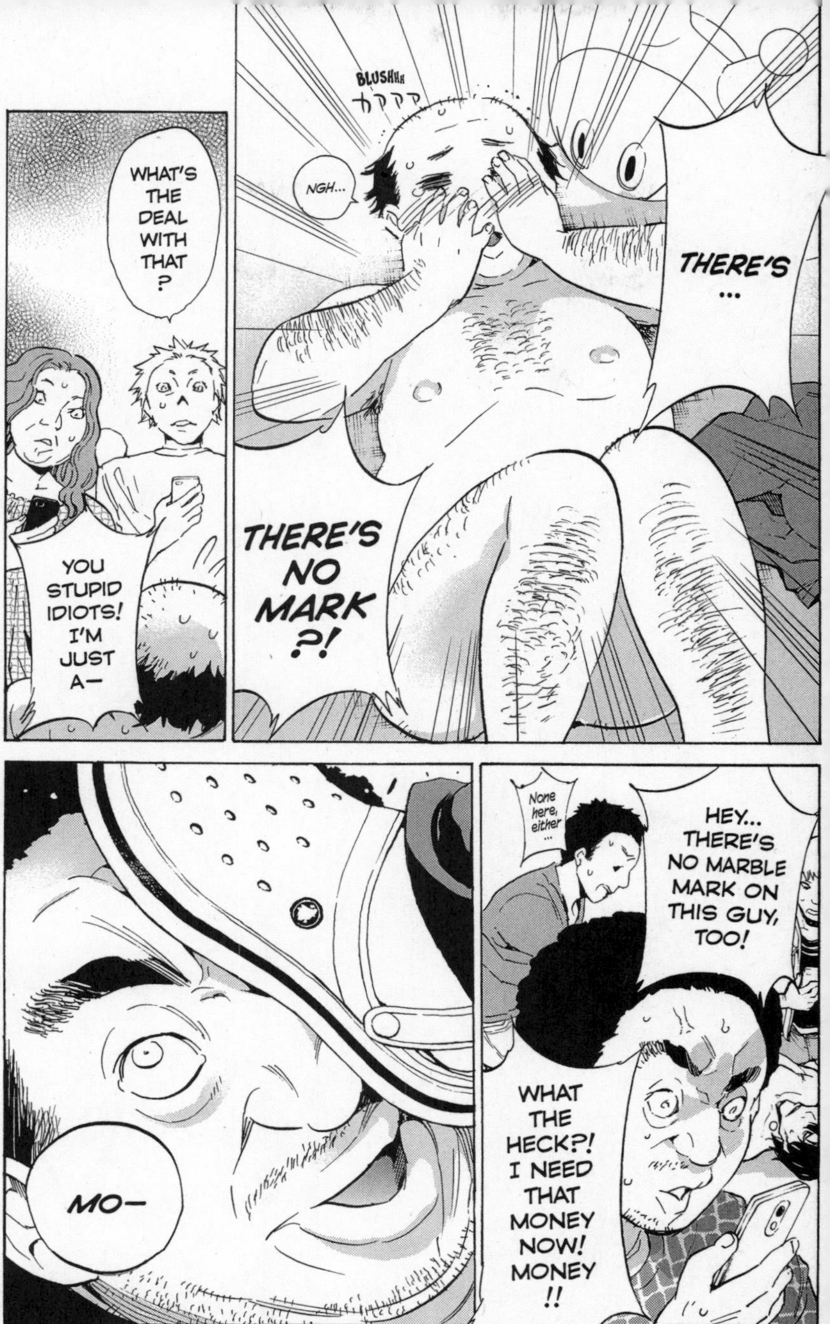
THERE'S ...
BLUSHHH
NGH...
THERE'S NO MARK ?!
WHAT'S THE DEAL WITH THAT ?
YOU STUPID IDIOTS! I'M JUST A—
HEY... THERE'S NO MARBLE MARK ON THIS GUY, TOO!
None here, either ...
WHAT THE HECK?! I NEED THAT MONEY NOW! MONEY !!
MO—

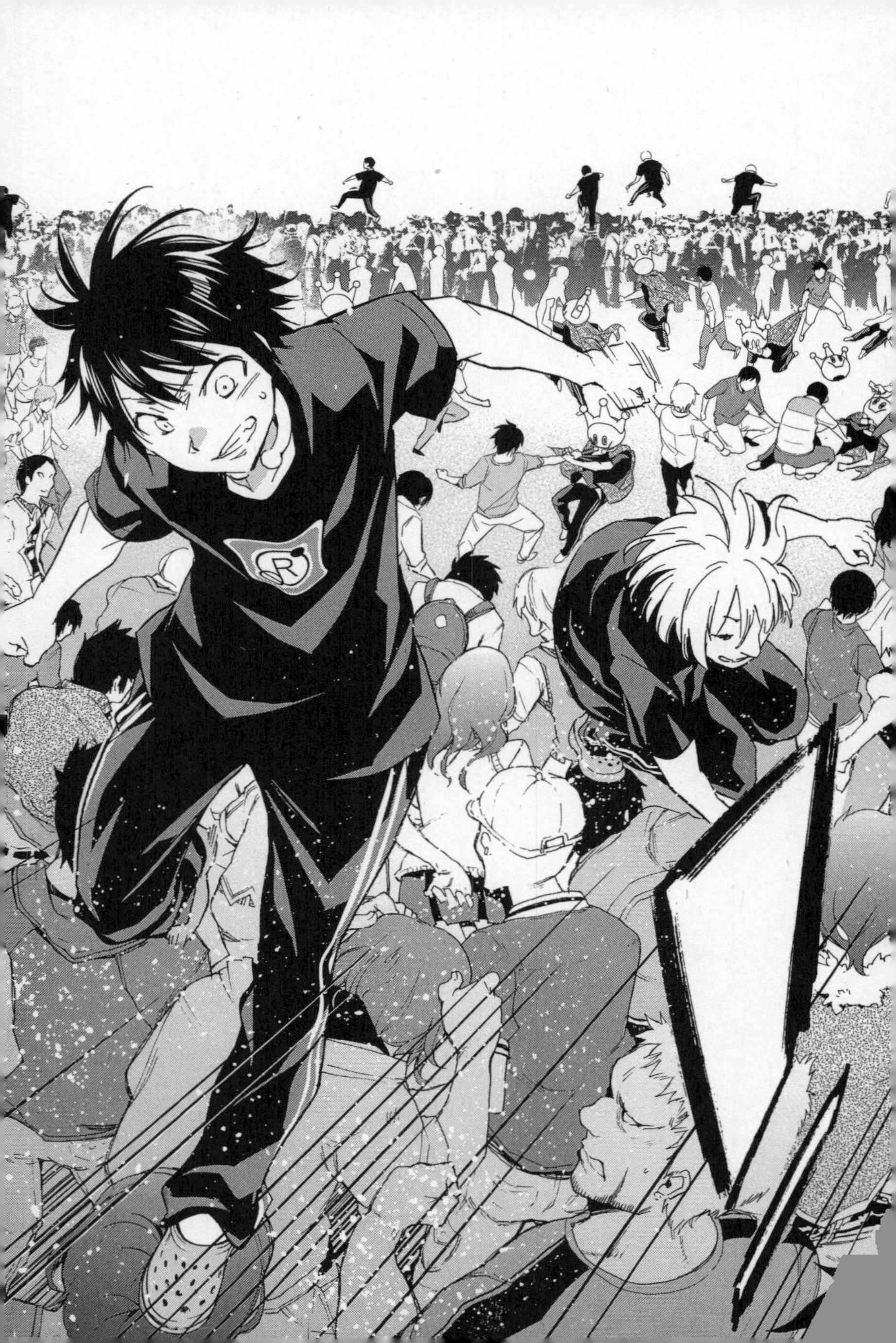

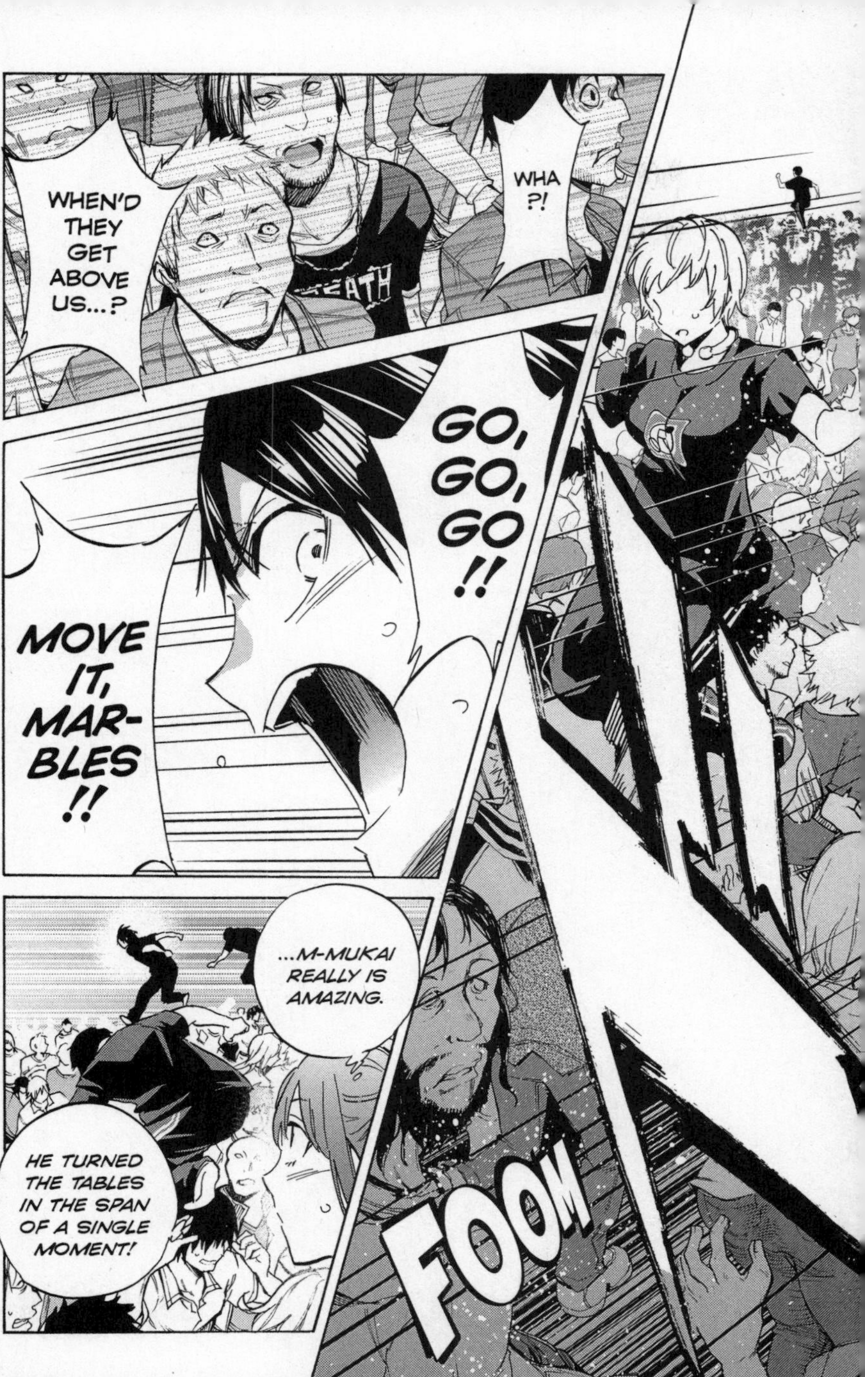
FOOM
WHA ?!
WHEN'D THEY GET ABOVE US...?
GO, GO, GO!!
MOVE IT, MAR-BLES!!
...M-MUKAI REALLY IS AMAZING.
HE TURNED THE TABLES IN THE SPAN OF A SINGLE MOMENT!

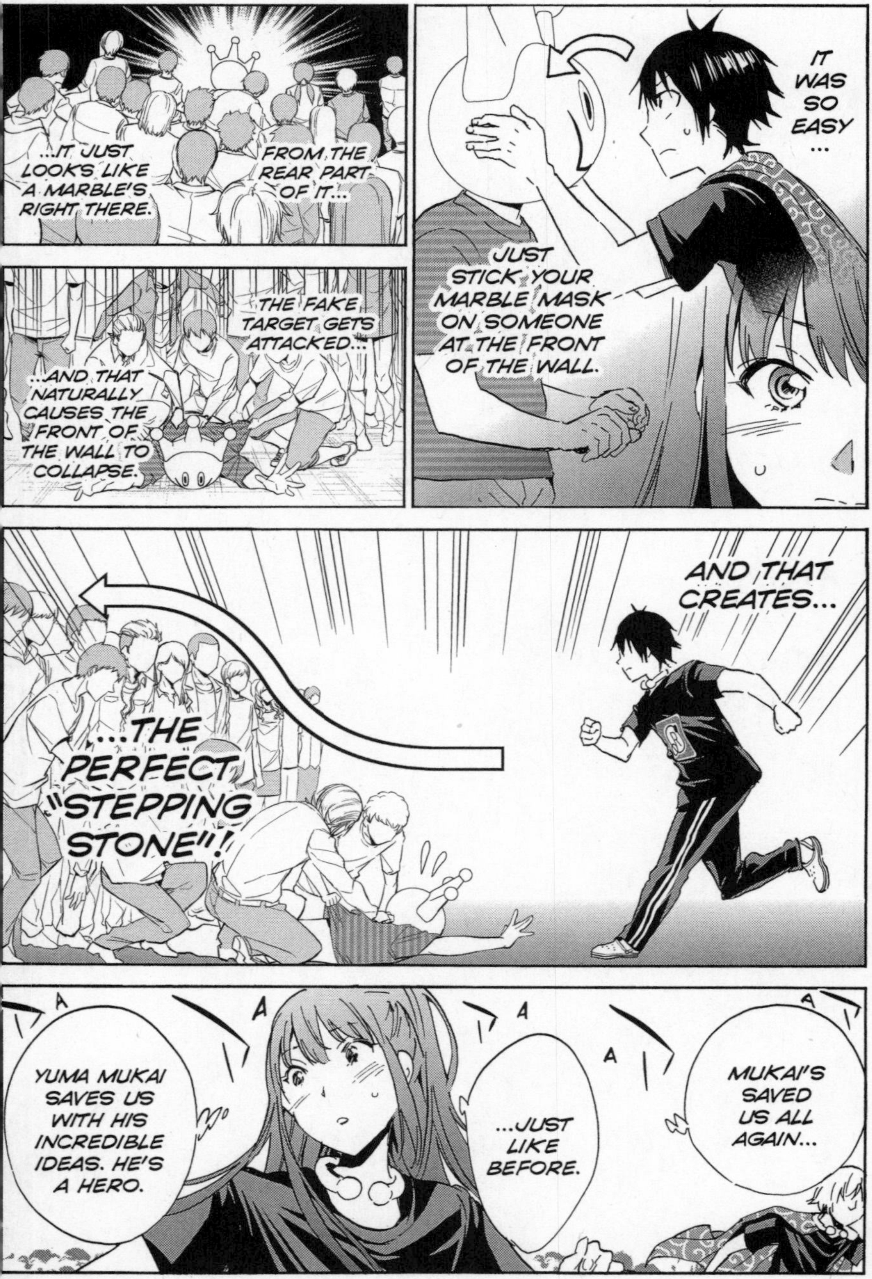
IT WAS SO EASY...
JUST STICK YOUR MARBLE MASK ON SOMEONE AT THE FRONT OF THE WALL.
FROM THE REAR PART OF IT...
...IT JUST LOOKS LIKE A MARBLE'S RIGHT THERE.
THE FAKE TARGET GETS ATTACKED...
...AND THAT NATURALLY CAUSES THE FRONT OF THE WALL TO COLLAPSE.
AND THAT CREATES...
...THE PERFECT "STEPPING STONE"!
MUKAI'S SAVED US ALL AGAIN...
...JUST LIKE BEFORE.
YUMA MUKAI SAVES US WITH HIS INCREDIBLE IDEAS. HE'S A HERO.

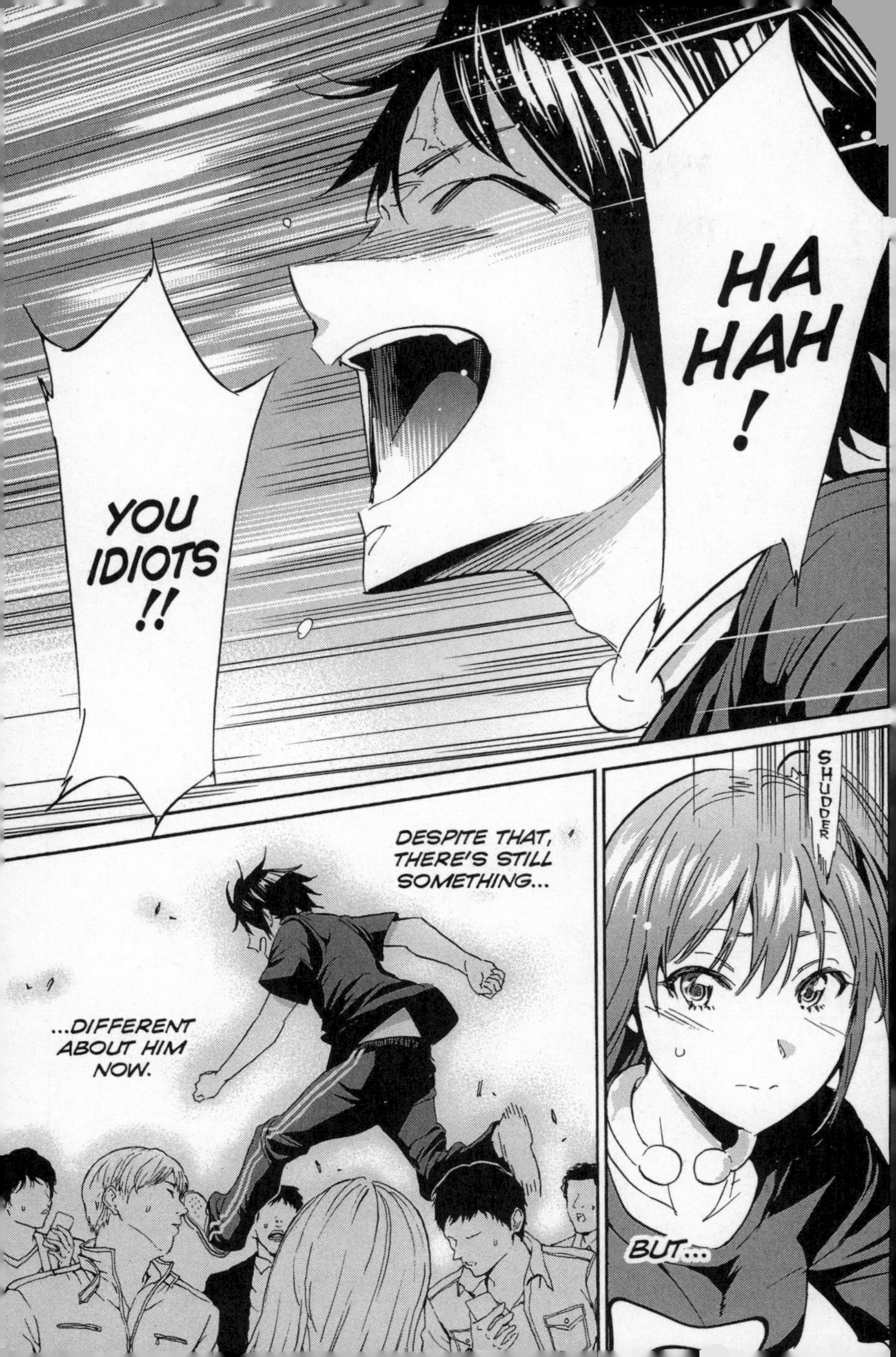
HA HAH!
YOU IDIOTS!!
SHUDDER
BUT...
DESPITE THAT, THERE'S STILL SOMETHING...
...DIFFERENT ABOUT HIM NOW.

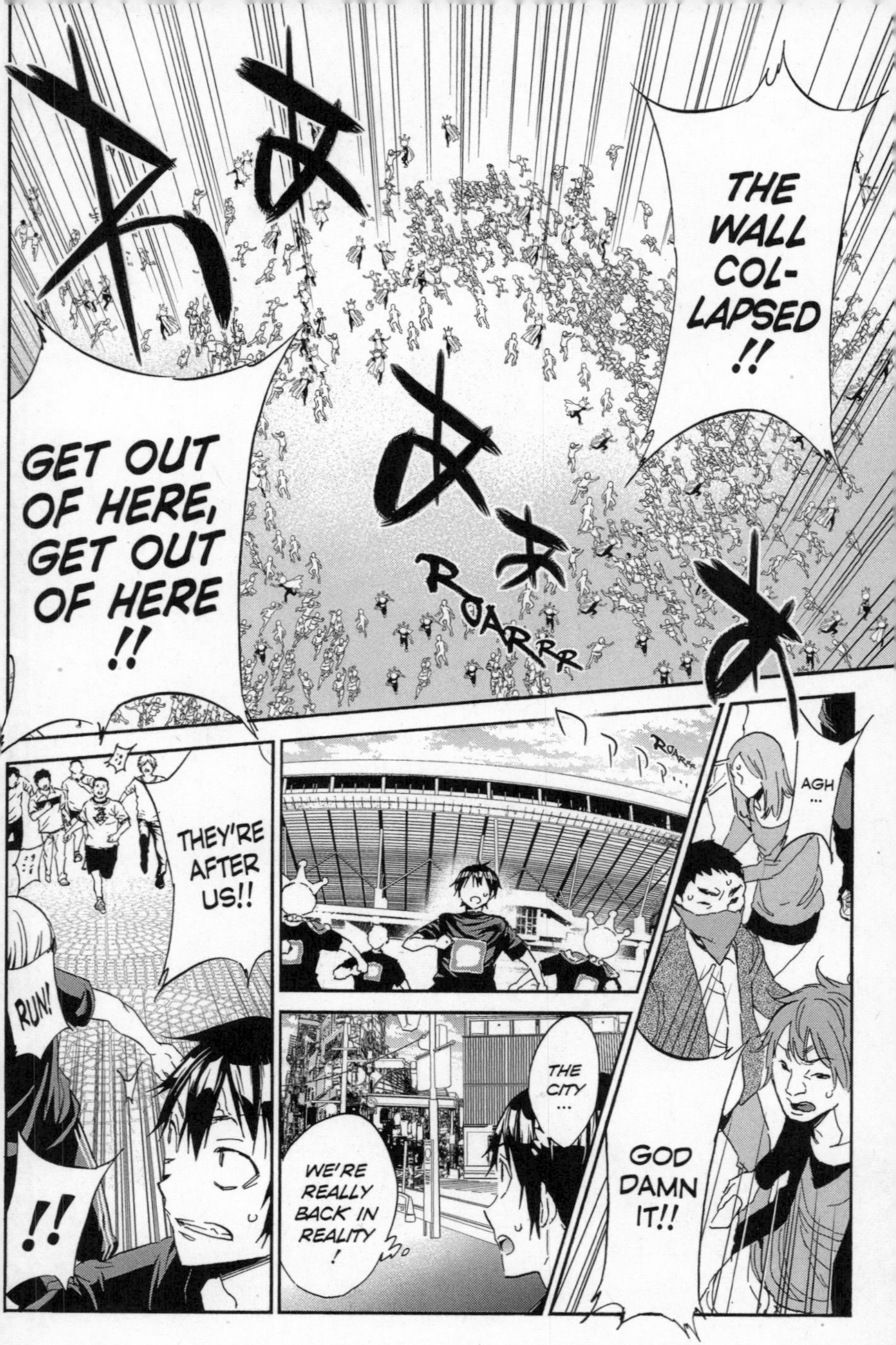
THE WALL COL-LAPSED!!
GET OUT OF HERE, GET OUT OF HERE!!
ROARRRR
AGH ...
GOD DAMN IT!!
ROARRR
THE CITY ...
WE'RE REALLY BACK IN REALITY!
THEY'RE AFTER US!!
RUN!
!!

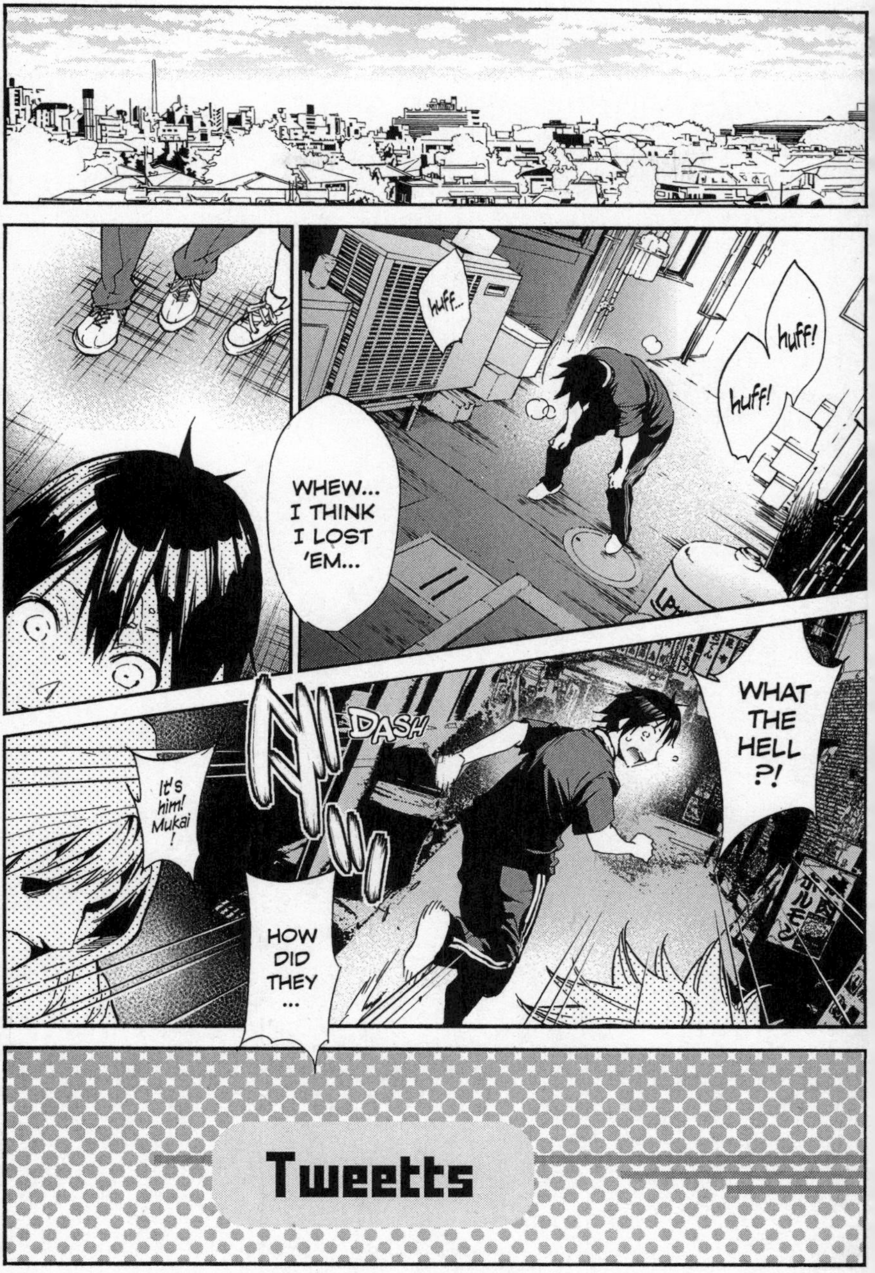
huff...
huff!
huff!
WHEW... I THINK I LOST 'EM...
WHAT THE HELL ?!
DASH
It's him! Mukai!
HOW DID THEY ...

Tweetts

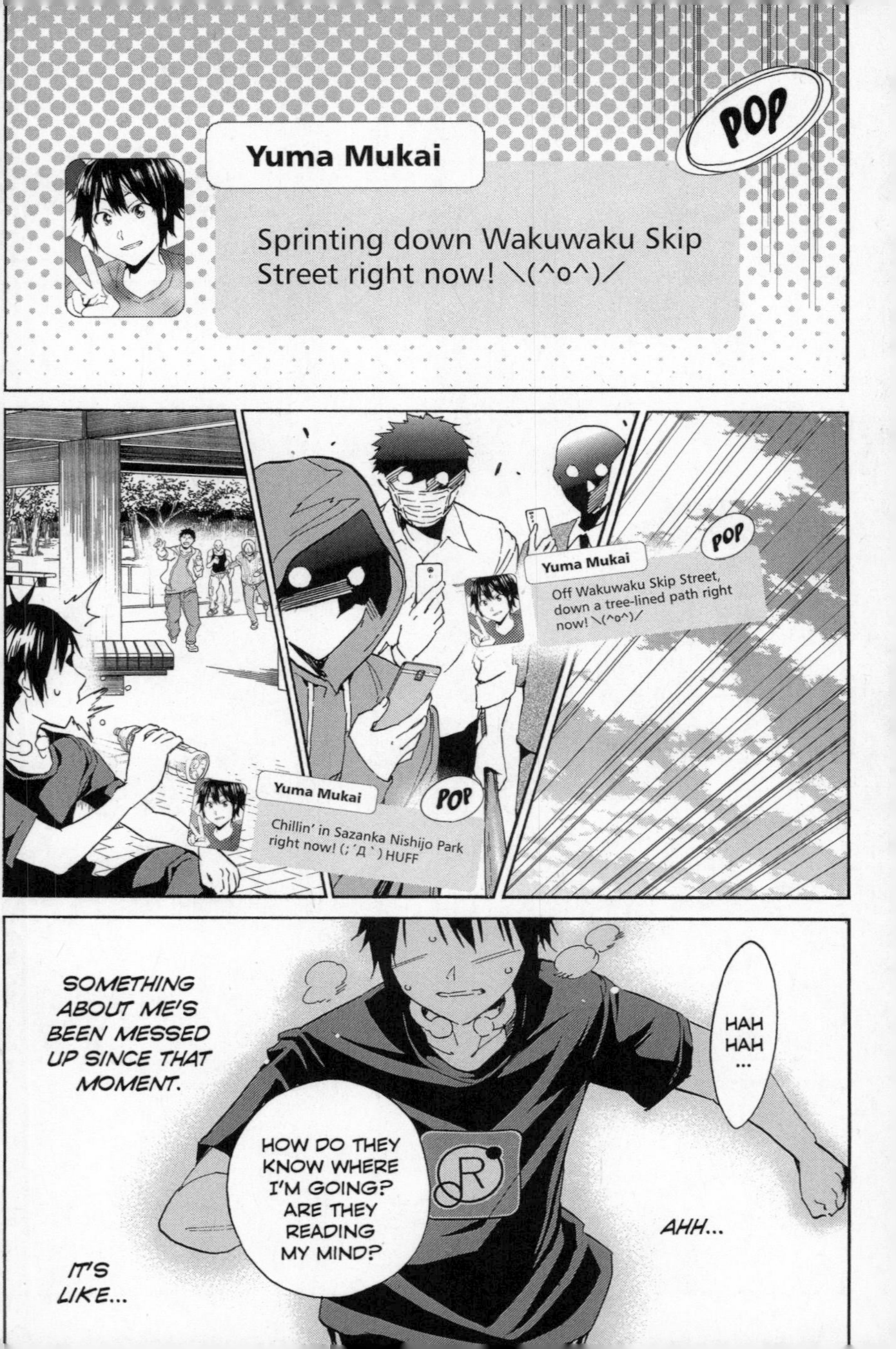
POP
Yuma Mukai
Sprinting down Wakuwaku Skip Street right now! ＼(^o^)／
POP
Yuma Mukai
Off Wakuwaku Skip Street, down a tree-lined path right now! ＼(^o^)／
POP
Yuma Mukai
Chillin' in Sazanka Nishijo Park right now! (;´Д`) HUFF
HAH HAH ...
SOMETHING ABOUT ME'S BEEN MESSED UP SINCE THAT MOMENT.
HOW DO THEY KNOW WHERE I'M GOING? ARE THEY READING MY MIND?
AHH...
IT'S LIKE...

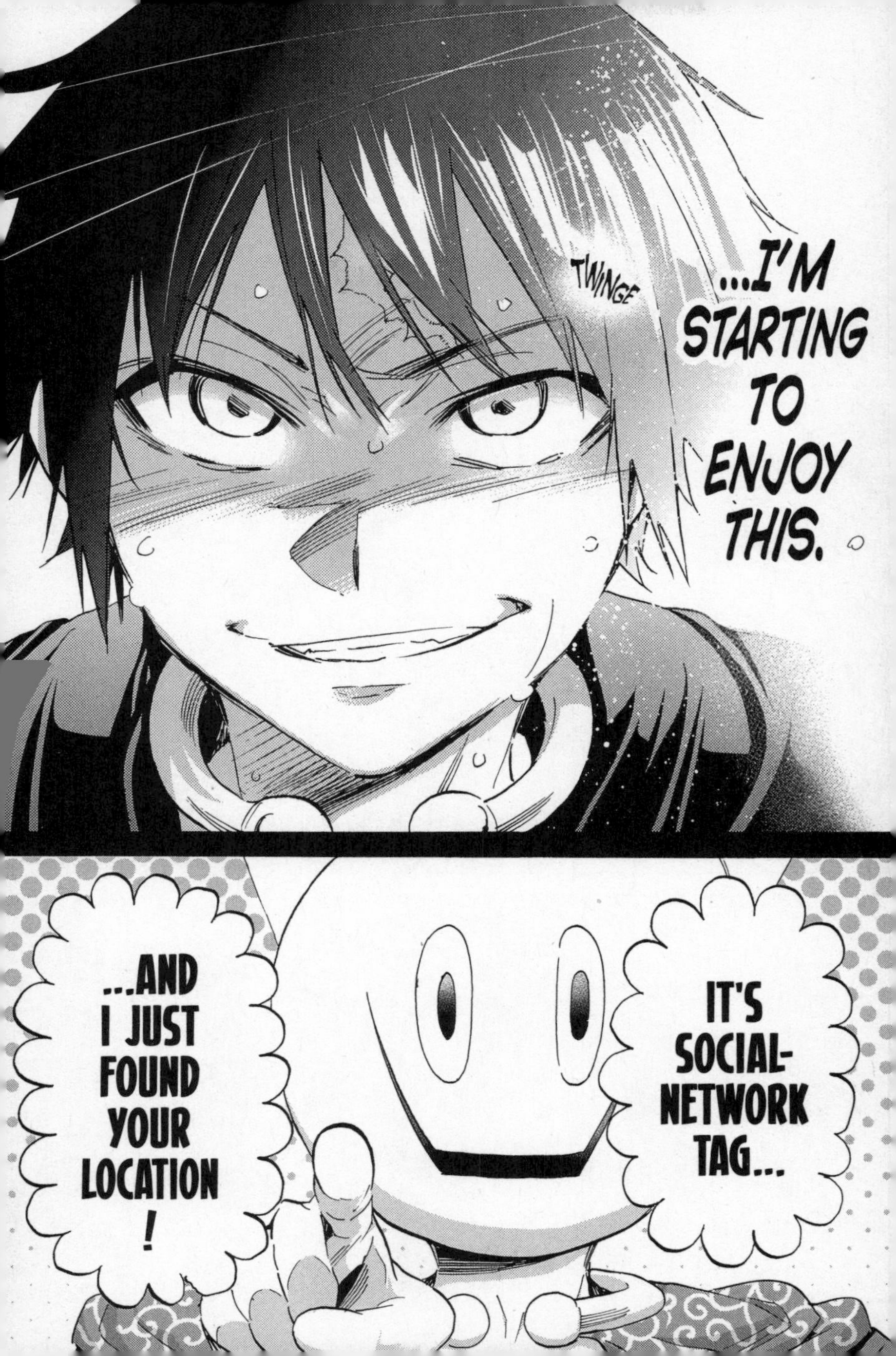
TWINGE
...I'M STARTING TO ENJOY THIS.
IT'S SOCIAL-NETWORK TAG...
...AND I JUST FOUND YOUR LOCATION!

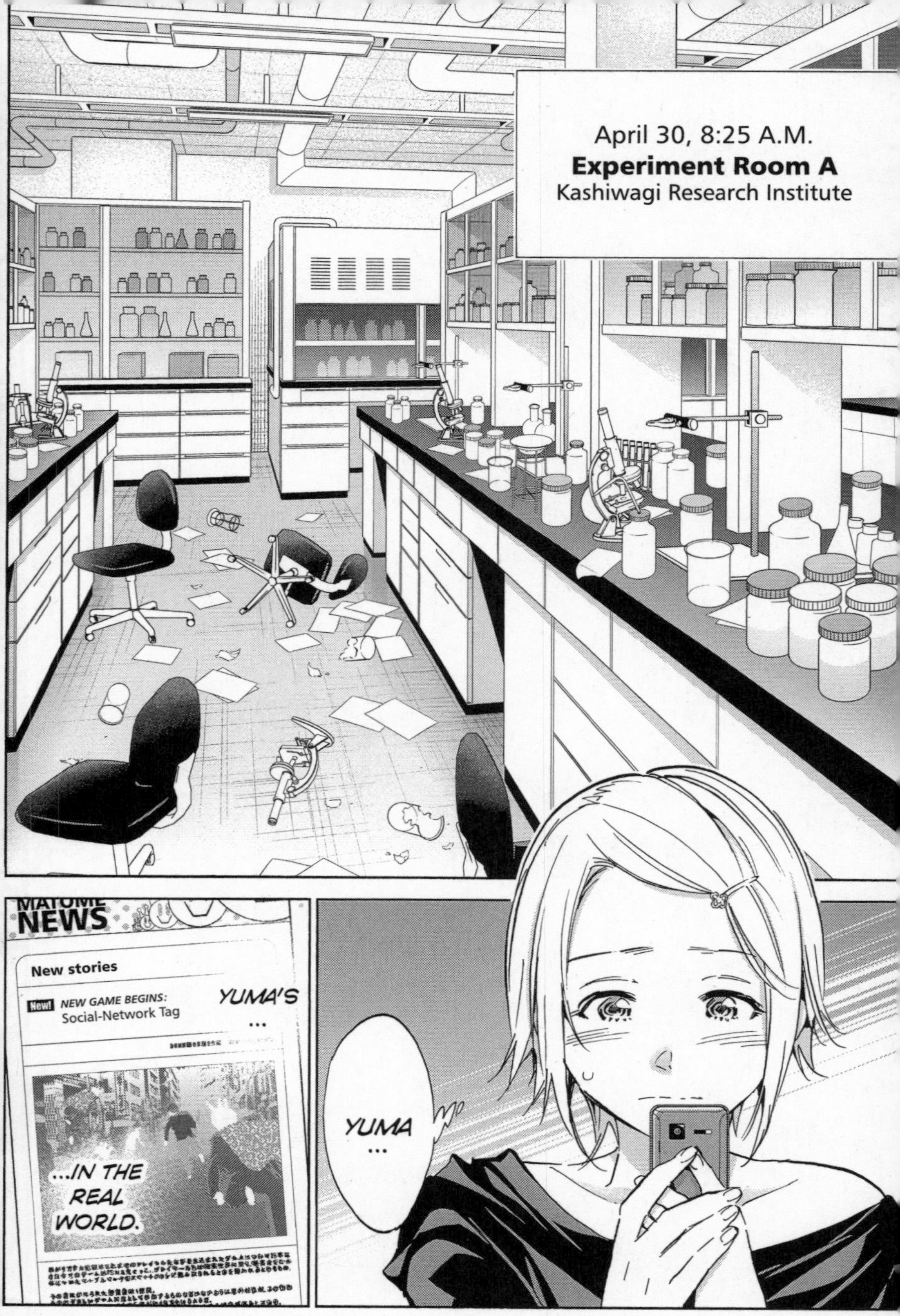
April 30, 8:25 A.M.
Experiment Room A
Kashiwagi Research Institute
YUMA ...
MATOME NEWS
New stories
New! NEW GAME BEGINS:
Social-Network Tag
YUMA'S ...
...IN THE REAL WORLD.

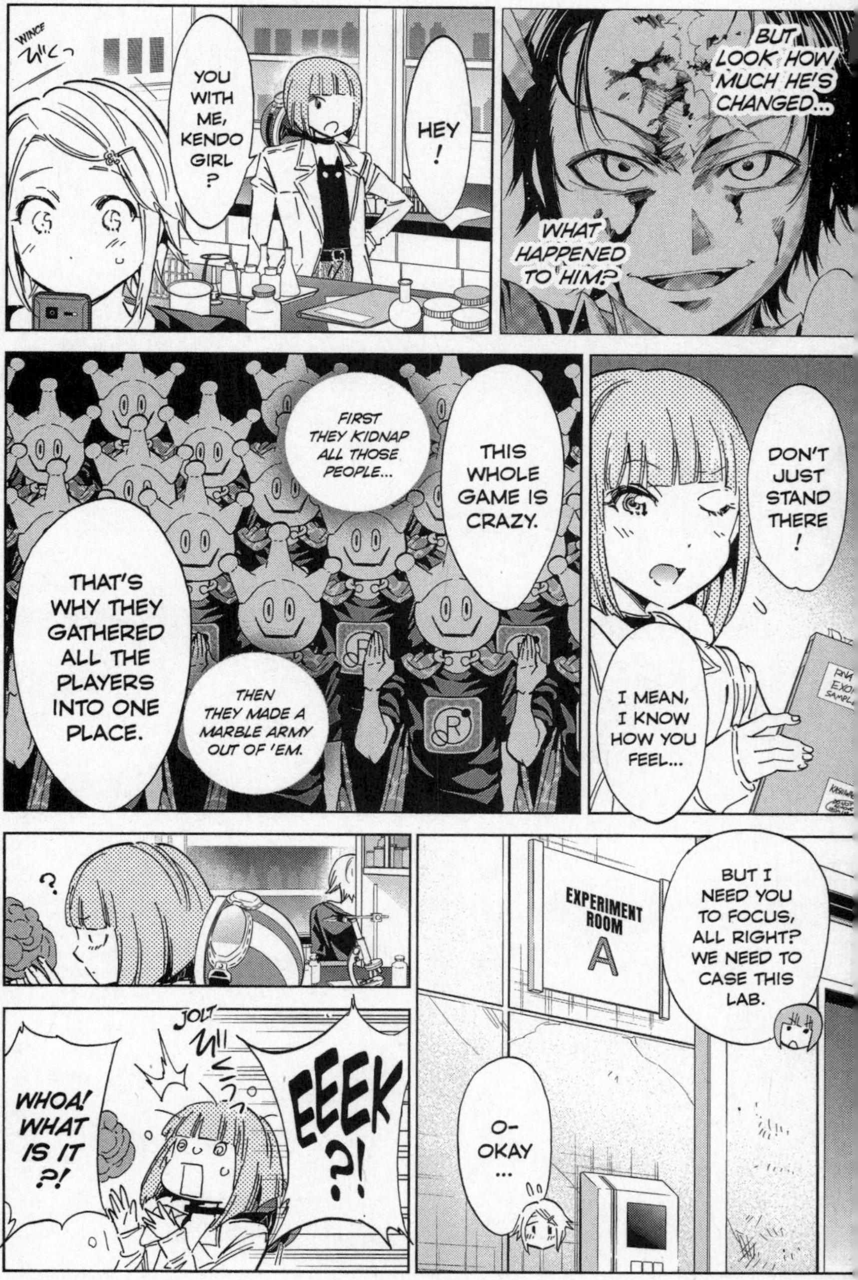
BUT LOOK HOW MUCH HE'S CHANGED...
WHAT HAPPENED TO HIM?
HEY!
YOU WITH ME, KENDO GIRL?
WINCE
びくっ
DON'T JUST STAND THERE!
I MEAN, I KNOW HOW YOU FEEL...
THIS WHOLE GAME IS CRAZY.
FIRST THEY KIDNAP ALL THOSE PEOPLE...
THEN THEY MADE A MARBLE ARMY OUT OF 'EM.
THAT'S WHY THEY GATHERED ALL THE PLAYERS INTO ONE PLACE.
EXPERIMENT ROOM A
BUT I NEED YOU TO FOCUS, ALL RIGHT? WE NEED TO CASE THIS LAB.
O-OKAY...
?
JOLT
EEEK?!
WHOA! WHAT IS IT?!

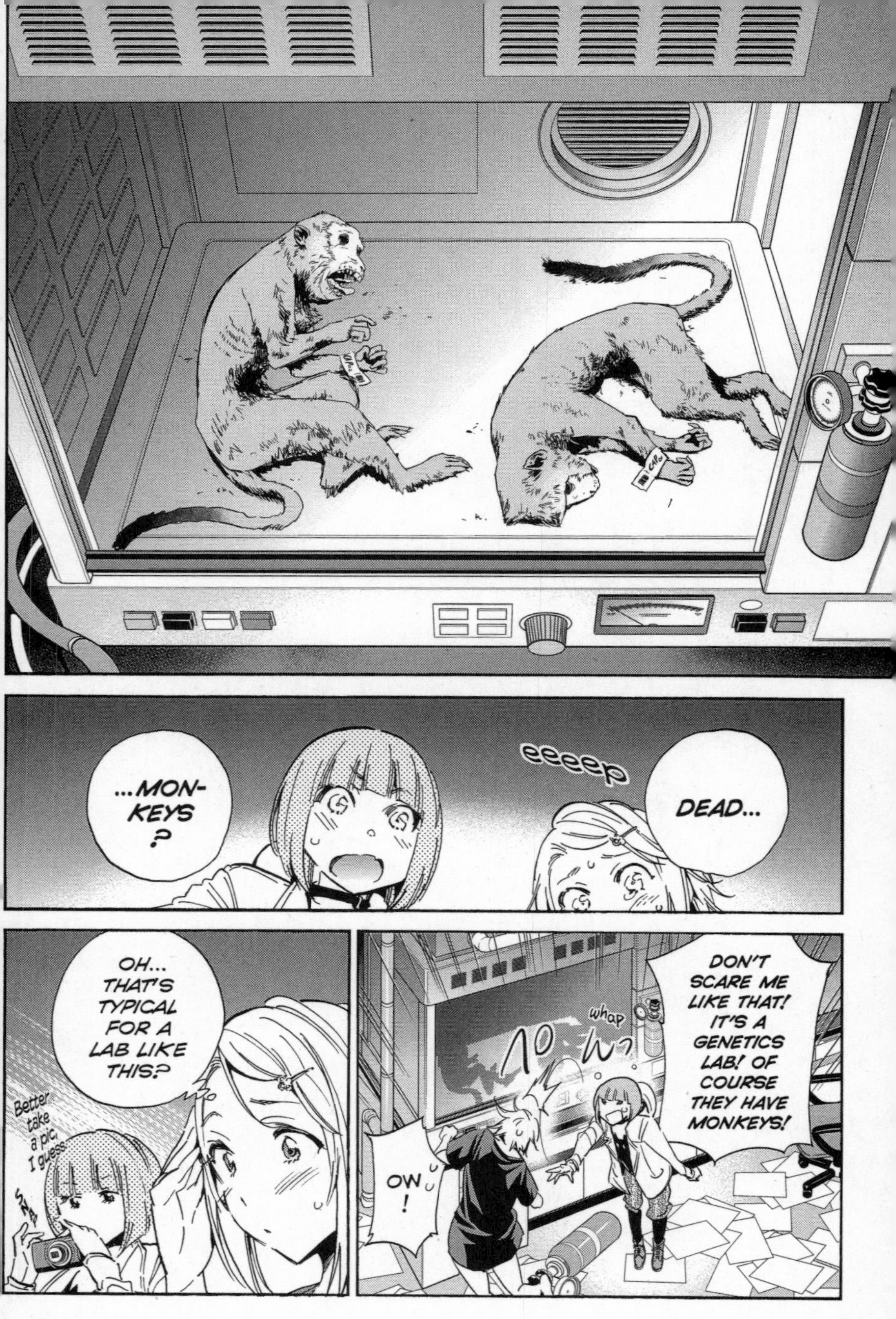
DEAD...
eeeep
...MON-KEYS?
DON'T SCARE ME LIKE THAT! IT'S A GENETICS LAB! OF COURSE THEY HAVE MONKEYS!
whap
OW!
OH... THAT'S TYPICAL FOR A LAB LIKE THIS?
Better take a pic, I guess
SNAP

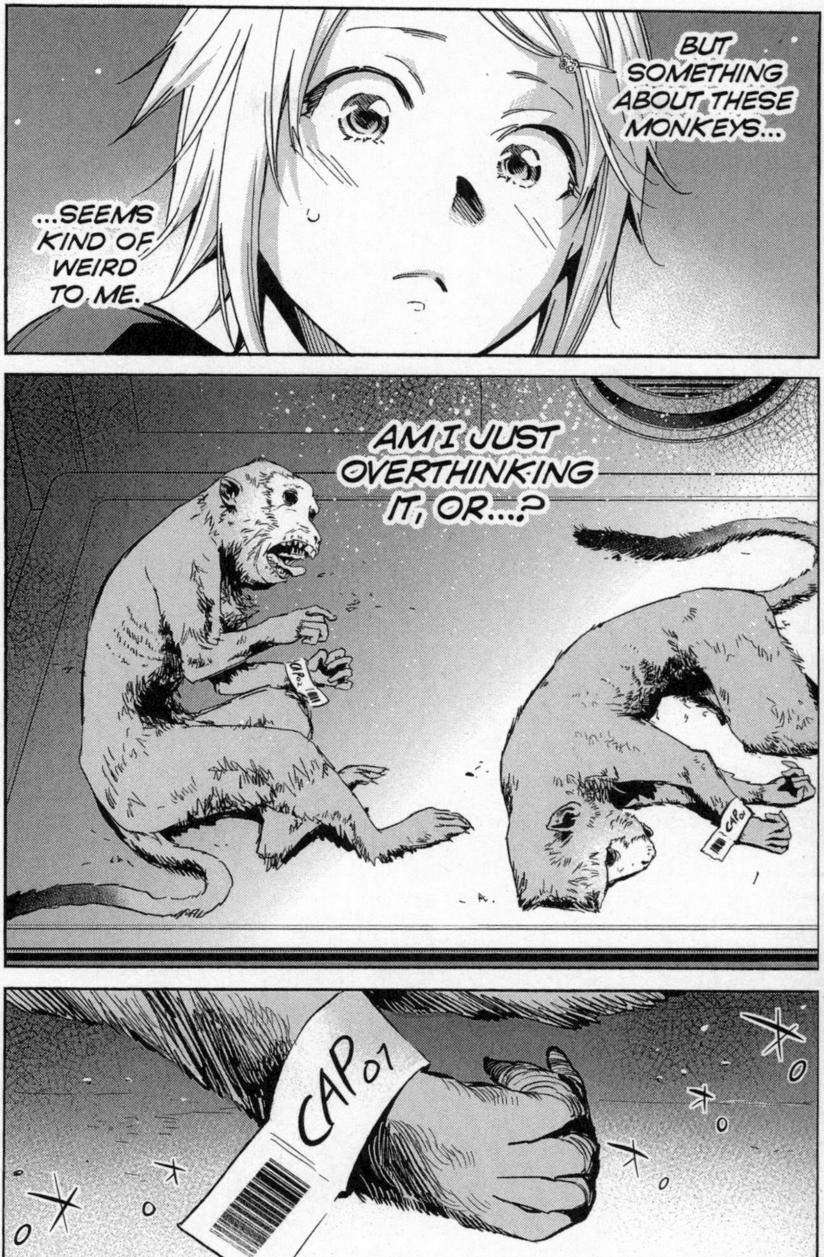
BUT SOMETHING ABOUT THESE MONKEYS...
...SEEMS KIND OF WEIRD TO ME.
AM I JUST OVERTHINKING IT, OR...?
CAP02
CAP01
CAP01

ACCOUNT 33 Resolve Across the Edge

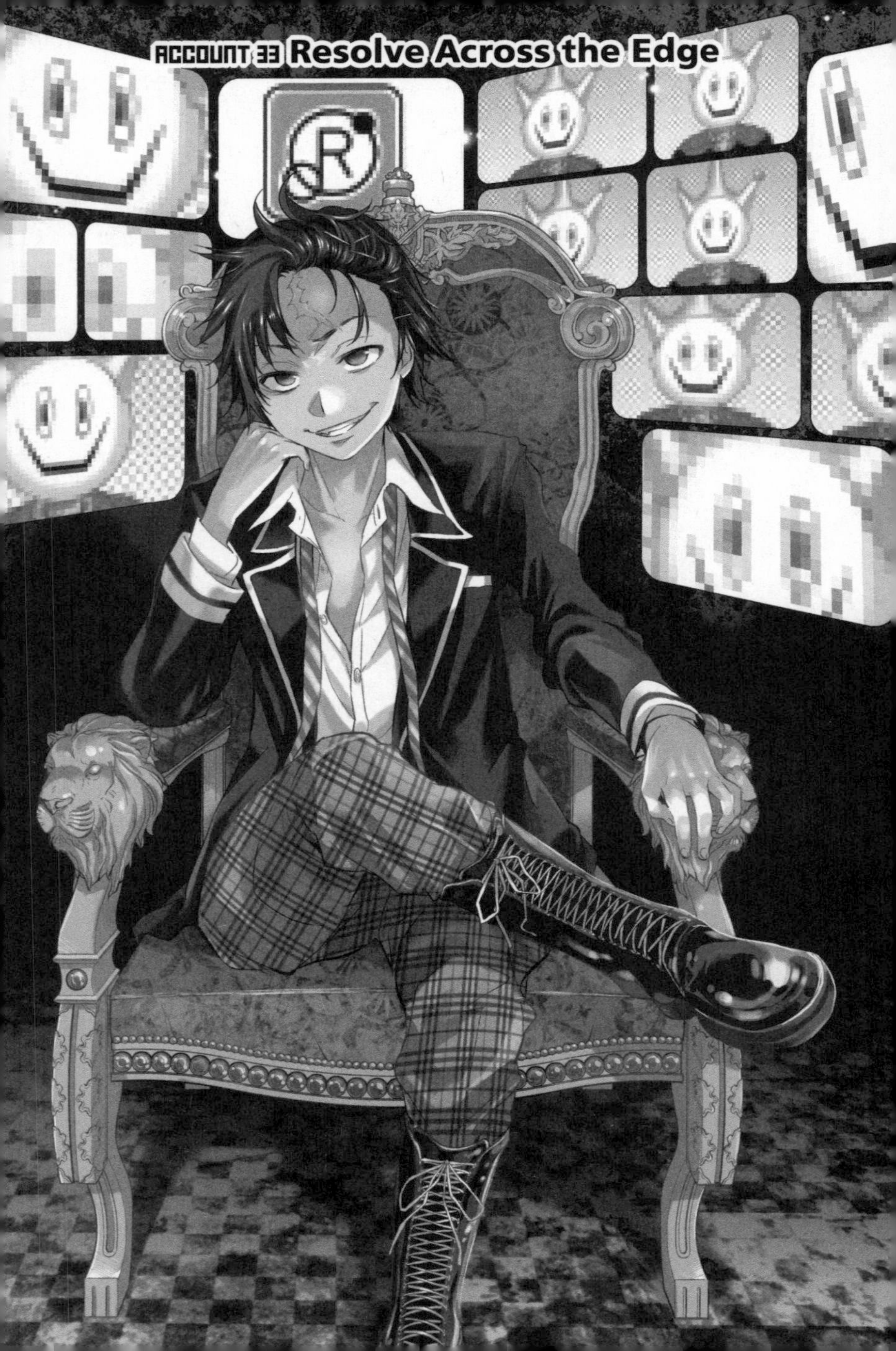

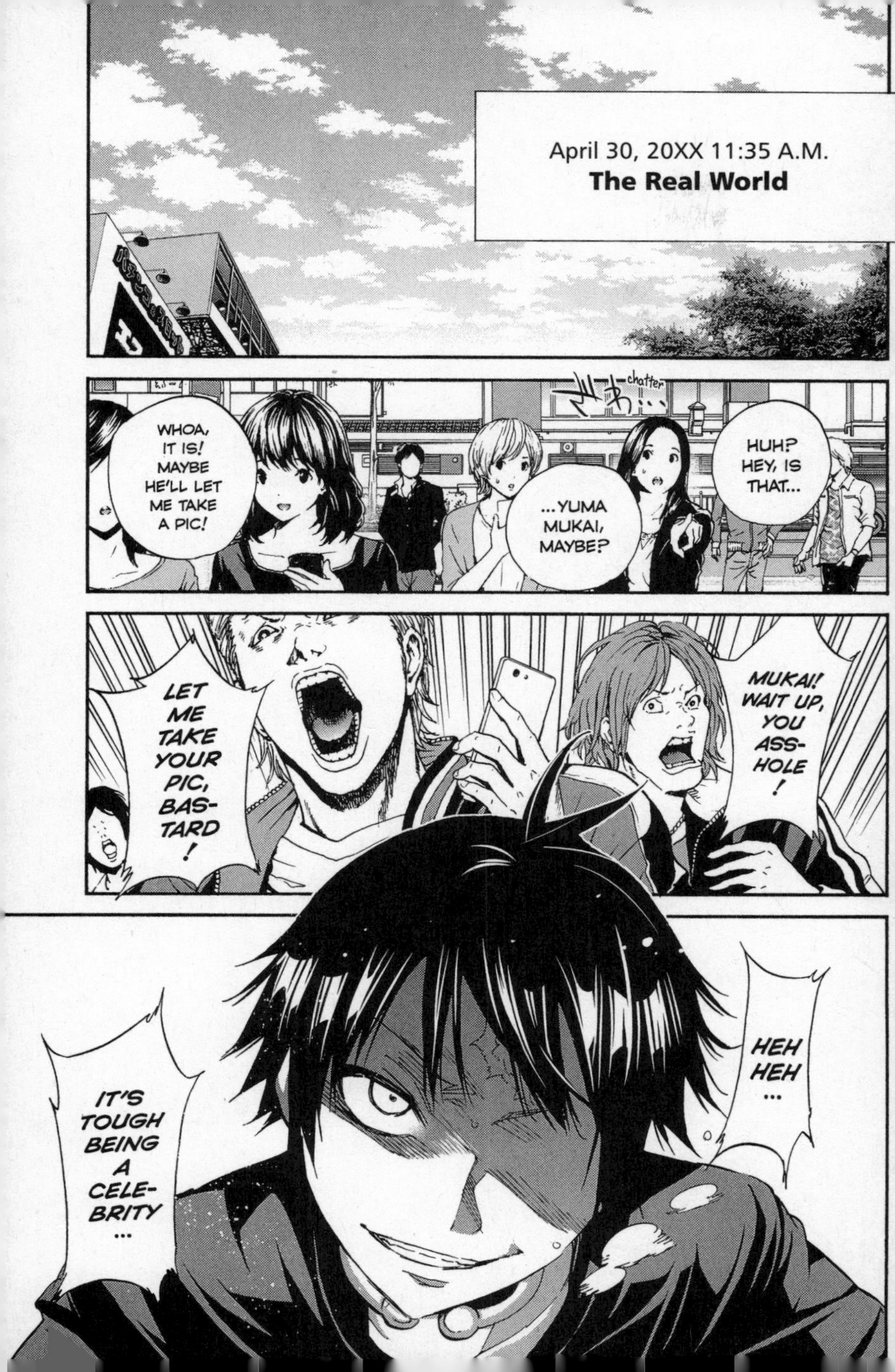
April 30, 20XX 11:35 A.M.
The Real World
chatter
HUH? HEY, IS THAT...
...YUMA MUKAI, MAYBE?
WHOA, IT IS! MAYBE HE'LL LET ME TAKE A PIC!
MUKAI! WAIT UP, YOU ASS-HOLE!
LET ME TAKE YOUR PIC, BAS-TARD!
HEH HEH...
IT'S TOUGH BEING A CELE-BRITY...

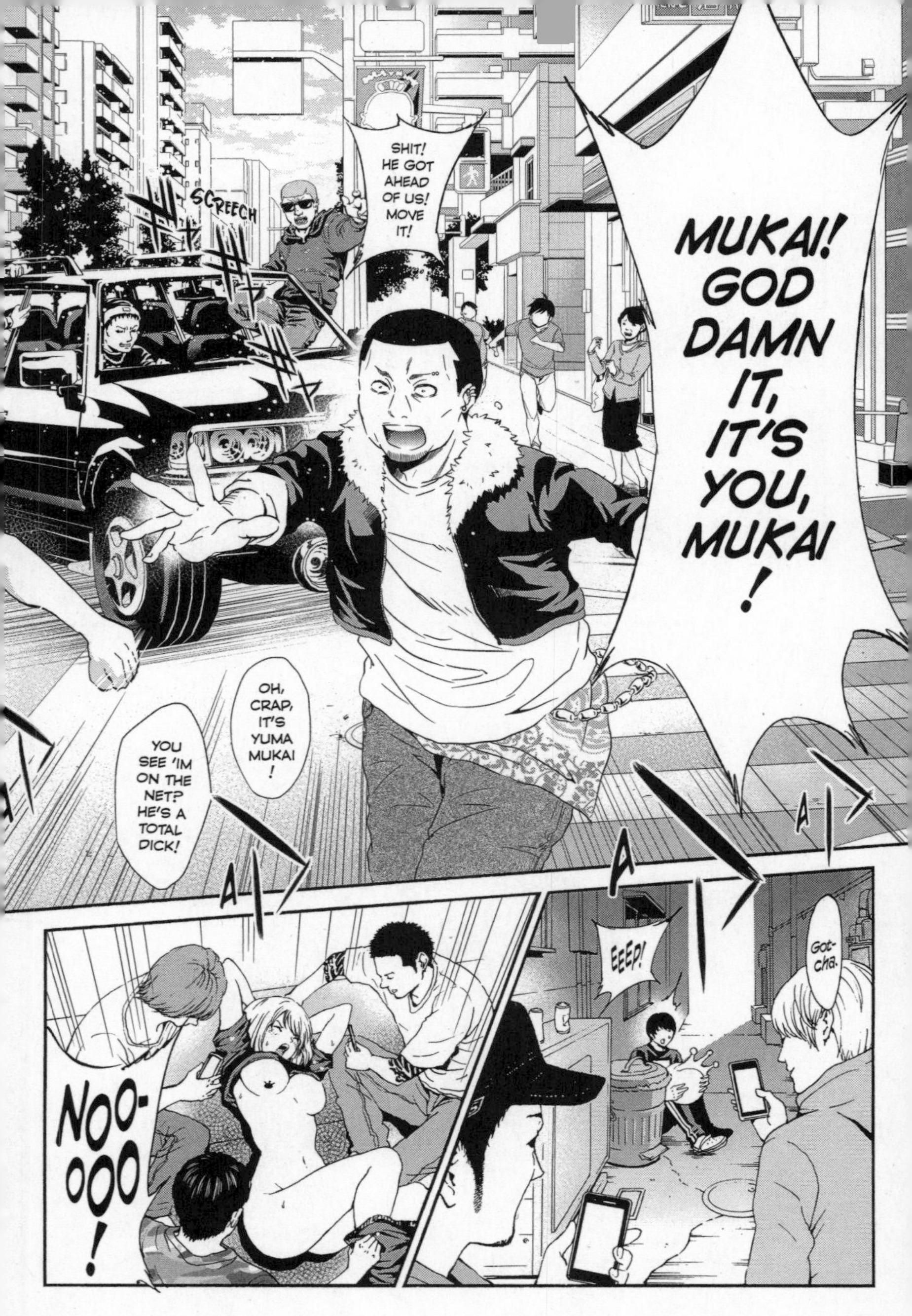
MUKAI! GOD DAMN IT, IT'S YOU, MUKAI!
SHIT! HE GOT AHEAD OF US! MOVE IT!
SCREECH
OH, CRAP, IT'S YUMA MUKAI!
YOU SEE 'IM ON THE NET? HE'S A TOTAL DICK!
Got-cha.
EEEp!
NOO-OOO!

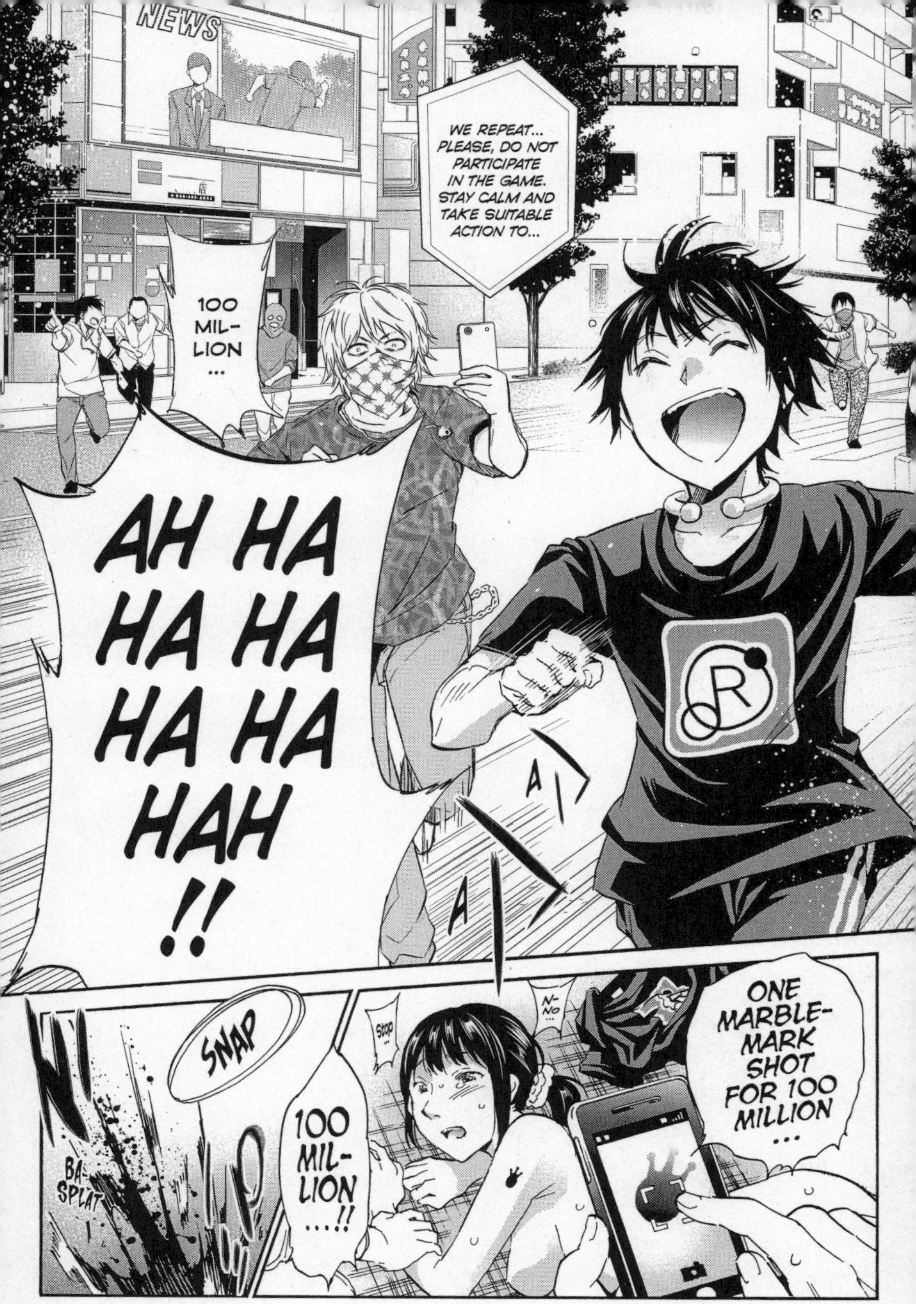
NEWS
WE REPEAT... PLEASE, DO NOT PARTICIPATE IN THE GAME. STAY CALM AND TAKE SUITABLE ACTION TO...
100 MIL-LION ...
AH HA HA HA HA HA HA HA HAH !!
A
A
ONE MARBLE-MARK SHOT FOR 100 MILLION ...
N-NO ...
Stop ...
100 MIL-LION ....!!
SNAP
BA-SPLAT

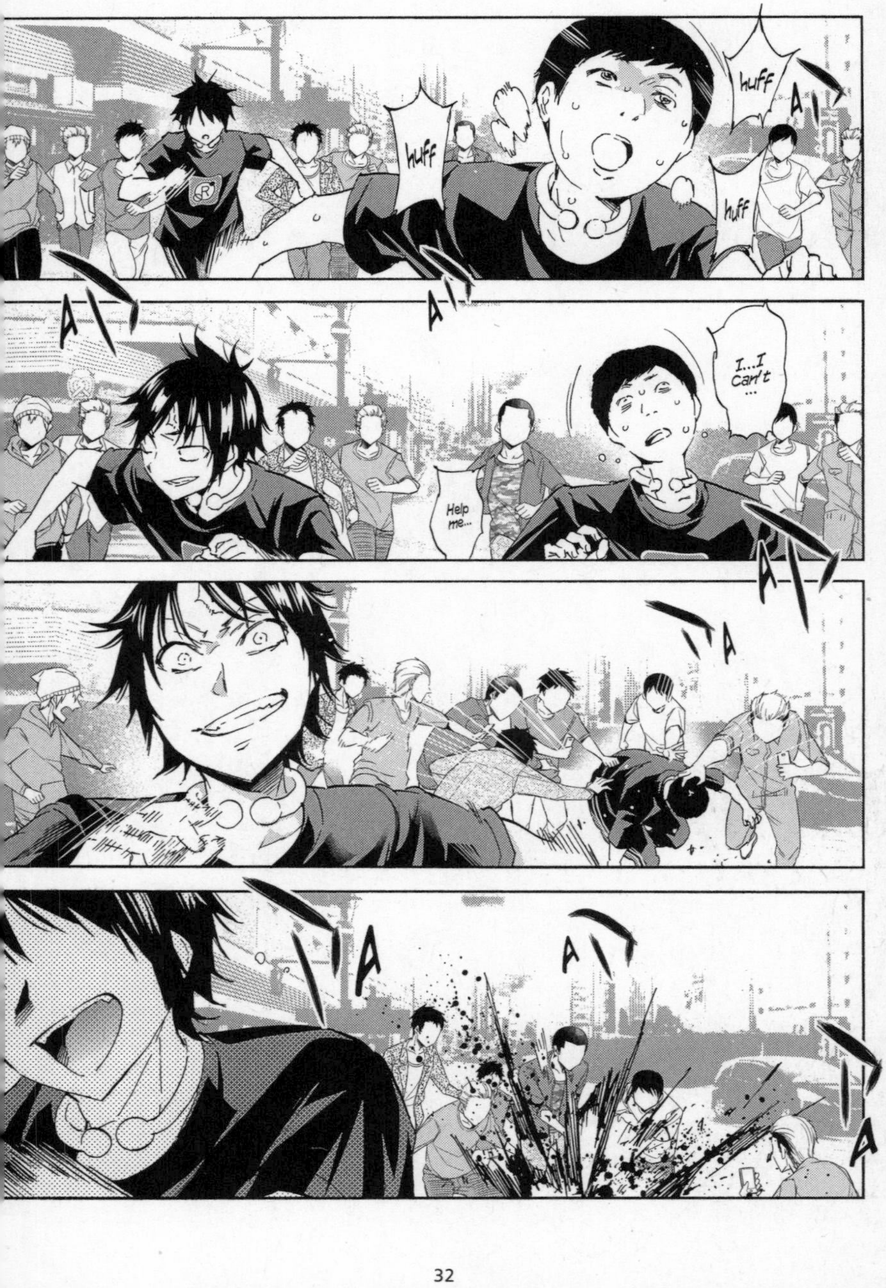
huff
huff
huff
I...I can't ...
Help me...

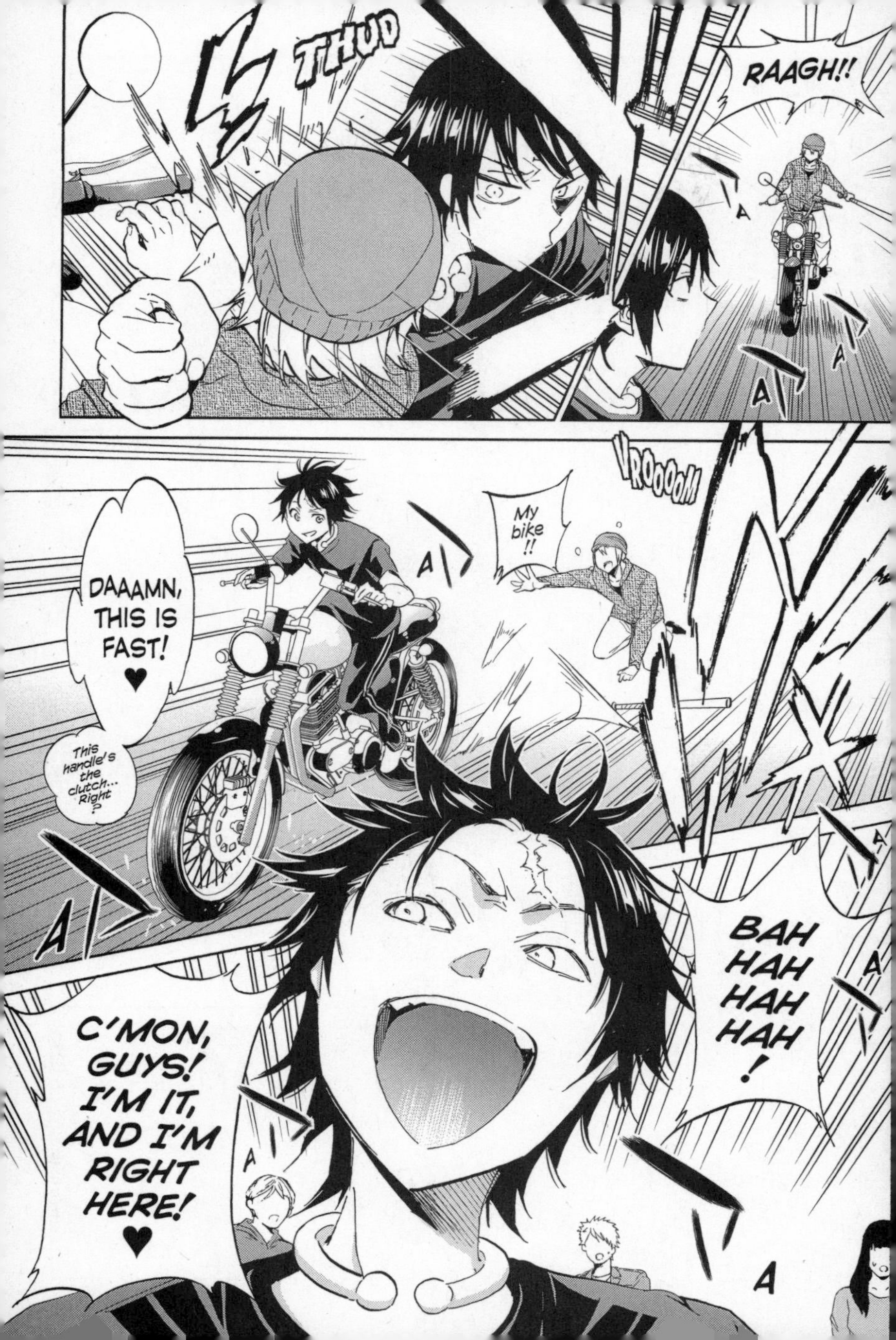
RAAGH!!
A A A A
THUD
VROOOOM
My bike!!
DAAAMN, THIS IS FAST! ♥
This handle's the clutch... Right?
A A
BAH HAH HAH HAH!
C'MON, GUYS! I'M IT, AND I'M RIGHT HERE! ♥
A A A A

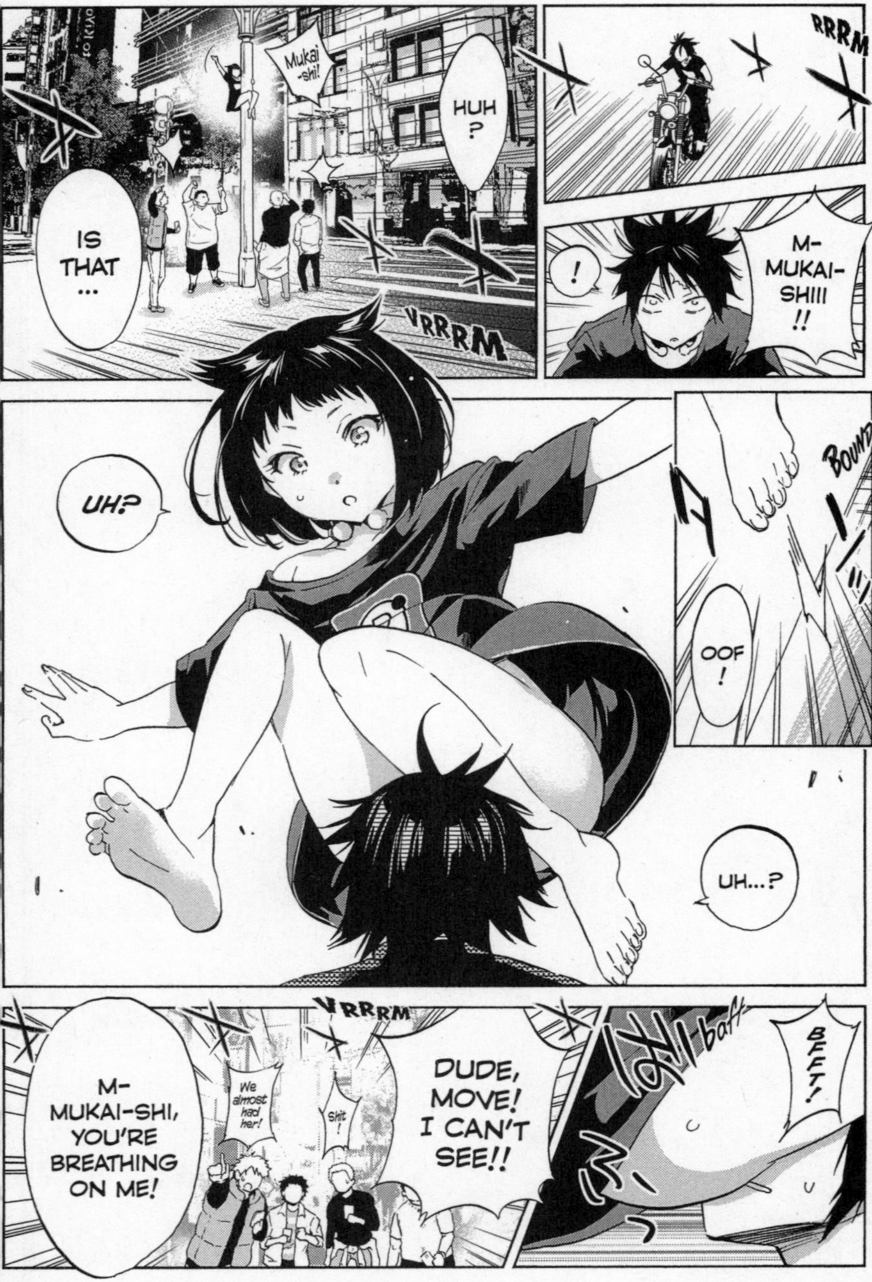
RRRM
M-MUKAI-SHIII!!
!
Mukai-shi!
HUH?
IS THAT...
VRRRM
BOUND
OOF!
UH...?
UH?
BEFT!
baff
DUDE, MOVE! I CAN'T SEE!!
VRRRM
Shit!
We almost had her!
M-MUKAI-SHI, YOU'RE BREATHING ON ME!

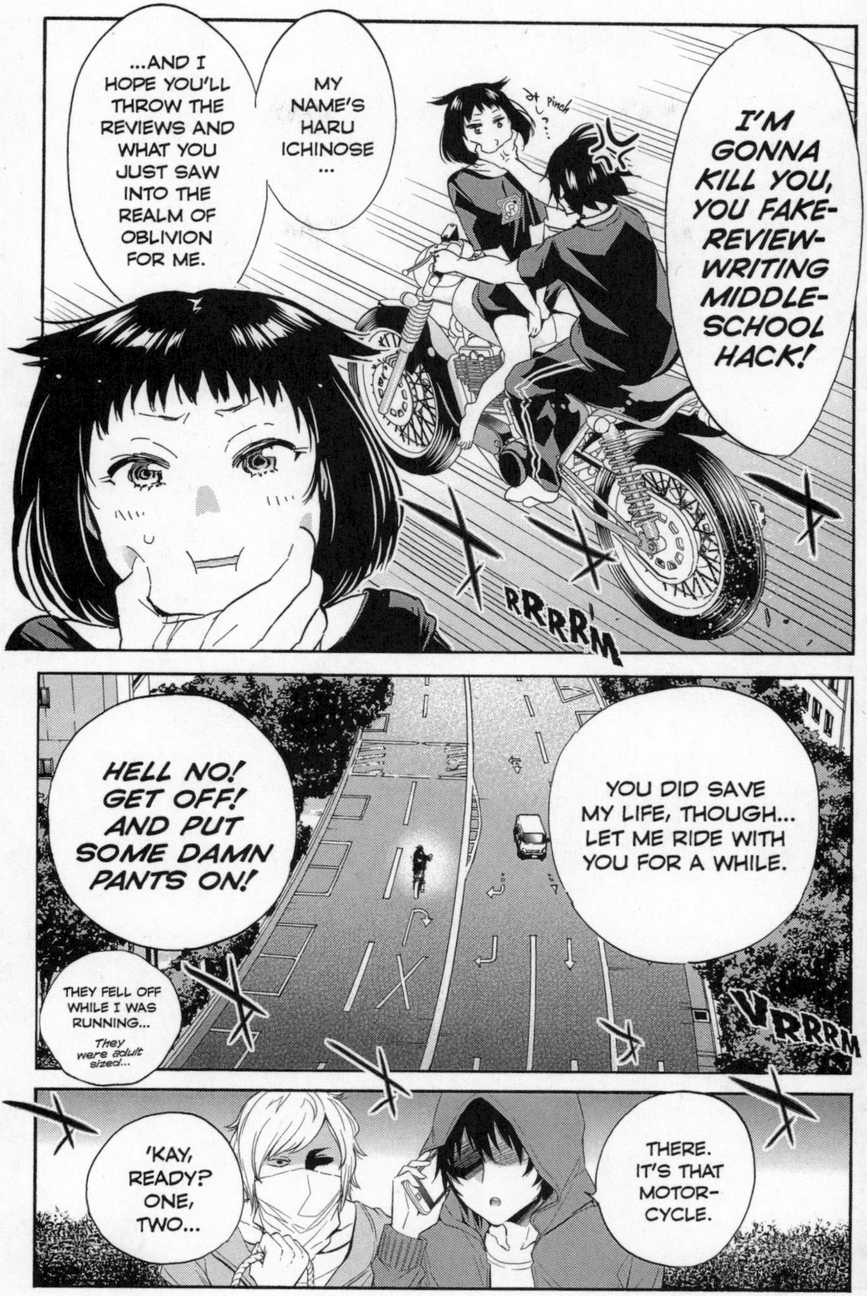
I'M GONNA KILL YOU, YOU FAKE-REVIEW-WRITING MIDDLE-SCHOOL HACK!
pinch
MY NAME'S HARU ICHINOSE...
...AND I HOPE YOU'LL THROW THE REVIEWS AND WHAT YOU JUST SAW INTO THE REALM OF OBLIVION FOR ME.
RRRRRM
YOU DID SAVE MY LIFE, THOUGH... LET ME RIDE WITH YOU FOR A WHILE.
VRRRM
HELL NO! GET OFF! AND PUT SOME DAMN PANTS ON!
THEY FELL OFF WHILE I WAS RUNNING...
They were adult sized...
THERE. IT'S THAT MOTOR-CYCLE.
'KAY, READY? ONE, TWO...

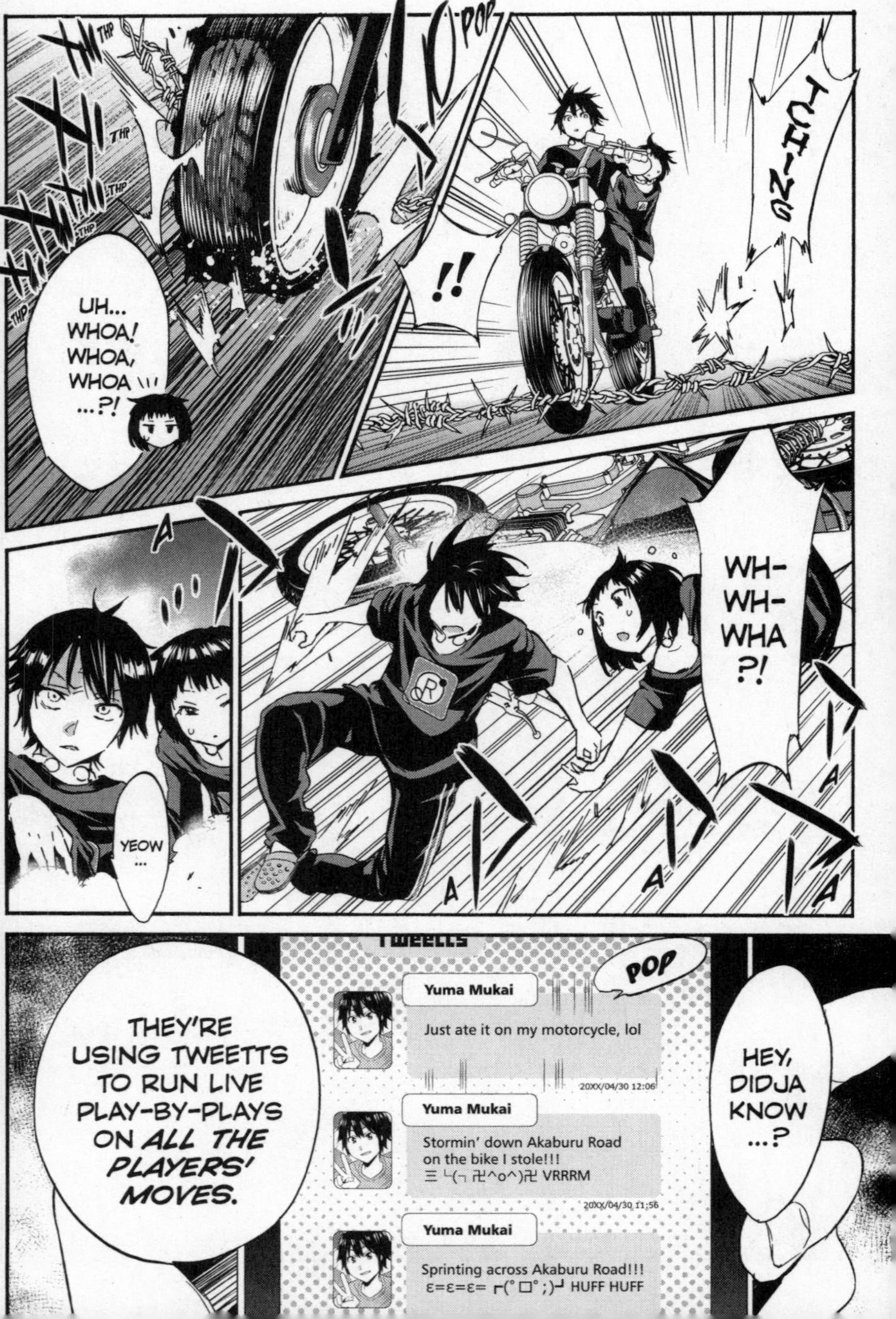
ICHING
!!
POP
THP THP THP THP THP
UH... WHOA! WHOA, WHOA ...?!
WH-WH-WHA ?!
YEOW ...
HEY, DIDJA KNOW ...?
TWEETTS
POP
Yuma Mukai
Just ate it on my motorcycle, lol
20XX/04/30 12:06
Yuma Mukai
Stormin' down Akaburu Road on the bike I stole!!! 三 ┗(┓卍^o^)卍 VRRRM
20XX/04/30 11:56
Yuma Mukai
Sprinting across Akaburu Road!!! ε=ε=ε= ┏(゜ロ゜;)┛ HUFF HUFF
THEY'RE USING TWEETTS TO RUN LIVE PLAY-BY-PLAYS ON *ALL THE PLAYERS'* MOVES.

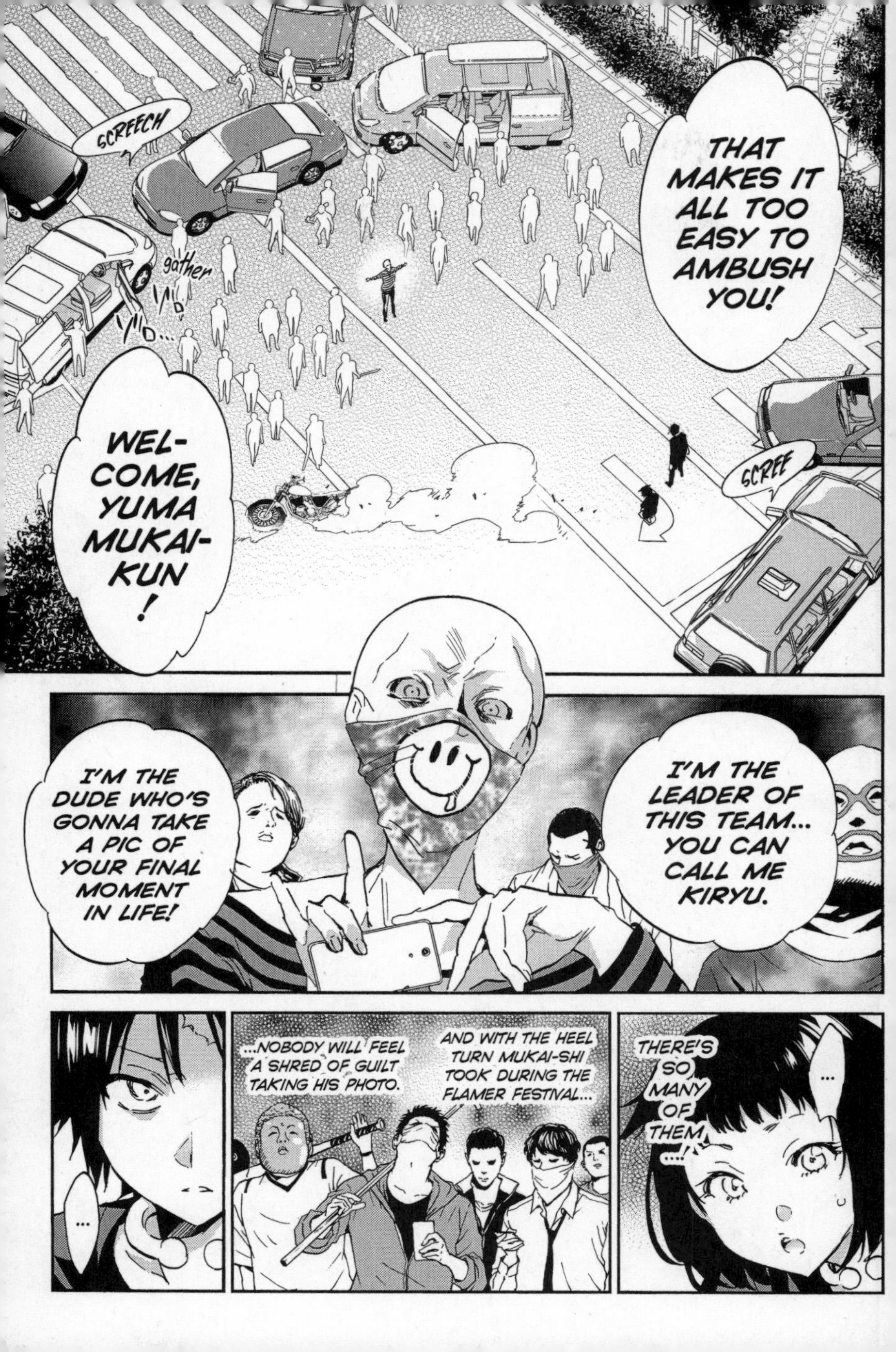
THAT MAKES IT ALL TOO EASY TO AMBUSH YOU!
SCREECH
gather
SCREE
WEL-COME, YUMA MUKAI-KUN!
I'M THE LEADER OF THIS TEAM... YOU CAN CALL ME KIRYU.
I'M THE DUDE WHO'S GONNA TAKE A PIC OF YOUR FINAL MOMENT IN LIFE!
THERE'S SO MANY OF THEM....!
...
AND WITH THE HEEL TURN MUKAI-SHI TOOK DURING THE FLAMER FESTIVAL...
...NOBODY WILL FEEL A SHRED OF GUILT TAKING HIS PHOTO.
...

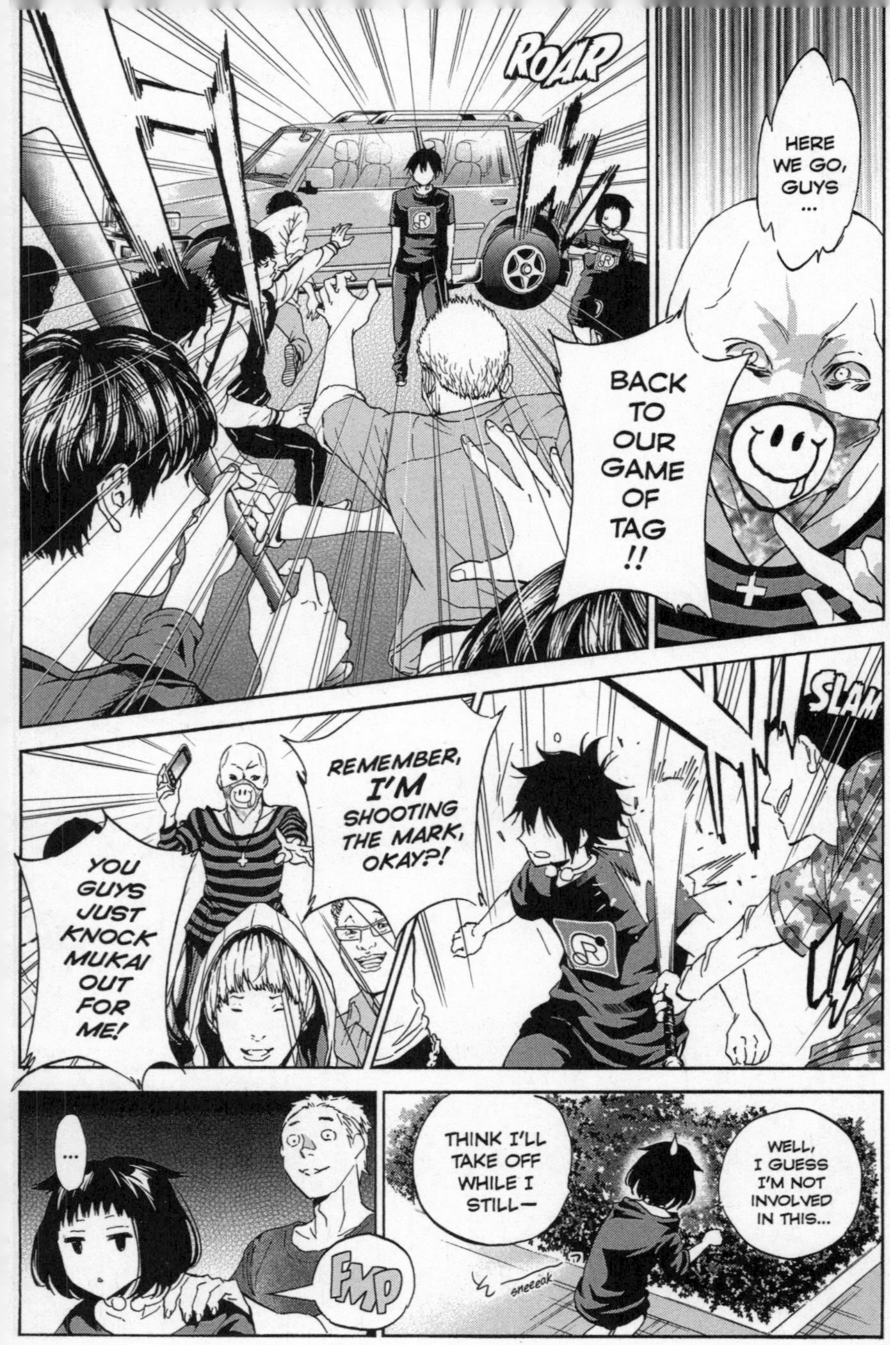
ROAR
HERE WE GO, GUYS...
BACK TO OUR GAME OF TAG!!
SLAM
REMEMBER, I'M SHOOTING THE MARK, OKAY?!
YOU GUYS JUST KNOCK MUKAI OUT FOR ME!
WELL, I GUESS I'M NOT INVOLVED IN THIS...
THINK I'LL TAKE OFF WHILE I STILL—
sneeeak
...
FMP

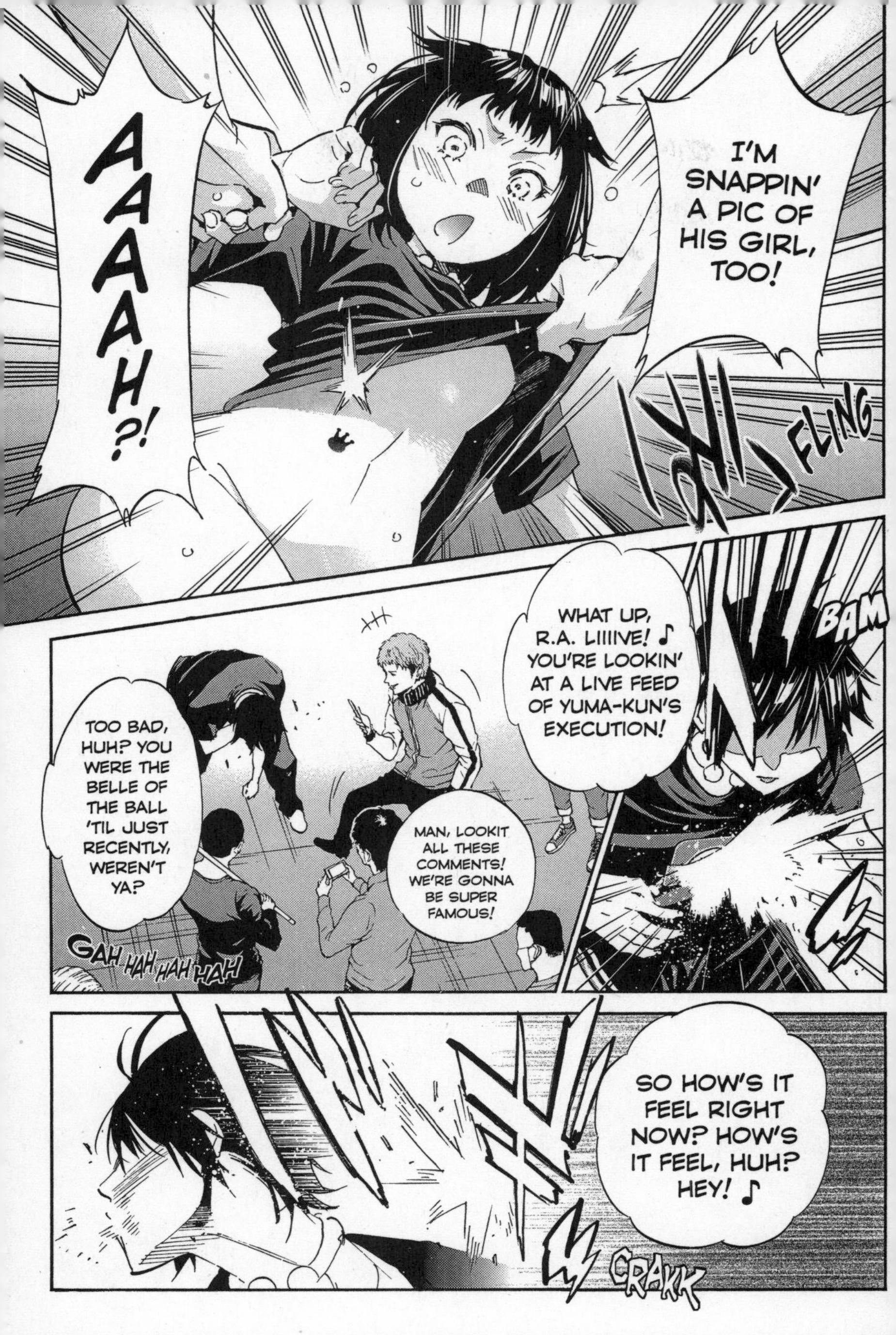
I'M SNAPPIN' A PIC OF HIS GIRL, TOO!
AAAAH?!
FLING
BAM
WHAT UP, R.A. LIIIIVE! ♪ YOU'RE LOOKIN' AT A LIVE FEED OF YUMA-KUN'S EXECUTION!
MAN, LOOKIT ALL THESE COMMENTS! WE'RE GONNA BE SUPER FAMOUS!
TOO BAD, HUH? YOU WERE THE BELLE OF THE BALL 'TIL JUST RECENTLY, WEREN'T YA?
GAH HAH HAH HAH
SO HOW'S IT FEEL RIGHT NOW? HOW'S IT FEEL, HUH? HEY! ♪
CRAKK

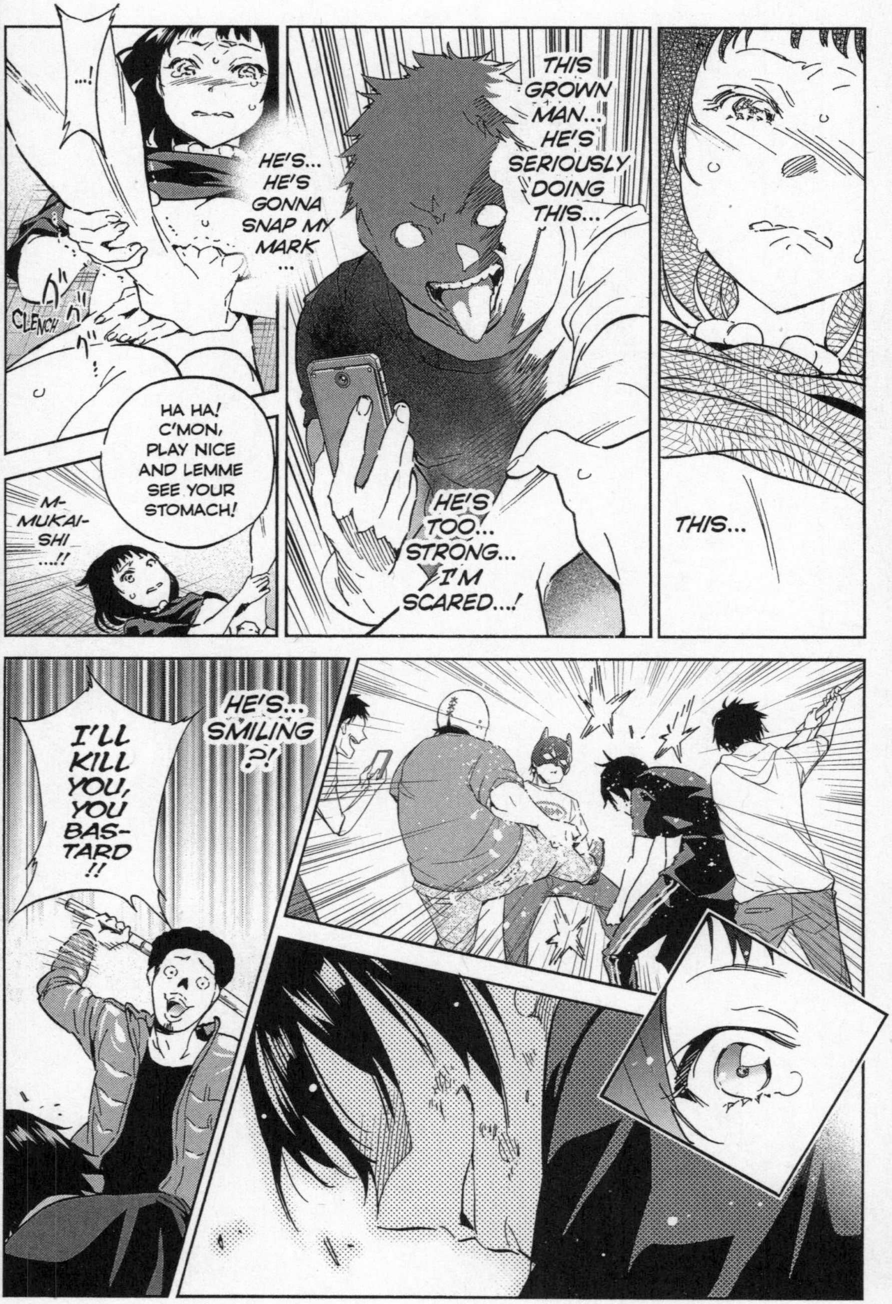
THIS...
THIS GROWN MAN... HE'S SERIOUSLY DOING THIS...
HE'S... HE'S GONNA SNAP MY MARK...
HE'S TOO... STRONG... I'M SCARED...!
...!
CLENCH
HA HA! C'MON, PLAY NICE AND LEMME SEE YOUR STOMACH!
M-MUKAISHI...!!
HE'S... SMILING?!
I'LL KILL YOU, YOU BASTARD!!

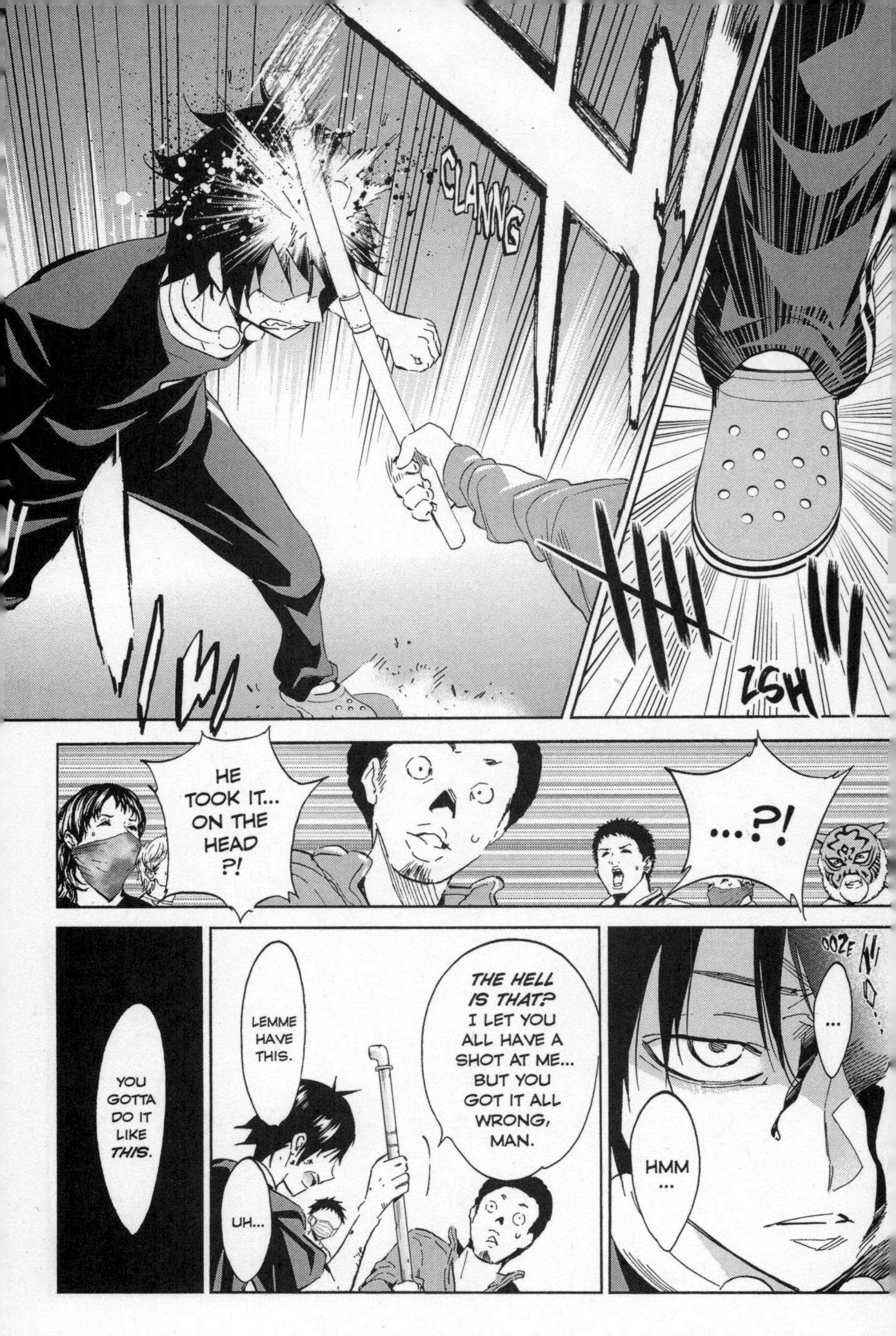
CLANNG
ZSH
...?!
HE TOOK IT... ON THE HEAD ?!
OOZE
...
HMM ...
THE HELL IS THAT? I LET YOU ALL HAVE A SHOT AT ME... BUT YOU GOT IT ALL WRONG, MAN.
LEMME HAVE THIS.
UH...
YOU GOTTA DO IT LIKE *THIS*.

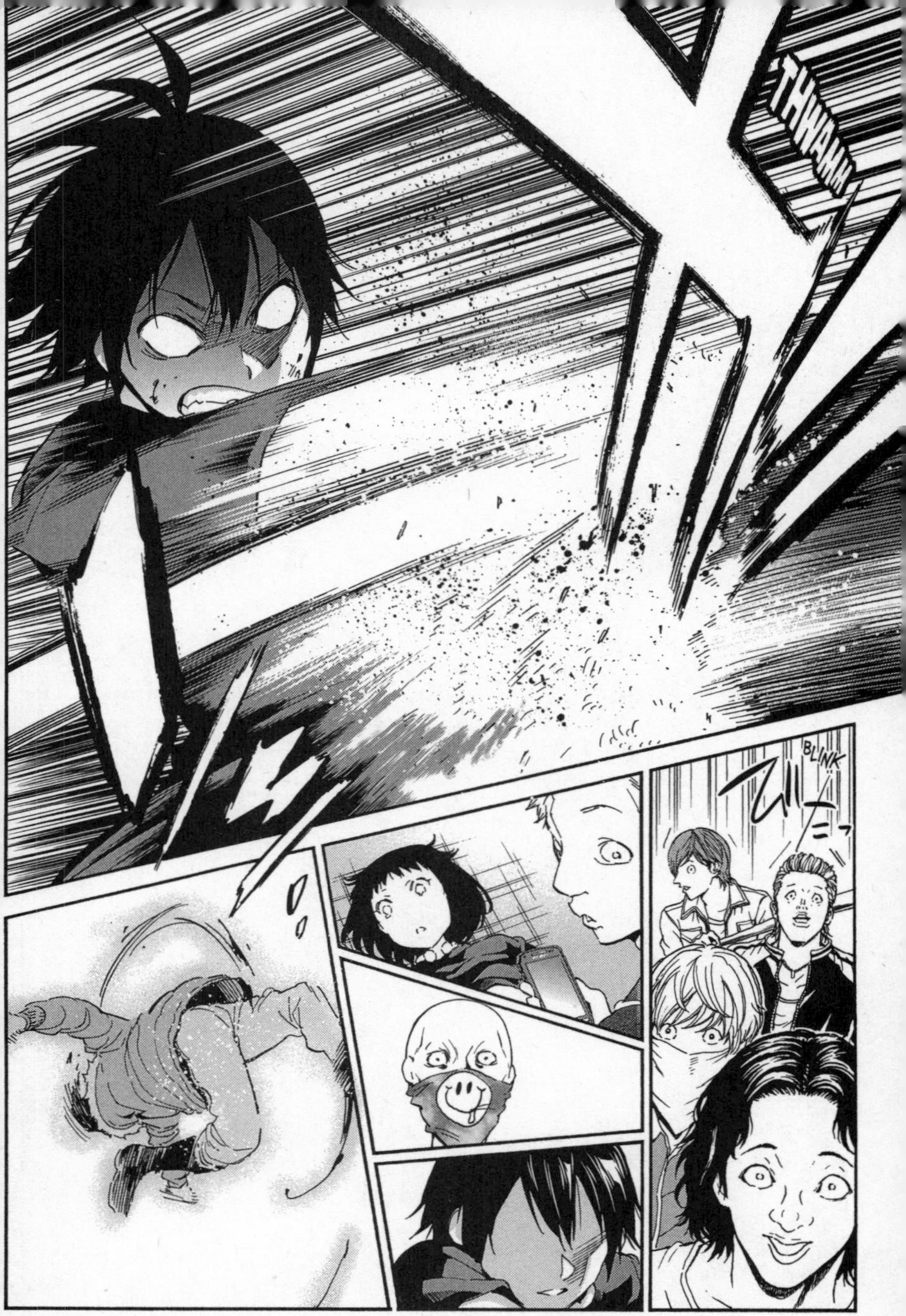
THWAM
BLINK

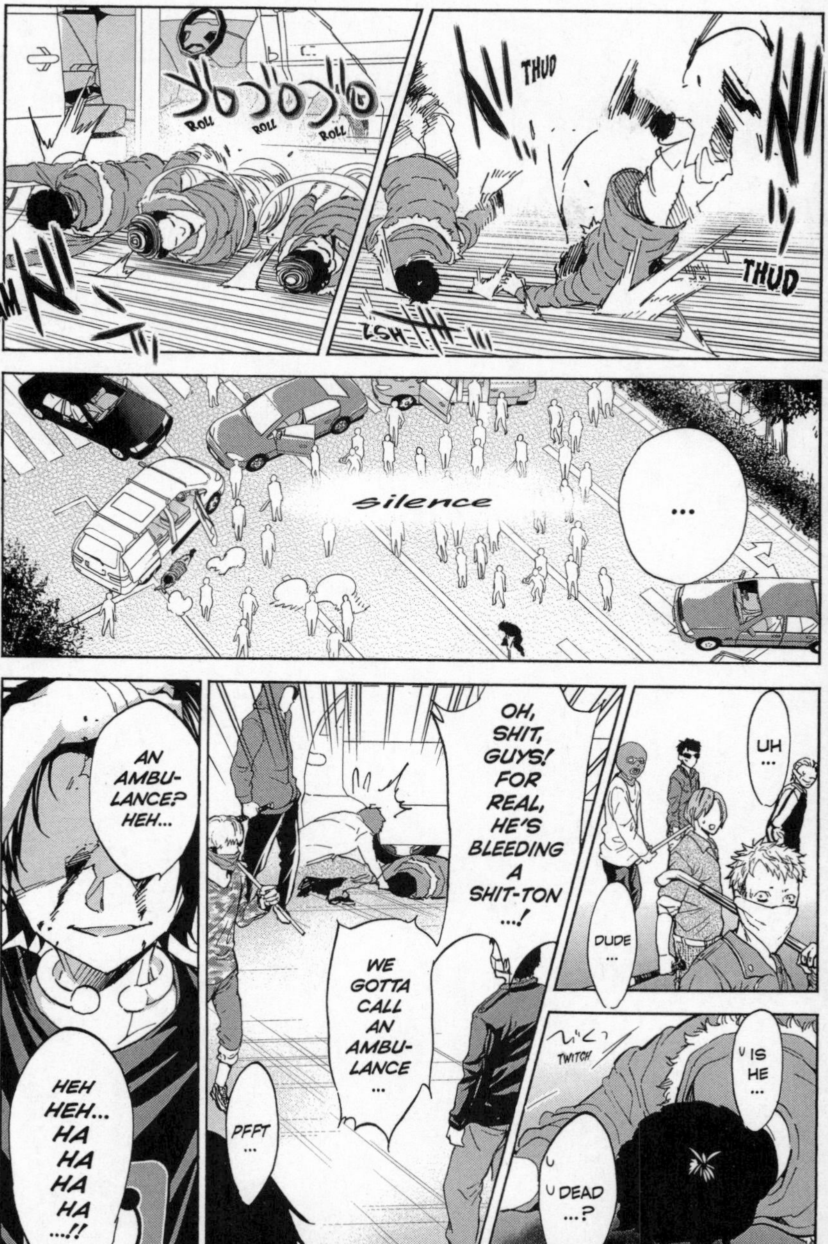
THUD
THUD
TSH
ROLL
ROLL
ROLL
BAM
silence
...
UH ...
DUDE ...
IS HE ...
DEAD ...?
TWITCH
PUDDLE
OH, SHIT, GUYS! FOR REAL, HE'S BLEEDING A SHIT-TON ...!
WE GOTTA CALL AN AMBULANCE ...
PFFT ...
AN AMBULANCE? HEH...
HEH HEH... HA HA HA HA ...!!

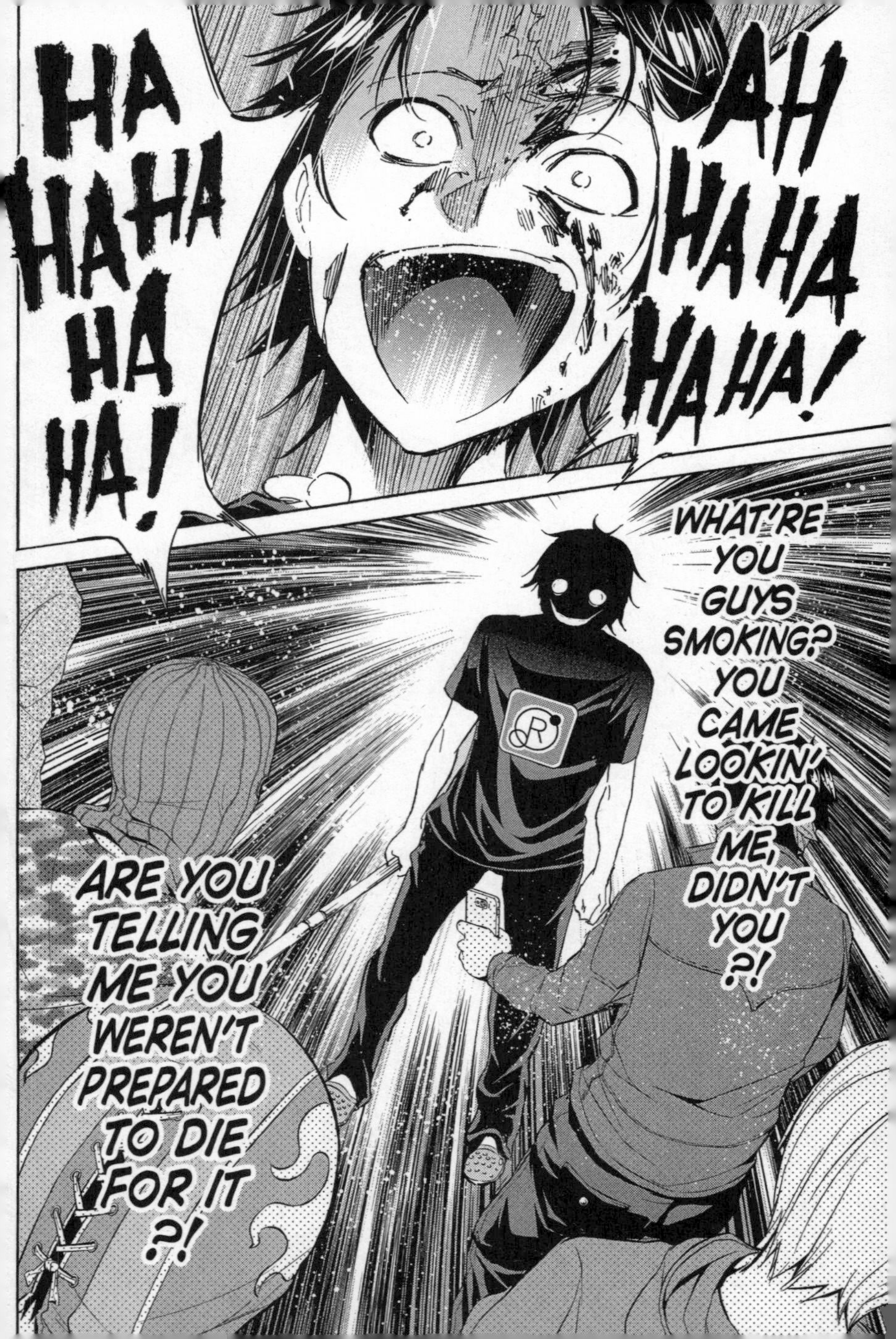
AH HAHAHA HAHAHA!
HA HAHAHA HA HA!
WHAT'RE YOU GUYS SMOKING? YOU CAME LOOKIN' TO KILL ME, DIDN'T YOU ?!
ARE YOU TELLING ME YOU WEREN'T PREPARED TO DIE FOR IT ?!

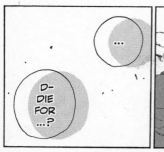

...

D-DIE FOR....?

JOLT

AH-AHH-HH!

CLANG

WHAT THE HELL? HE'S SWING-ING LIKE...

SHUDDER

...

UGHH...

CLANG

WHUMP

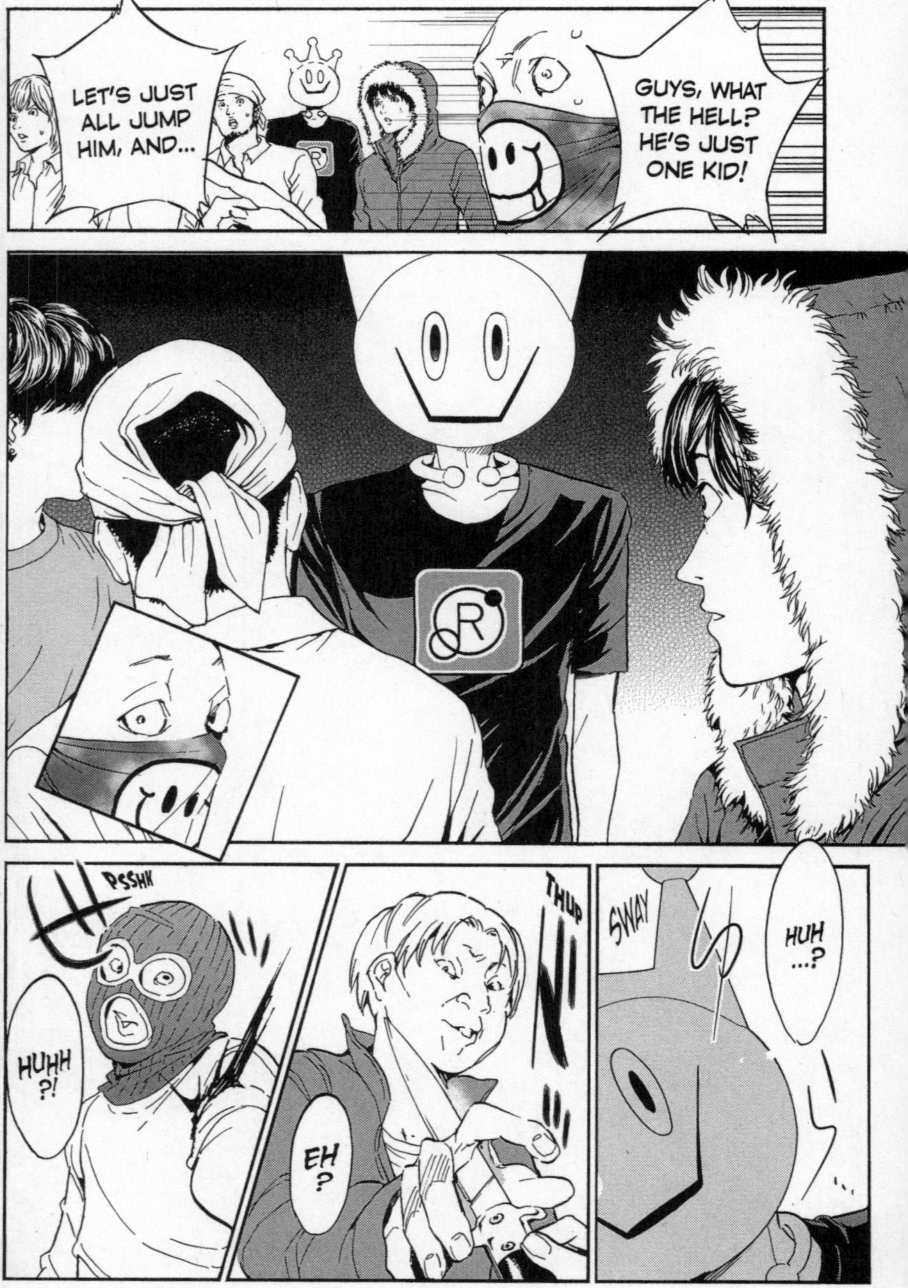
GUYS, WHAT THE HELL? HE'S JUST ONE KID!
LET'S JUST ALL JUMP HIM, AND...
SWAY
HUH ...?
THUP
EH?
PSSHK
HUHH ?!

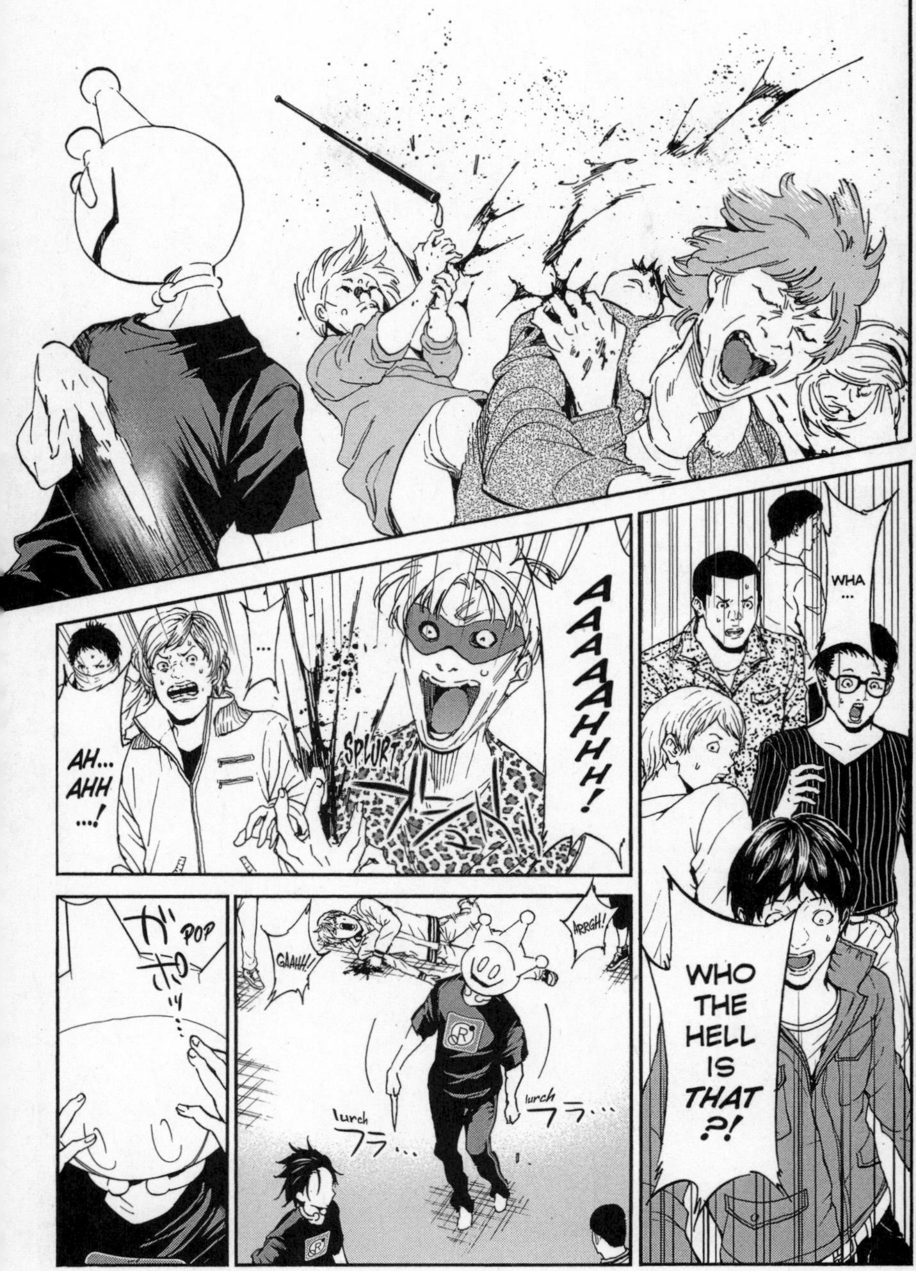
WHA ...
WHO THE HELL IS THAT?!
AAAAAHHH!
SPLURT
...
AH... AHH ...!
ARRGH!
GAAHH!
lurch フラ...
lurch フラ...
ガポッ
POP

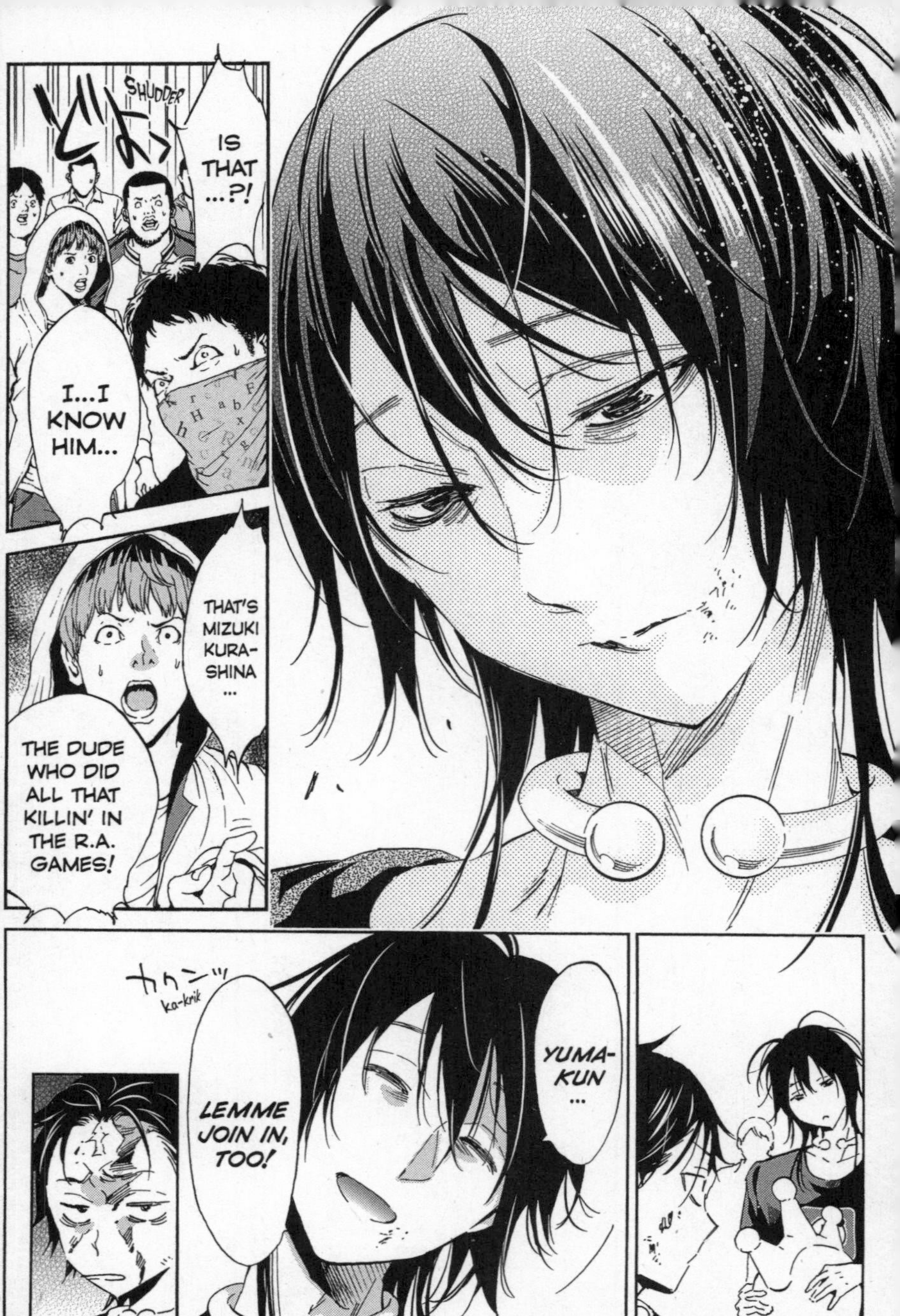
SHUDDER
IS THAT ...?!
I...I KNOW HIM...
THAT'S MIZUKI KURA-SHINA ...
THE DUDE WHO DID ALL THAT KILLIN' IN THE R.A. GAMES!
YUMA-KUN ...
LEMME JOIN IN, TOO!
ka-krik

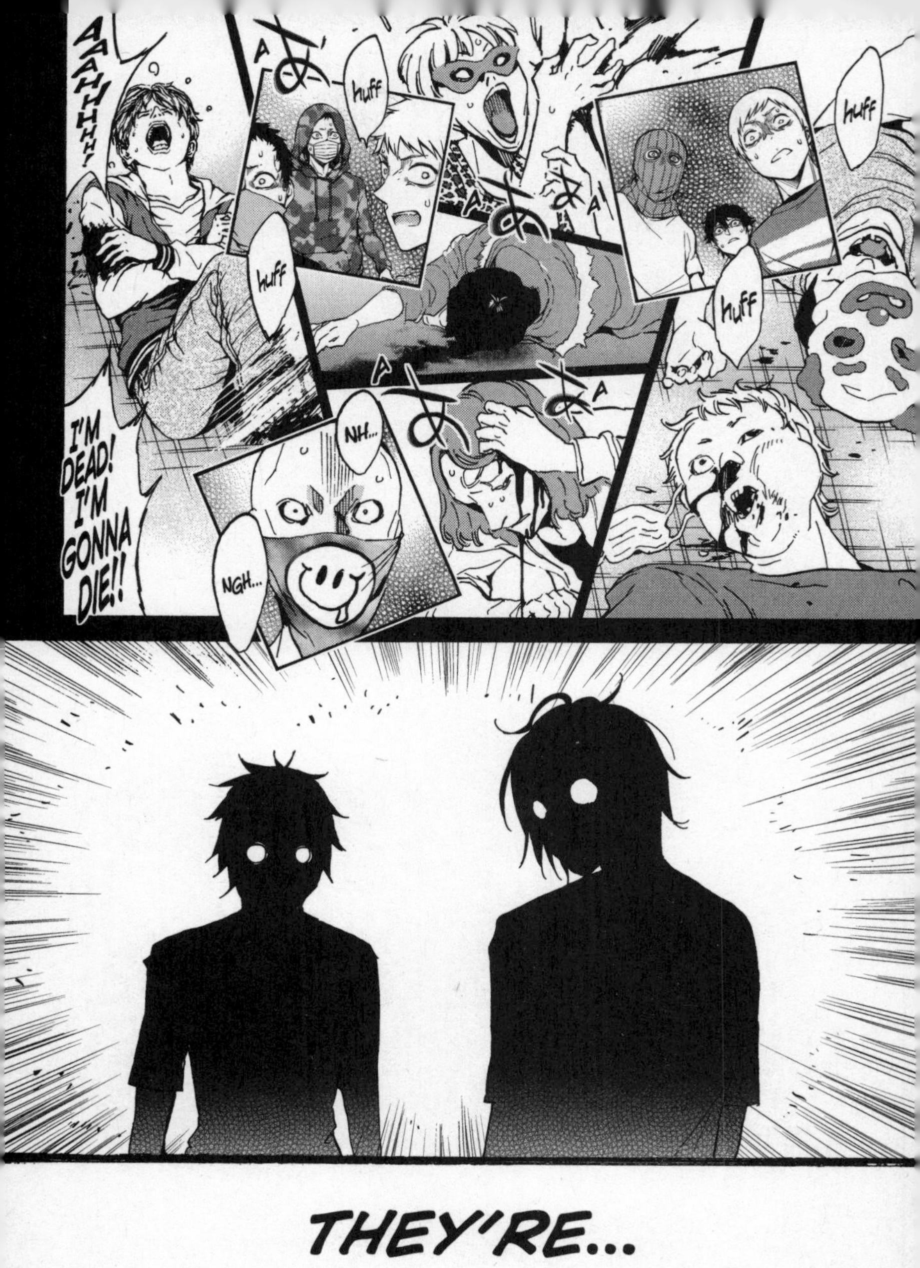
huff
A
huff
A
A
huff
A
huff
A
AAAHHHHH!
NH...
NGH...
I'M DEAD! I'M GONNA DIE!!

THEY'RE...

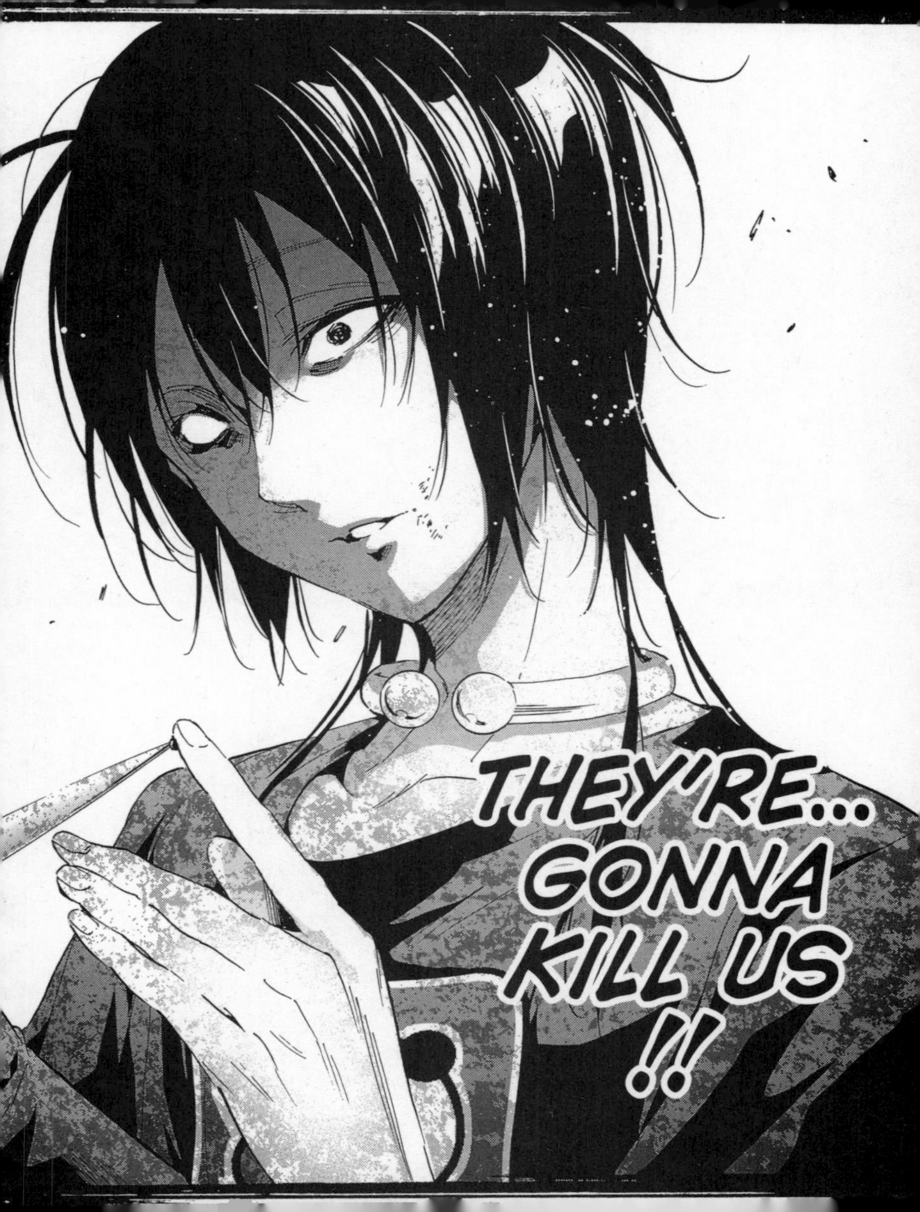
THEY'RE... GONNA KILL US !!

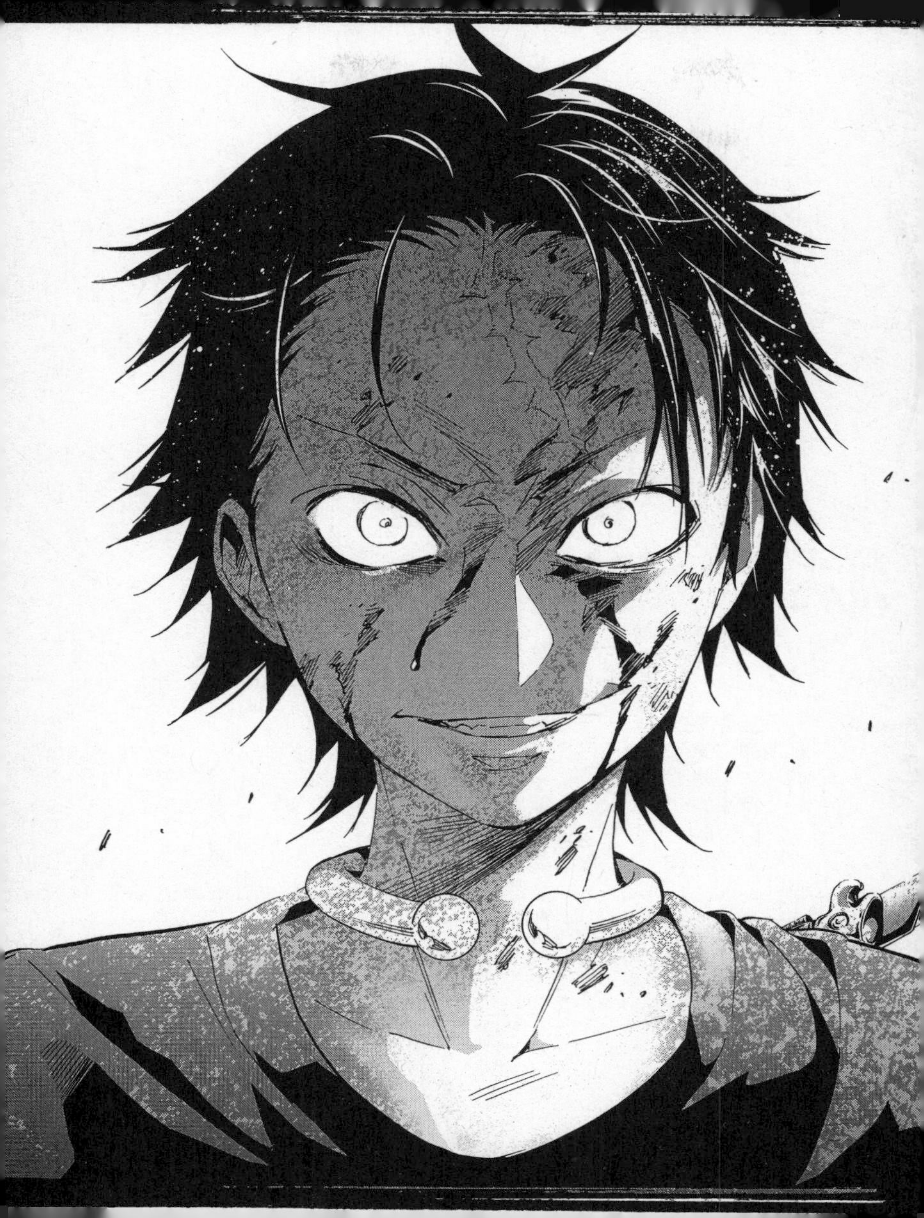

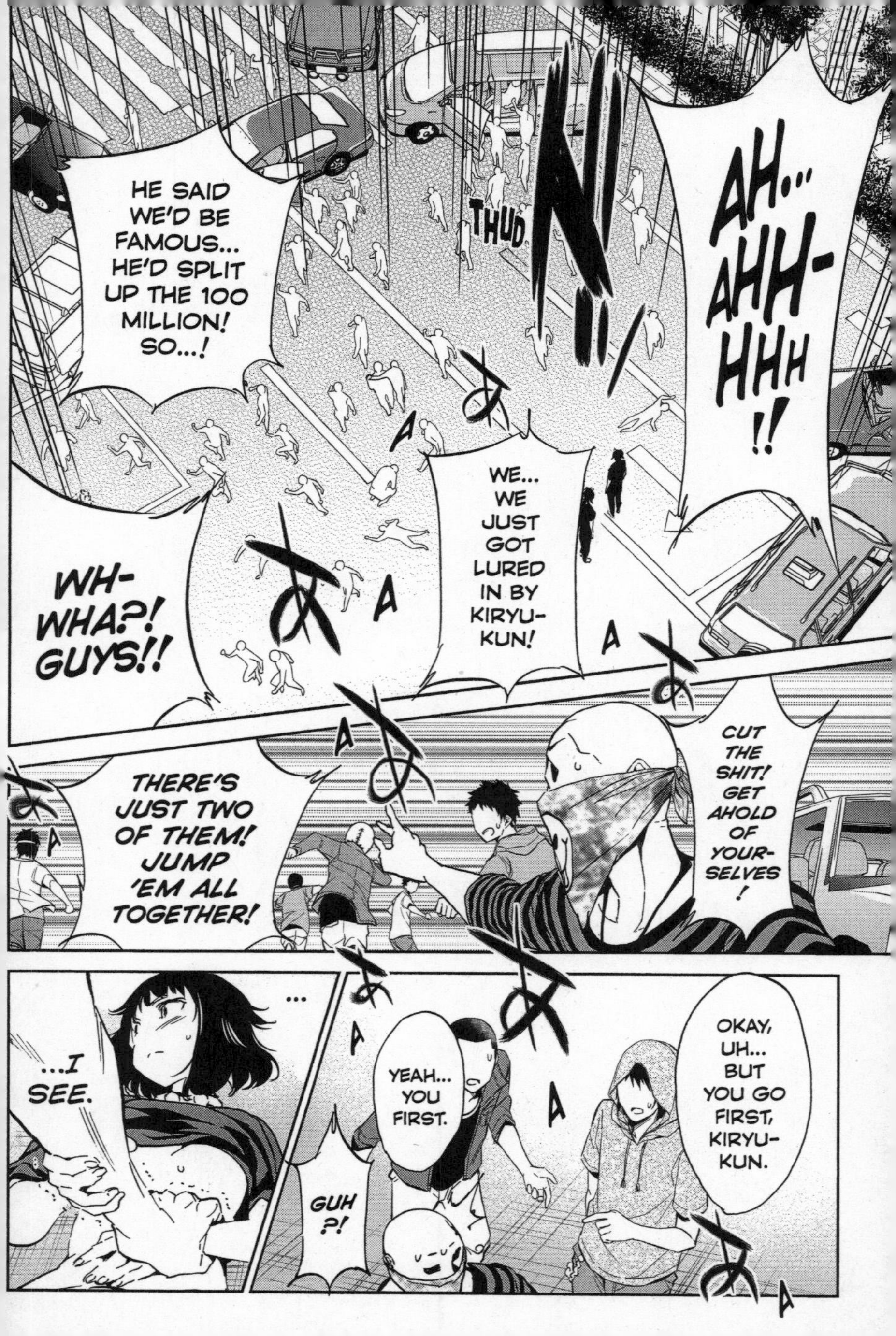

AH... AHH-HHH!!
N!!
THUD
HE SAID WE'D BE FAMOUS... HE'D SPLIT UP THE 100 MILLION! SO...!
WE... WE JUST GOT LURED IN BY KIRYU-KUN!
WH-WHA?! GUYS!!
CUT THE SHIT! GET AHOLD OF YOURSELVES!
THERE'S JUST TWO OF THEM! JUMP 'EM ALL TOGETHER!
OKAY, UH... BUT YOU GO FIRST, KIRYU-KUN.
YEAH... YOU FIRST.
GUH?!
...
...I SEE.

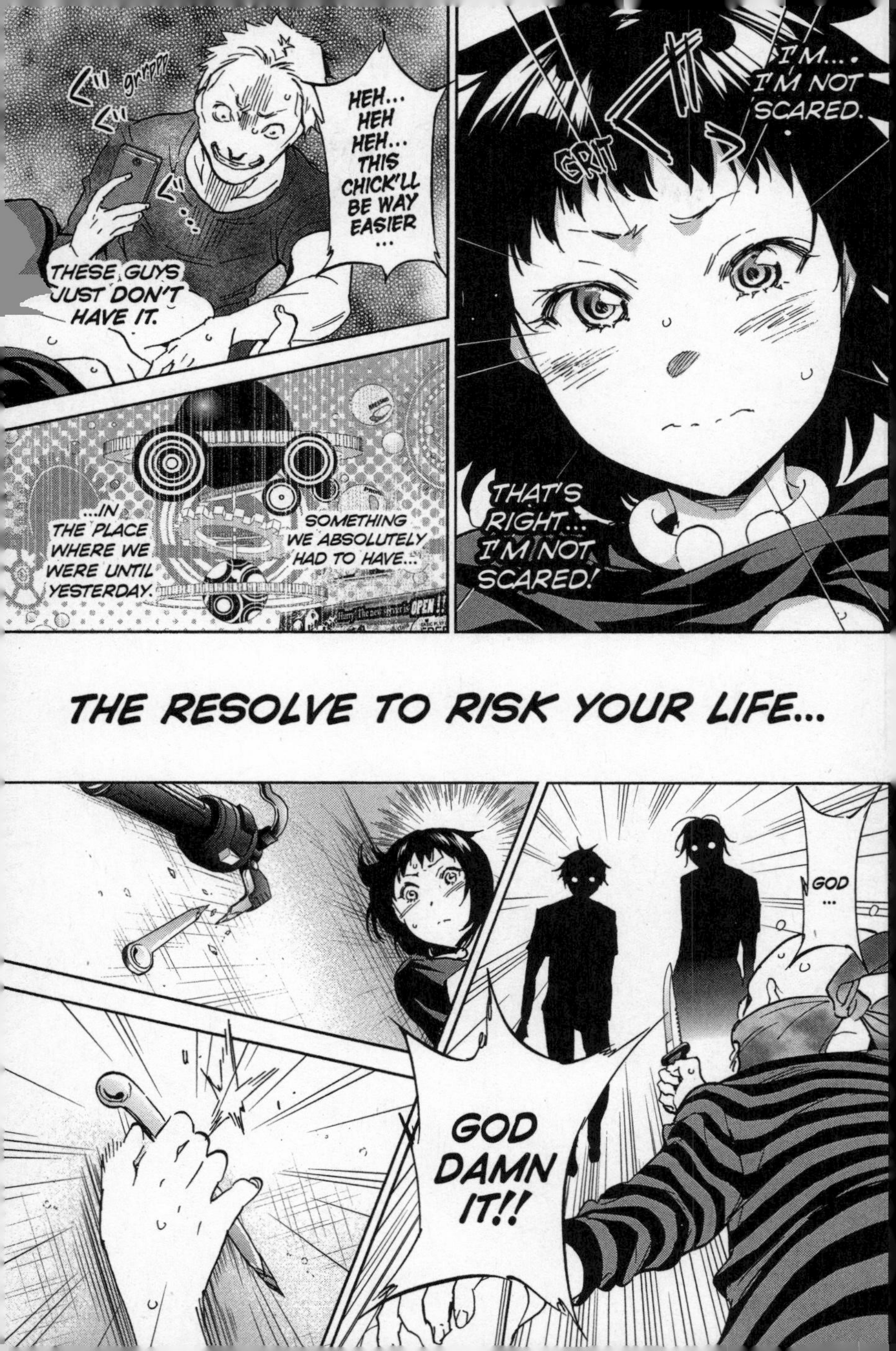
GRIT
I'M... I'M NOT SCARED.
THAT'S RIGHT... I'M NOT SCARED!
HEH... HEH HEH... THIS CHICK'LL BE WAY EASIER...
THESE GUYS JUST DON'T HAVE IT.
SOMETHING WE ABSOLUTELY HAD TO HAVE...
...IN THE PLACE WHERE WE WERE UNTIL YESTERDAY.
THE RESOLVE TO RISK YOUR LIFE...
GOD...
GOD DAMN IT!!

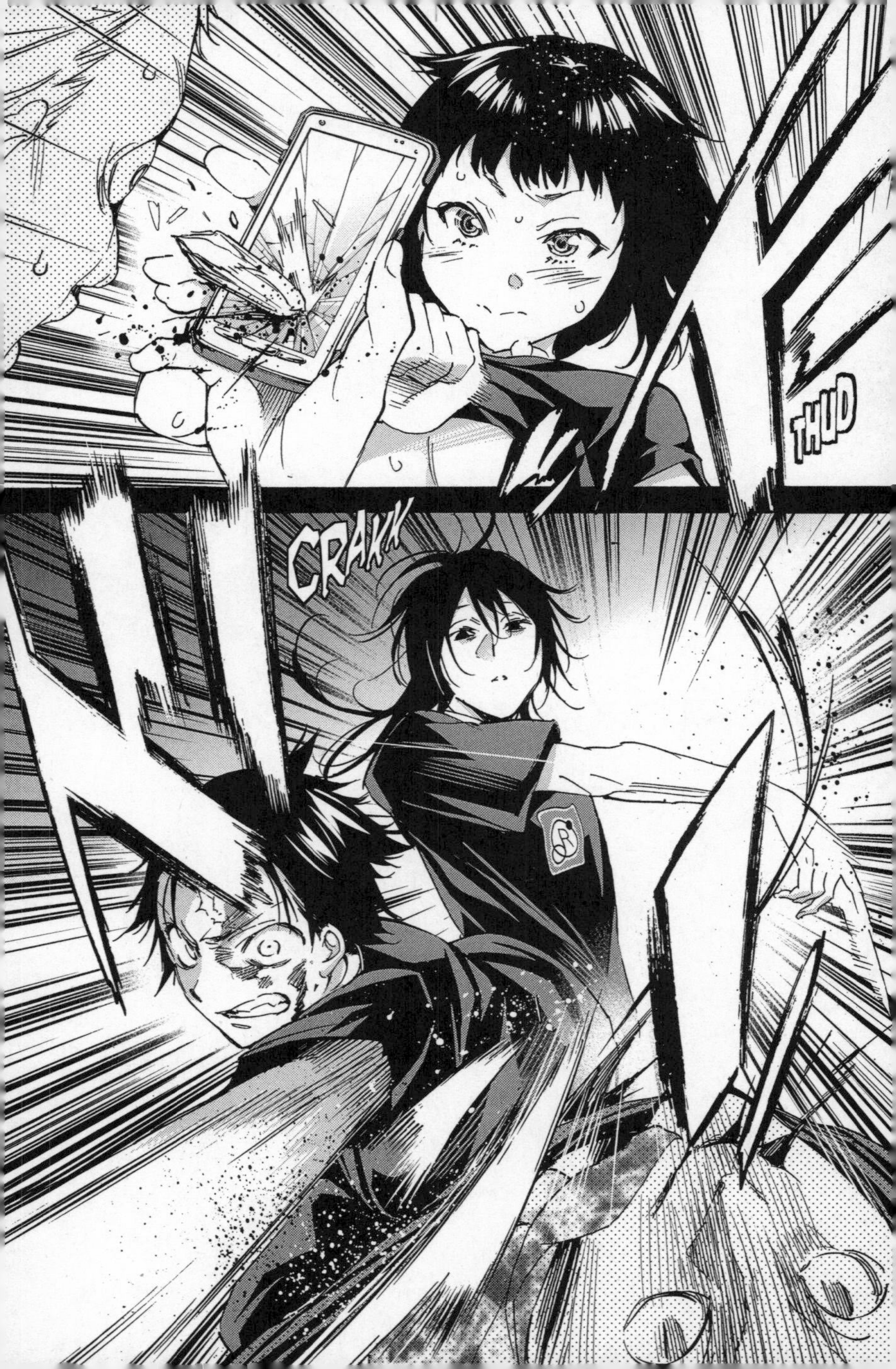
THUD
CRAKK

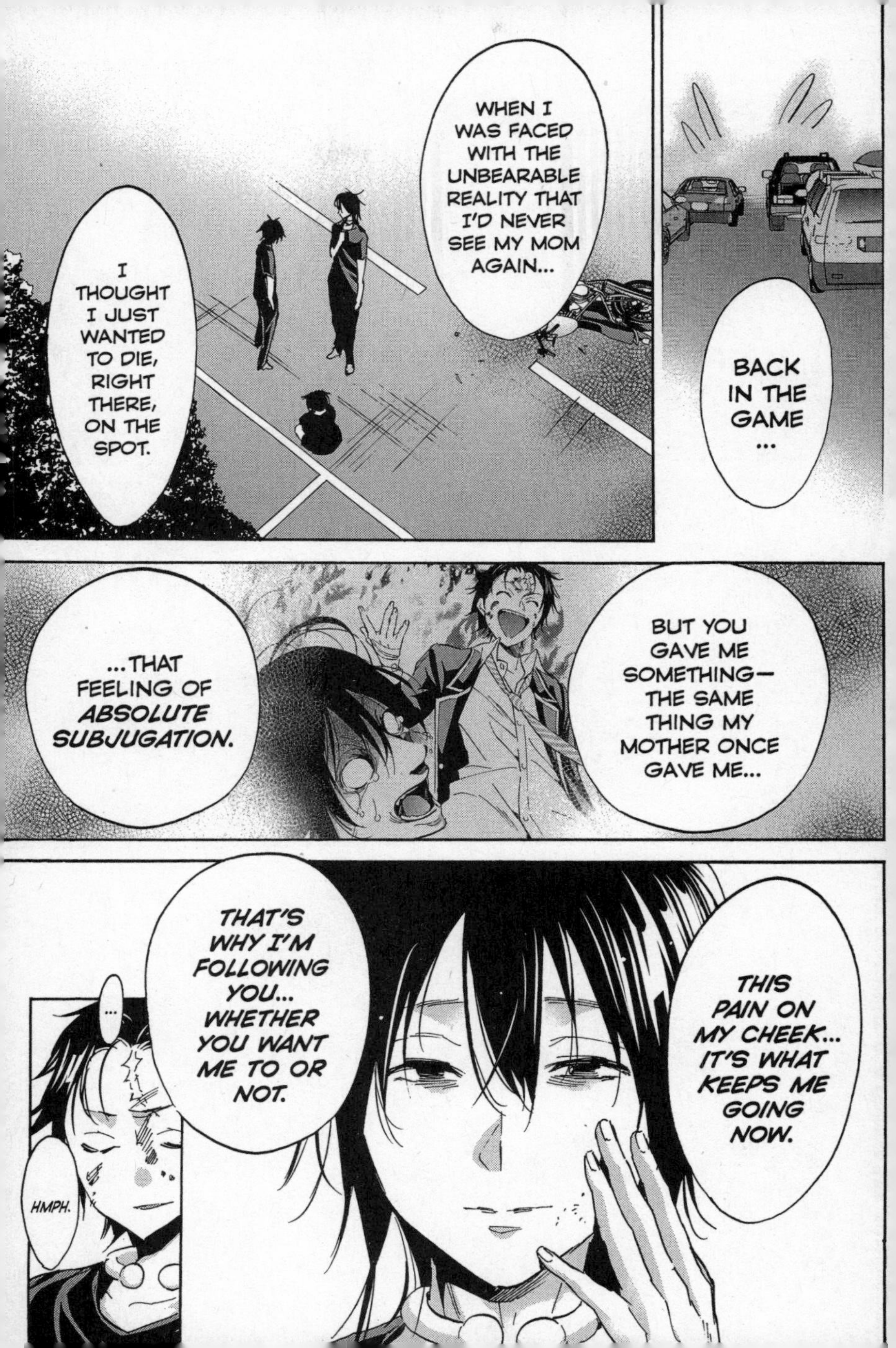
BACK IN THE GAME ...
WHEN I WAS FACED WITH THE UNBEARABLE REALITY THAT I'D NEVER SEE MY MOM AGAIN...
I THOUGHT I JUST WANTED TO DIE, RIGHT THERE, ON THE SPOT.
BUT YOU GAVE ME SOMETHING— THE SAME THING MY MOTHER ONCE GAVE ME...
...THAT FEELING OF ABSOLUTE SUBJUGATION.
THIS PAIN ON MY CHEEK... IT'S WHAT KEEPS ME GOING NOW.
THAT'S WHY I'M FOLLOWING YOU... WHETHER YOU WANT ME TO OR NOT.
...
HMPH.

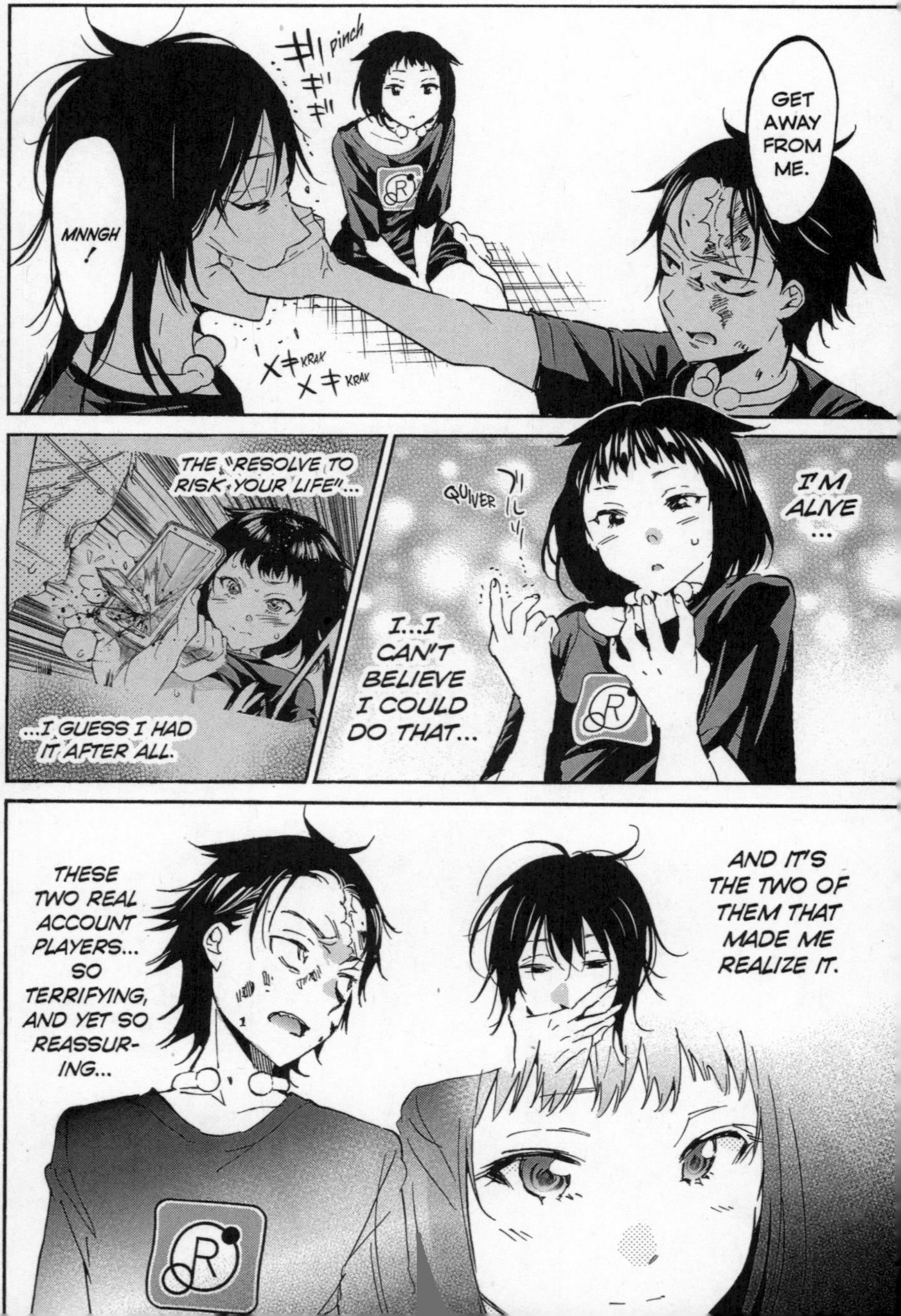
GET AWAY FROM ME.
pinch
MNNGH!
KRAK
KRAK
I'M ALIVE...
QUIVER
I...I CAN'T BELIEVE I COULD DO THAT...
THE "RESOLVE TO RISK YOUR LIFE"...
...I GUESS I HAD IT AFTER ALL.
AND IT'S THE TWO OF THEM THAT MADE ME REALIZE IT.
THESE TWO REAL ACCOUNT PLAYERS... SO TERRIFYING, AND YET SO REASSURING...

ACCOUNT 33 Epilogue

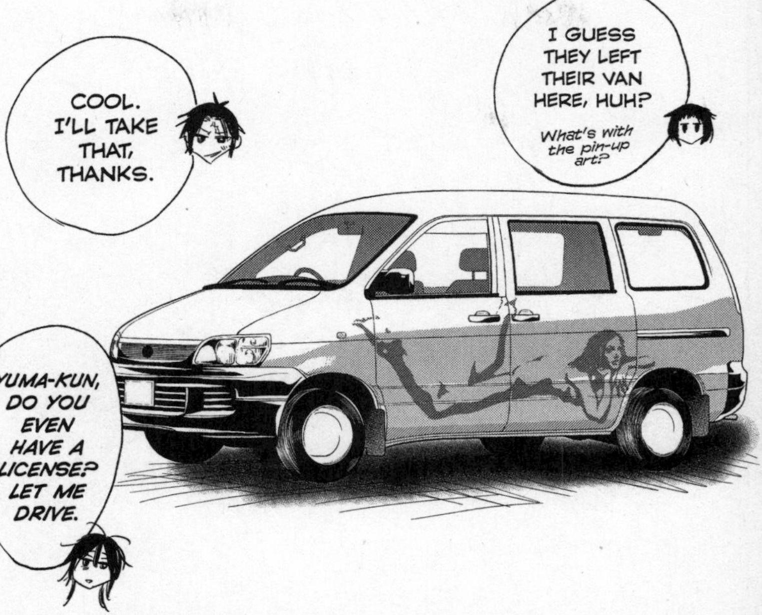

I GUESS THEY LEFT THEIR VAN HERE, HUH?
What's with the pin-up art?
COOL. I'LL TAKE THAT, THANKS.
YUMA-KUN, DO YOU EVEN HAVE A LICENSE? LET ME DRIVE.

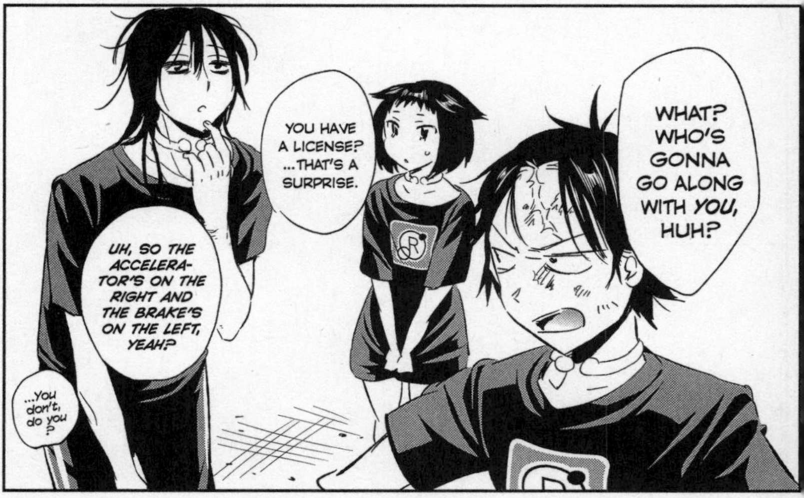

WHAT? WHO'S GONNA GO ALONG WITH YOU, HUH?
YOU HAVE A LICENSE? ...THAT'S A SURPRISE.
UH, SO THE ACCELERATOR'S ON THE RIGHT AND THE BRAKE'S ON THE LEFT, YEAH?
...You don't, do you?

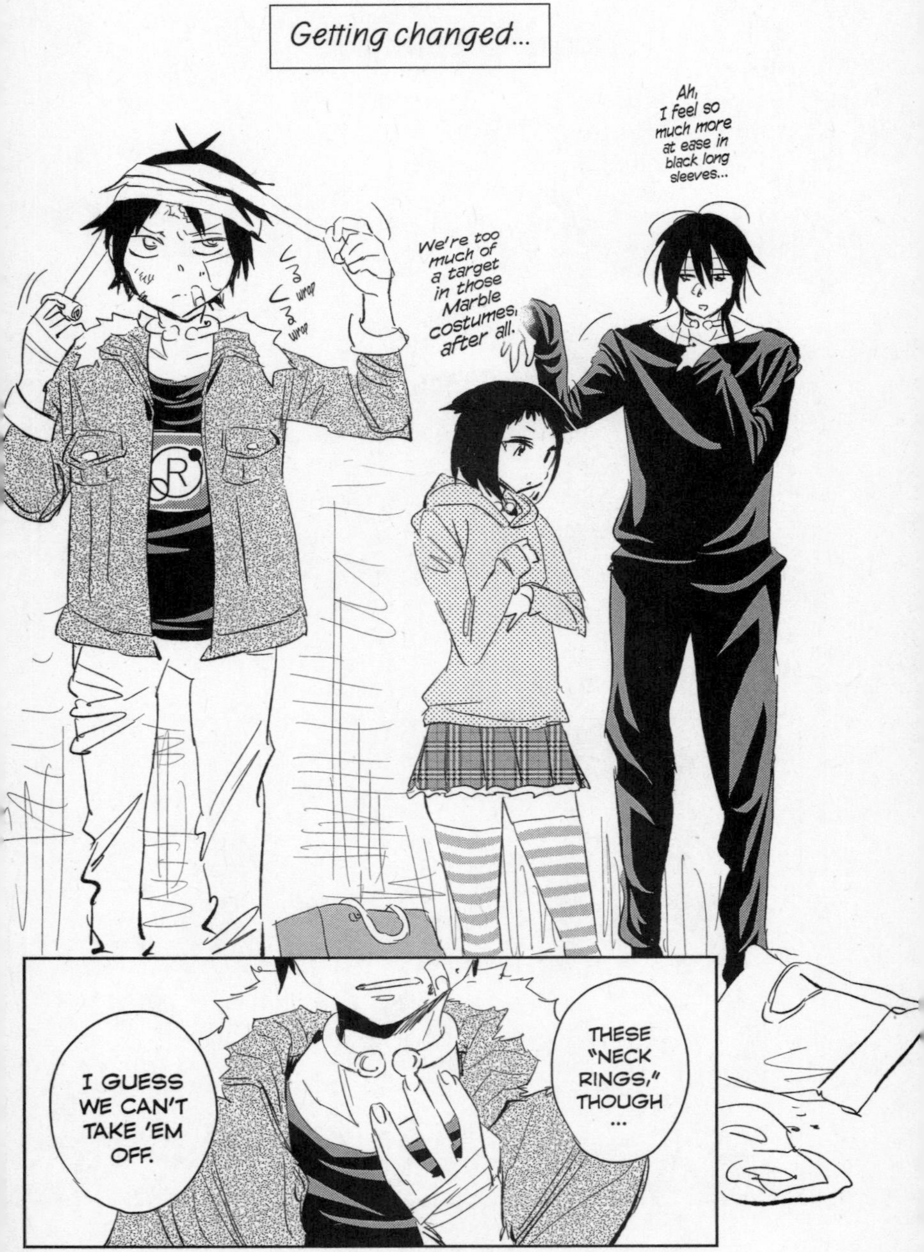
Getting changed...
Ah, I feel so much more at ease in black long sleeves...
We're too much of a target in those Marble costumes, after all.
wrap wrap
THESE "NECK RINGS," THOUGH...
I GUESS WE CAN'T TAKE 'EM OFF.

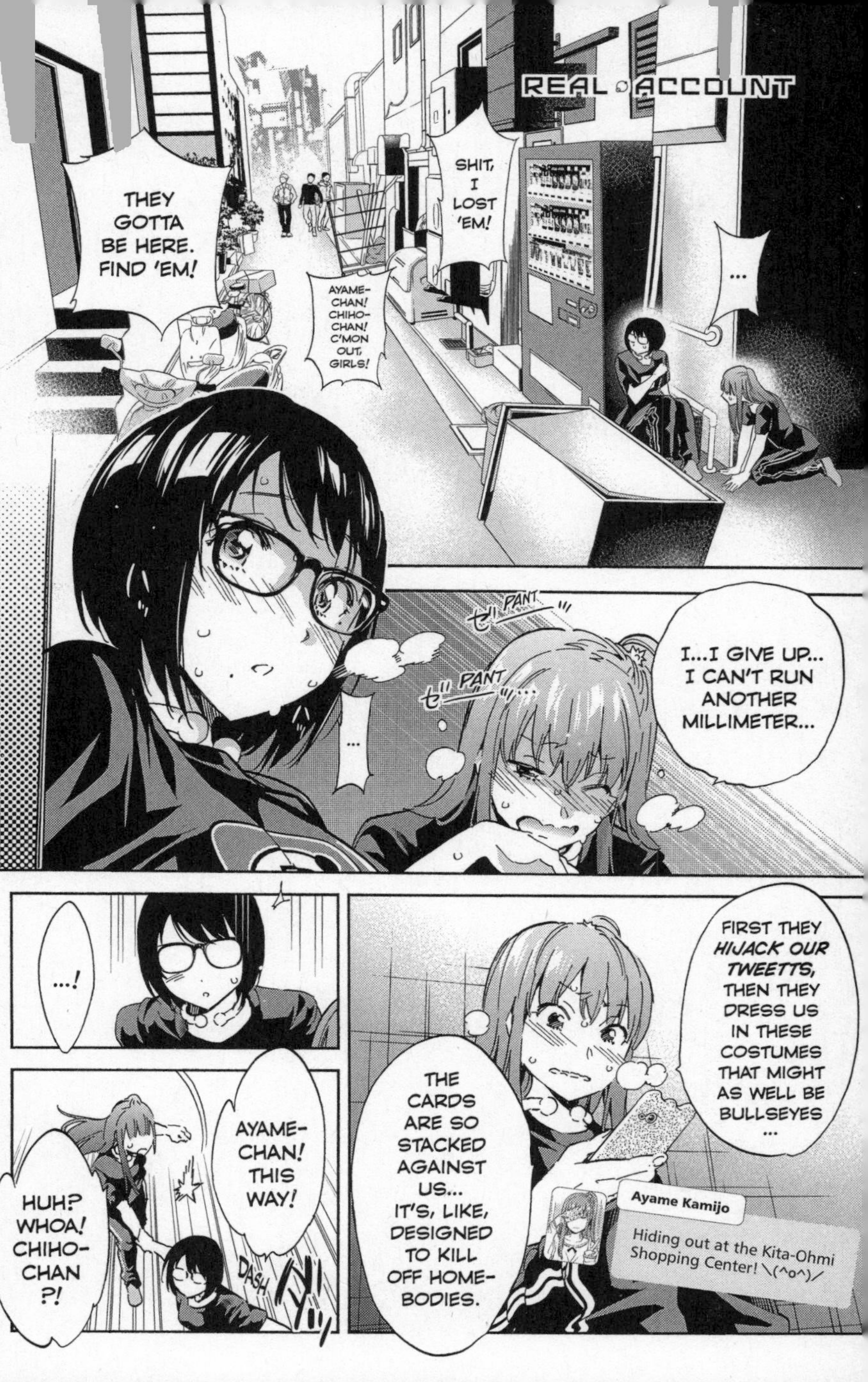
...
SHIT, I LOST 'EM!
THEY GOTTA BE HERE. FIND 'EM!
AYAME-CHAN! CHIHO-CHAN! C'MON OUT, GIRLS!
PANT
PANT
I...I GIVE UP... I CAN'T RUN ANOTHER MILLIMETER...
...
FIRST THEY *HIJACK OUR TWEETTS*, THEN THEY DRESS US IN THESE COSTUMES THAT MIGHT AS WELL BE BULLSEYES ...
THE CARDS ARE SO STACKED AGAINST US... IT'S, LIKE, DESIGNED TO KILL OFF HOME-BODIES.
Ayame Kamijo
Hiding out at the Kita-Ohmi Shopping Center! \(^o^)/
...!
AYAME-CHAN! THIS WAY!
HUH? WHOA! CHIHO-CHAN?!
DASH

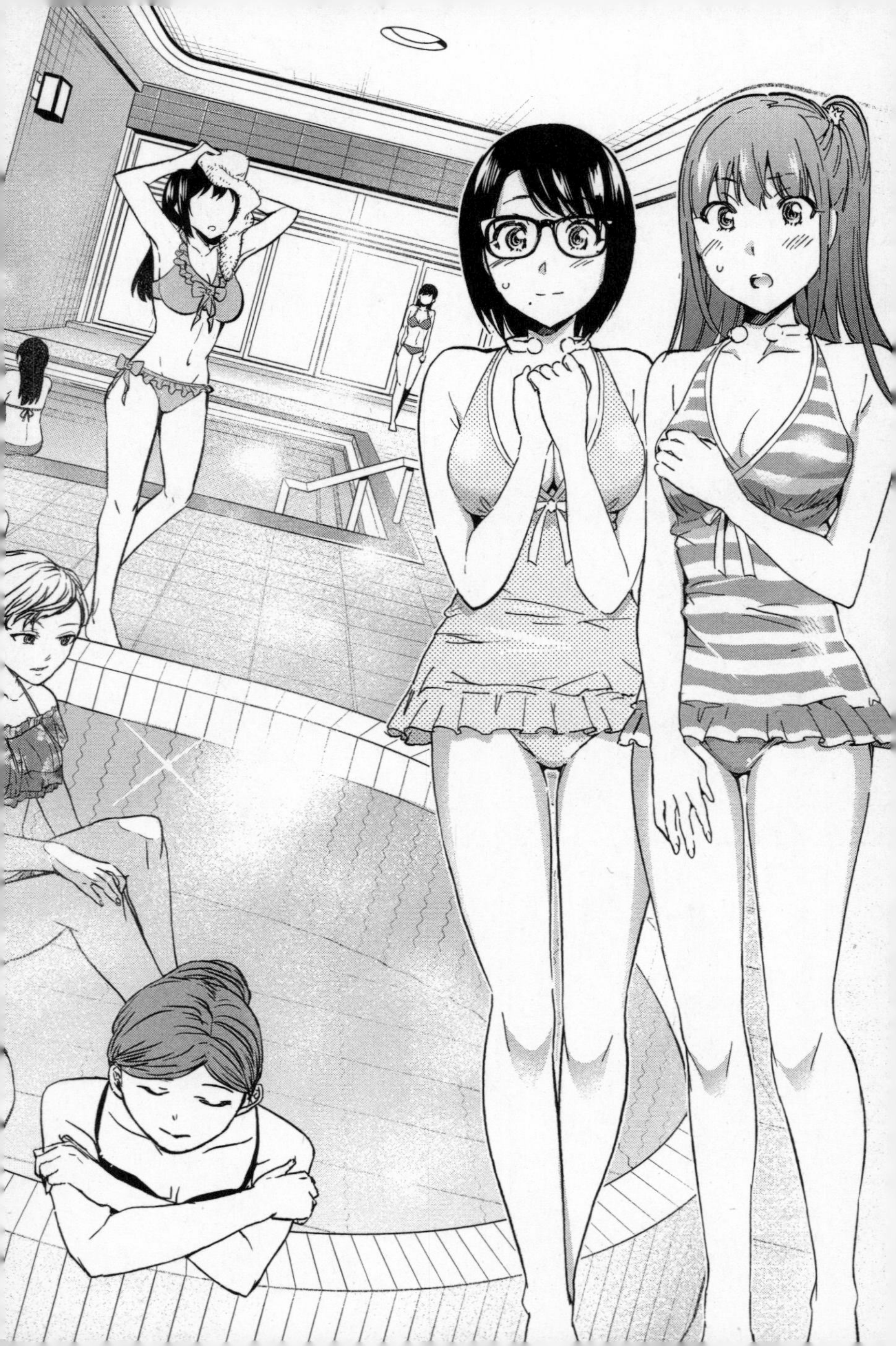

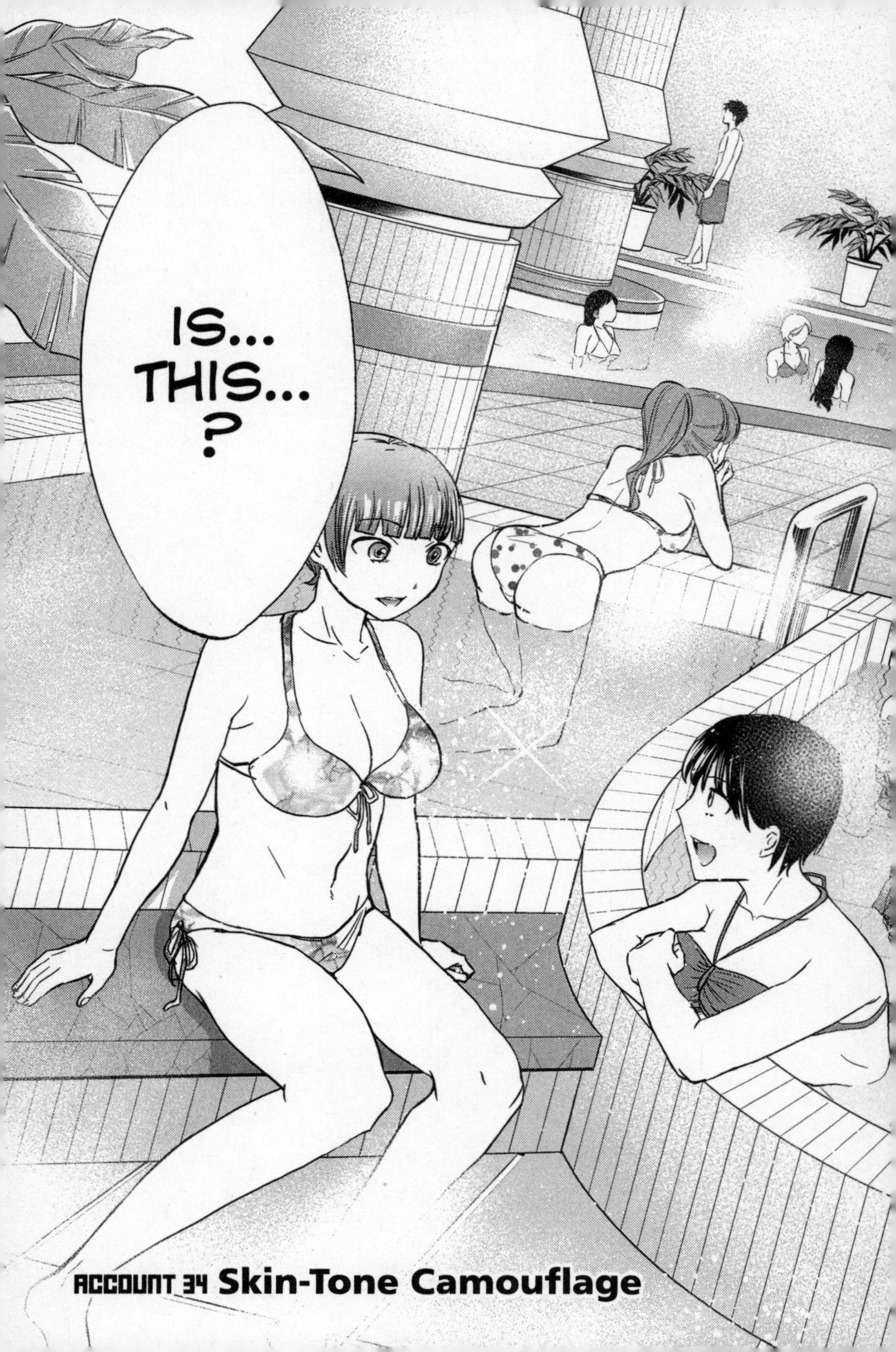
IS... THIS... ?

ACCOUNT 34 Skin-Tone Camouflage

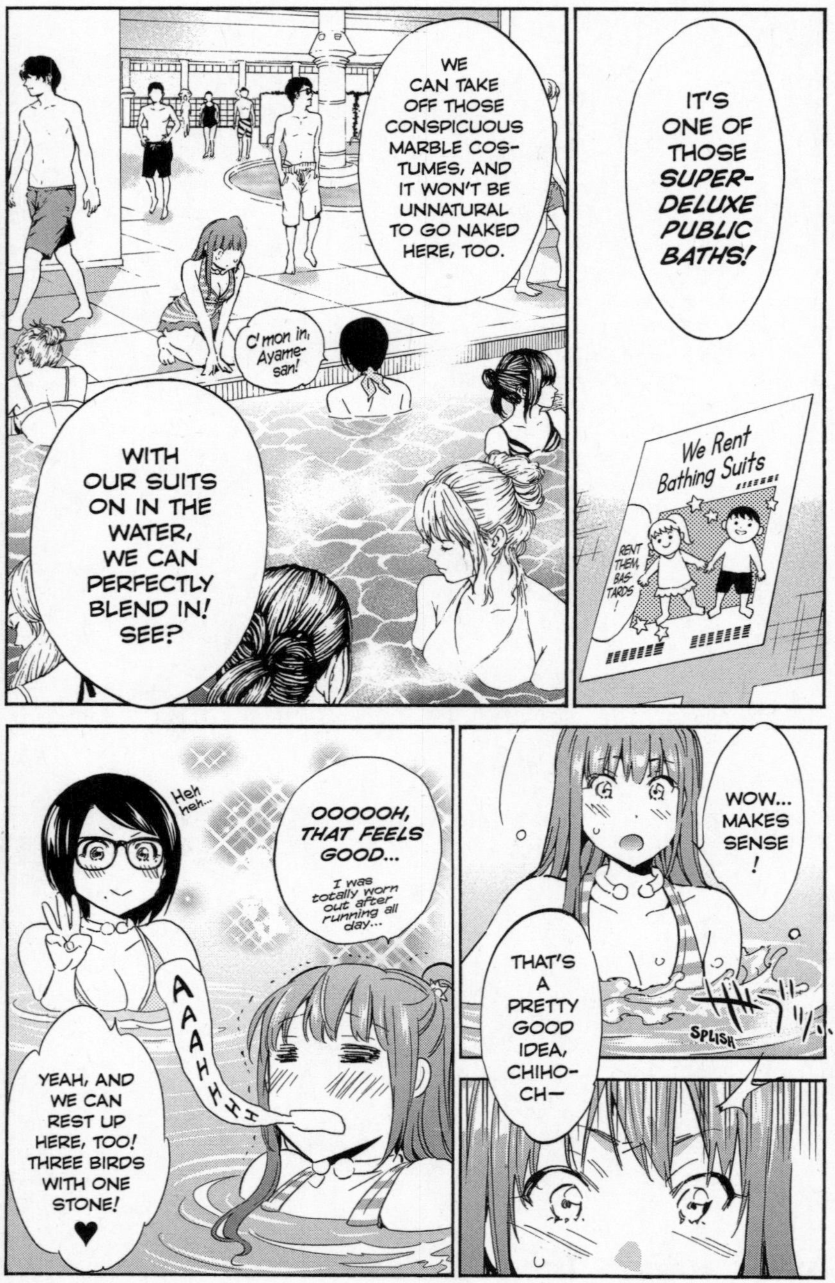

IT'S ONE OF THOSE SUPER-DELUXE PUBLIC BATHS!
We Rent Bathing Suits
RENT THEM, BASTARDS!
WE CAN TAKE OFF THOSE CONSPICUOUS MARBLE COS-TUMES, AND IT WON'T BE UNNATURAL TO GO NAKED HERE, TOO.
C'mon in, Ayame-san!
WITH OUR SUITS ON IN THE WATER, WE CAN PERFECTLY BLEND IN! SEE?
WOW... MAKES SENSE!
THAT'S A PRETTY GOOD IDEA, CHIHO-CH—
SPLISH
OOOOOH, THAT FEELS GOOD...
I was totally worn out after running all day...
Heh heh...
AAAHHH
YEAH, AND WE CAN REST UP HERE, TOO! THREE BIRDS WITH ONE STONE! ♥

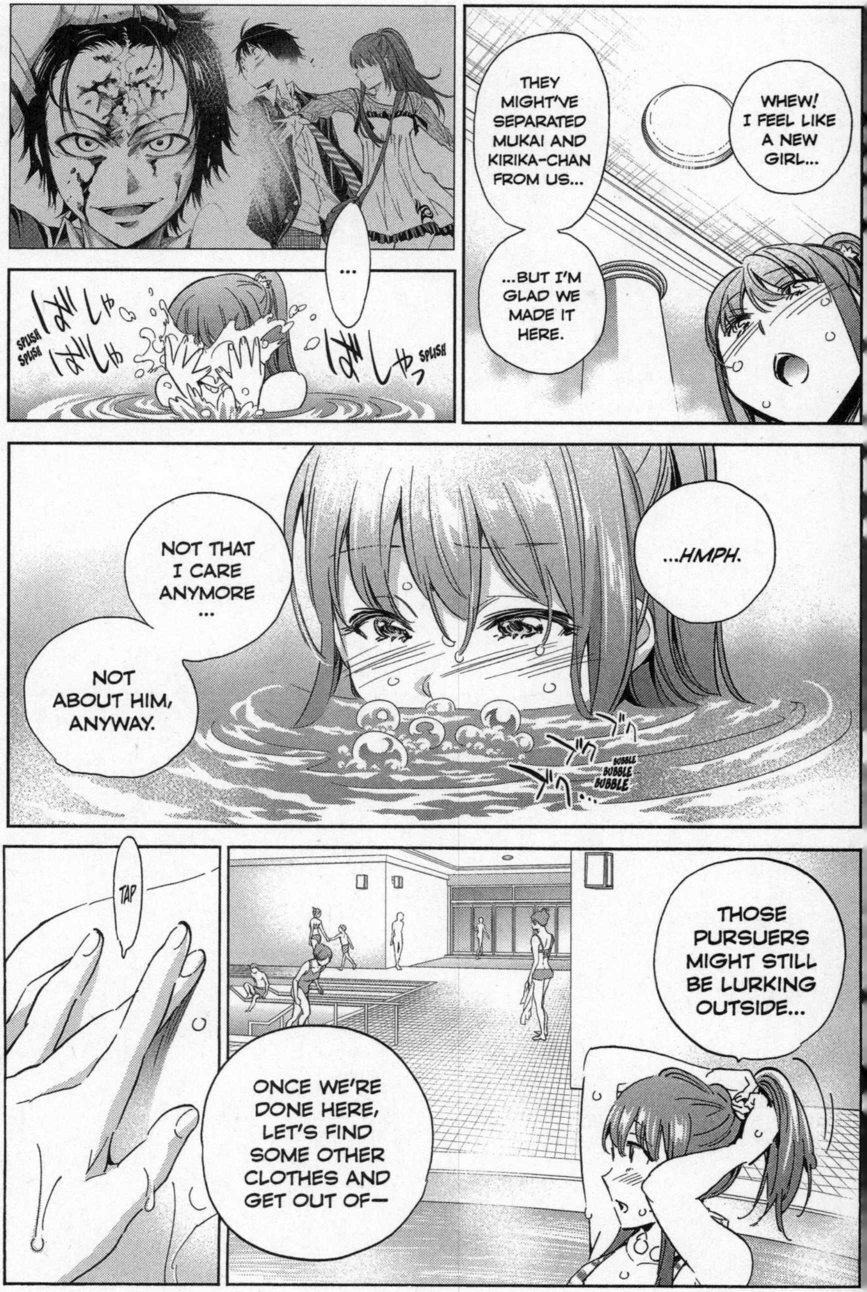
WHEW! I FEEL LIKE A NEW GIRL...
THEY MIGHT'VE SEPARATED MUKAI AND KIRIKA-CHAN FROM US...
...BUT I'M GLAD WE MADE IT HERE.
...
ばしゃっ SPLISH
ばしゃ ばしゃ SPLISH SPLISH
...HMPH.
NOT THAT I CARE ANYMORE ...
NOT ABOUT HIM, ANYWAY.
ブクブクブク... BUBBLE BUBBLE BUBBLE
THOSE PURSUERS MIGHT STILL BE LURKING OUTSIDE...
ONCE WE'RE DONE HERE, LET'S FIND SOME OTHER CLOTHES AND GET OUT OF—
TAP

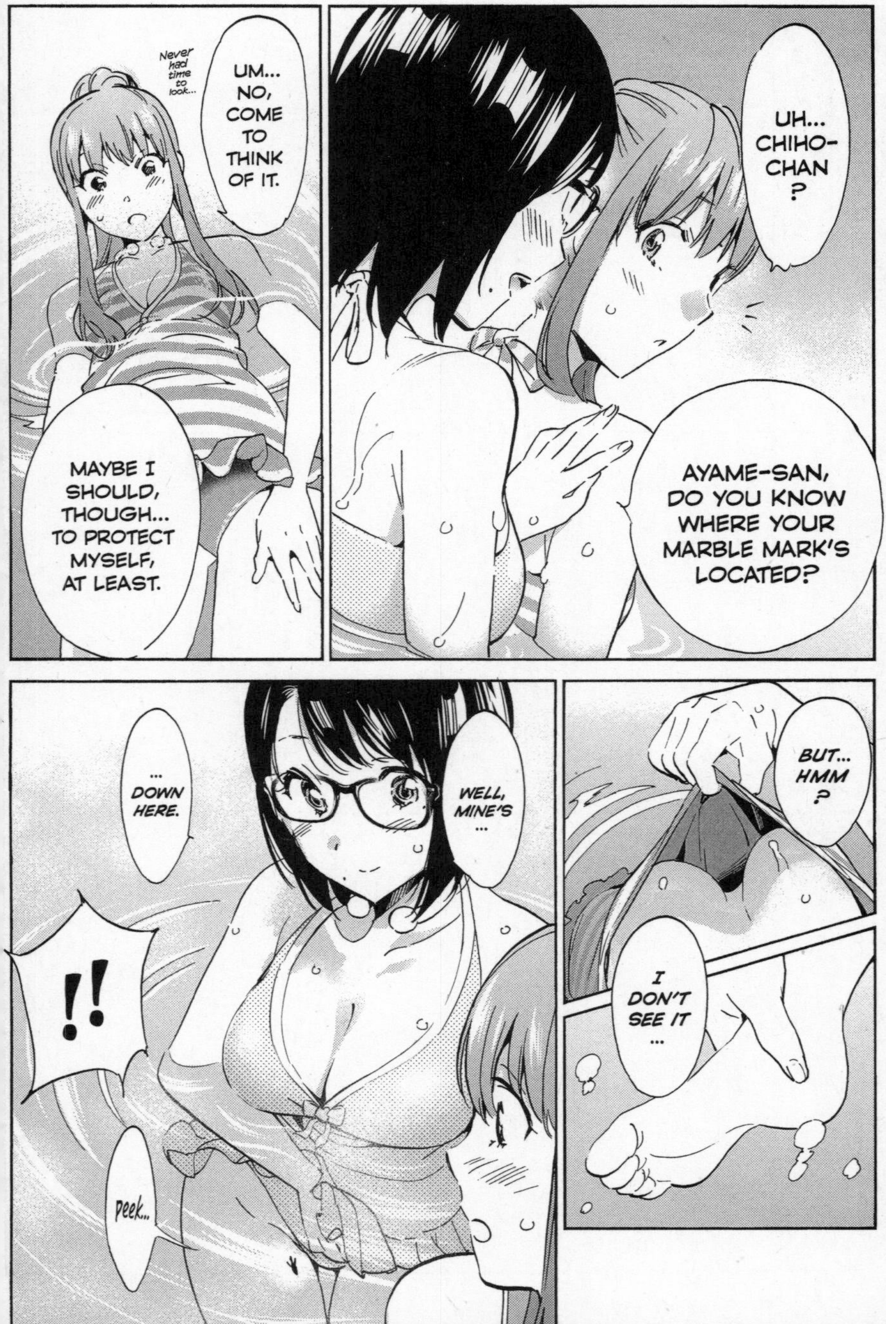
UH... CHIHO-CHAN?
AYAME-SAN, DO YOU KNOW WHERE YOUR MARBLE MARK'S LOCATED?
UM... NO, COME TO THINK OF IT.
Never had time to look...
MAYBE I SHOULD, THOUGH... TO PROTECT MYSELF, AT LEAST.
BUT... HMM?
I DON'T SEE IT...
WELL, MINE'S ...
... DOWN HERE.
!!
peek...

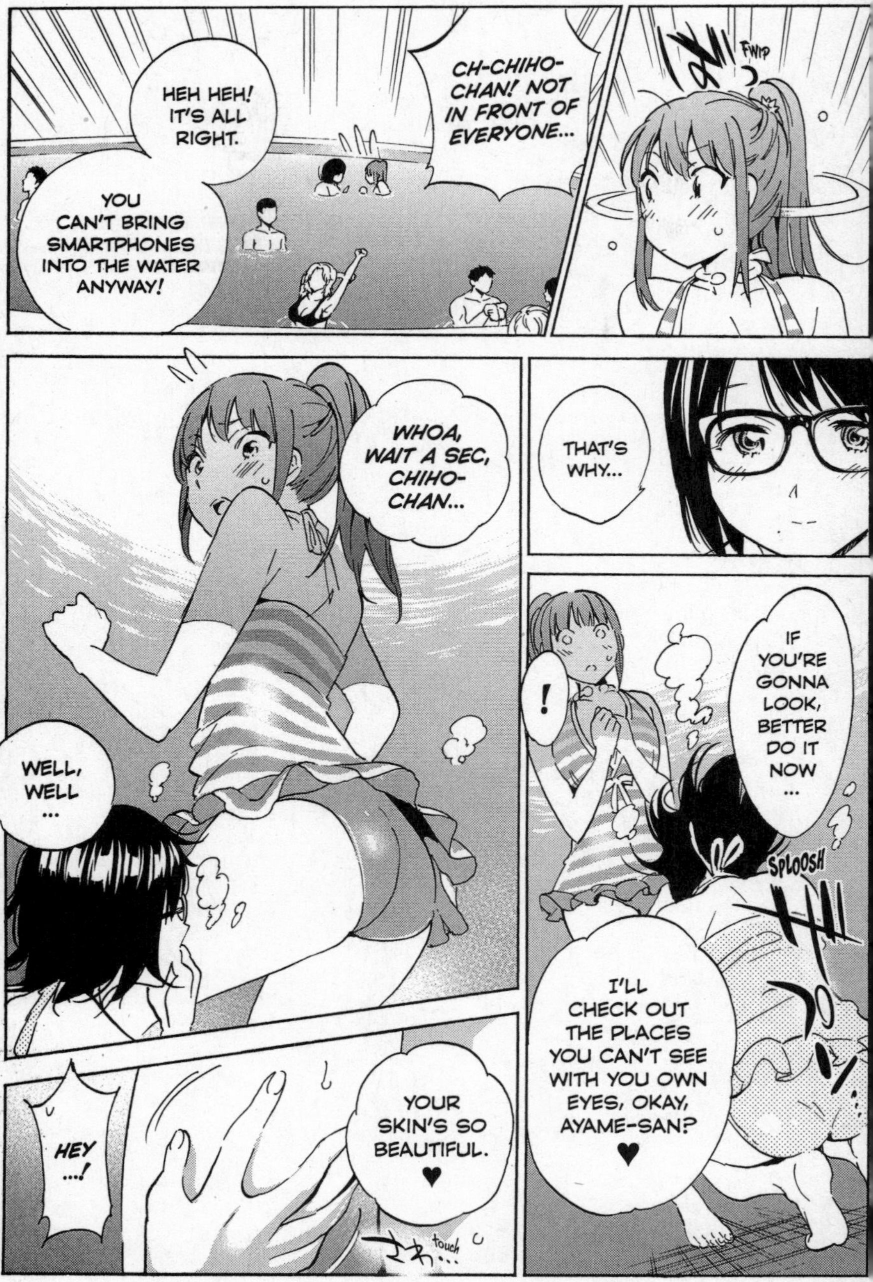
FWIP
CH-CHIHO-CHAN! NOT IN FRONT OF EVERYONE...
HEH HEH! IT'S ALL RIGHT.
YOU CAN'T BRING SMARTPHONES INTO THE WATER ANYWAY!
THAT'S WHY...
IF YOU'RE GONNA LOOK, BETTER DO IT NOW ...
!
SPLOOSH
I'LL CHECK OUT THE PLACES YOU CAN'T SEE WITH YOU OWN EYES, OKAY, AYAME-SAN? ♥
WHOA, WAIT A SEC, CHIHO-CHAN...
WELL, WELL ...
YOUR SKIN'S SO BEAUTIFUL. ♥
HEY ...!
touch

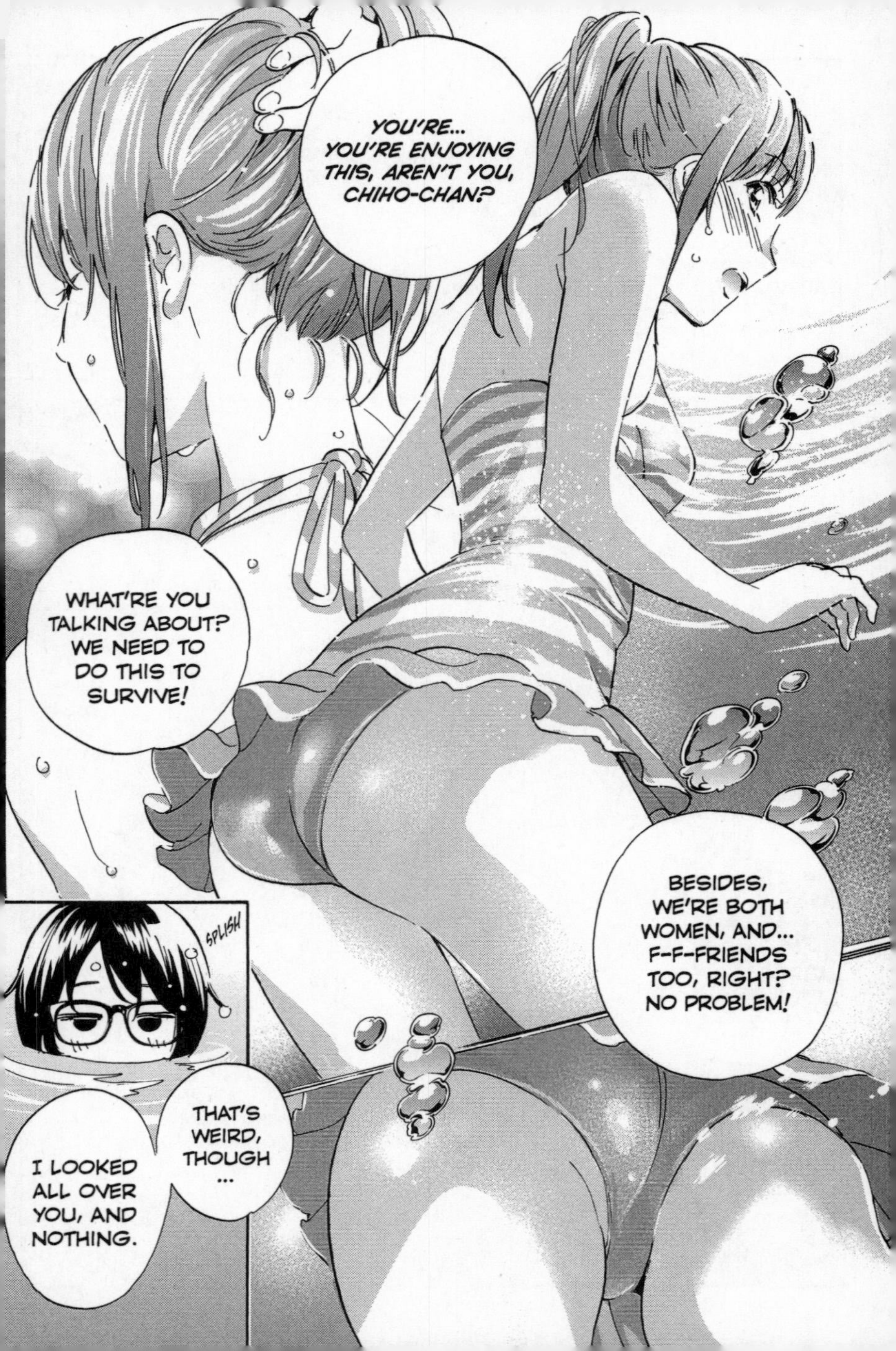
YOU'RE... YOU'RE ENJOYING THIS, AREN'T YOU, CHIHO-CHAN?
WHAT'RE YOU TALKING ABOUT? WE NEED TO DO THIS TO SURVIVE!
BESIDES, WE'RE BOTH WOMEN, AND... F-F-FRIENDS TOO, RIGHT? NO PROBLEM!
SPLISH
THAT'S WEIRD, THOUGH ...
I LOOKED ALL OVER YOU, AND NOTHING.

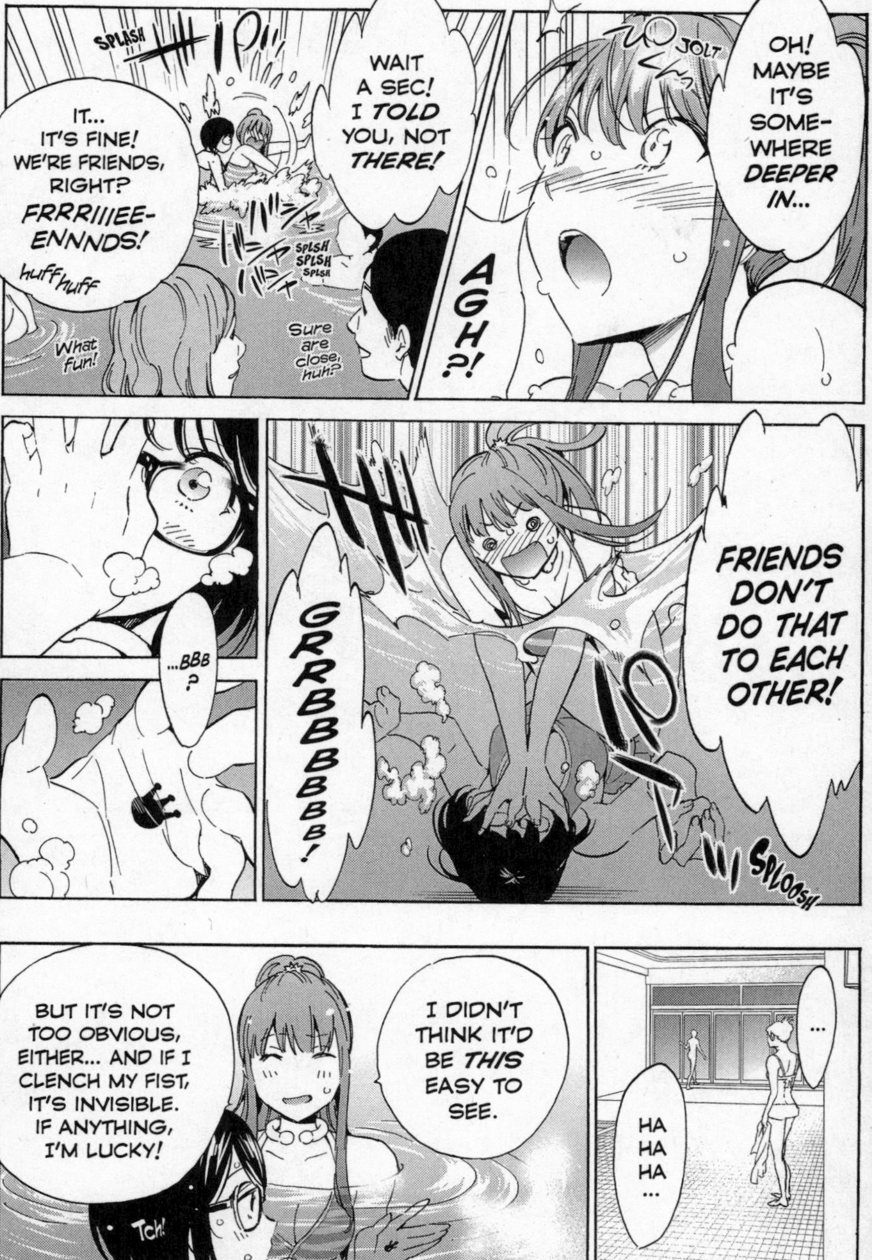
JOLT
OH! MAYBE IT'S SOMEWHERE DEEPER IN...
AGH?!
WAIT A SEC! I TOLD YOU, NOT THERE!
SPLASH
IT... IT'S FINE! WE'RE FRIENDS, RIGHT? FRRRIIIEE-ENNNDS!
huff huff
SPLSH SPLSH SPLSH
Sure are close, huh?
What fun!
FRIENDS DON'T DO THAT TO EACH OTHER!
GRRBBBBBBB!
SPLOOSH
...BBB?
...
HA HA HA...
I DIDN'T THINK IT'D BE THIS EASY TO SEE.
BUT IT'S NOT TOO OBVIOUS, EITHER... AND IF I CLENCH MY FIST, IT'S INVISIBLE. IF ANYTHING, I'M LUCKY!
Tch!

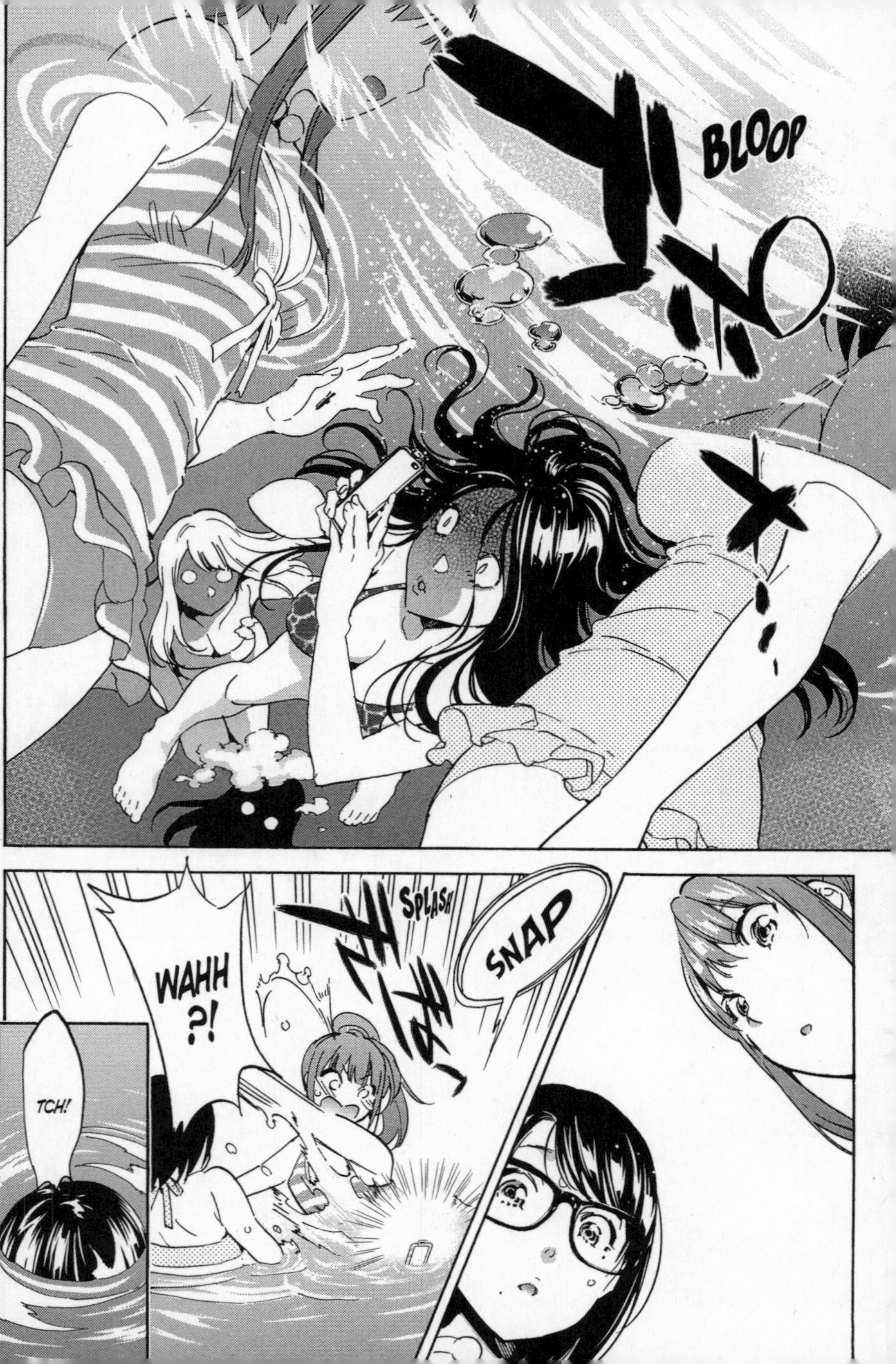
BLOOP
SNAP
SPLASH
WAHH ?!
TCH!

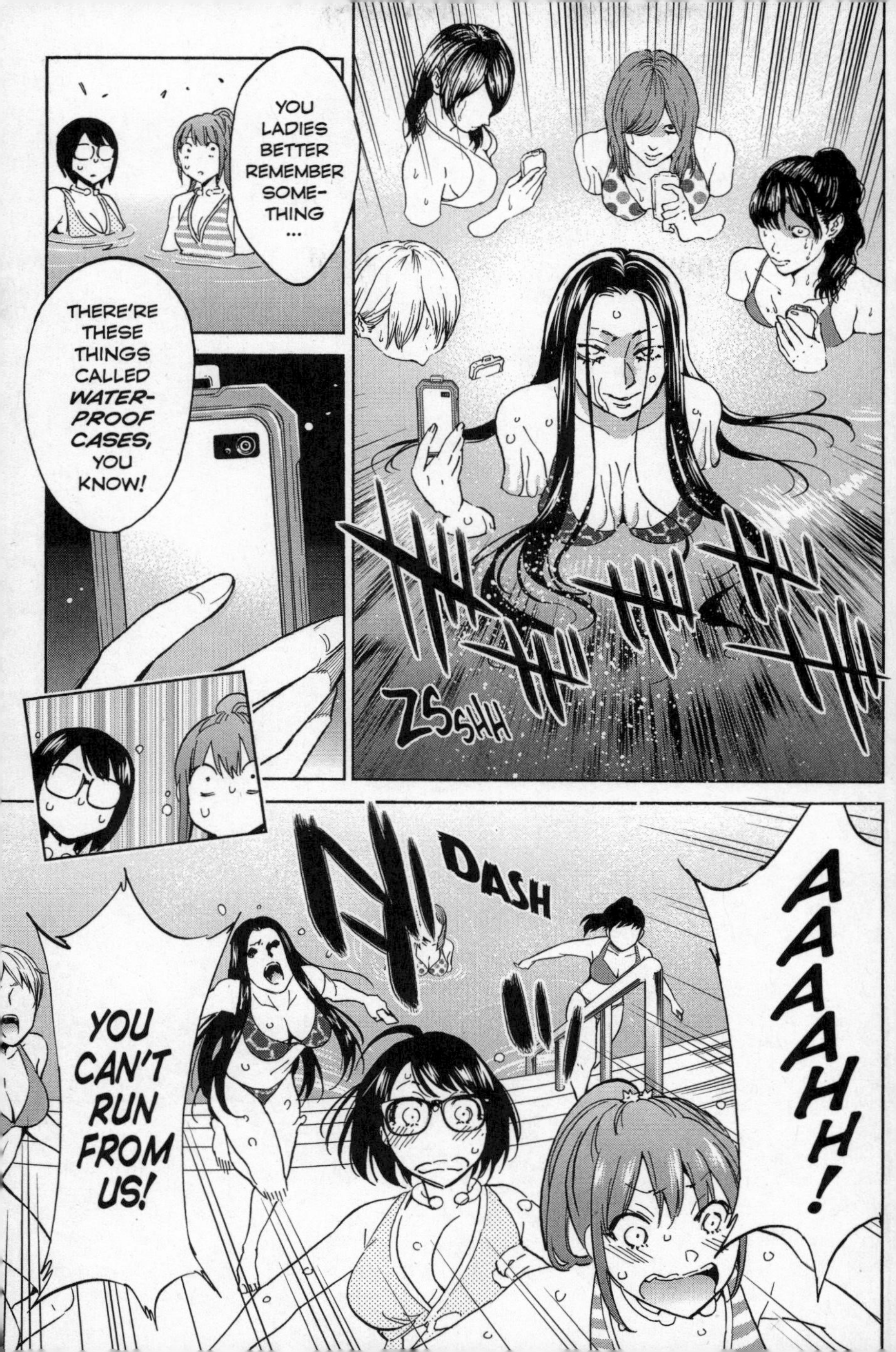
ZSSHH
YOU LADIES BETTER REMEMBER SOMETHING ...
THERE'RE THESE THINGS CALLED *WATER-PROOF* CASES, YOU KNOW!
AAAAHH!
DASH
YOU CAN'T RUN FROM US!

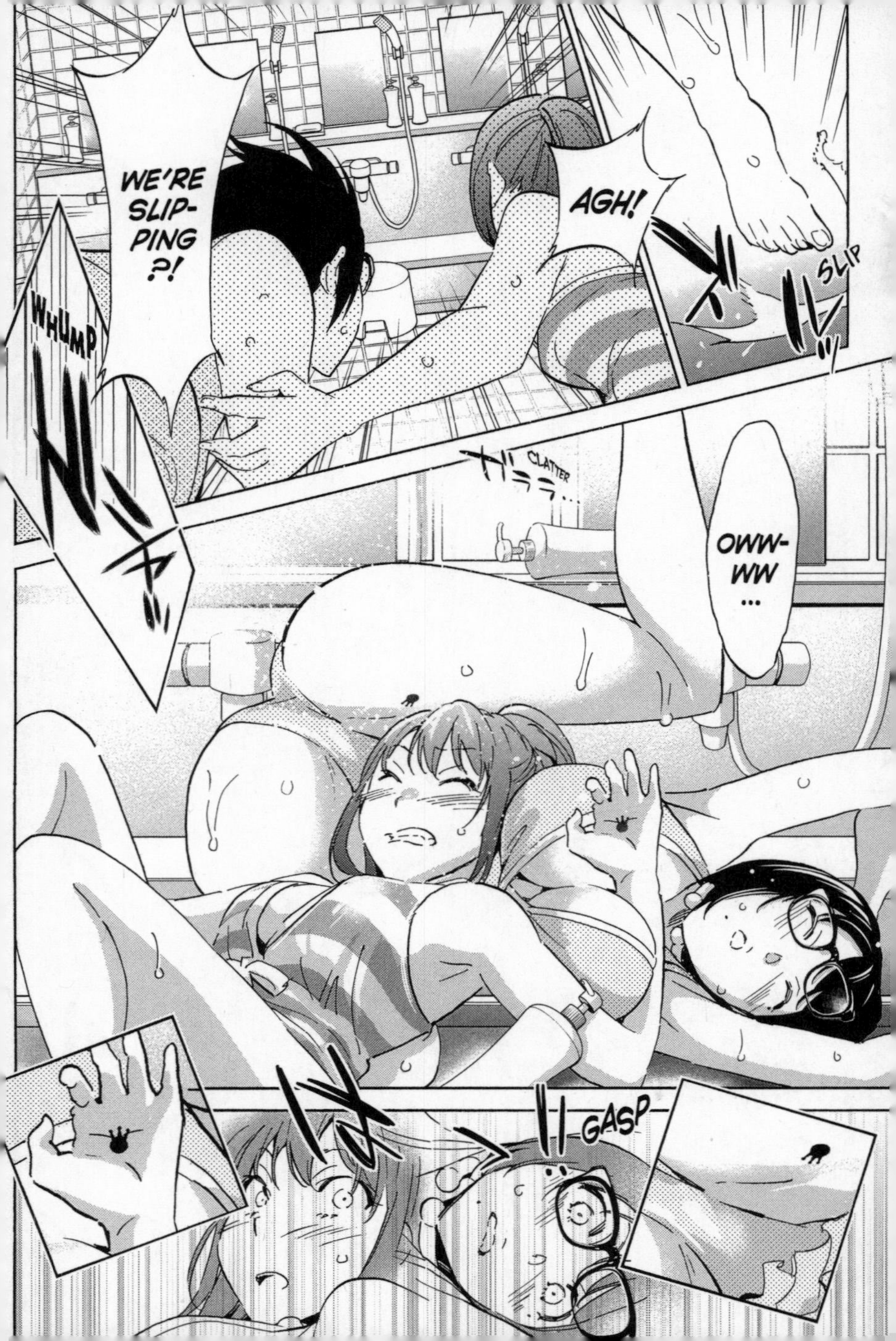
SLIP
AGH!
WE'RE SLIP-PING?!
WHUMP
OWW-WW...
CLATTER
GASP

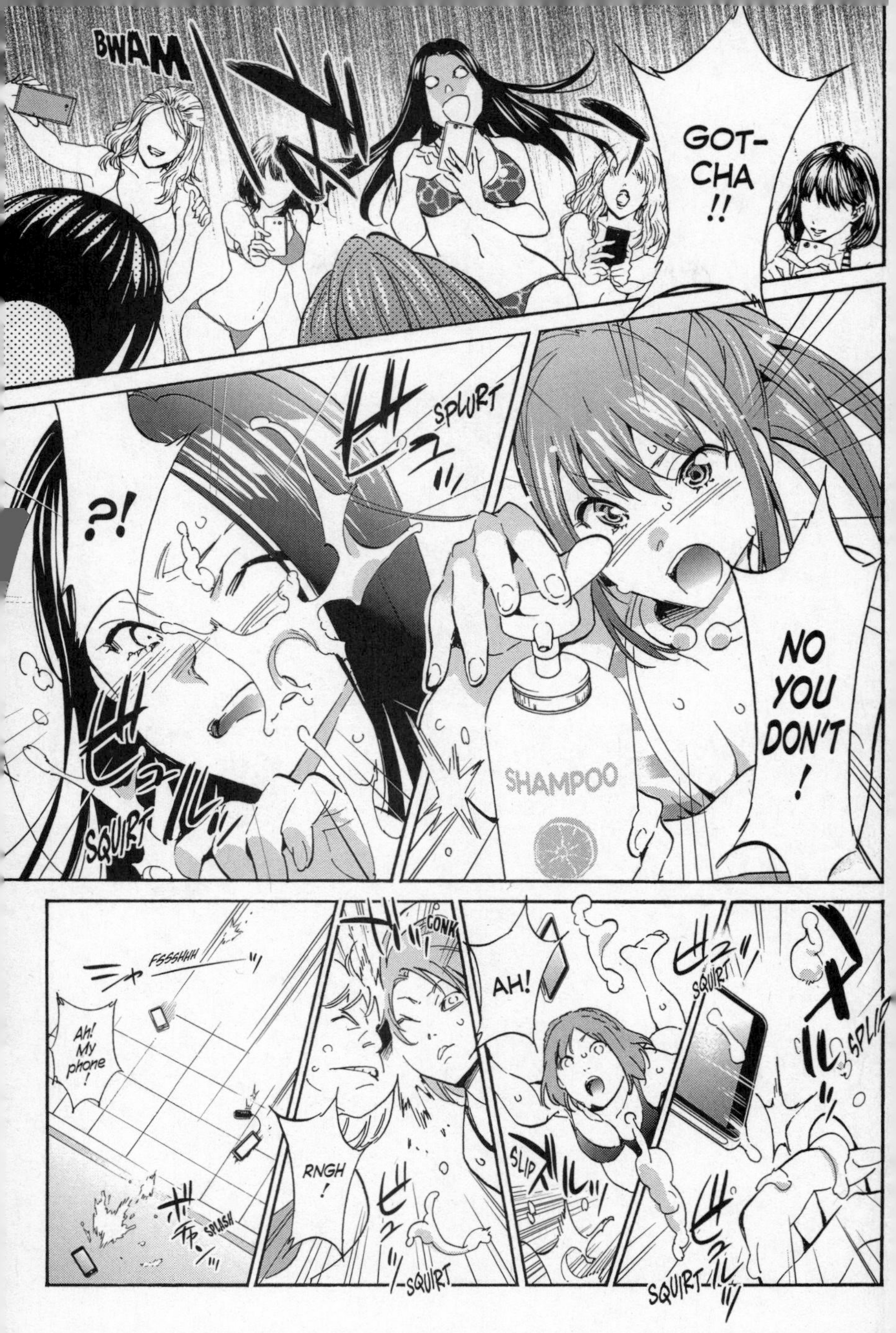
GOT-CHA !!
BWAM
NO YOU DON'T !
SHAMPOO
SPLURT
?!
SQUIRT
SPLIP
SQUIRT
SQUIRT
AH!
SLIP
CONK
RNGH !
SQUIRT
FSSSHHH
Ah! My phone !
SPLASH

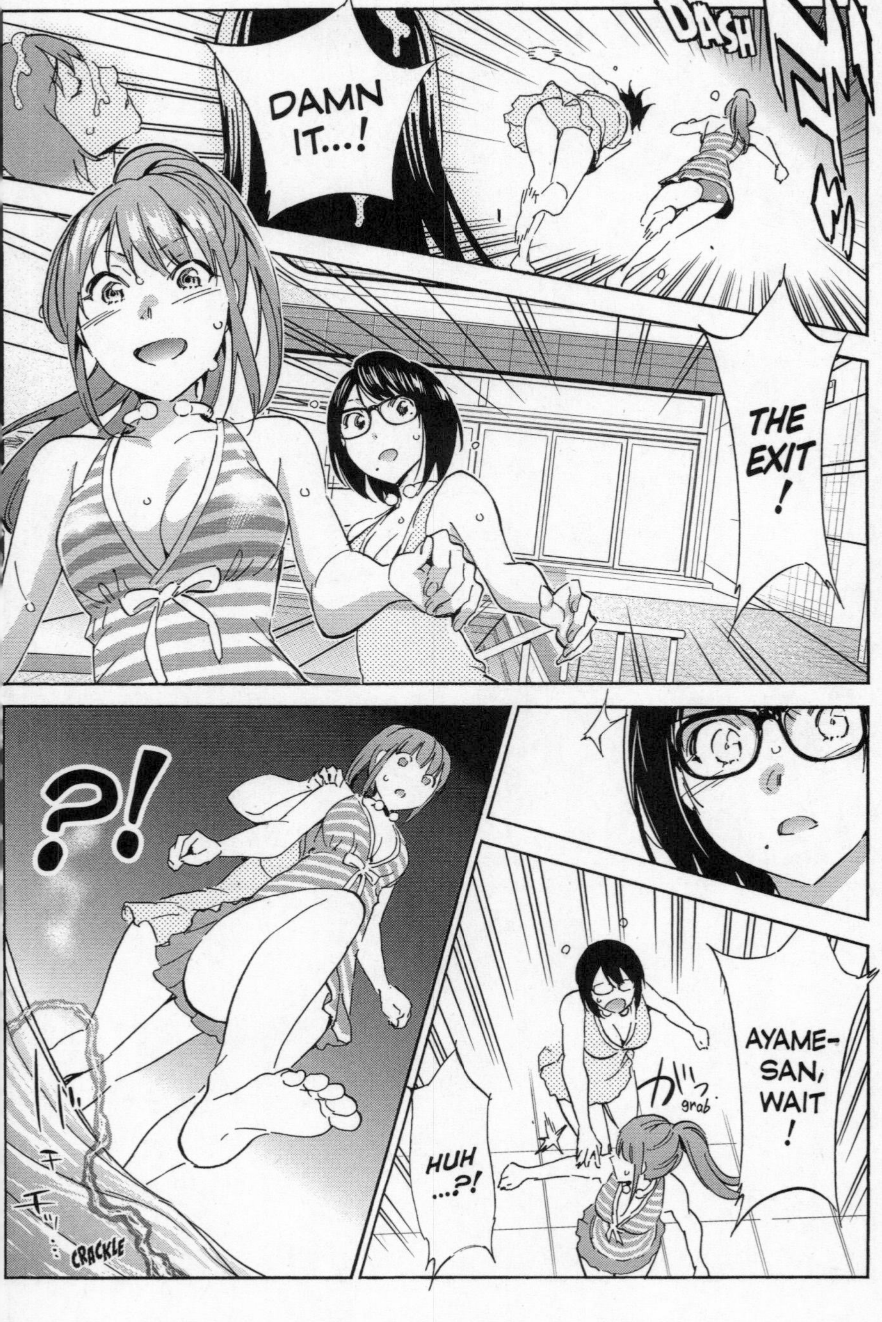
DASH
DAMN IT...!
THE EXIT!
AYAME-SAN, WAIT!
grab
HUH...?!
?!
CRACKLE

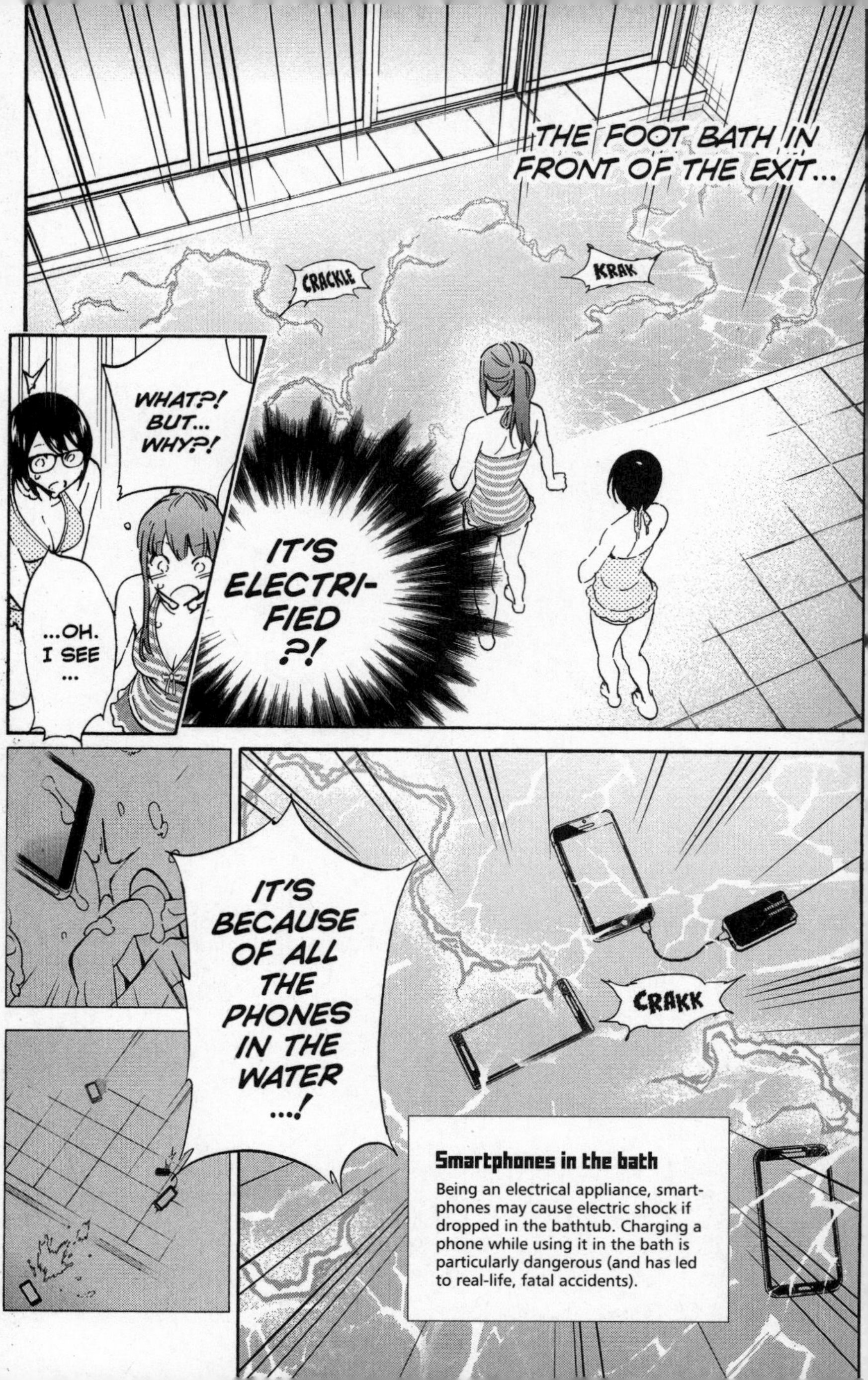
THE FOOT BATH IN FRONT OF THE EXIT...
KRAK
CRACKLE
IT'S ELECTRIFIED?!
WHAT?! BUT... WHY?!
...OH. I SEE ...
CRAKK
IT'S BECAUSE OF ALL THE PHONES IN THE WATER ...!
Smartphones in the bath
Being an electrical appliance, smartphones may cause electric shock if dropped in the bathtub. Charging a phone while using it in the bath is particularly dangerous (and has led to real-life, fatal accidents).

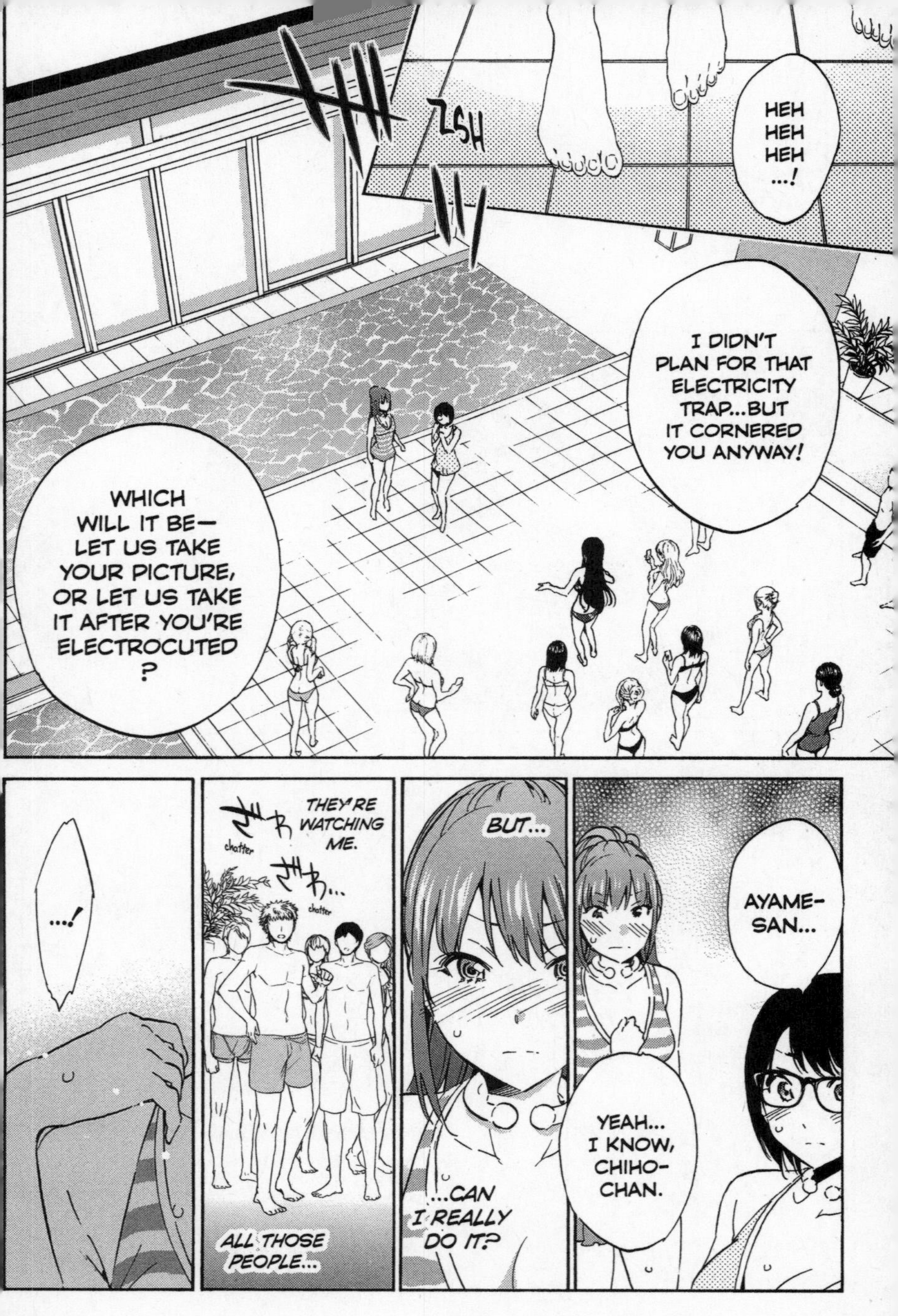
HEH HEH HEH ...!
ZSH
I DIDN'T PLAN FOR THAT ELECTRICITY TRAP...BUT IT CORNERED YOU ANYWAY!
WHICH WILL IT BE— LET US TAKE YOUR PICTURE, OR LET US TAKE IT AFTER YOU'RE ELECTROCUTED ?
AYAME-SAN...
YEAH... I KNOW, CHIHO-CHAN.
BUT...
...CAN I REALLY DO IT?
THEY'RE WATCHING ME.
ざわ
chatter
ざわ...
chatter
ALL THOSE PEOPLE...
...!

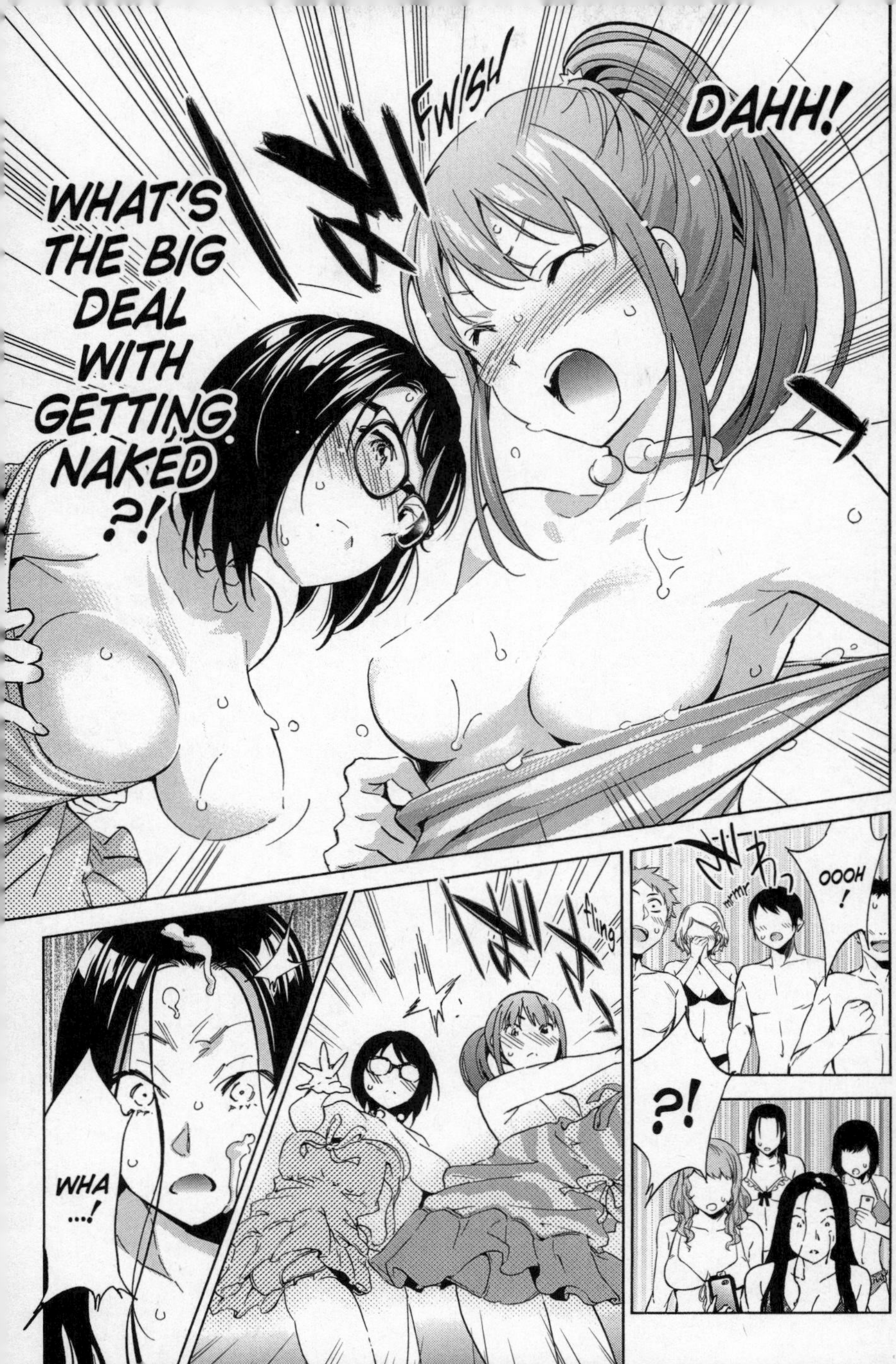
DAHH!
FWISH
WHAT'S THE BIG DEAL WITH GETTING NAKED ?!
OOOH !
mrmr
?!
fling
WHA ...!

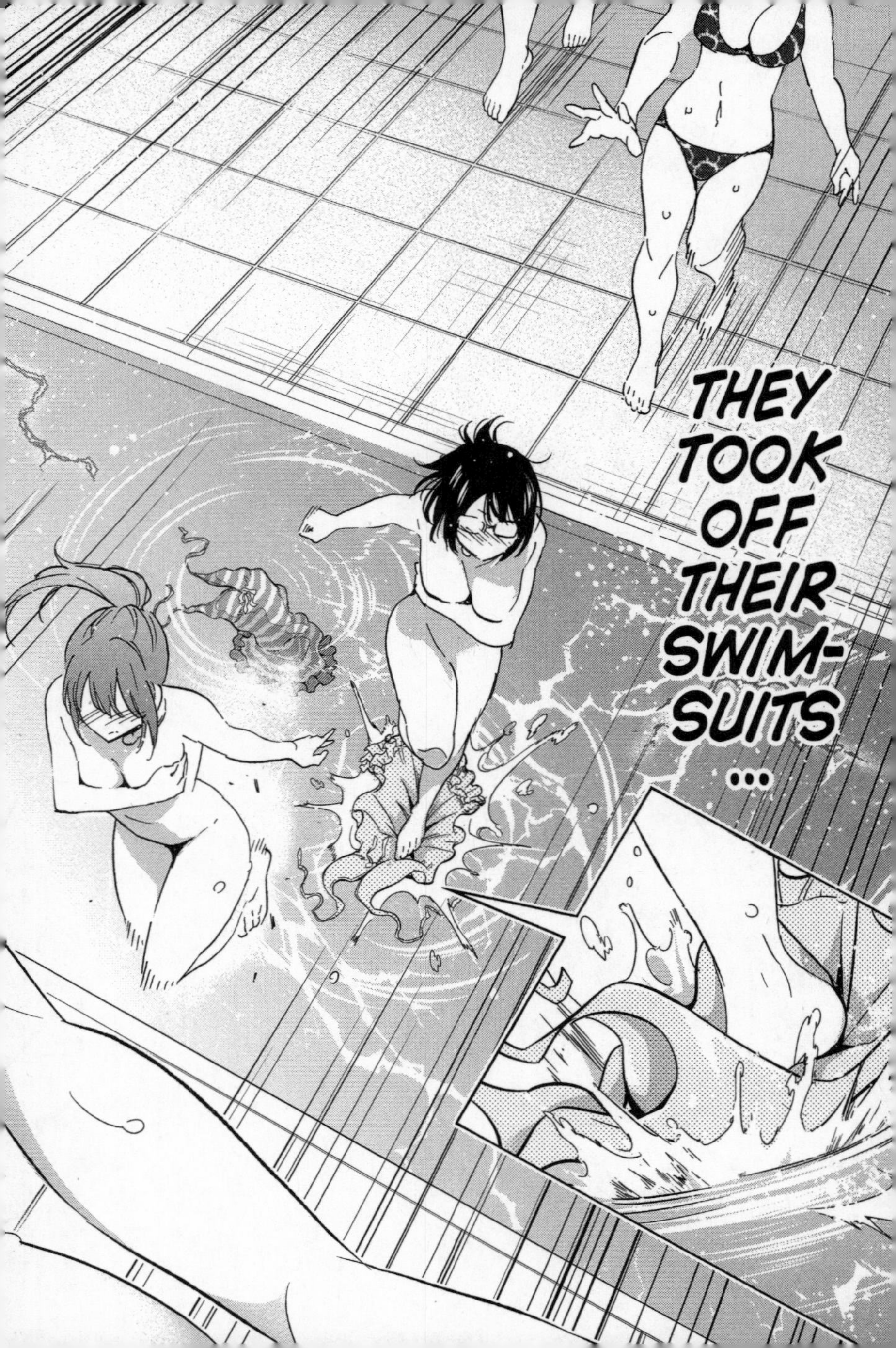
THEY TOOK OFF THEIR SWIM-SUITS ...

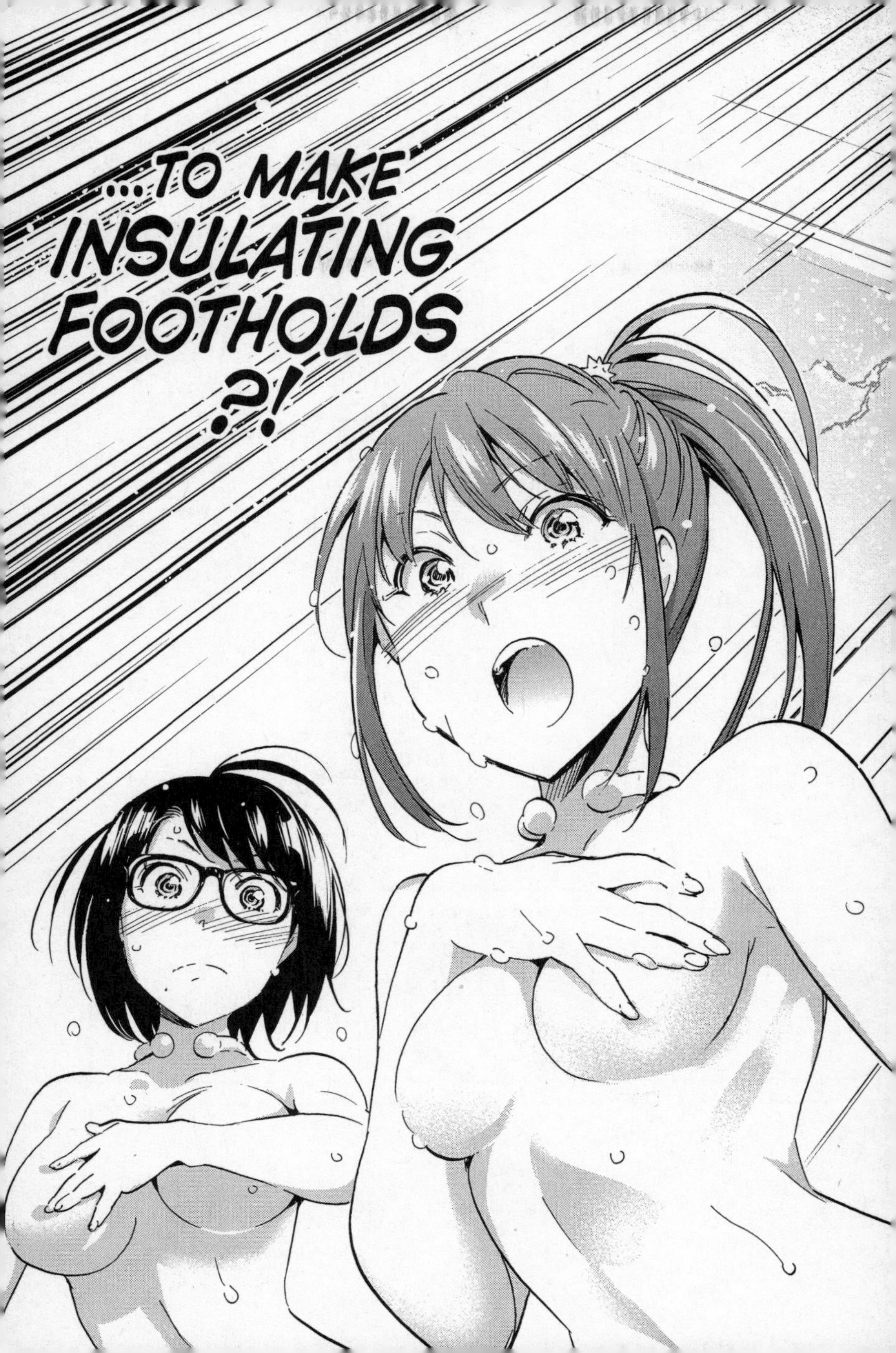
...TO MAKE INSULATING FOOTHOLDS ?!

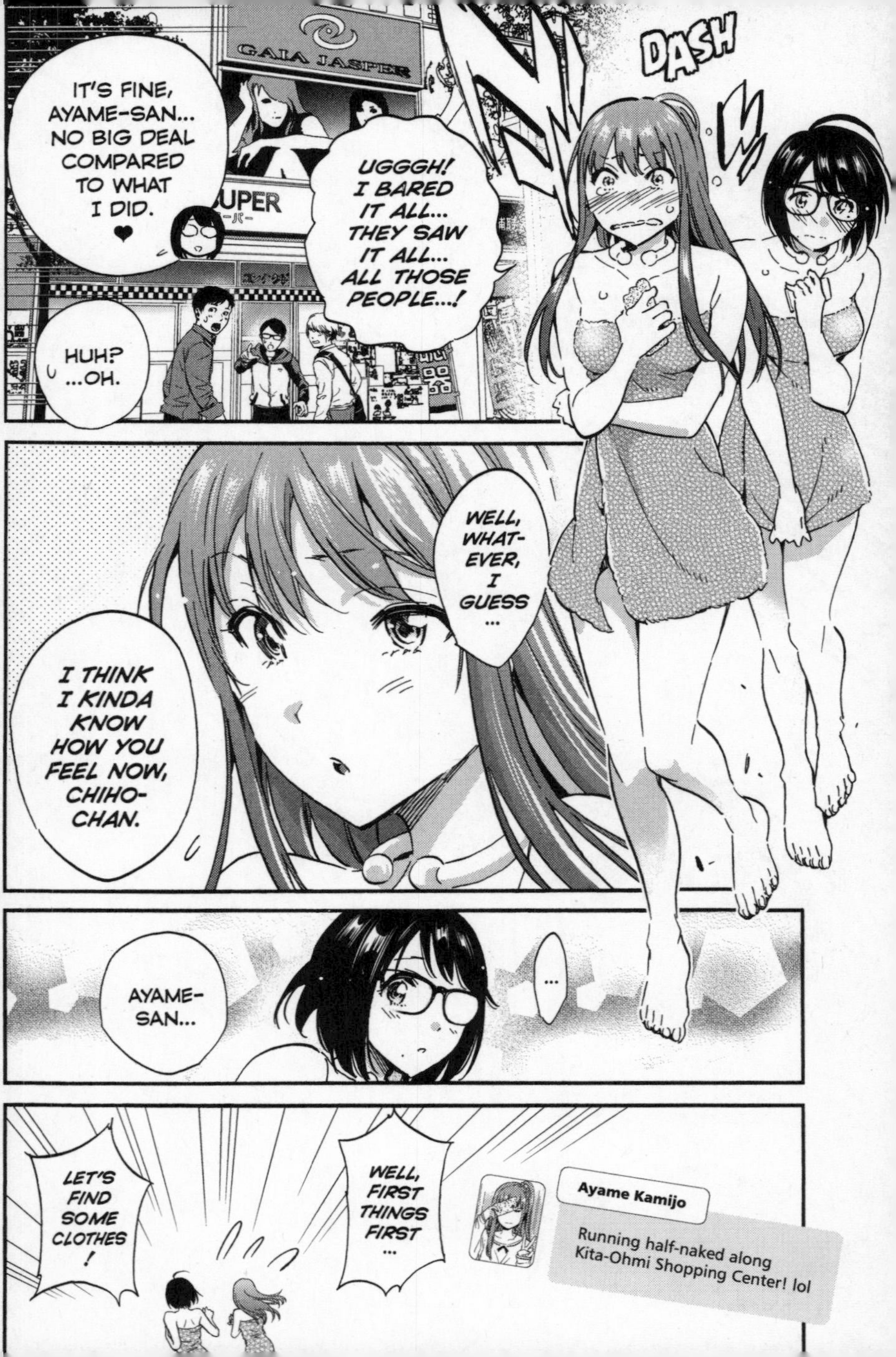
DASH
GAIA JASPER
UGGGH! I BARED IT ALL... THEY SAW IT ALL... ALL THOSE PEOPLE...!
IT'S FINE, AYAME-SAN... NO BIG DEAL COMPARED TO WHAT I DID. ❤
HUH? ...OH.
WELL, WHATEVER, I GUESS...
I THINK I KINDA KNOW HOW YOU FEEL NOW, CHIHO-CHAN.
...
AYAME-SAN...
Ayame Kamijo
Running half-naked along Kita-Ohmi Shopping Center! lol
WELL, FIRST THINGS FIRST...
LET'S FIND SOME CLOTHES!

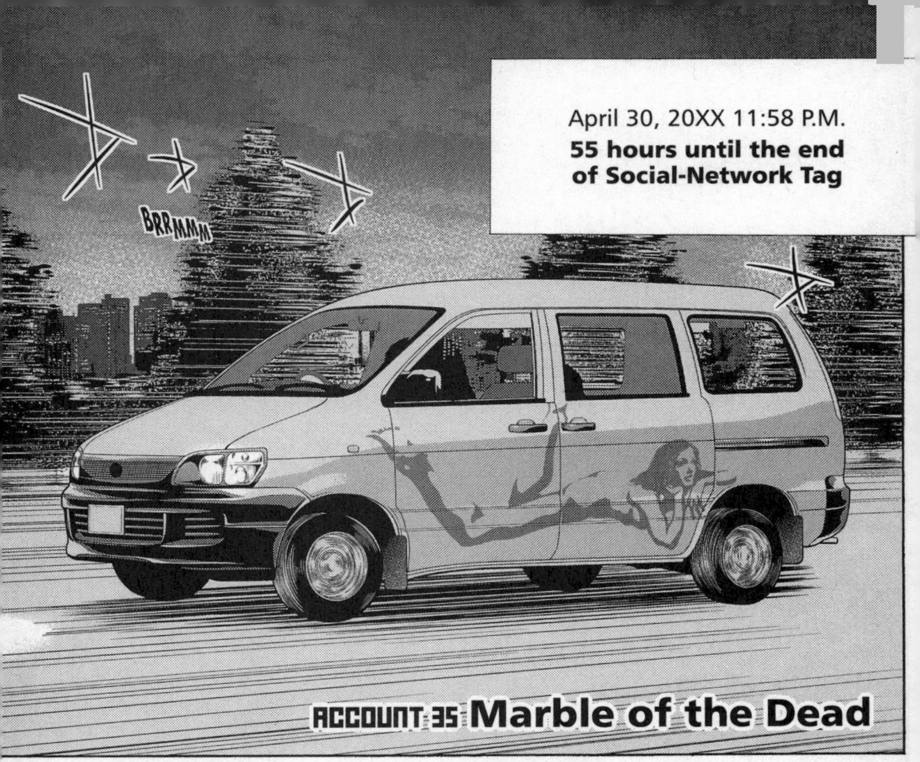
April 30, 20XX 11:58 P.M.
55 hours until the end of Social-Network Tag
BRRMMM

ACCOUNT 35 Marble of the Dead

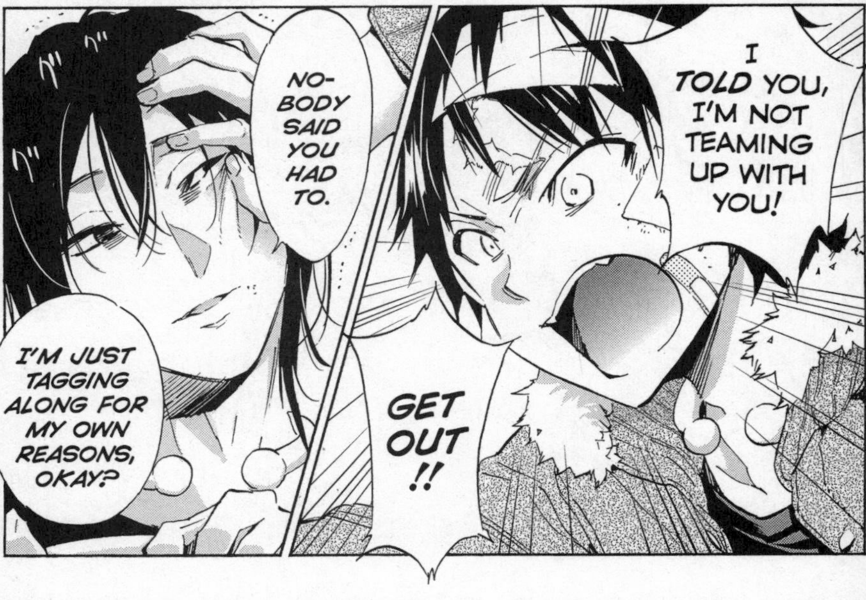
I TOLD YOU, I'M NOT TEAMING UP WITH YOU!
GET OUT !!
NO-BODY SAID YOU HAD TO.
I'M JUST TAGGING ALONG FOR MY OWN REASONS, OKAY?

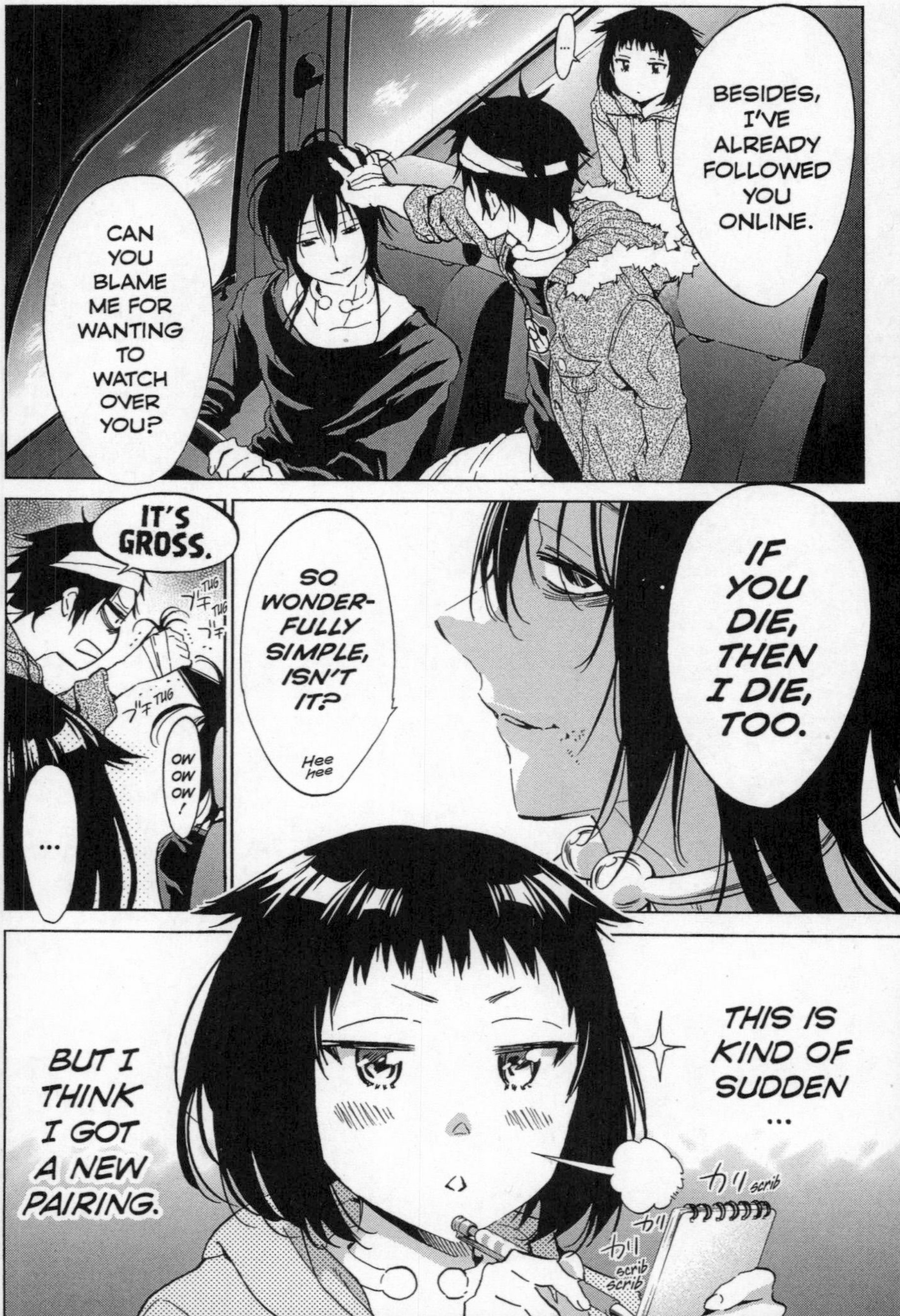
BESIDES, I'VE ALREADY FOLLOWED YOU ONLINE.
...
CAN YOU BLAME ME FOR WANTING TO WATCH OVER YOU?
IF YOU DIE, THEN I DIE, TOO.
SO WONDERFULLY SIMPLE, ISN'T IT?
Hee hee
IT'S GROSS.
ブチ TUG
ブチ TUG
ブチ TUG
OW OW OW!
...
THIS IS KIND OF SUDDEN...
BUT I THINK I GOT A NEW PAIRING.
カリ scrib
カリ
カリ scrib scrib

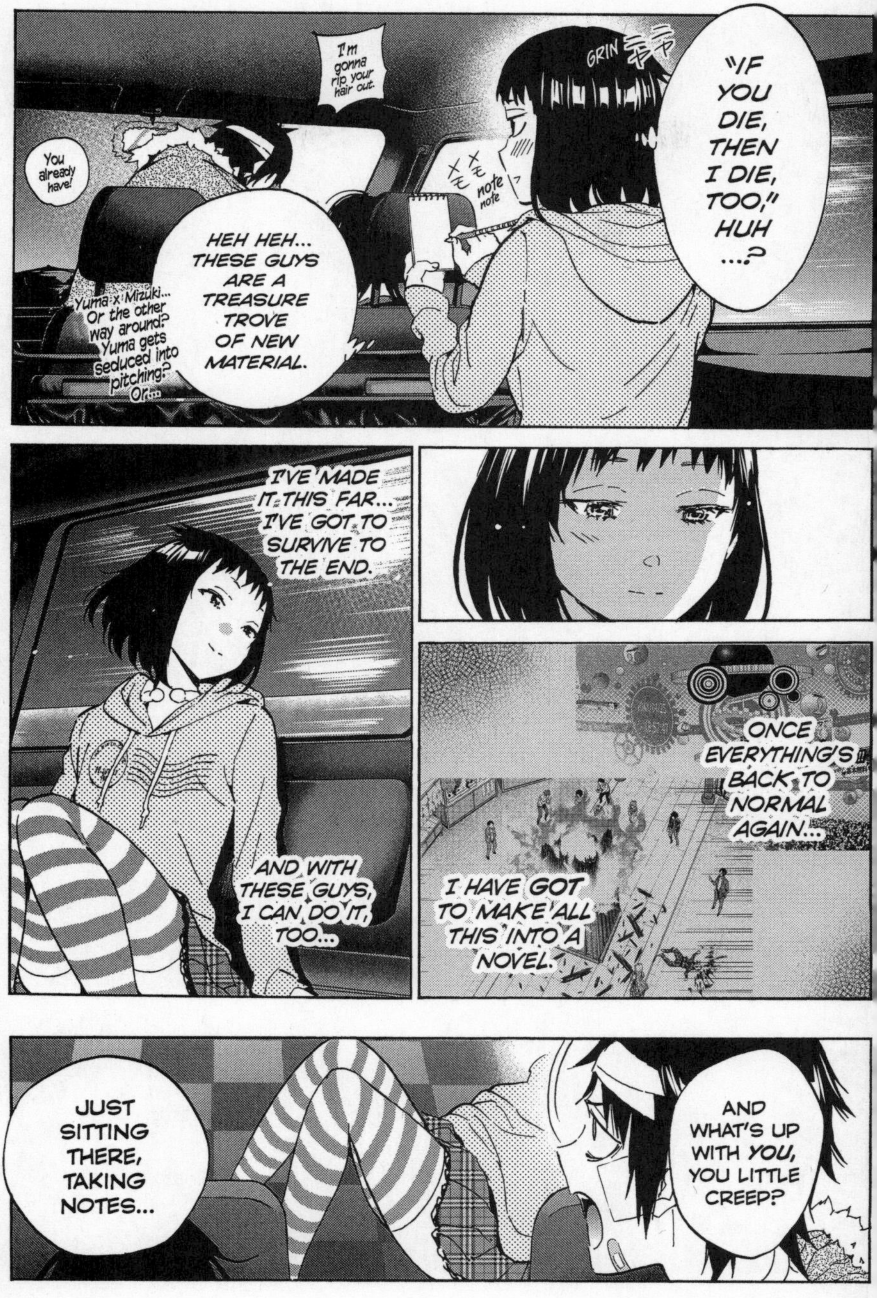
GRIN
"IF YOU DIE, THEN I DIE, TOO," HUH ...?
I'm gonna rip your hair out.
You already have!
メモ メモ
note note
HEH HEH... THESE GUYS ARE A TREASURE TROVE OF NEW MATERIAL.
Yuma x Mizuki... Or the other way around? Yuma gets seduced into pitching? Or...
ONCE EVERYTHING'S BACK TO NORMAL AGAIN...
I HAVE GOT TO MAKE ALL THIS INTO A NOVEL.
I'VE MADE IT THIS FAR... I'VE GOT TO SURVIVE TO THE END.
AND WITH THESE GUYS, I CAN DO IT, TOO...
AND WHAT'S UP WITH YOU, YOU LITTLE CREEP?
JUST SITTING THERE, TAKING NOTES...

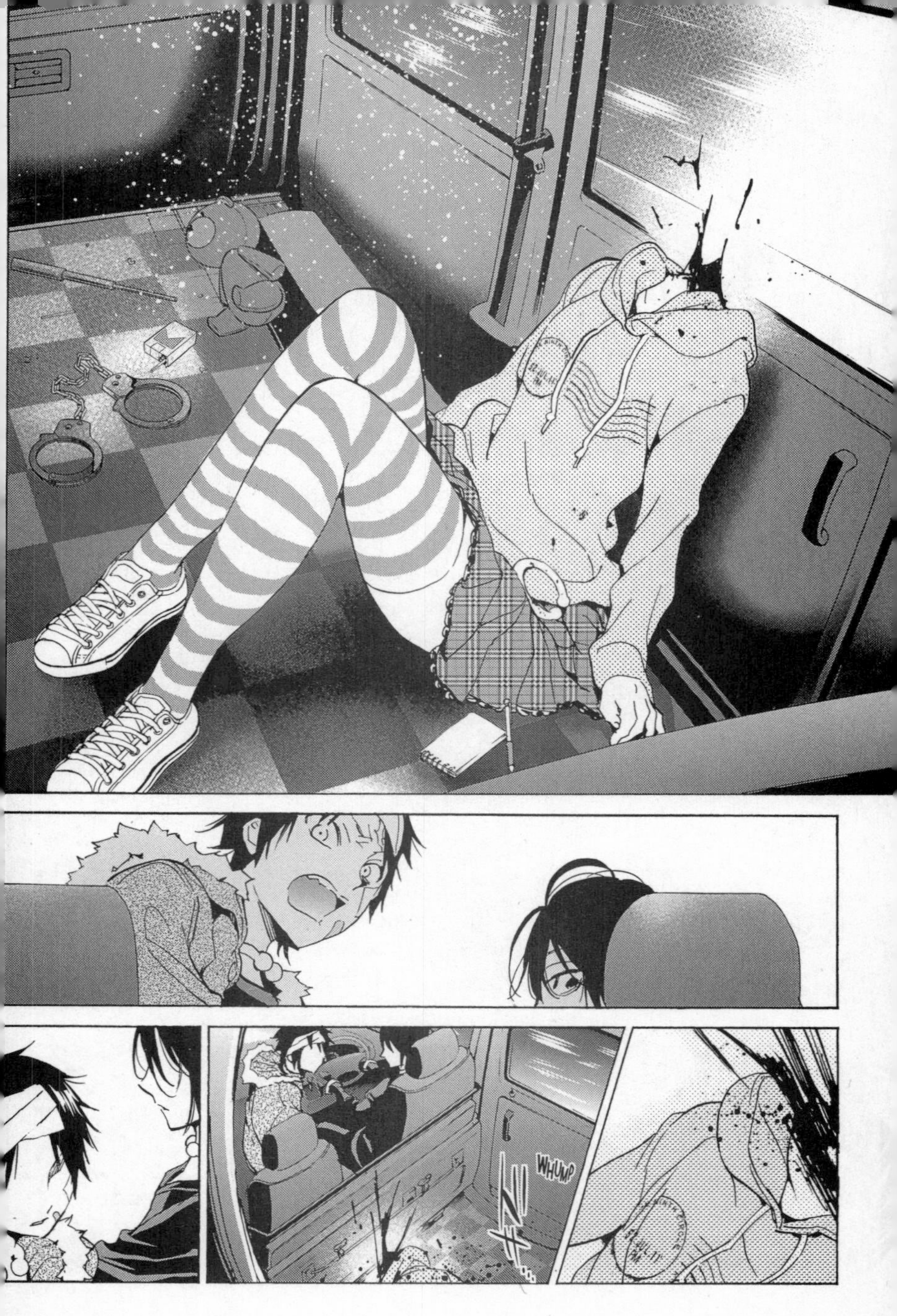
WHUMP

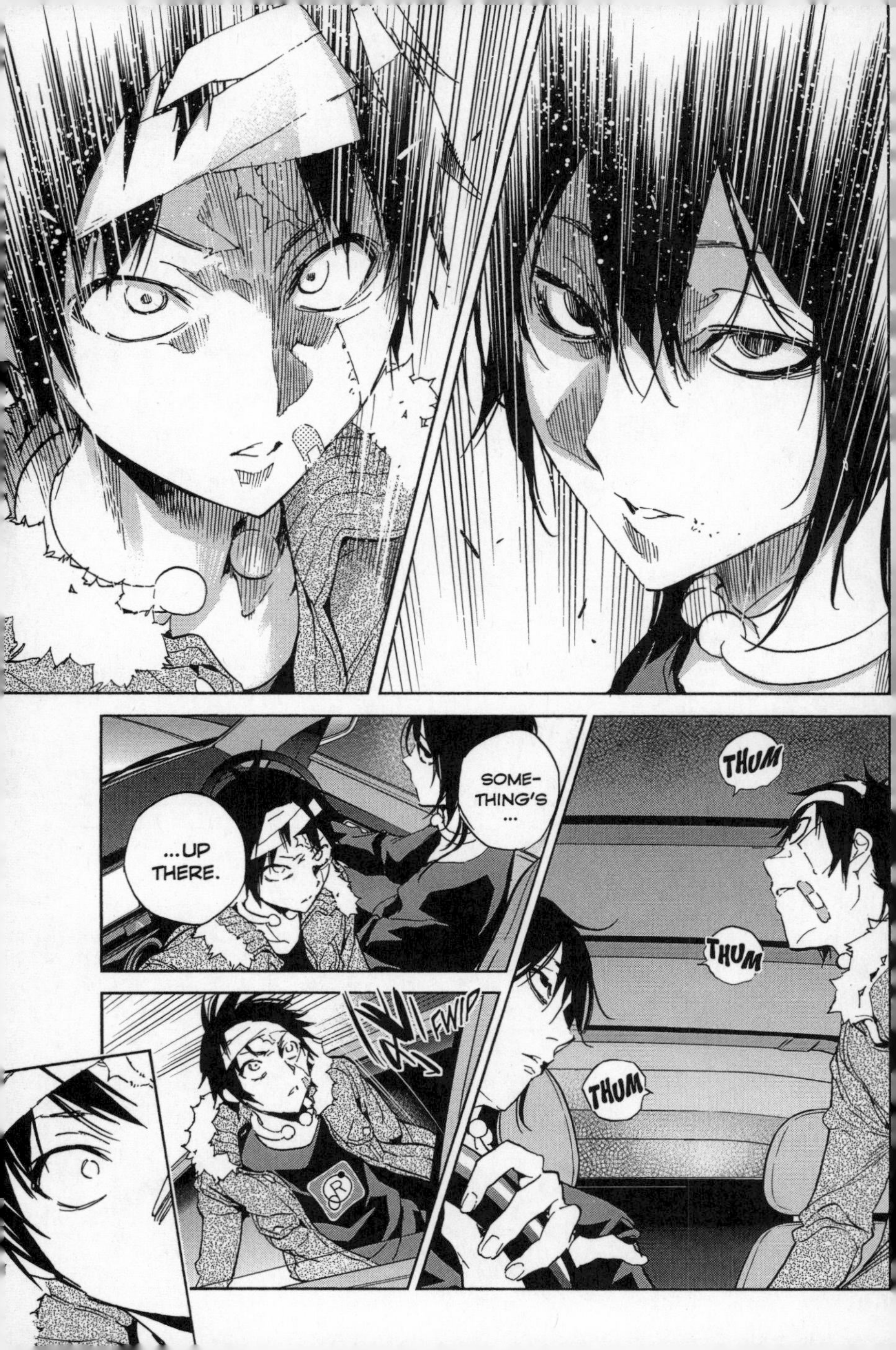
THUM
THUM
THUM
SOME-THING'S ...
...UP THERE.
FWIP

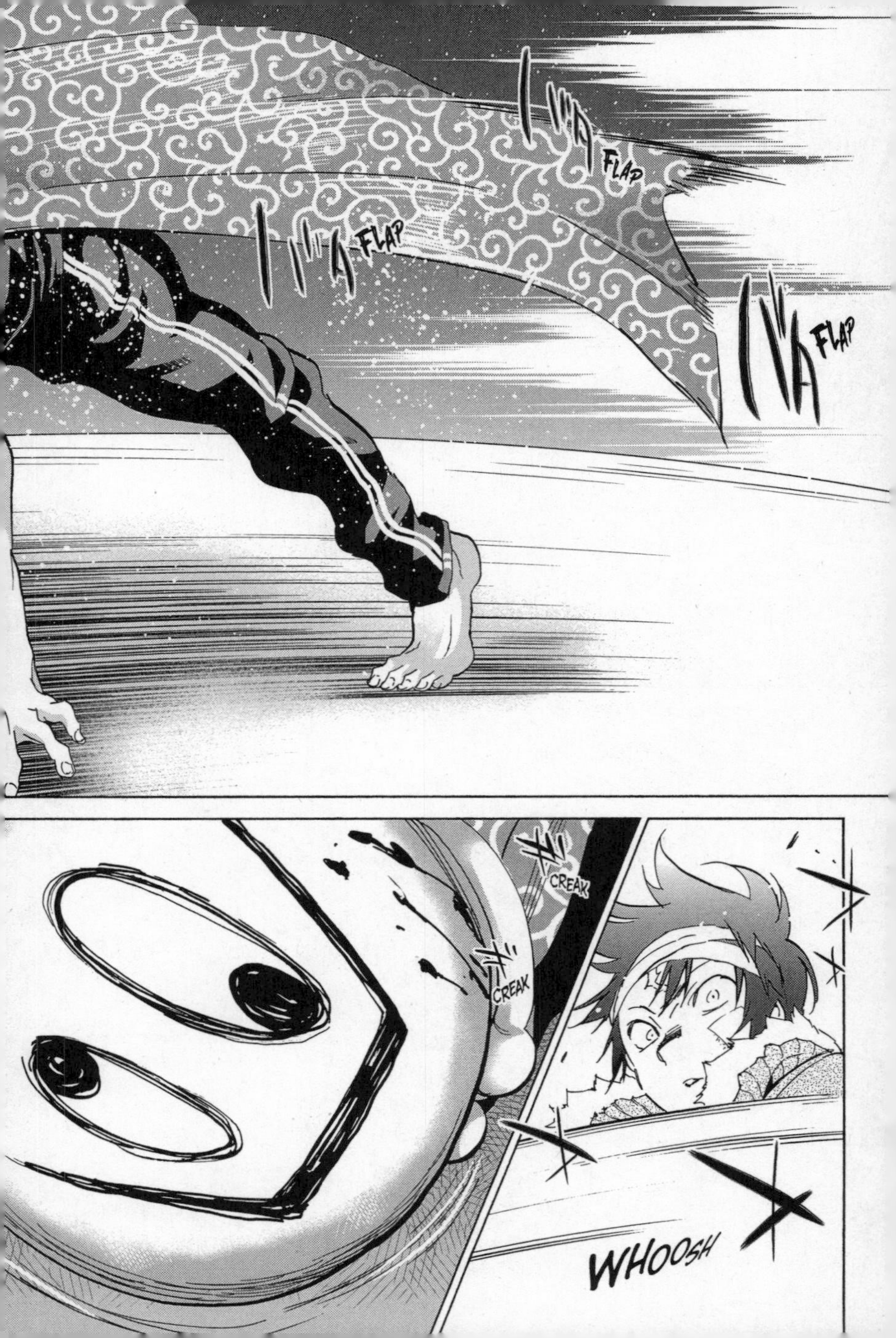
FLAP
FLAP
FLAP
CREAK
CREAK
WHOOSH

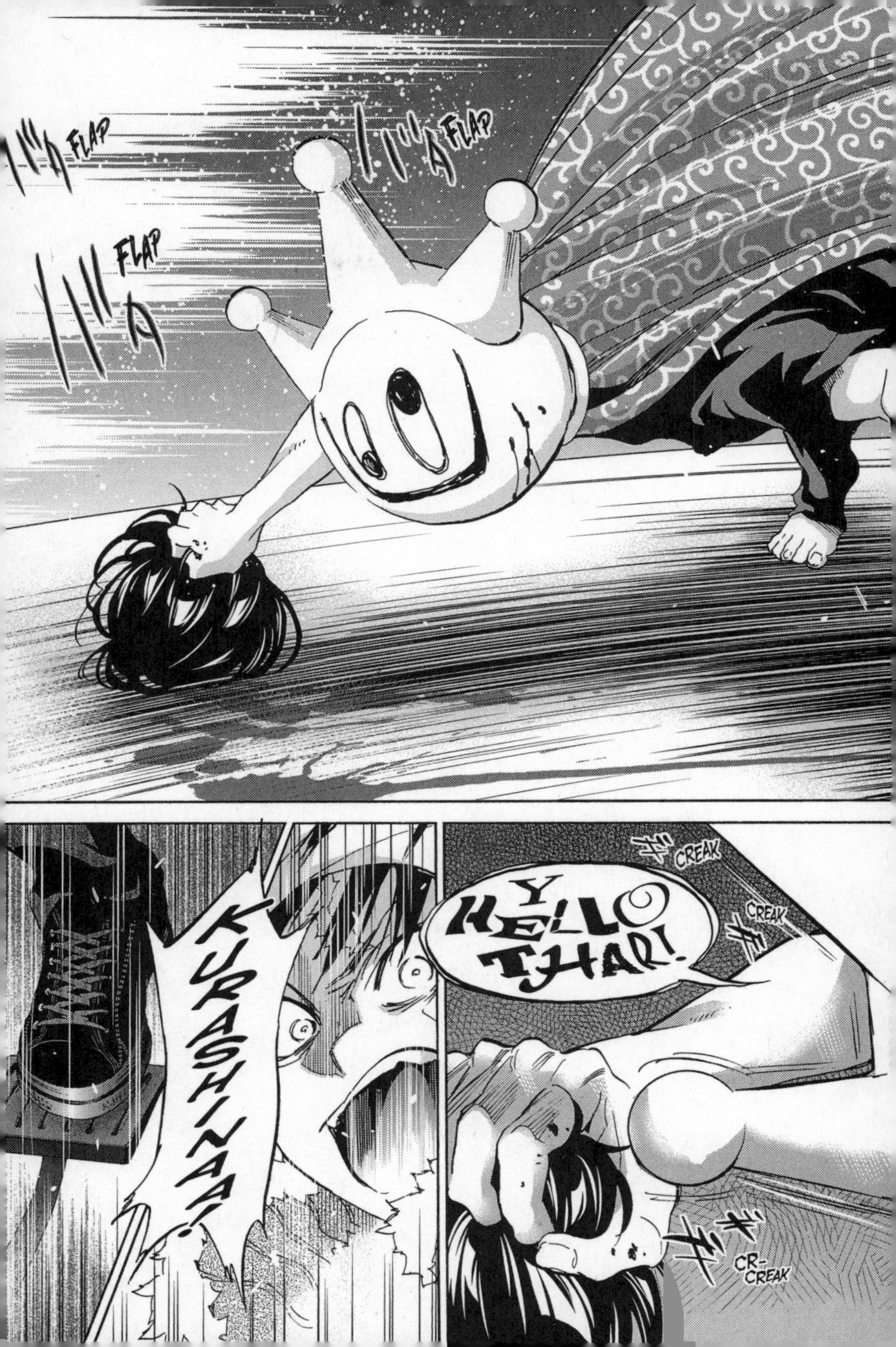
FLAP
FLAP
FLAP
CREAK
CREAK
Y HELLO THAR!
CR-CREAK
KURASHINAA!

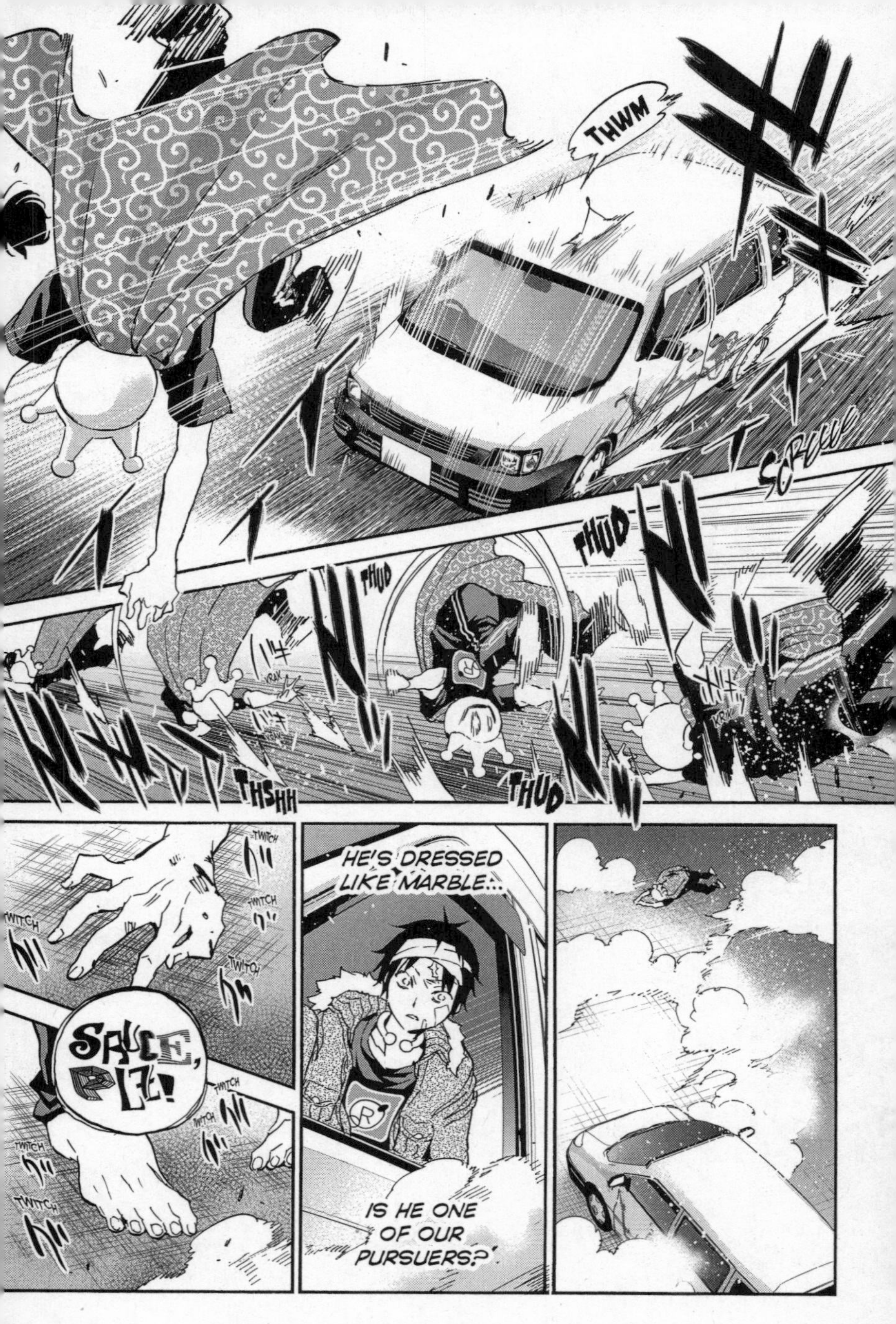
THWM
THUD
THUD
THUD
THSHH
HE'S DRESSED LIKE MARBLE...
IS HE ONE OF OUR PURSUERS?
TWITCH
TWITCH
TWITCH
TWITCH
TWITCH
TWITCH
TWITCH
SAUCE, PLZ!

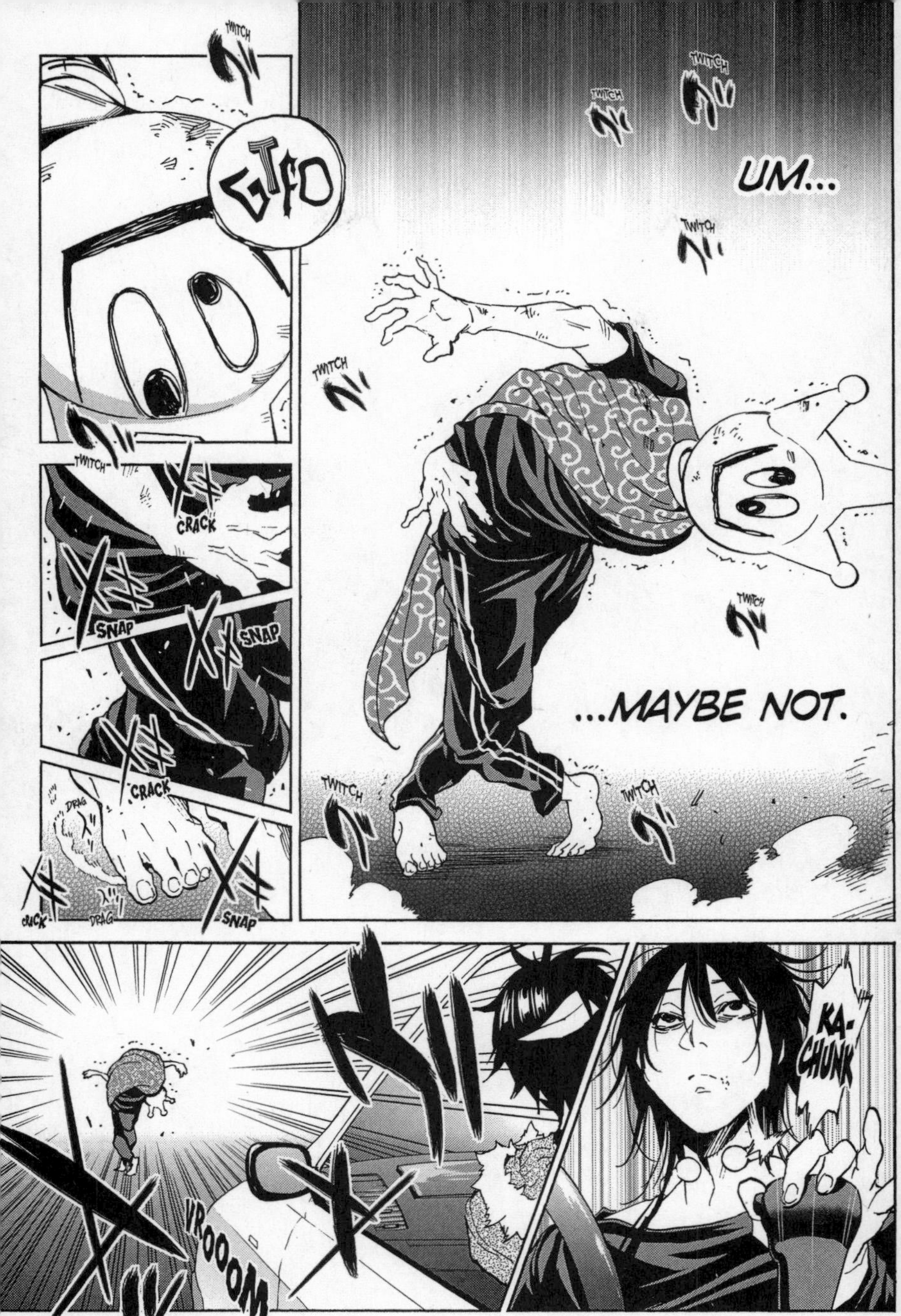
TWITCH
TWITCH
UM...
TWITCH
TWITCH
TWITCH
...MAYBE NOT.
TWITCH
TWITCH
TWITCH
GTFO
TWITCH
CRACK
SNAP
SNAP
CRACK
DRAG
DRAG
CRACK
SNAP
KA-CHUNK
VROOOM

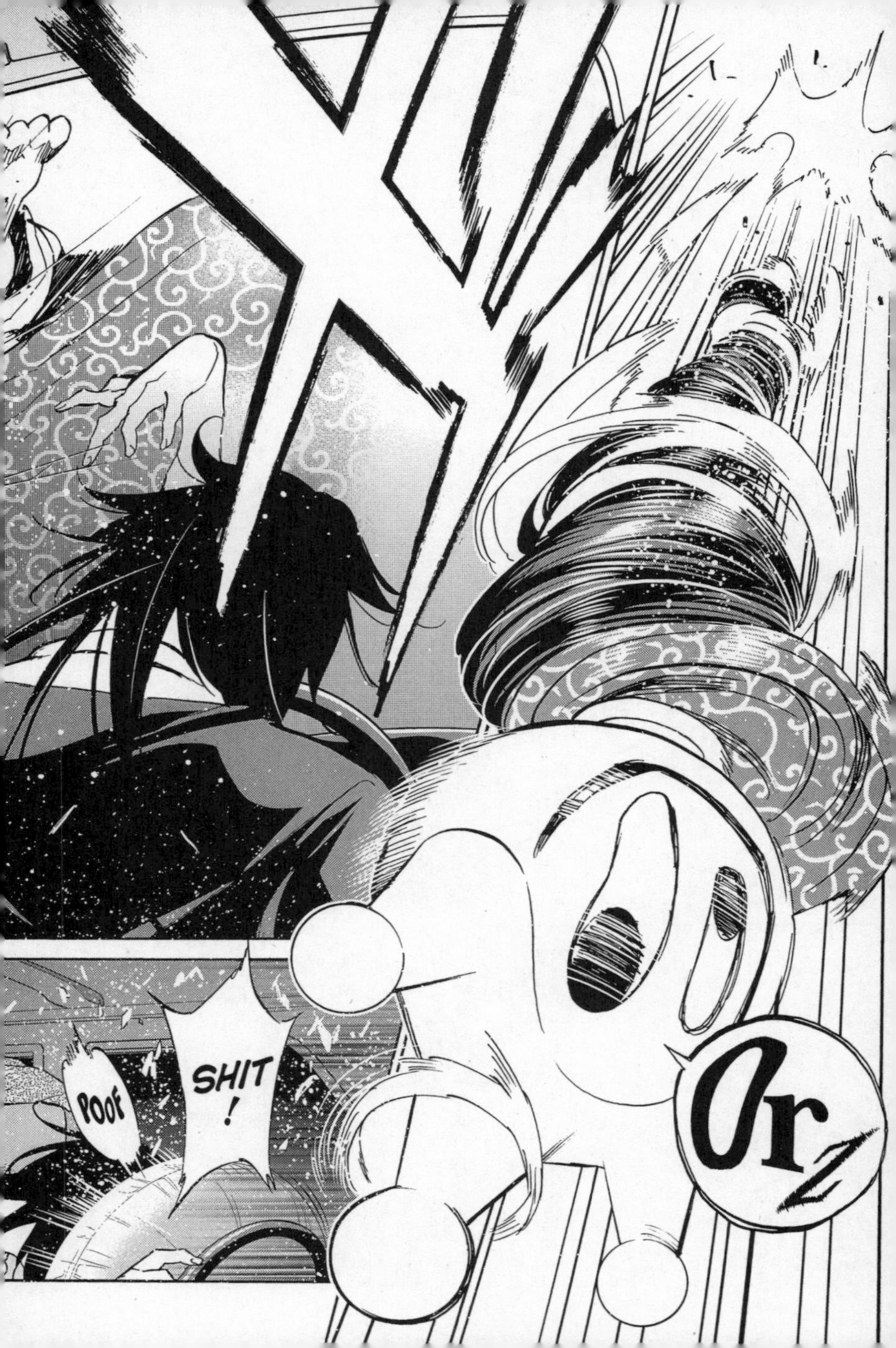
Orz
SHIT!
POOF

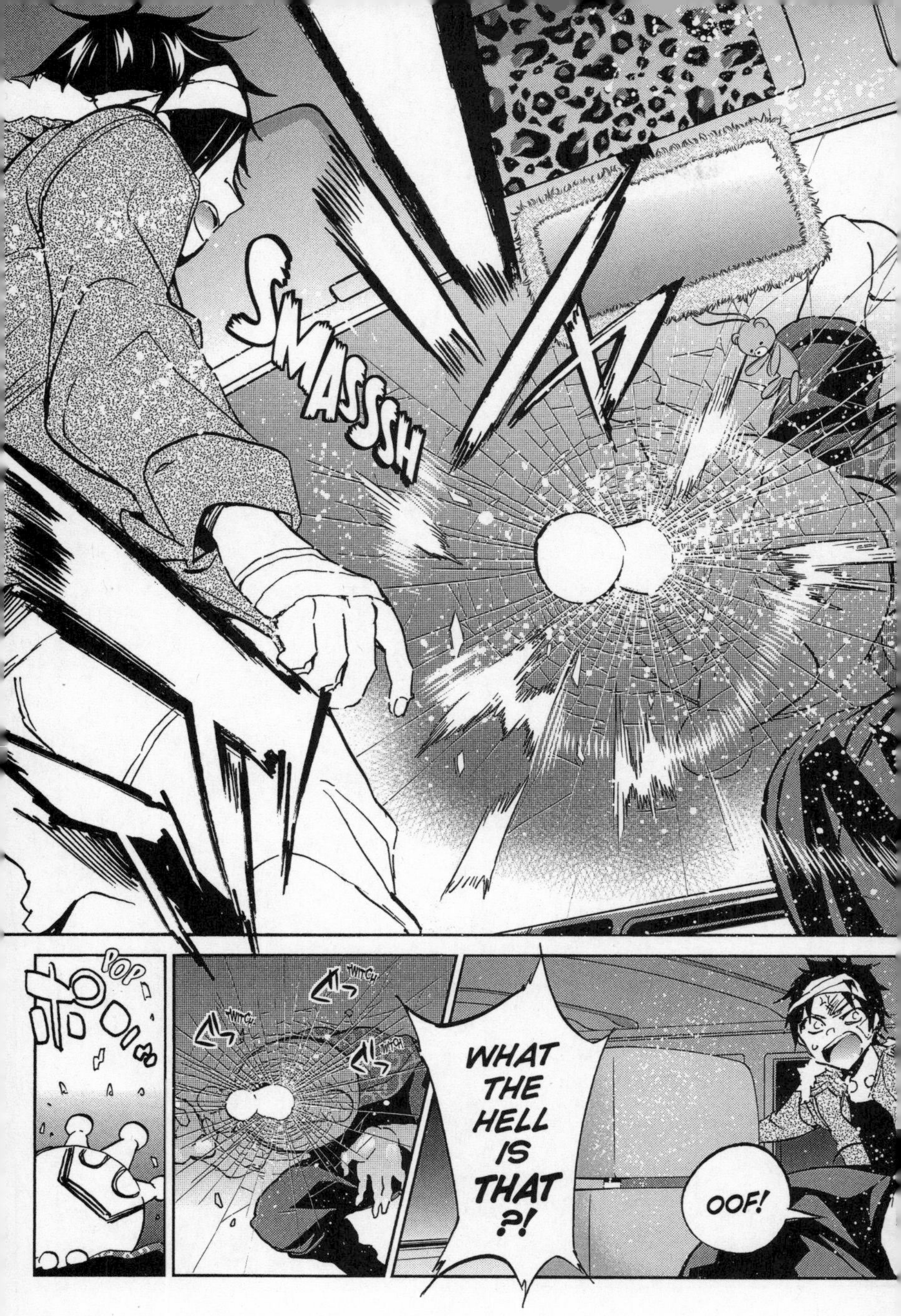
SMASSSH
OOF!
WHAT THE HELL IS THAT?!
TWITCH
TWITCH
TWITCH
POP

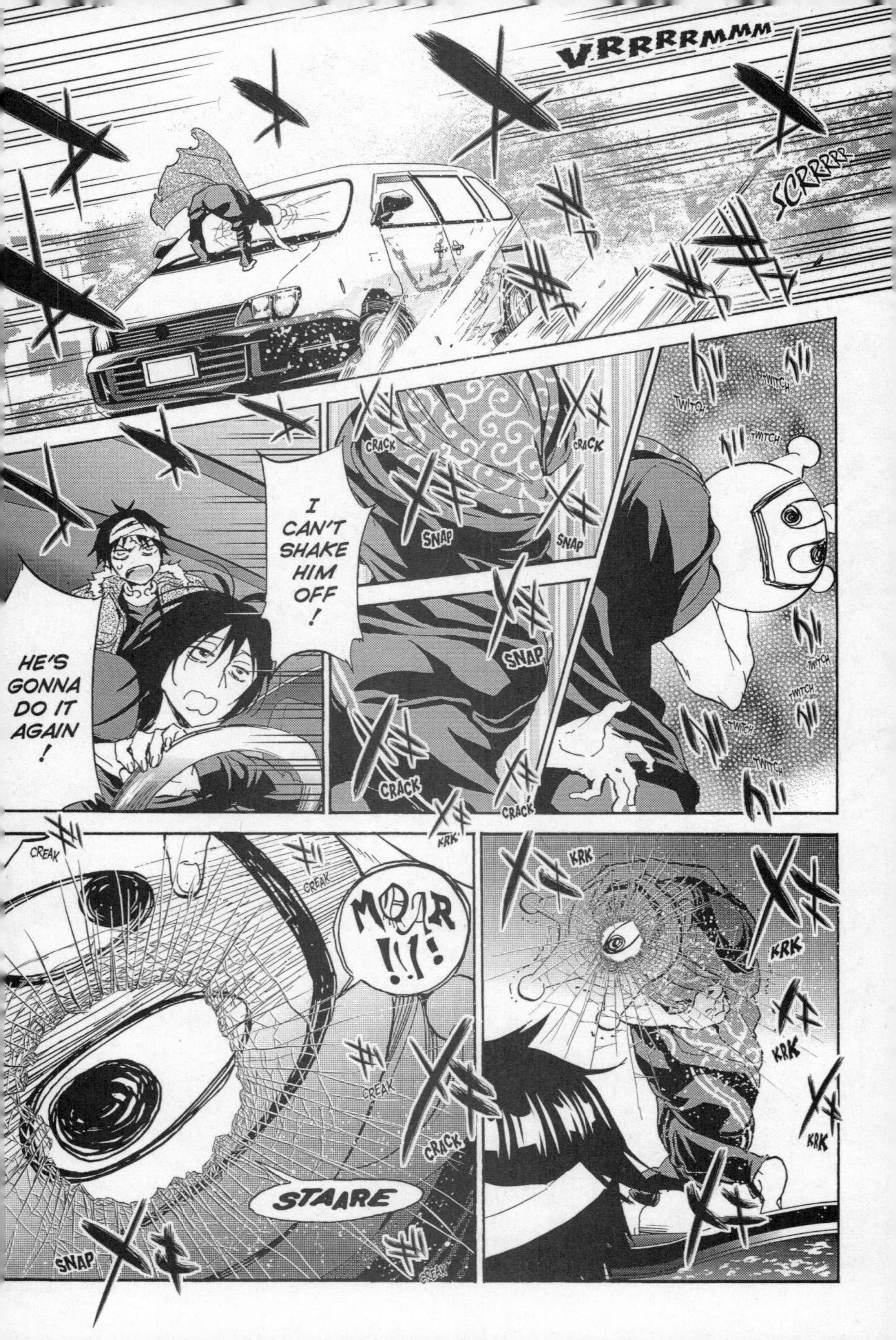
VRRRRMMM
SCRRRRR
TWITCH
TWITCH
TWITCH
TWITCH
TWITCH
TWITCH
CRACK
CRACK
I CAN'T SHAKE HIM OFF!
SNAP
SNAP
SNAP
CRACK
CRACK
HE'S GONNA DO IT AGAIN!
KRK
KRK
KRK
KRK
KRK
CREAK
CREAK
MOAR!!!
CREAK
CRACK
STAARE
SNAP
CREAK

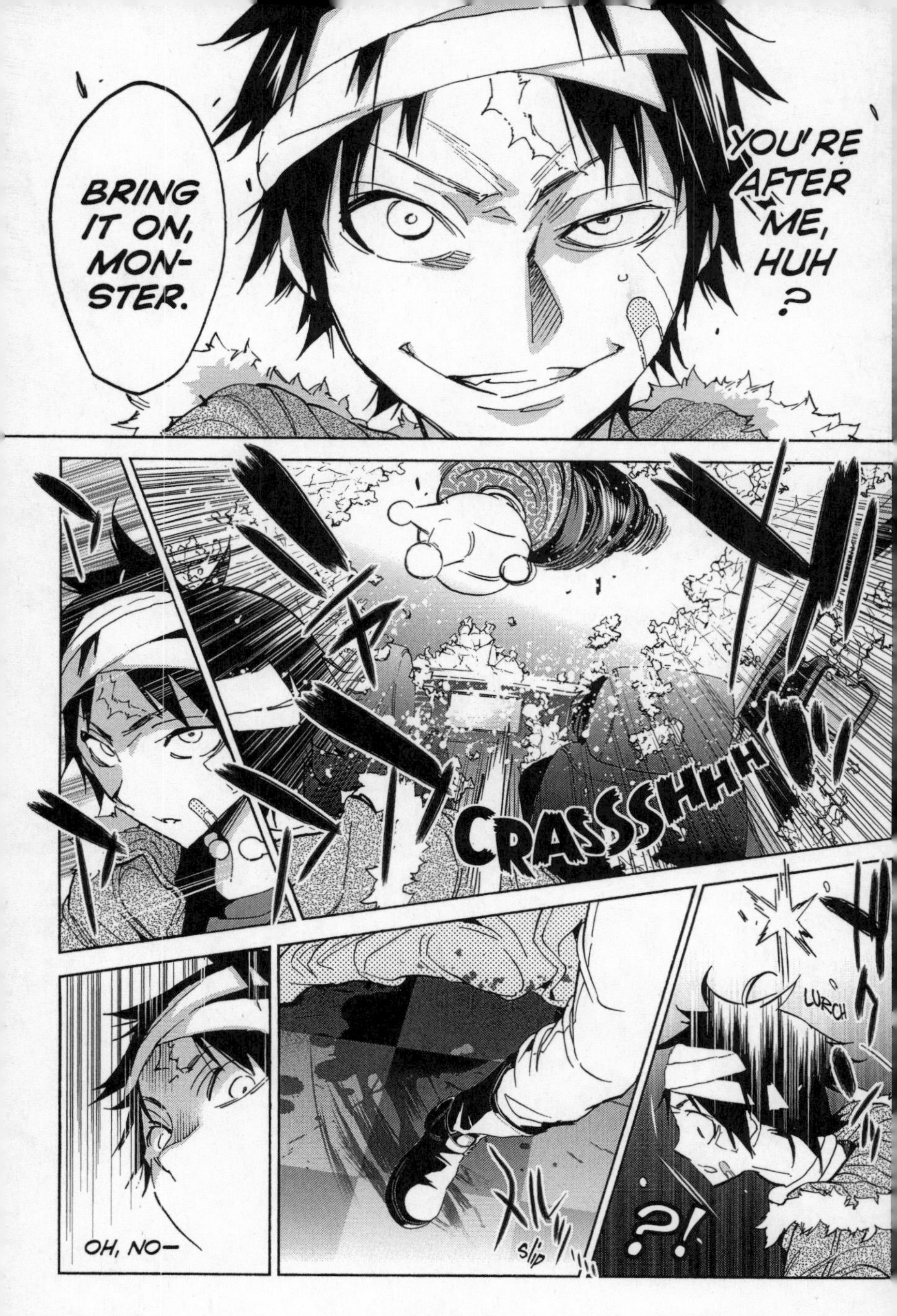
YOU'RE AFTER ME, HUH?
BRING IT ON, MONSTER.
CRASSSHHH
LURCH
?!
SLIP
OH, NO—

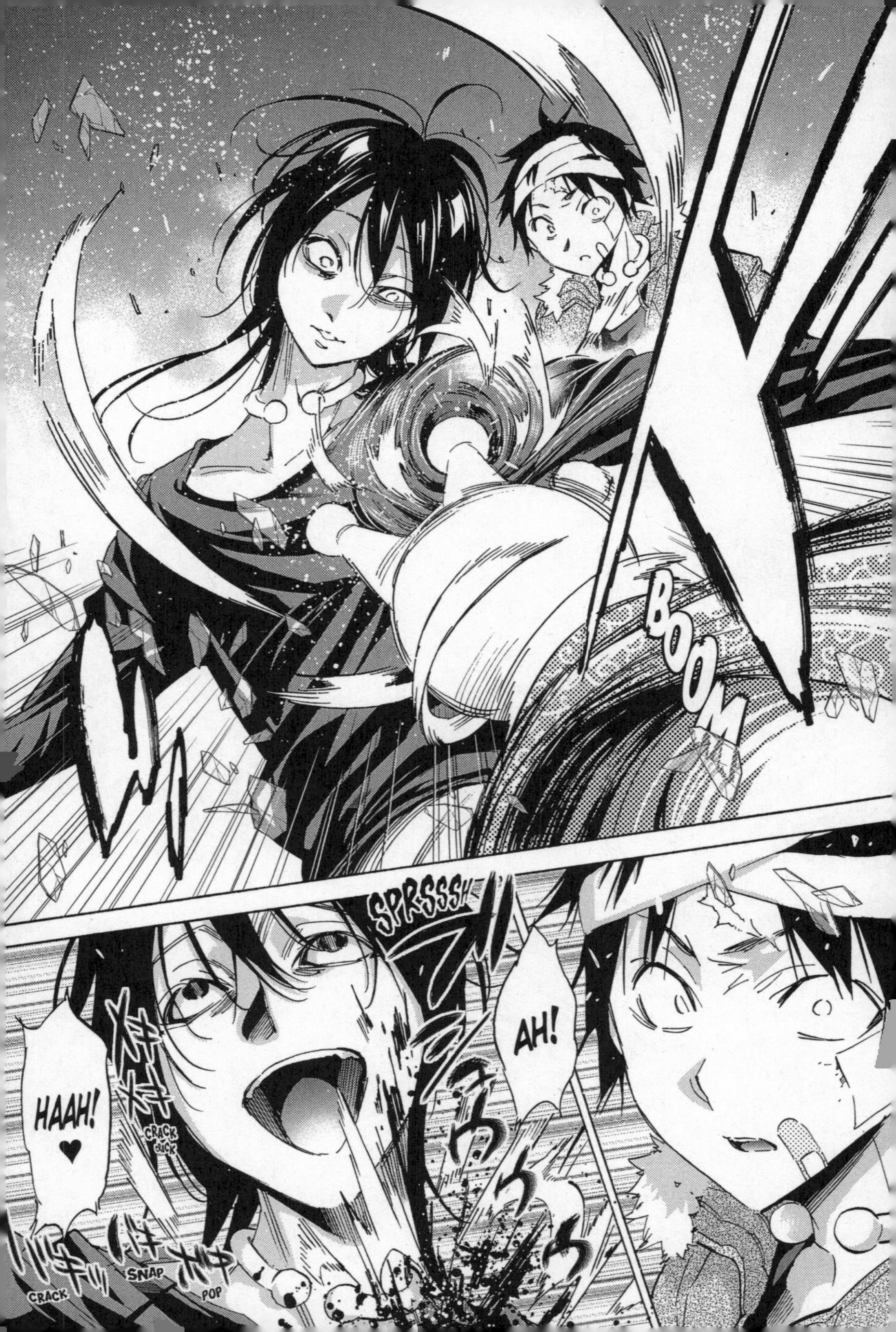
BOOM
SPRSSSH
AH!
HAAH! ♥
CRACK
CRACK
SNAP
POP
CRACK

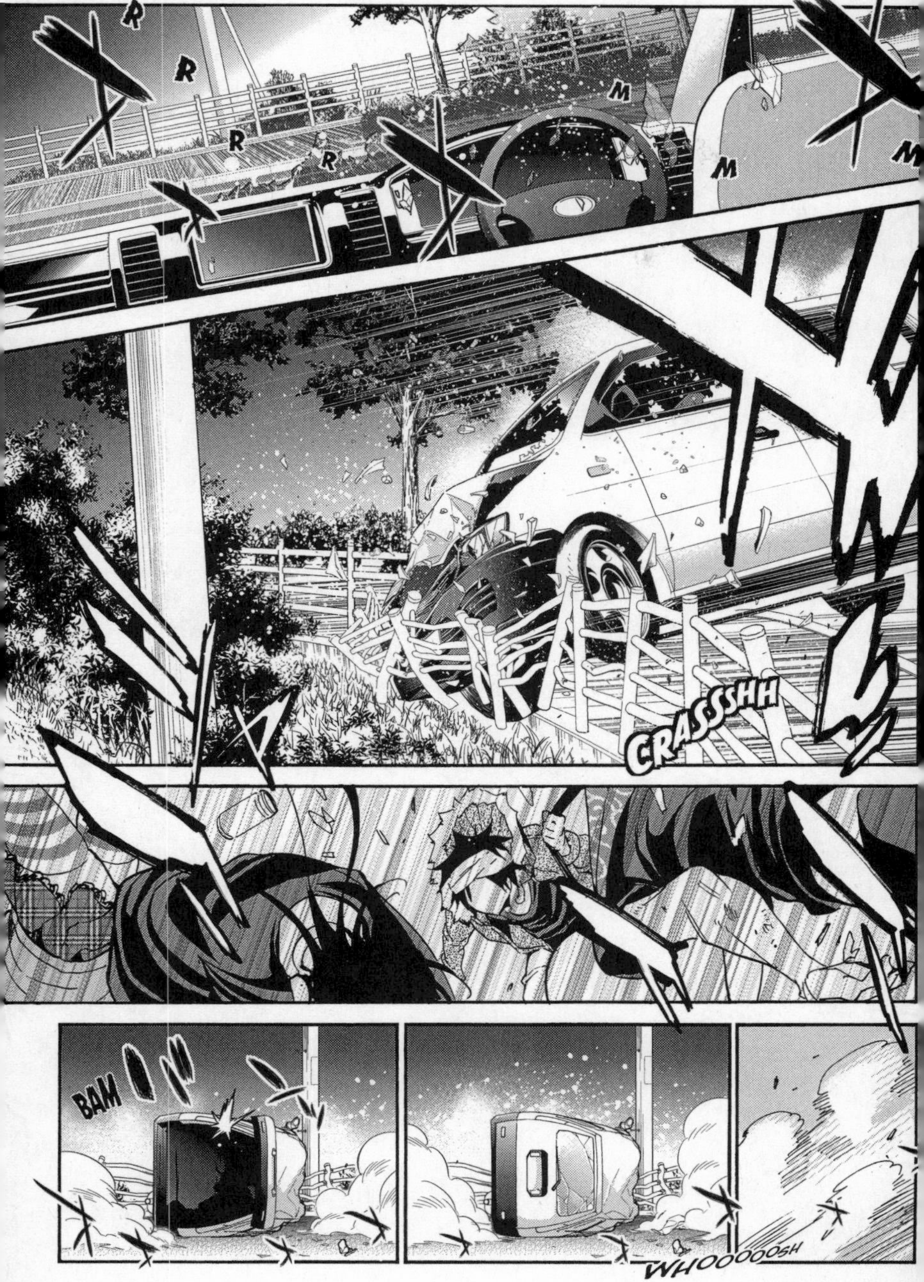
M M M
R R R R
CRASSSHH
WHOOOOOSH
BAM

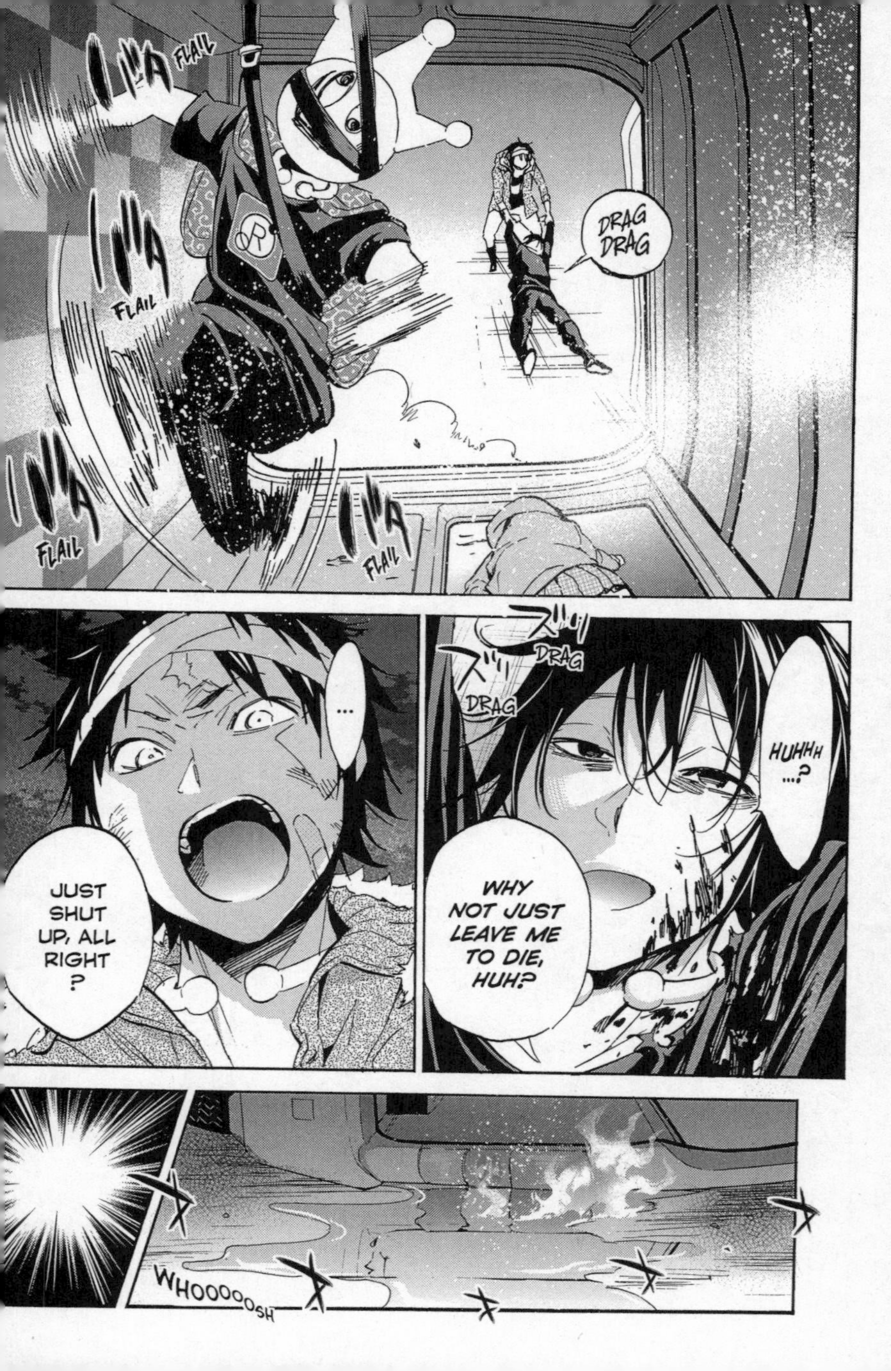
DRAG DRAG
FLAIL
FLAIL
FLAIL
FLAIL
DRAG
DRAG
HUHHH ...?
WHY NOT JUST LEAVE ME TO DIE, HUH?
...
JUST SHUT UP, ALL RIGHT?
WHOOOOOOSH

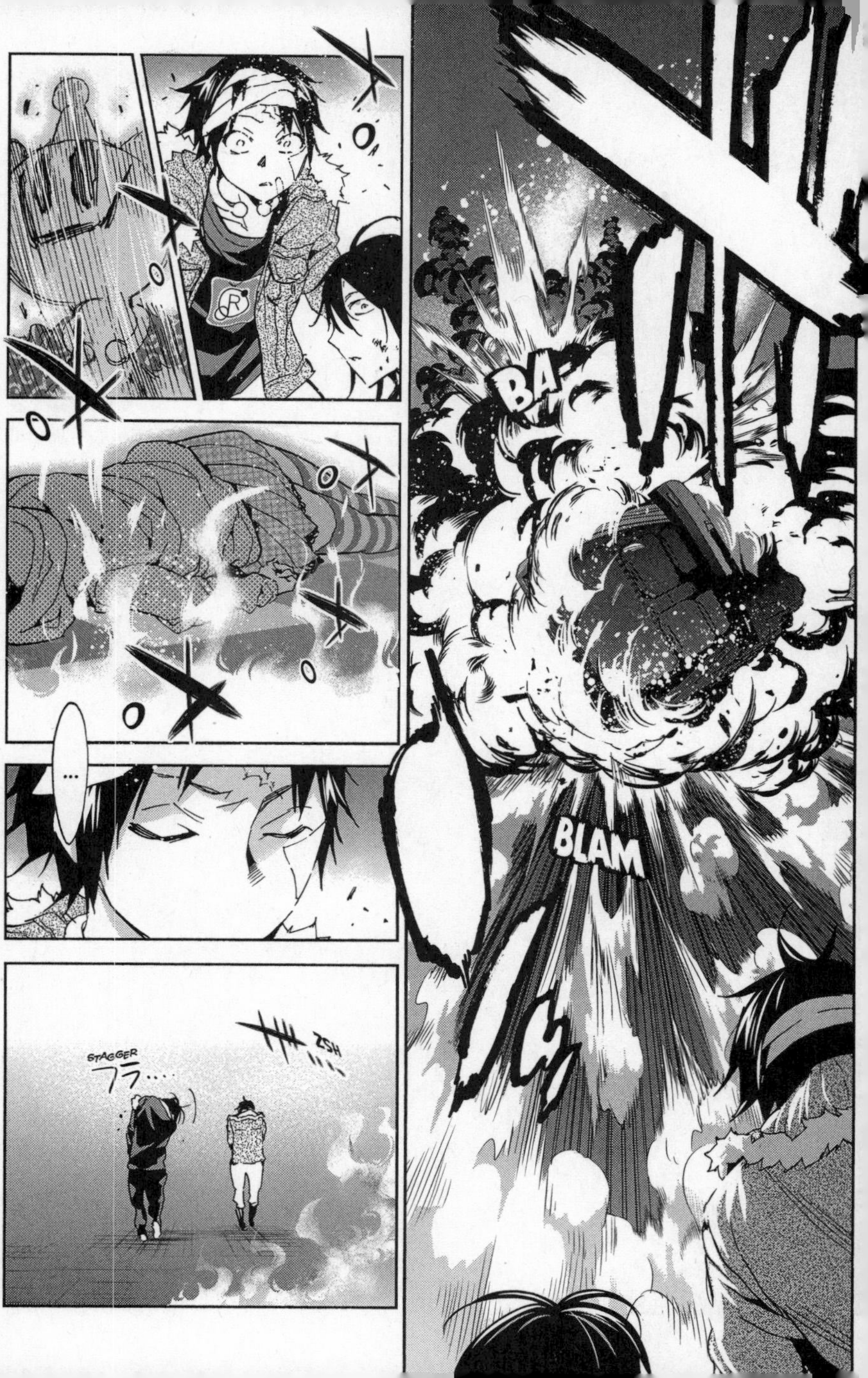
BA-
BLAM
...
STAGGER
フラ...
ZSH

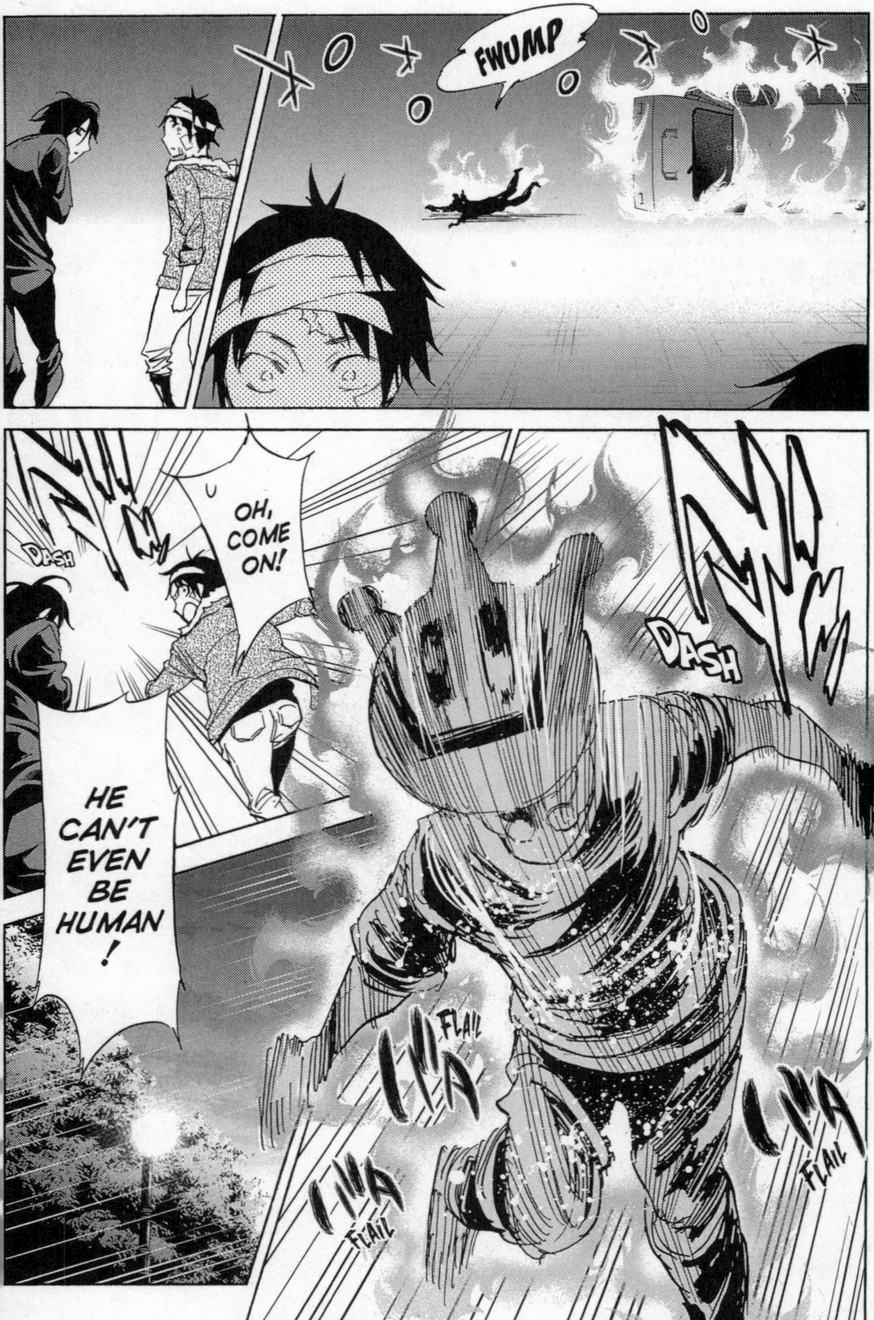
FWUMP
DASH
OH, COME ON!
DASH
HE CAN'T EVEN BE HUMAN!
FLAIL
FLAIL
FLAIL

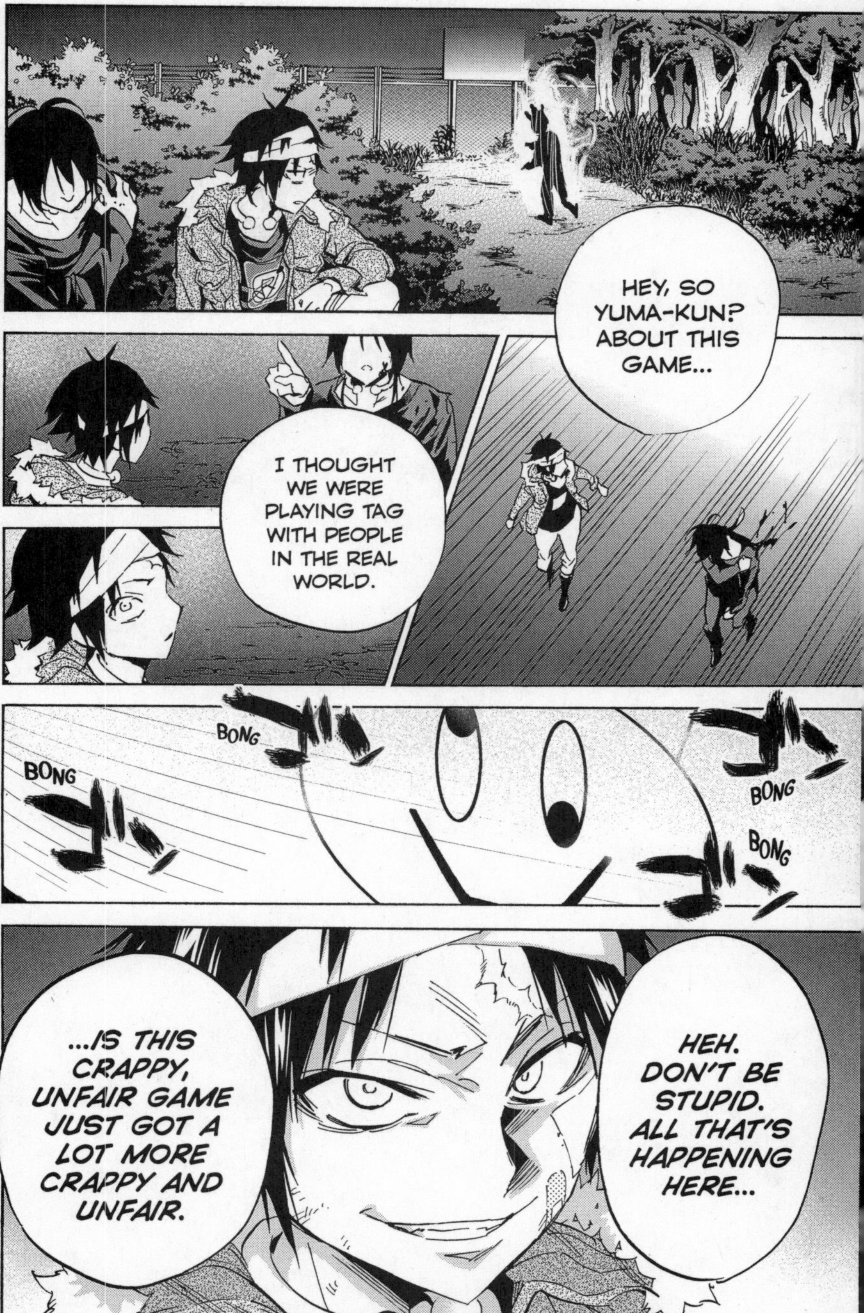
HEY, SO YUMA-KUN? ABOUT THIS GAME...
I THOUGHT WE WERE PLAYING TAG WITH PEOPLE IN THE REAL WORLD.
BONG
BONG
BONG
BONG
HEH. DON'T BE STUPID. ALL THAT'S HAPPENING HERE...
...IS THIS CRAPPY, UNFAIR GAME JUST GOT A LOT MORE CRAPPY AND UNFAIR.

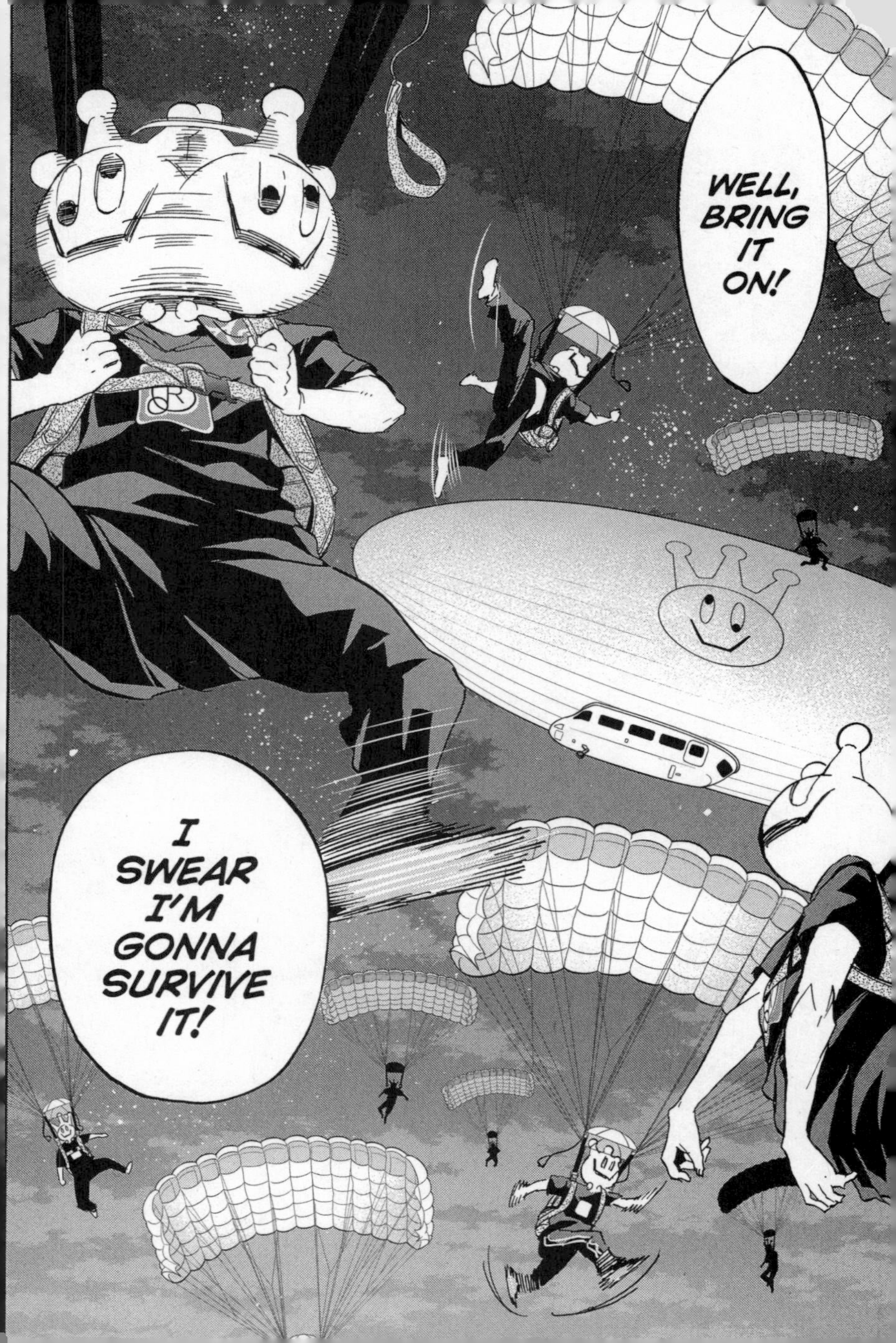
WELL, BRING IT ON!
I SWEAR I'M GONNA SURVIVE IT!

ACCOUNT 36 The Derp Marbles

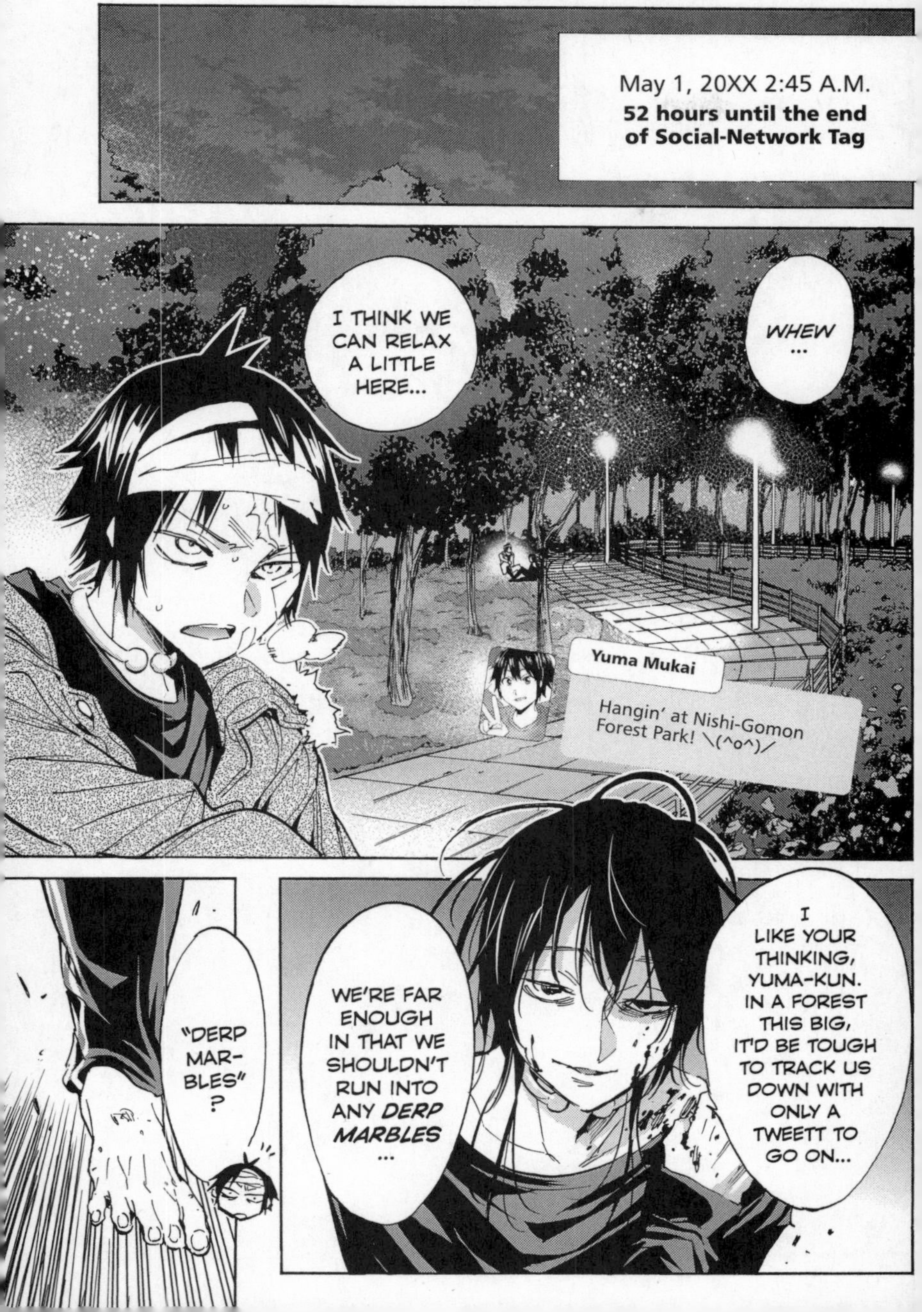
May 1, 20XX 2:45 A.M.
52 hours until the end of Social-Network Tag
WHEW ...
I THINK WE CAN RELAX A LITTLE HERE...
Yuma Mukai
Hangin' at Nishi-Gomon Forest Park! \(^o^)/
I LIKE YOUR THINKING, YUMA-KUN. IN A FOREST THIS BIG, IT'D BE TOUGH TO TRACK US DOWN WITH ONLY A TWEETT TO GO ON...
WE'RE FAR ENOUGH IN THAT WE SHOULDN'T RUN INTO ANY *DERP MARBLES* ...
"DERP MAR-BLES" ?

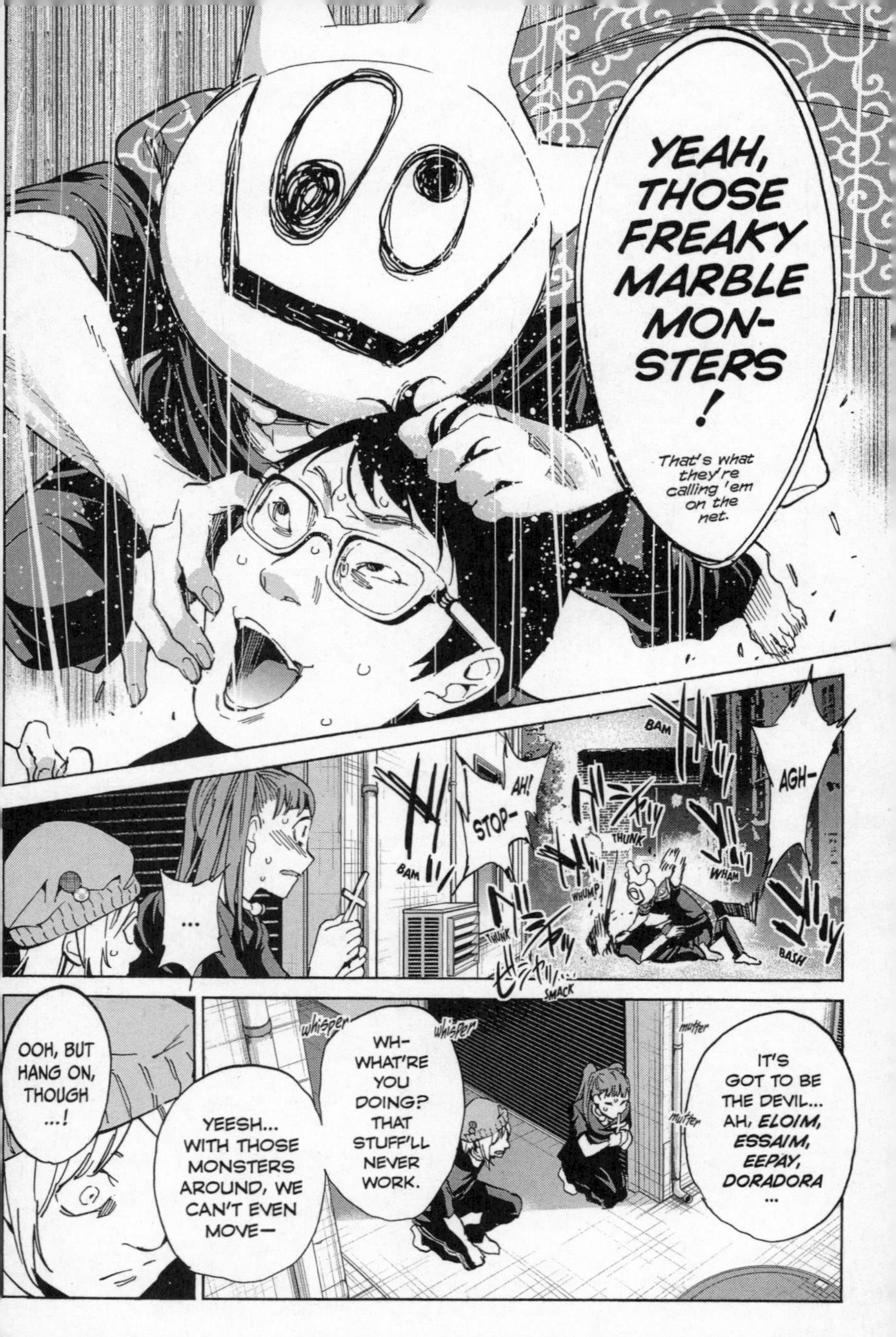
YEAH, THOSE FREAKY MARBLE MONSTERS!
That's what they're calling 'em on the net.
BAM
AGH-
AH!
STOP-
THUNK
WHAM
WHUMP
BAM
BASH
THUNK
SMACK
...
mutter
mutter
IT'S GOT TO BE THE DEVIL... AH, ELOIM, ESSAIM, EEPAY, DORADORA ...
whisper
whisper
WH-WHAT'RE YOU DOING? THAT STUFF'LL NEVER WORK.
YEESH... WITH THOSE MONSTERS AROUND, WE CAN'T EVEN MOVE—
OOH, BUT HANG ON, THOUGH ...!

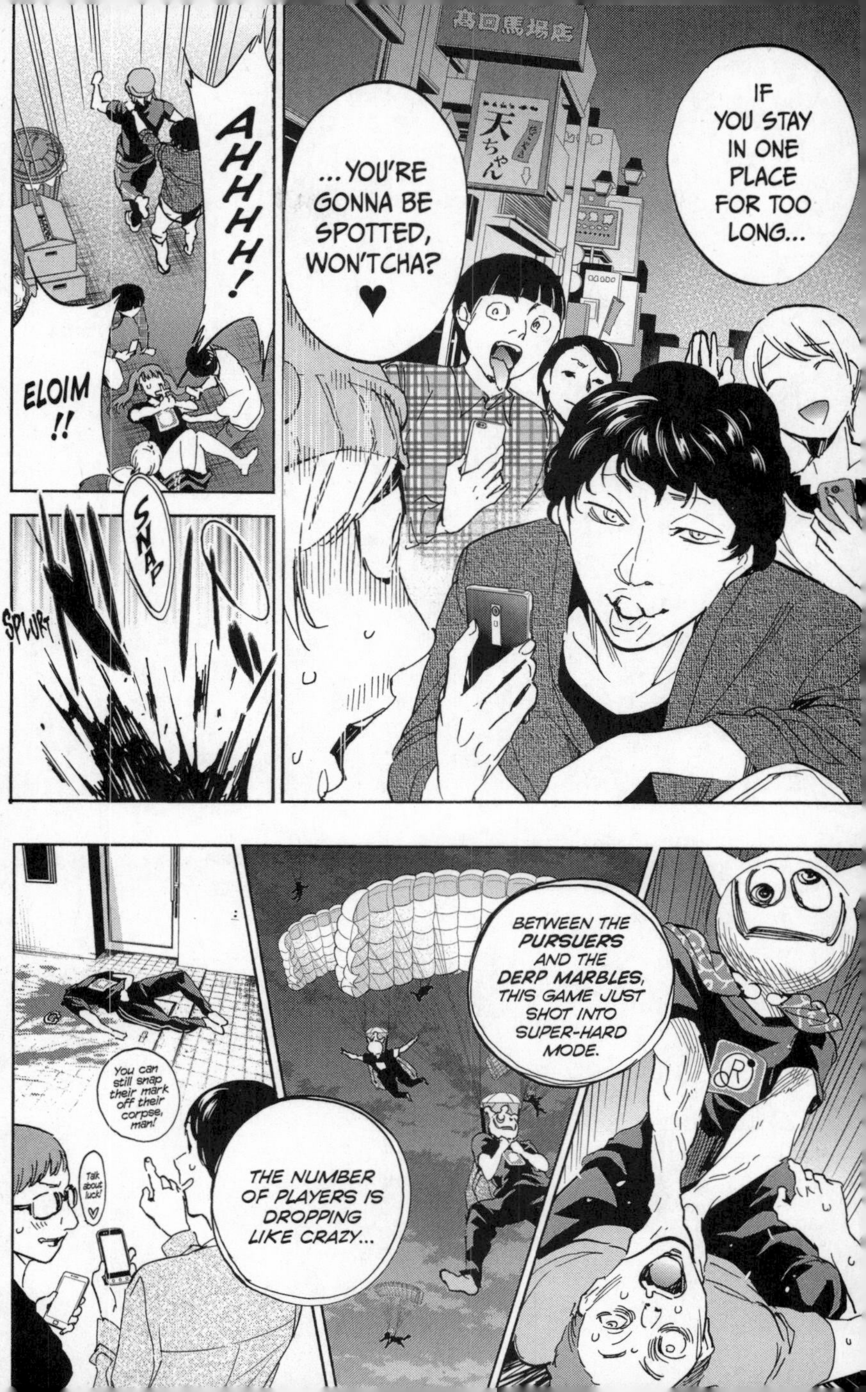

IF YOU STAY IN ONE PLACE FOR TOO LONG...
...YOU'RE GONNA BE SPOTTED, WON'TCHA? ♥
AHHHH!
ELOIM!!
SNAP
SPLURT
BETWEEN THE PURSUERS AND THE DERP MARBLES, THIS GAME JUST SHOT INTO SUPER-HARD MODE.
THE NUMBER OF PLAYERS IS DROPPING LIKE CRAZY...
You can still snap their mark off their corpse, man!
Talk about luck! ♥

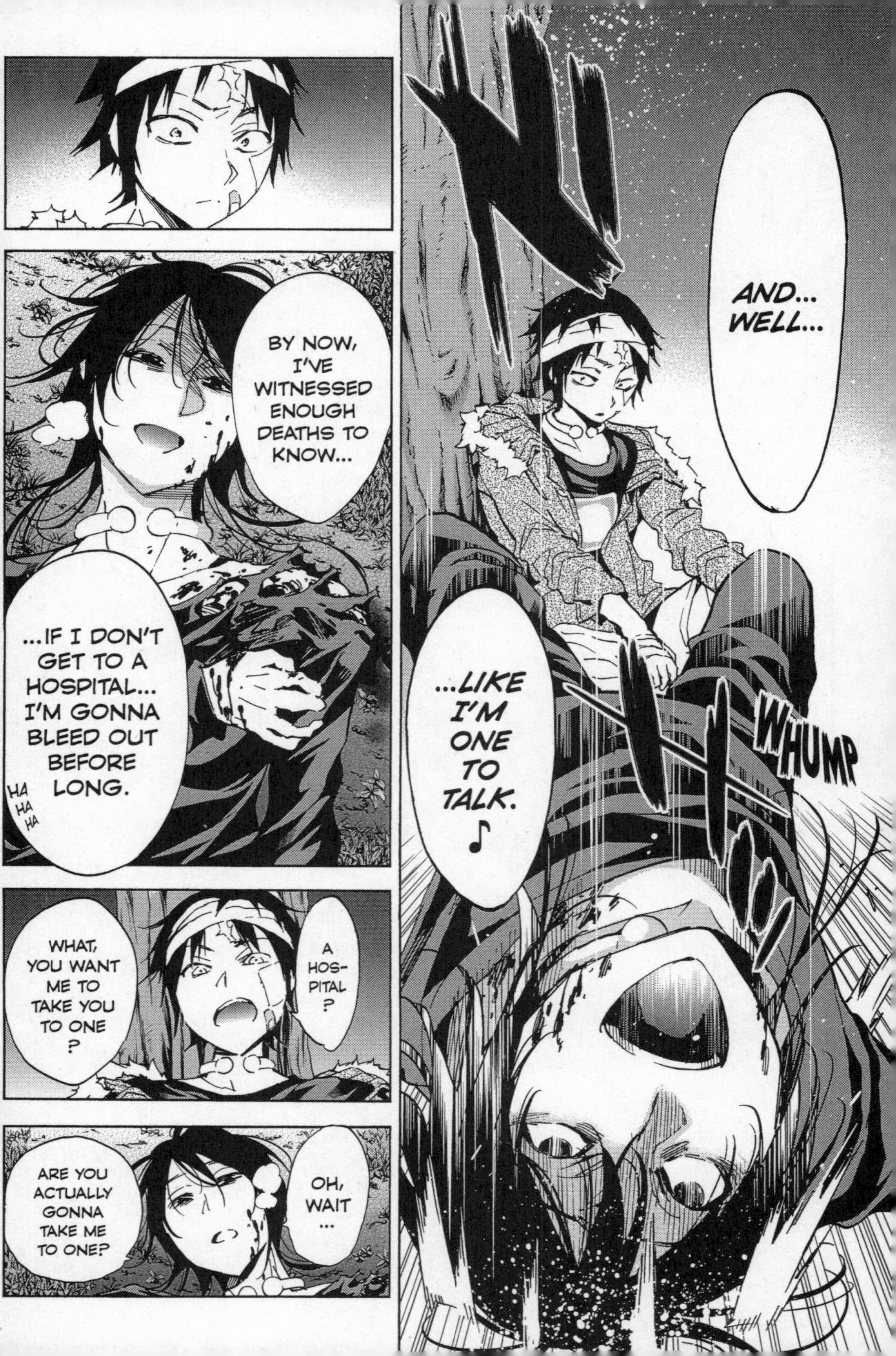
AND... WELL...
...LIKE I'M ONE TO TALK. ♪
WHUMP
BY NOW, I'VE WITNESSED ENOUGH DEATHS TO KNOW...
...IF I DON'T GET TO A HOSPITAL... I'M GONNA BLEED OUT BEFORE LONG.
HA HA HA
A HOS-PITAL?
WHAT, YOU WANT ME TO TAKE YOU TO ONE?
OH, WAIT...
ARE YOU ACTUALLY GONNA TAKE ME TO ONE?

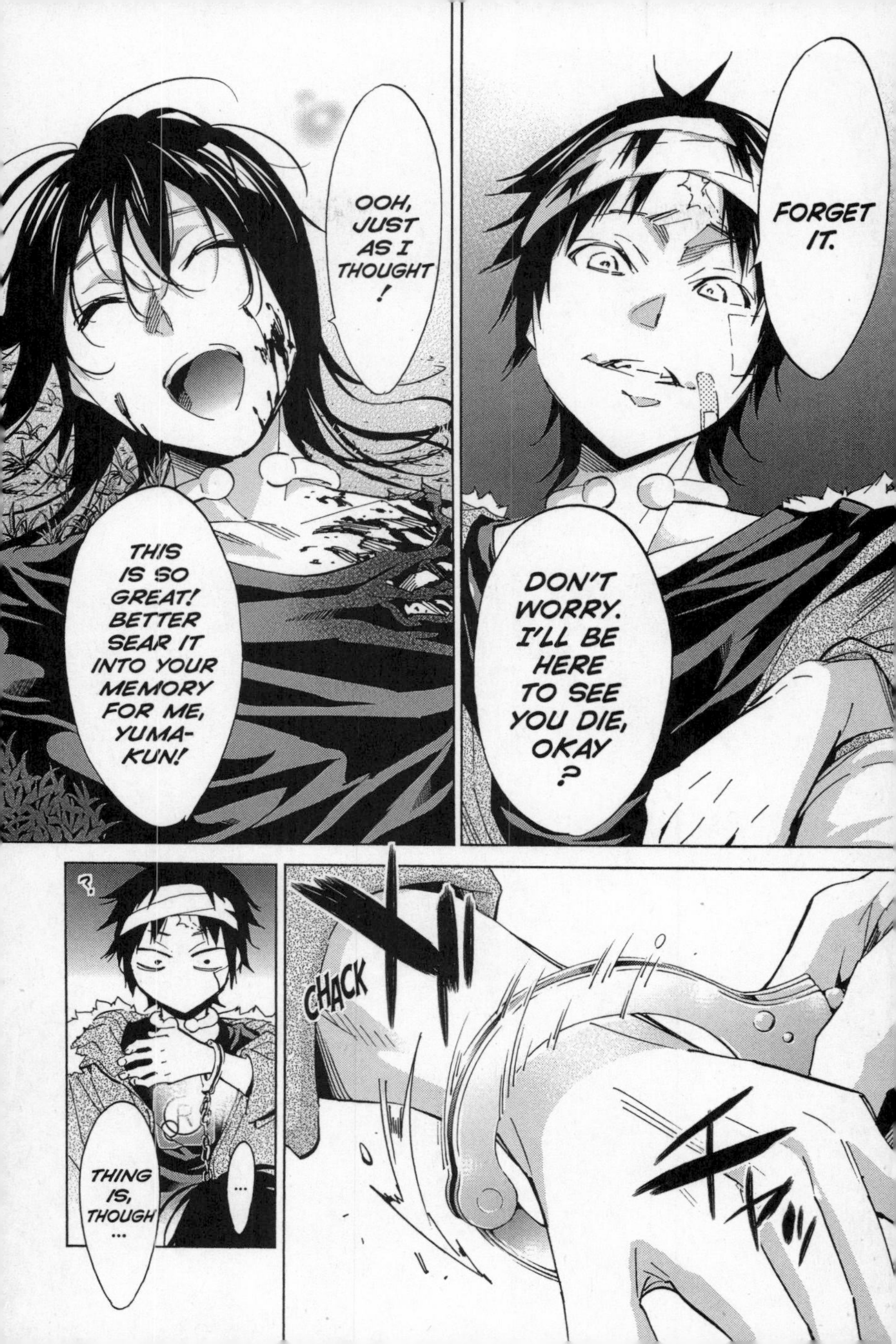
FORGET IT.
DON'T WORRY. I'LL BE HERE TO SEE YOU DIE, OKAY?
OOH, JUST AS I THOUGHT!
THIS IS SO GREAT! BETTER SEAR IT INTO YOUR MEMORY FOR ME, YUMA-KUN!
CHACK
?
...
THING IS, THOUGH...

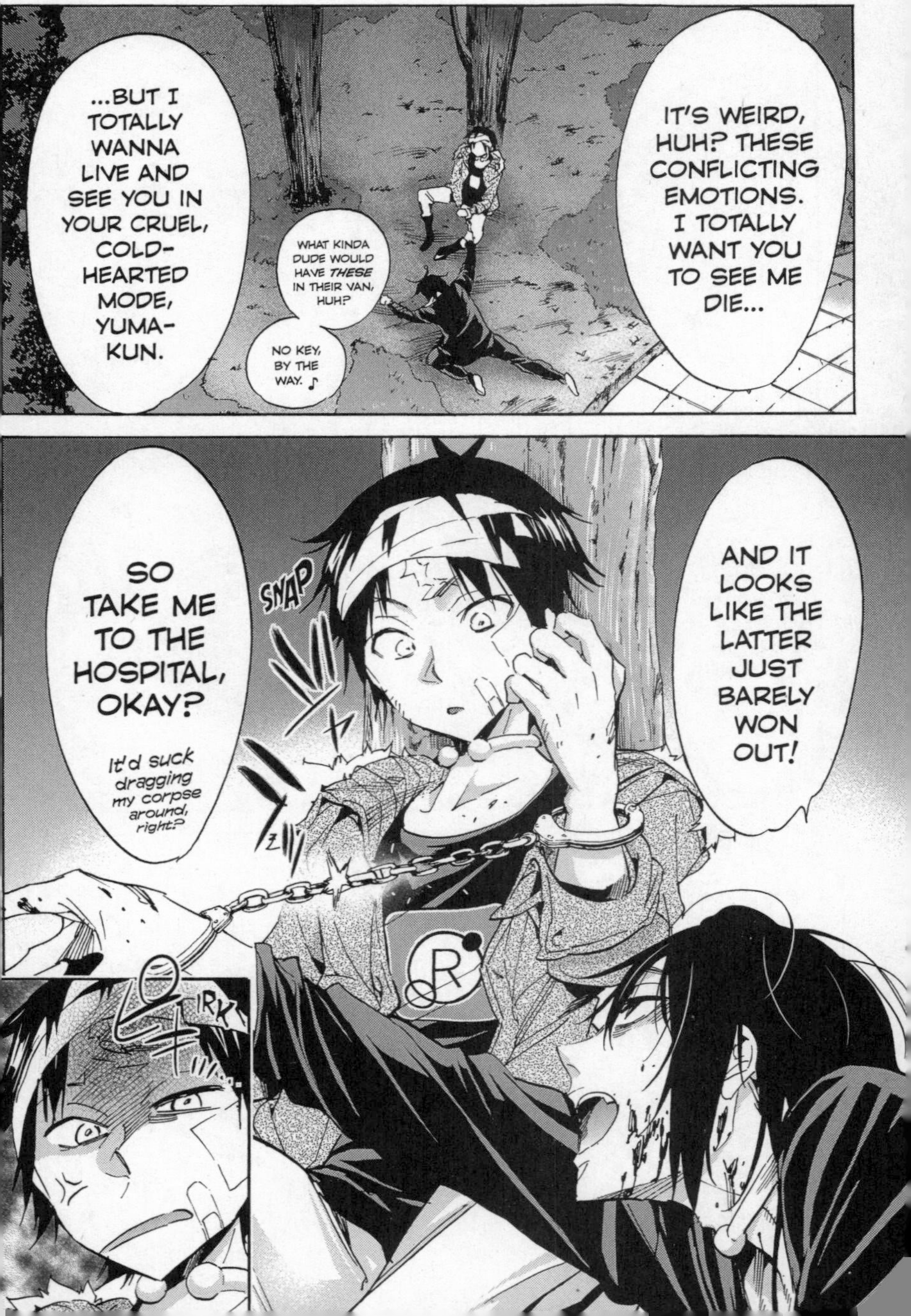
IT'S WEIRD, HUH? THESE CONFLICTING EMOTIONS. I TOTALLY WANT YOU TO SEE ME DIE...
WHAT KINDA DUDE WOULD HAVE *THESE* IN THEIR VAN, HUH?
NO KEY, BY THE WAY. ♪
...BUT I TOTALLY WANNA LIVE AND SEE YOU IN YOUR CRUEL, COLD-HEARTED MODE, YUMA-KUN.
AND IT LOOKS LIKE THE LATTER JUST BARELY WON OUT!
SNAP
SO TAKE ME TO THE HOSPITAL, OKAY?
It'd suck dragging my corpse around, right?
IRK

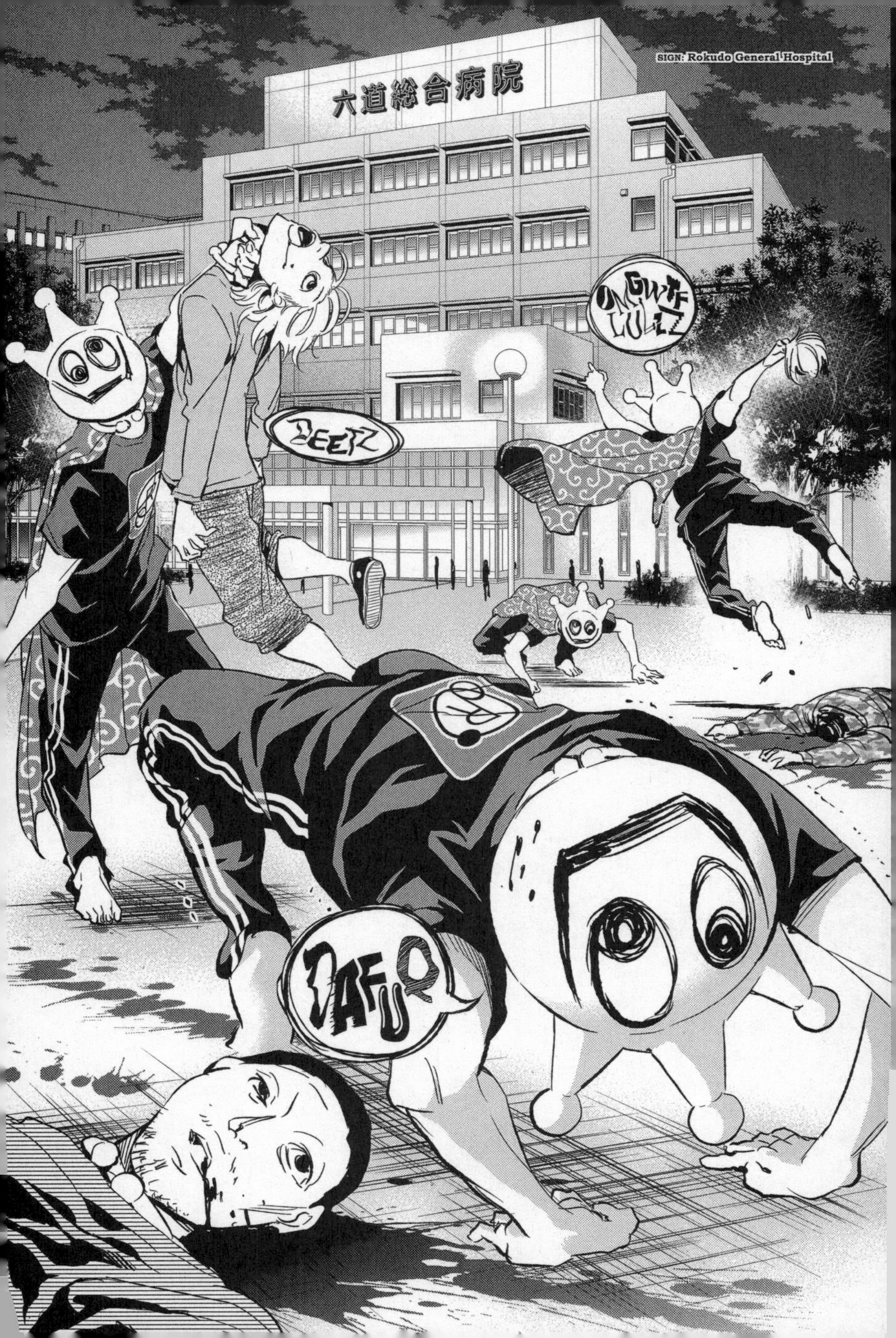
SIGN: Rokudo General Hospital
六道総合病院
OMGWTF LULZZ
DEERZ
DAFUQ

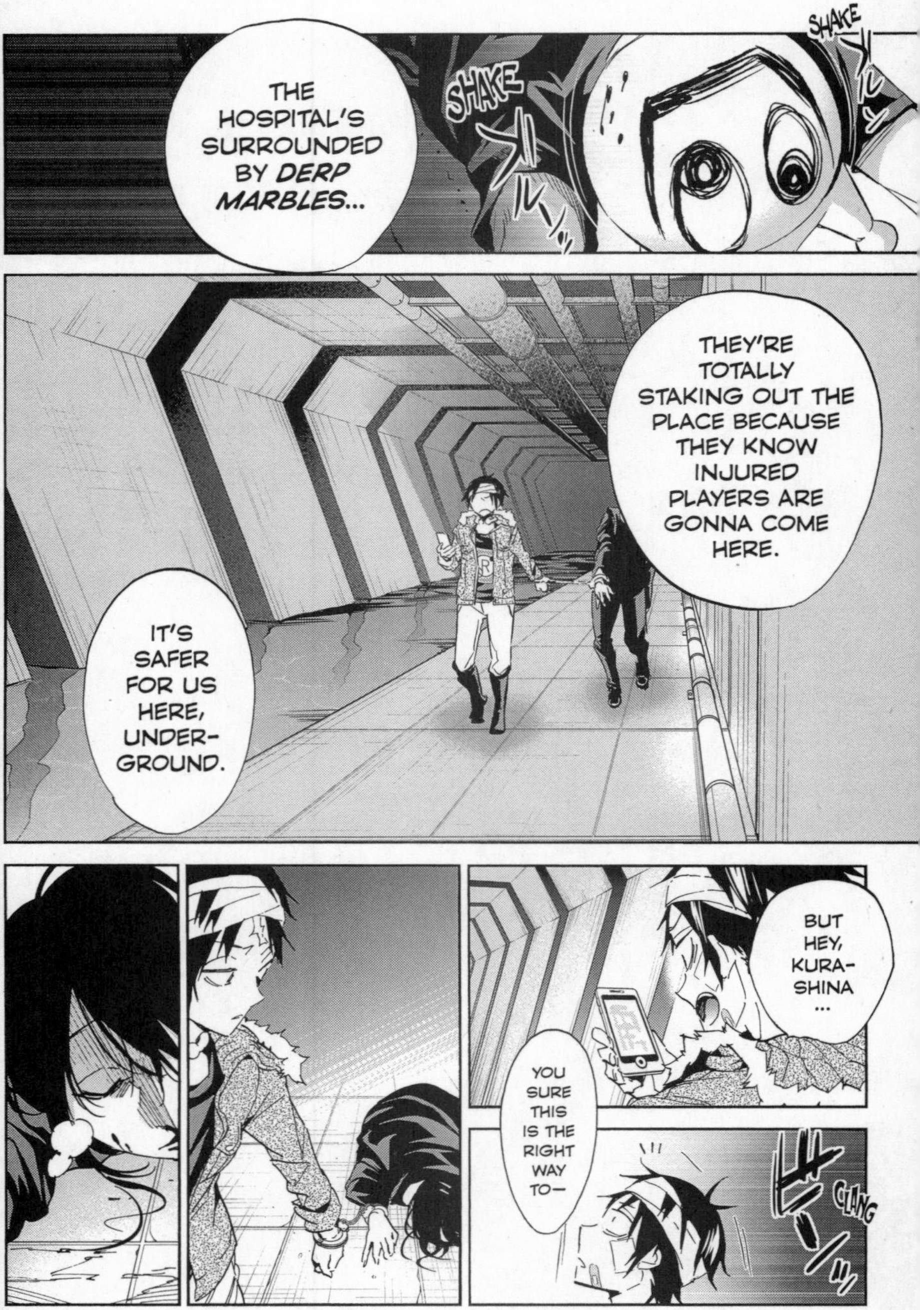
SHAKE
SHAKE
THE HOSPITAL'S SURROUNDED BY *DERP MARBLES*...
THEY'RE TOTALLY STAKING OUT THE PLACE BECAUSE THEY KNOW INJURED PLAYERS ARE GONNA COME HERE.
IT'S SAFER FOR US HERE, UNDER-GROUND.
BUT HEY, KURA-SHINA...
YOU SURE THIS IS THE RIGHT WAY TO—
CLANG

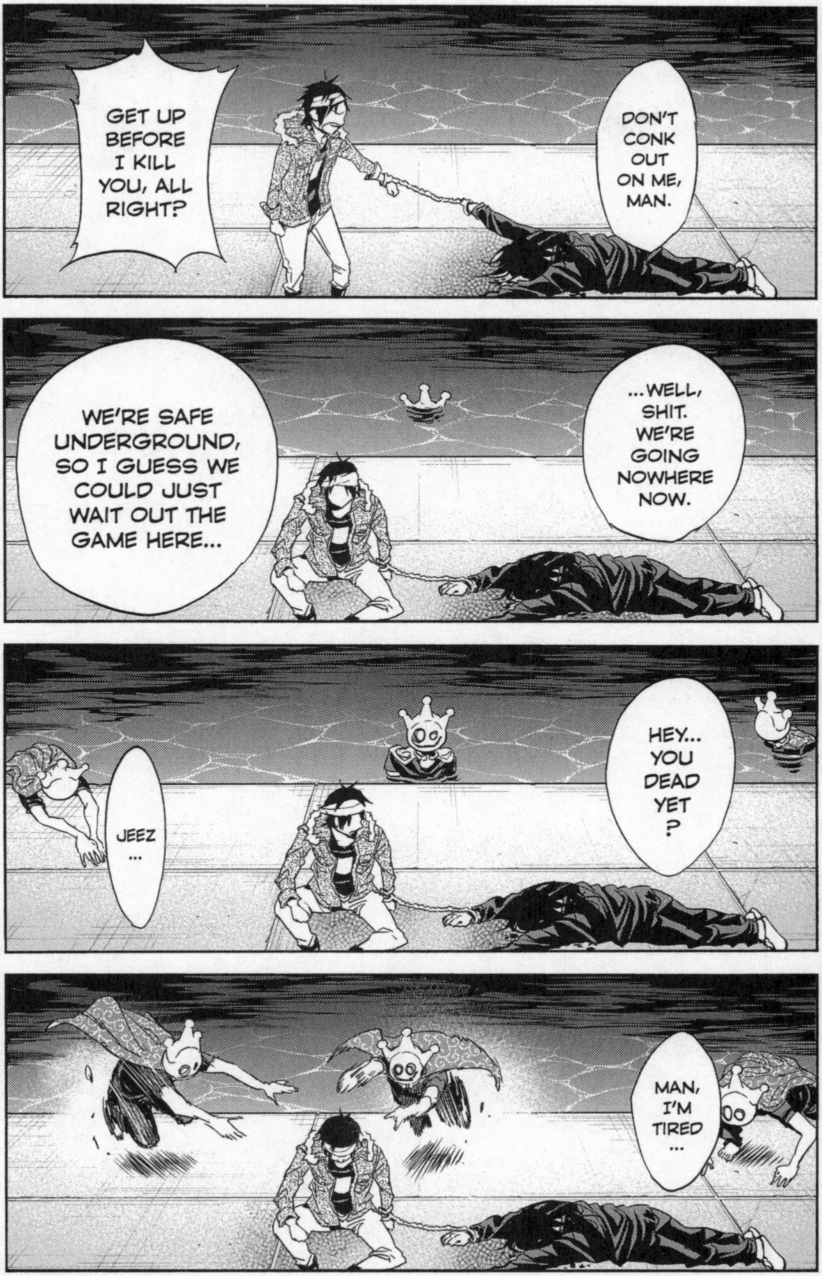
DON'T CONK OUT ON ME, MAN.
GET UP BEFORE I KILL YOU, ALL RIGHT?
...WELL, SHIT. WE'RE GOING NOWHERE NOW.
WE'RE SAFE UNDERGROUND, SO I GUESS WE COULD JUST WAIT OUT THE GAME HERE...
HEY... YOU DEAD YET?
JEEZ...
MAN, I'M TIRED...

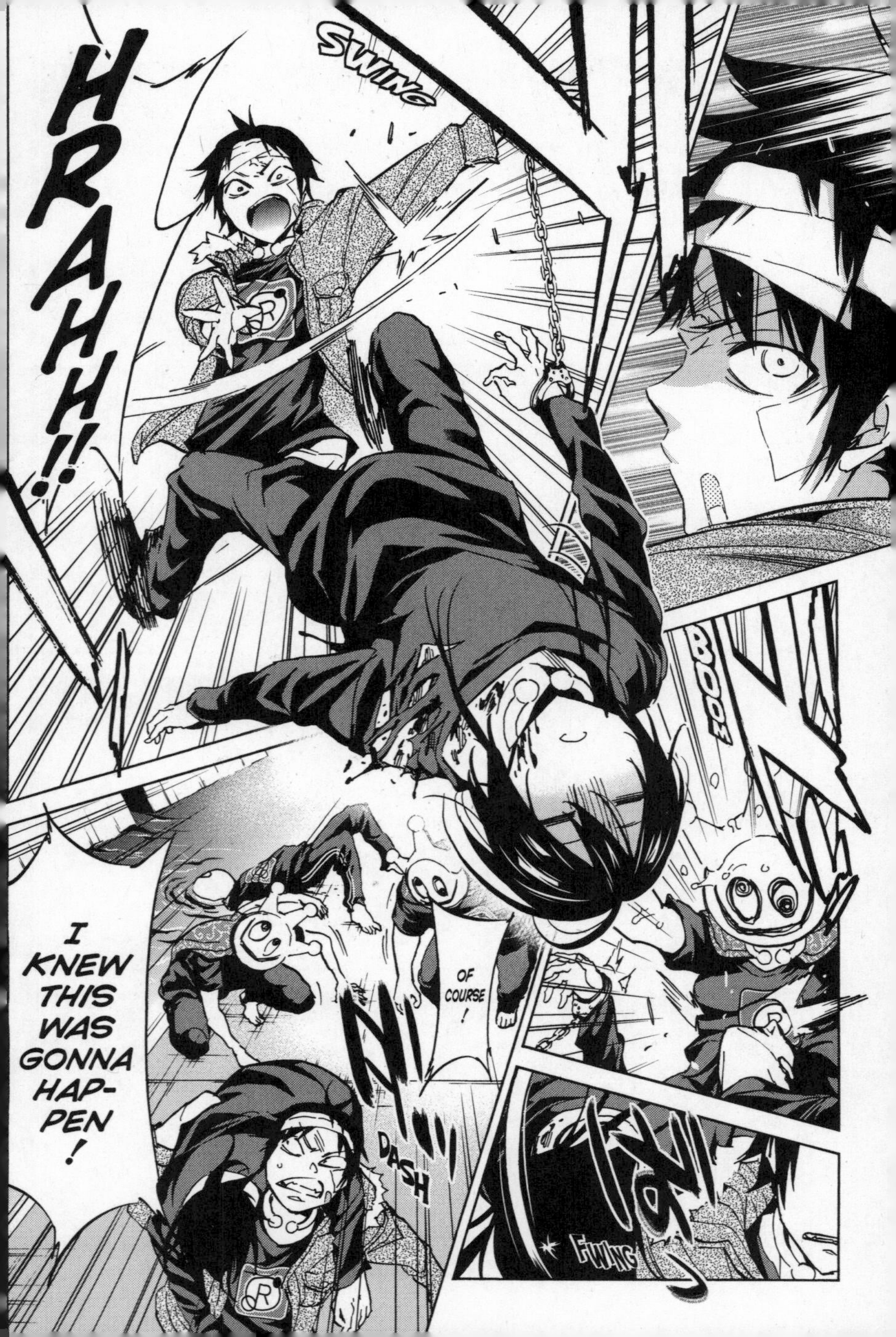
SWING
HRAHHH!!
BOOM
OF COURSE!
FWING
DASH
I KNEW THIS WAS GONNA HAP-PEN!

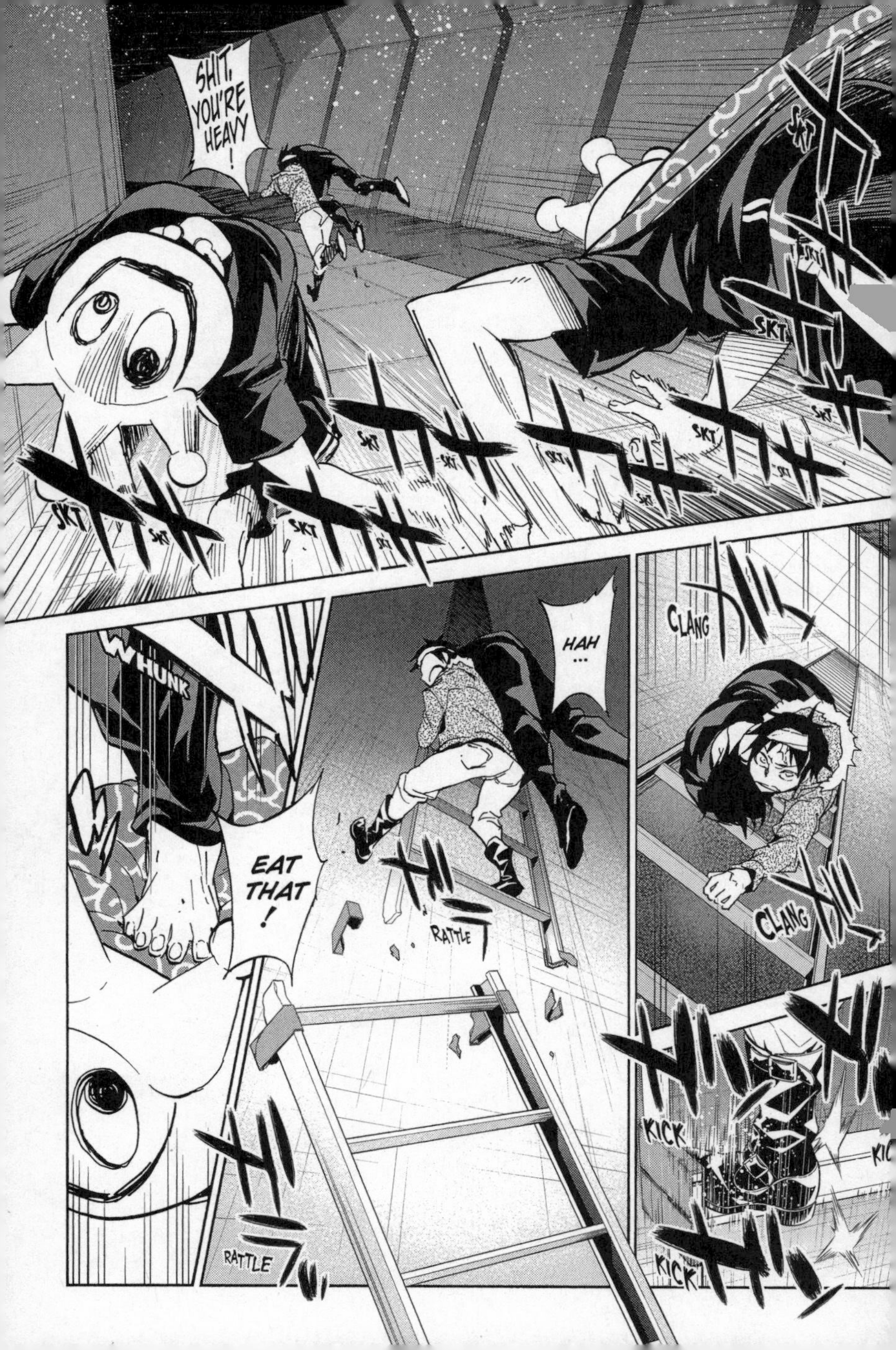
SHIT, YOU'RE HEAVY!
SKT
SKT
SKT
SKT
SKT
SKT
SKT
SKT
SKT
SKT
SKT
SKT
SKT
CLANG
CLANG
KICK
KICK
KICK
HAH...
RATTLE
WHUNK
EAT THAT!
RATTLE

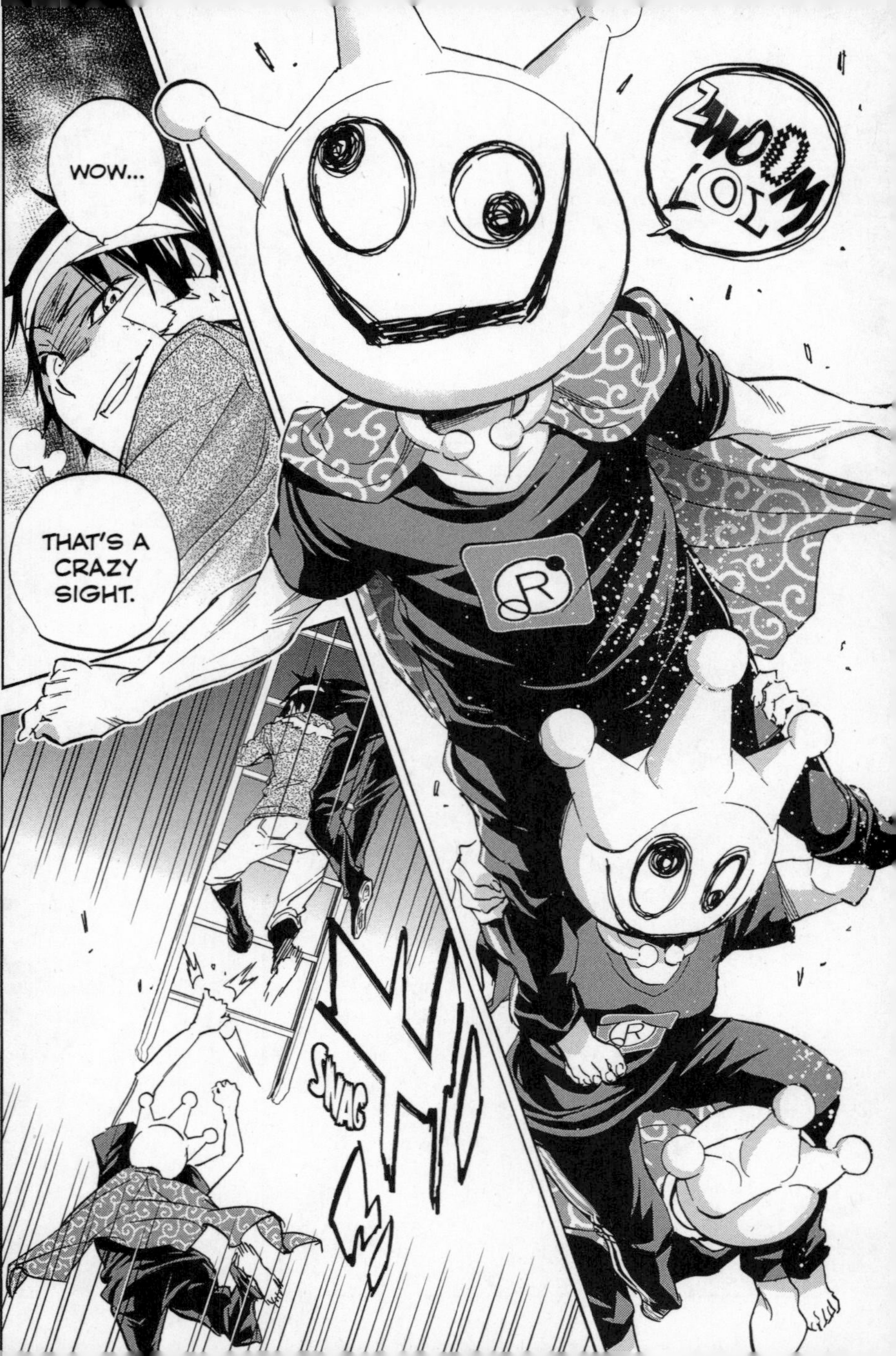
ZWOOM
WOW...
THAT'S A CRAZY SIGHT.
SNAG

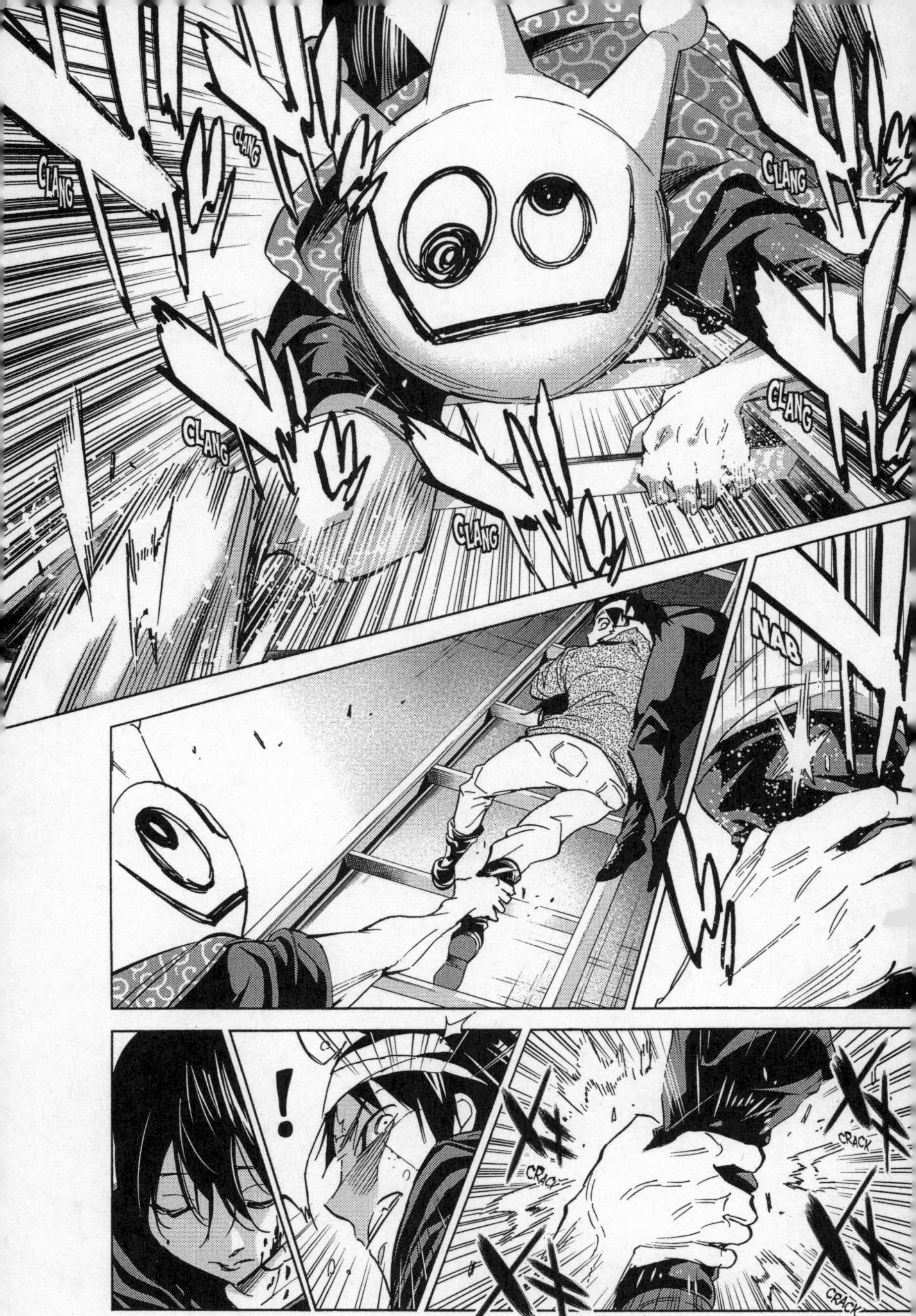
CLANG
CLANG
CLANG
CLANG
CLANG
CLANG
NAB
CRACK
CRACK
CRACK
CRACK
!

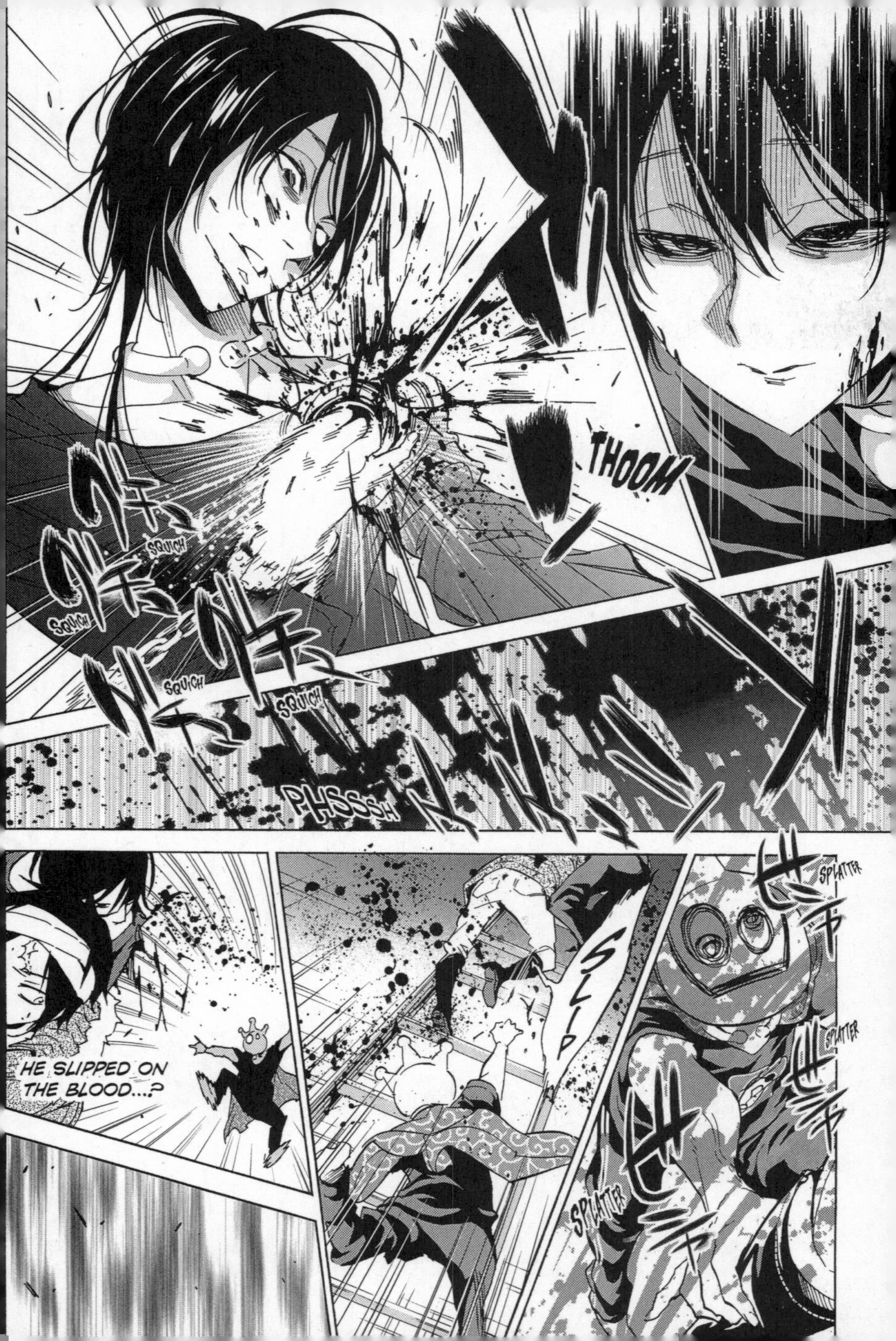

THOOM
SQUICH
SQUICH
SQUICH
SQUICH
PHSSSH
SPLATTER
SPLATTER
SPLATTER
SLIP
HE SLIPPED ON THE BLOOD...?

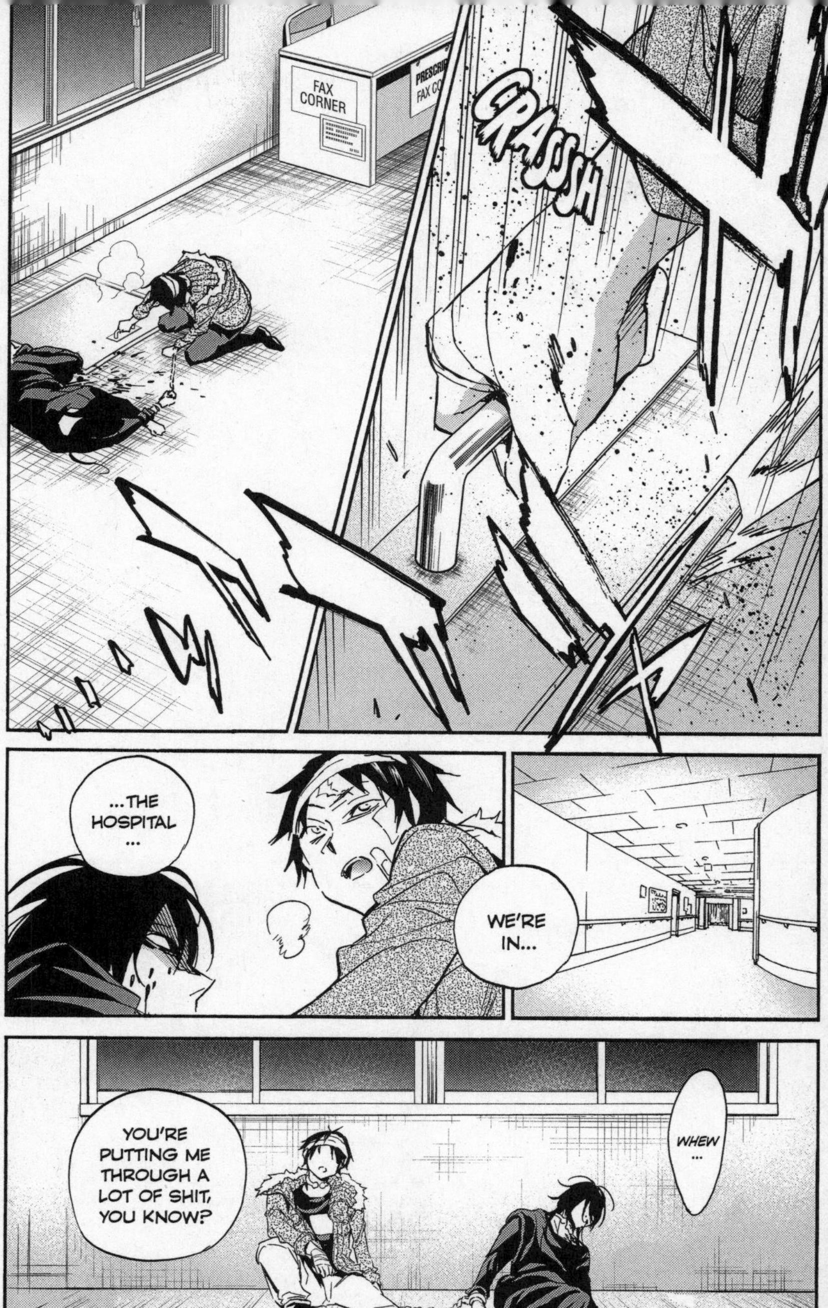
FAX CORNER
CRASSSH
WE'RE IN...
...THE HOSPITAL...
WHEW...
YOU'RE PUTTING ME THROUGH A LOT OF SHIT, YOU KNOW?

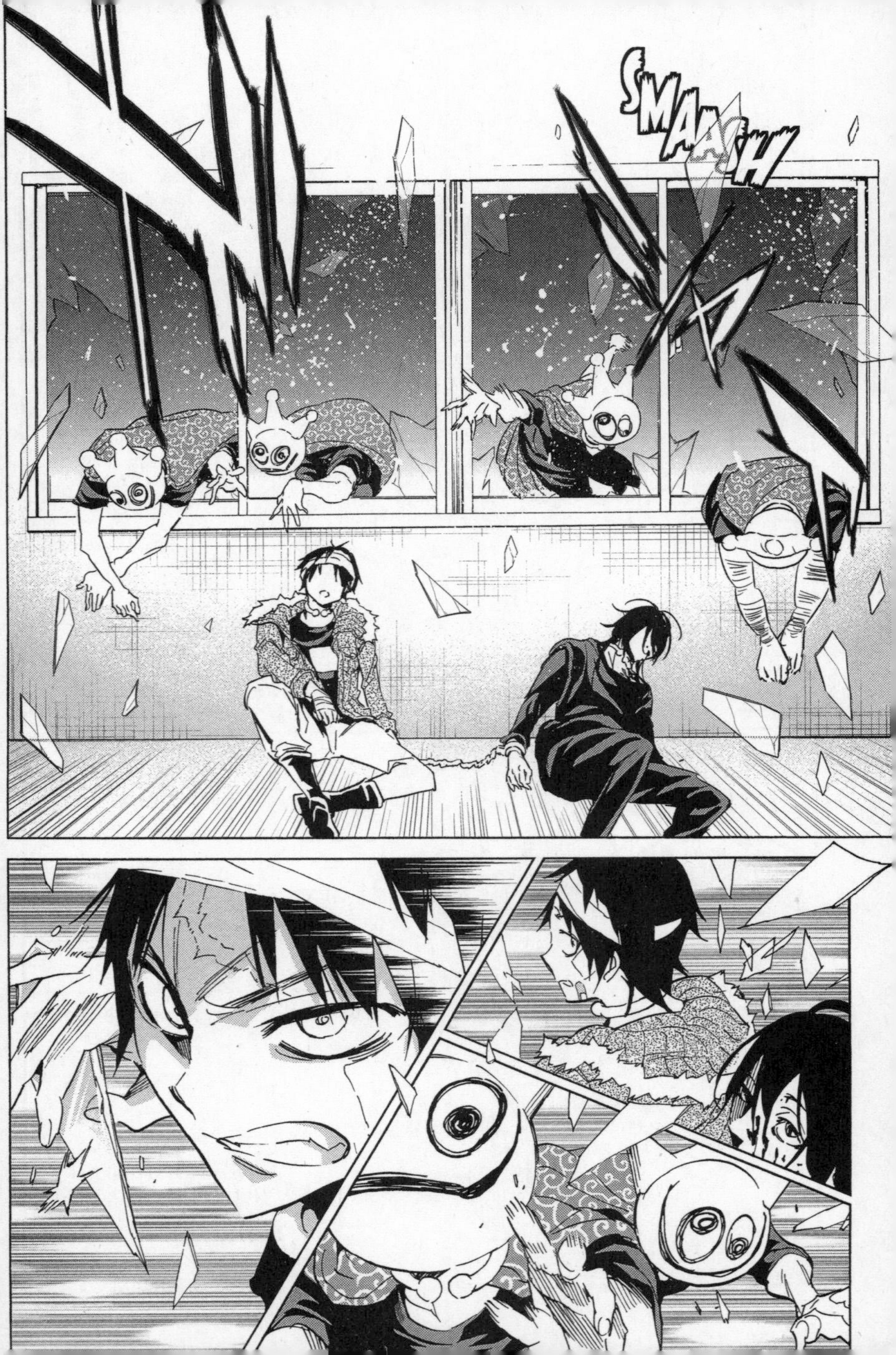
SMAAASH

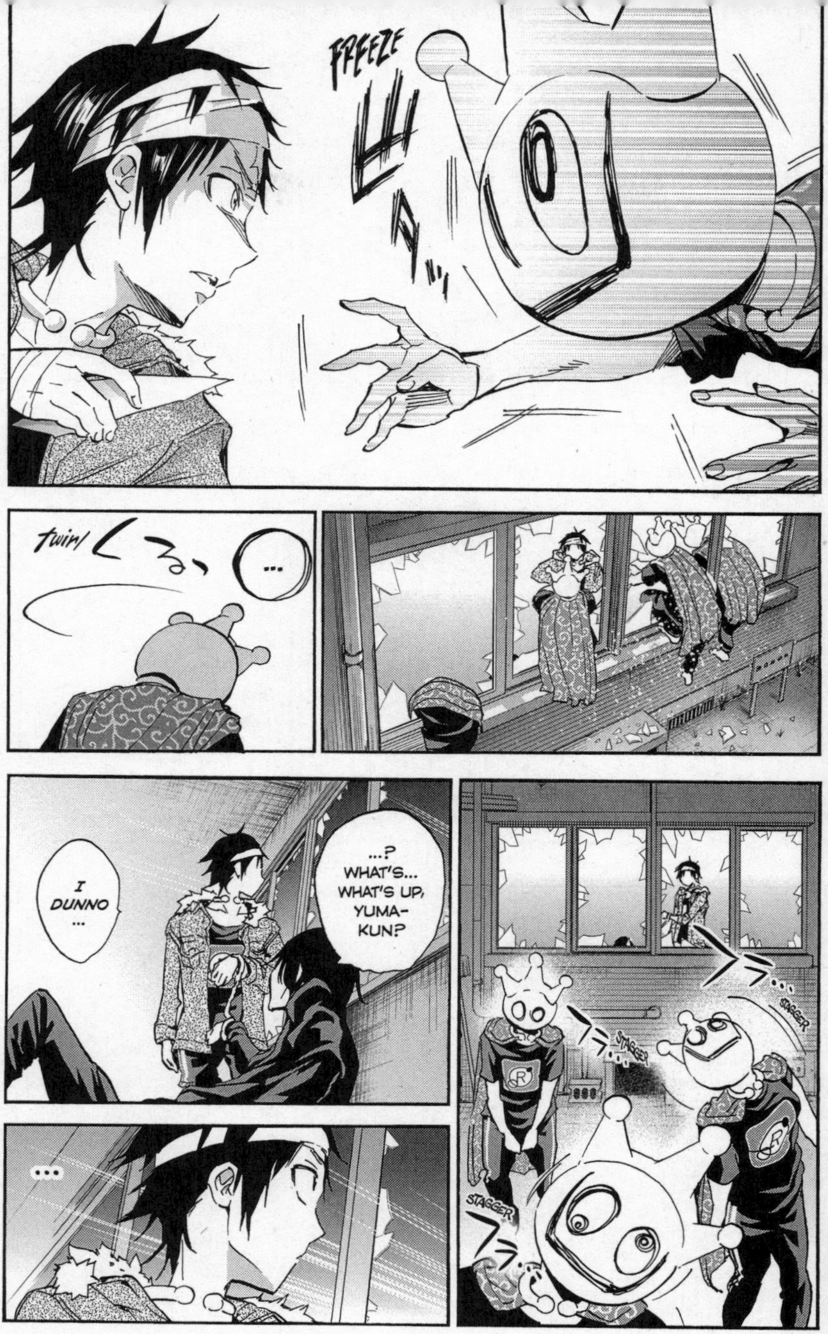
FREEZE
twirl くるっ
...
STAGGER
STAGGER
STAGGER
...? WHAT'S... WHAT'S UP, YUMA-KUN?
I DUNNO ...
...

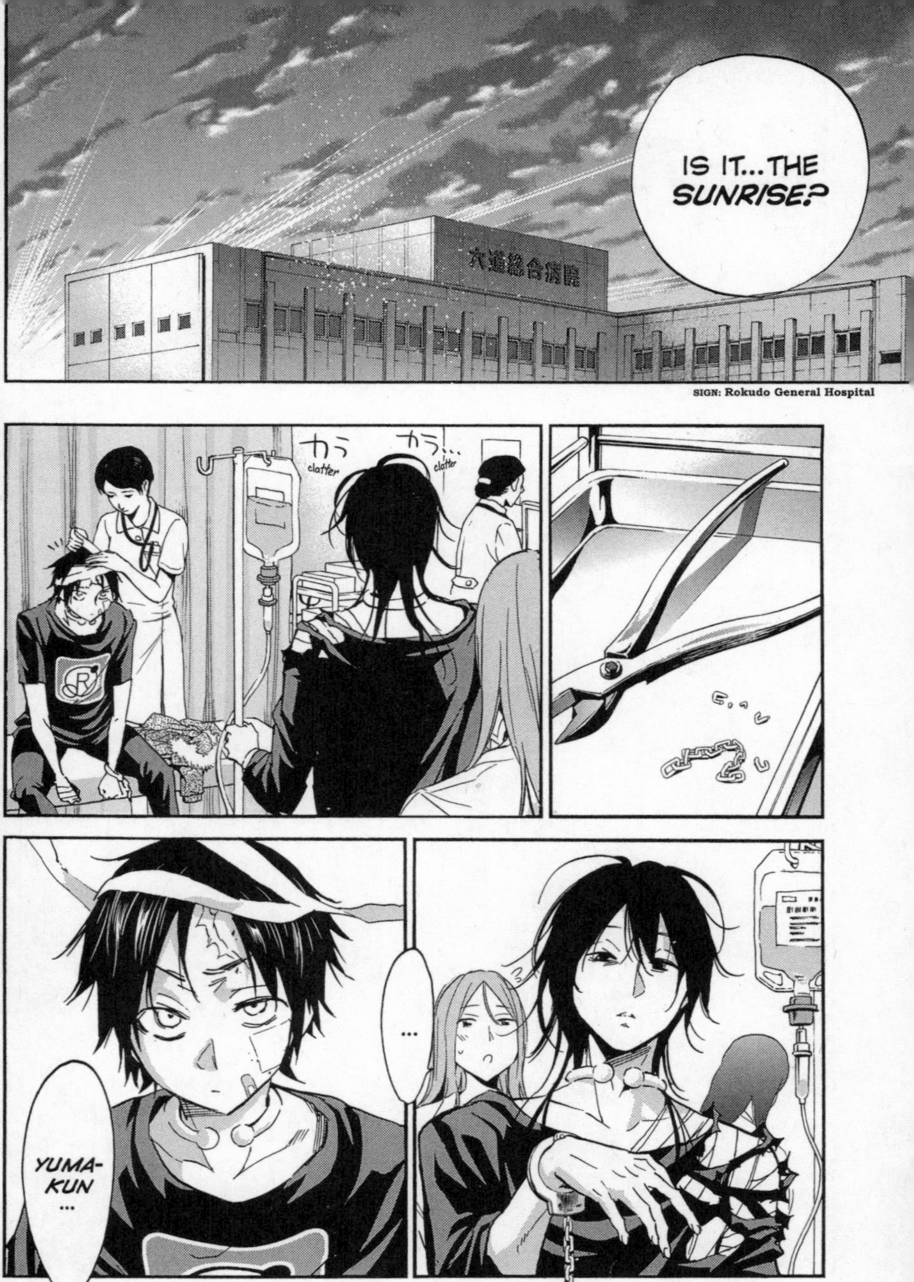
IS IT...THE SUNRISE?
SIGN: Rokudo General Hospital
カラ
clatter
カラ...
clatter
...
YUMA-KUN ...

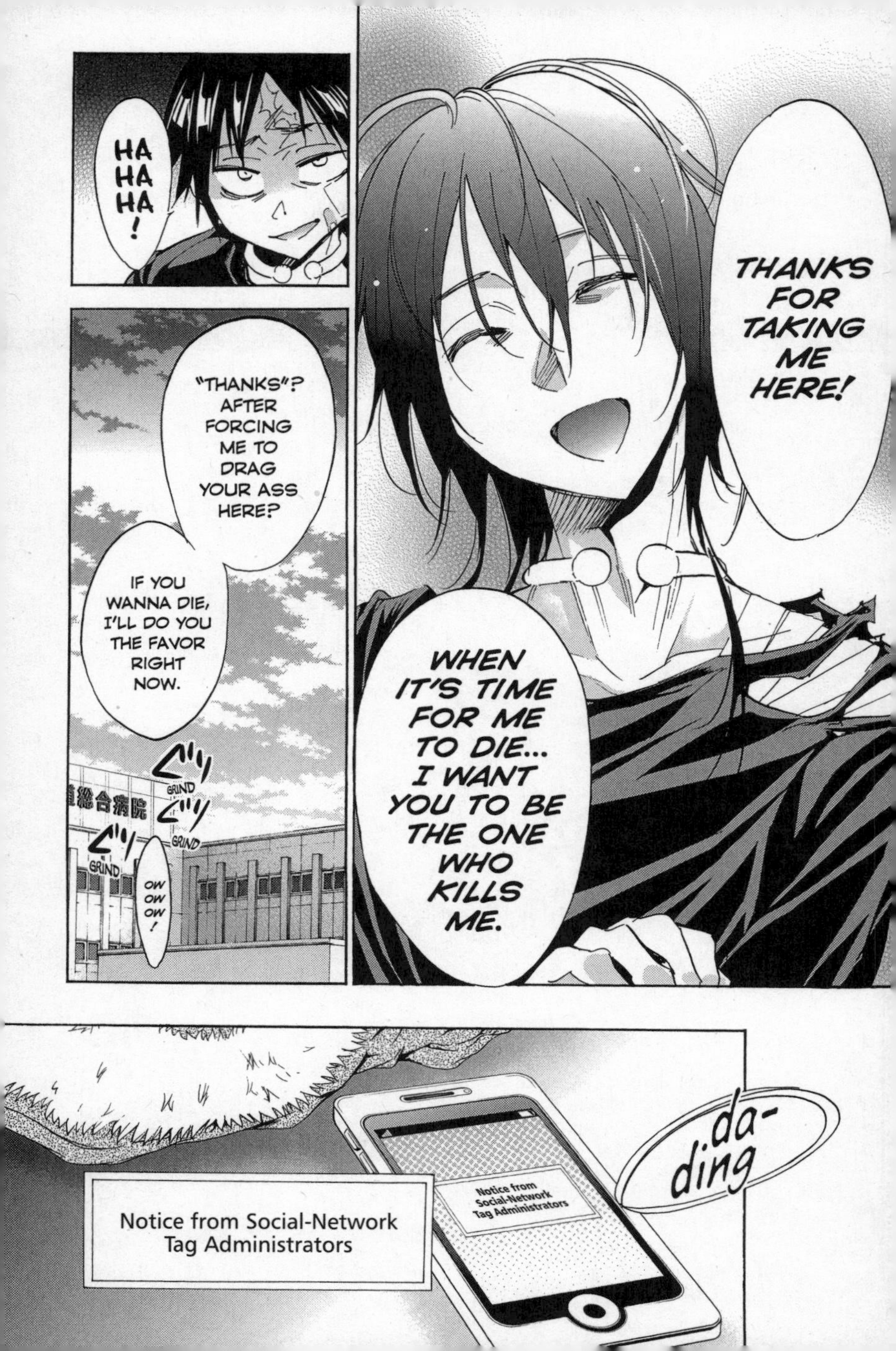
THANKS FOR TAKING ME HERE!
WHEN IT'S TIME FOR ME TO DIE... I WANT YOU TO BE THE ONE WHO KILLS ME.
HA HA HA!
"THANKS"? AFTER FORCING ME TO DRAG YOUR ASS HERE?
IF YOU WANNA DIE, I'LL DO YOU THE FAVOR RIGHT NOW.
GRIND
GRIND
GRIND
OW OW OW!
da-ding
Notice from Social-Network Tag Administrators
Notice from Social-Network Tag Administrators

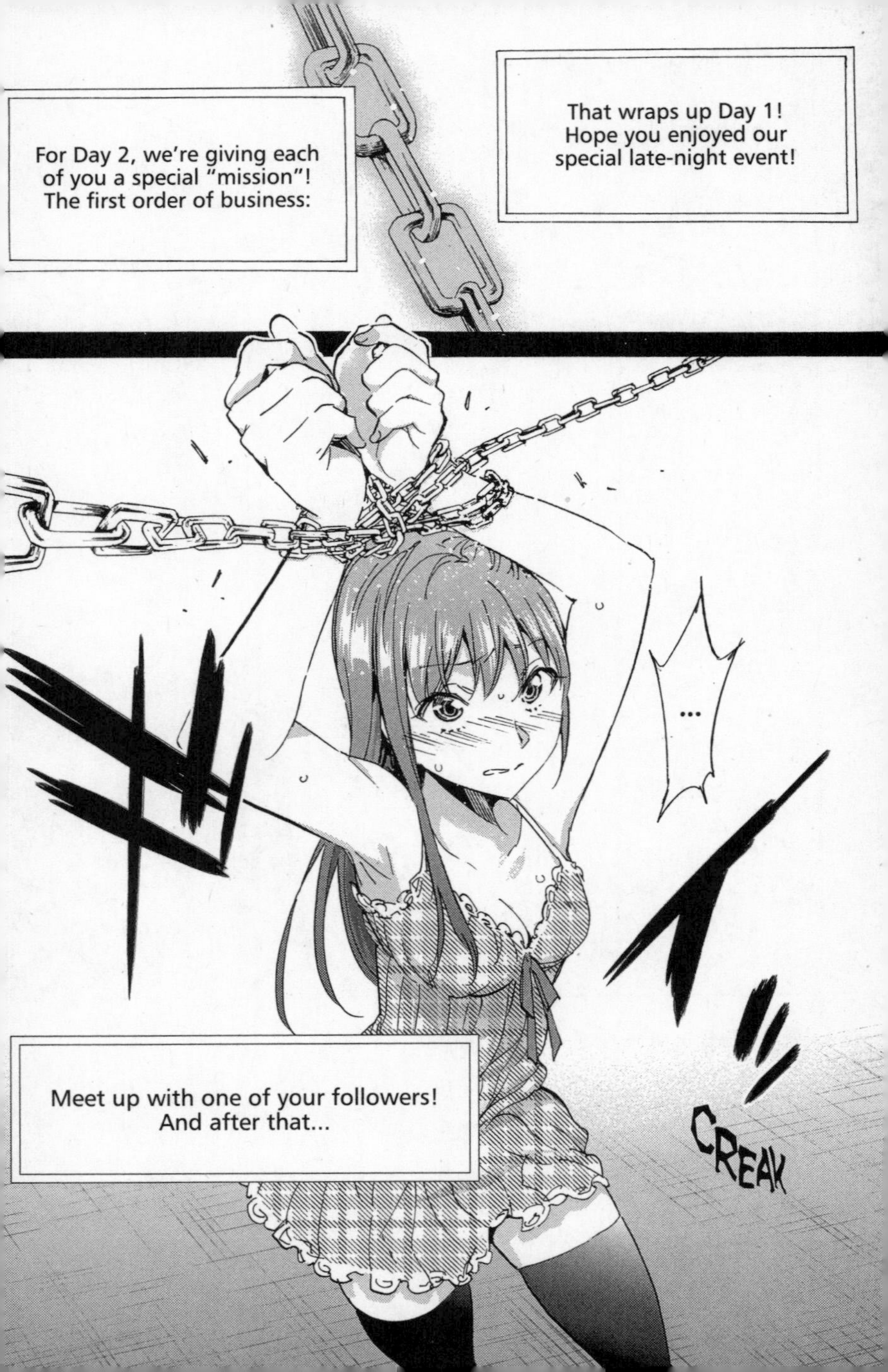
That wraps up Day 1! Hope you enjoyed our special late-night event!
For Day 2, we're giving each of you a special "mission"! The first order of business:
...
Meet up with one of your followers! And after that...
CREAK

The rules of Social-Network Tag:
Players ***die immediately*** if someone uses a smartphone to snap a picture of the ***Marble Mark*** hidden somewhere on their bodies.

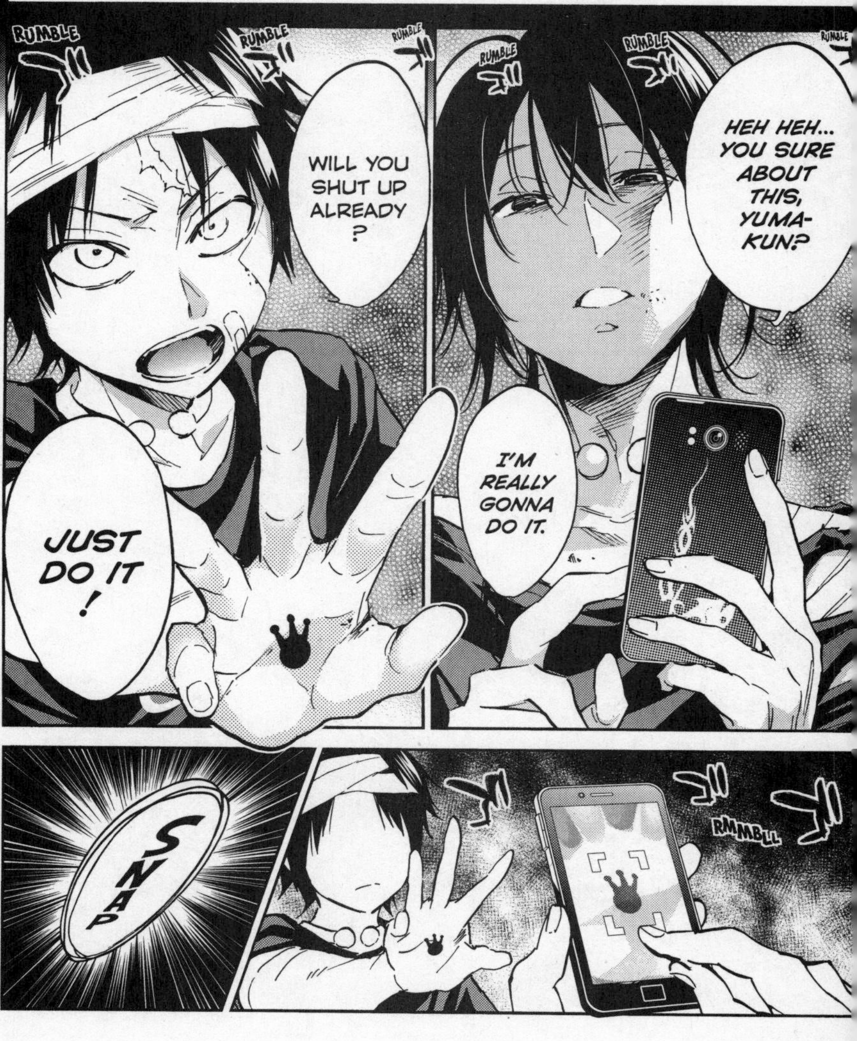
RUMBLE
RUMBLE
HEH HEH... YOU SURE ABOUT THIS, YUMA-KUN?
I'M REALLY GONNA DO IT.
RUMBLE
RUMBLE
RUMBLE
WILL YOU SHUT UP ALREADY?
JUST DO IT!
RMMBLL
SNAP

ACCOUNT 37 Mission Impossible

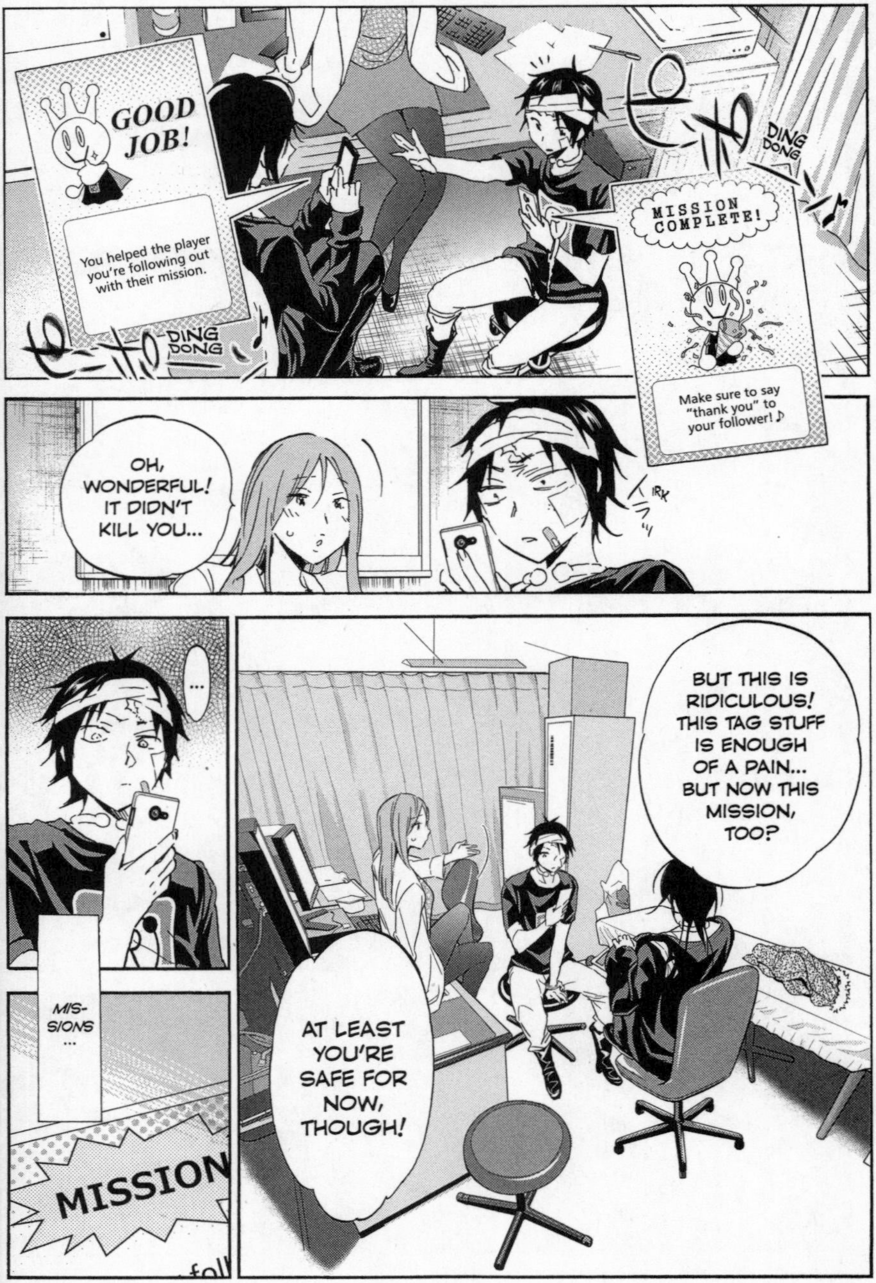
DING DONG
MISSION COMPLETE!
Make sure to say "thank you" to your follower!♪
GOOD JOB!
You helped the player you're following out with their mission.
DING DONG
IRK
OH, WONDERFUL! IT DIDN'T KILL YOU...
BUT THIS IS RIDICULOUS! THIS TAG STUFF IS ENOUGH OF A PAIN... BUT NOW THIS MISSION, TOO?
AT LEAST YOU'RE SAFE FOR NOW, THOUGH!
...
MIS-SIONS ...
MISSION

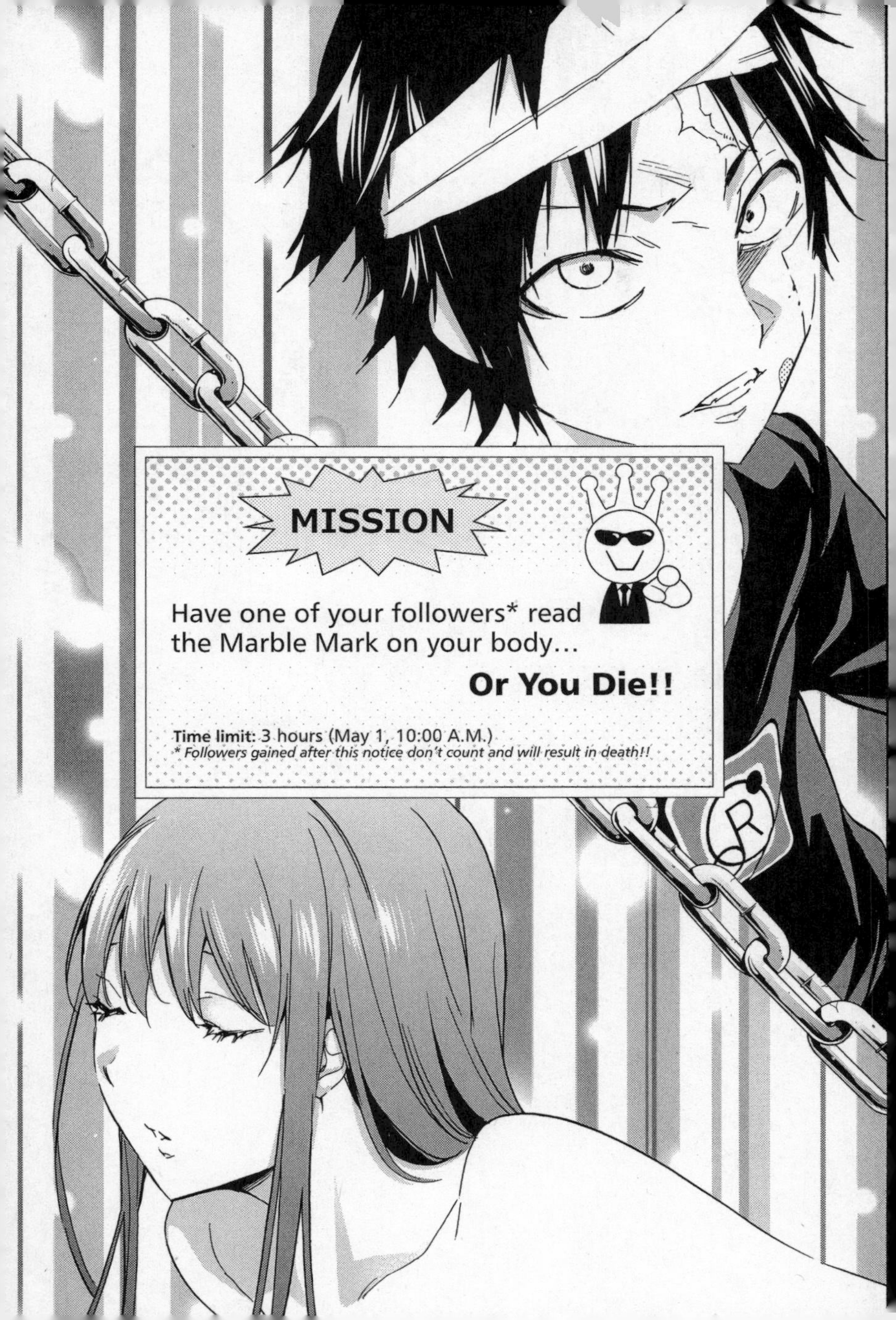

MISSION
Have one of your followers* read the Marble Mark on your body...
Or You Die!!
Time limit: 3 hours (May 1, 10:00 A.M.)
* Followers gained after this notice don't count and will result in death!!
R

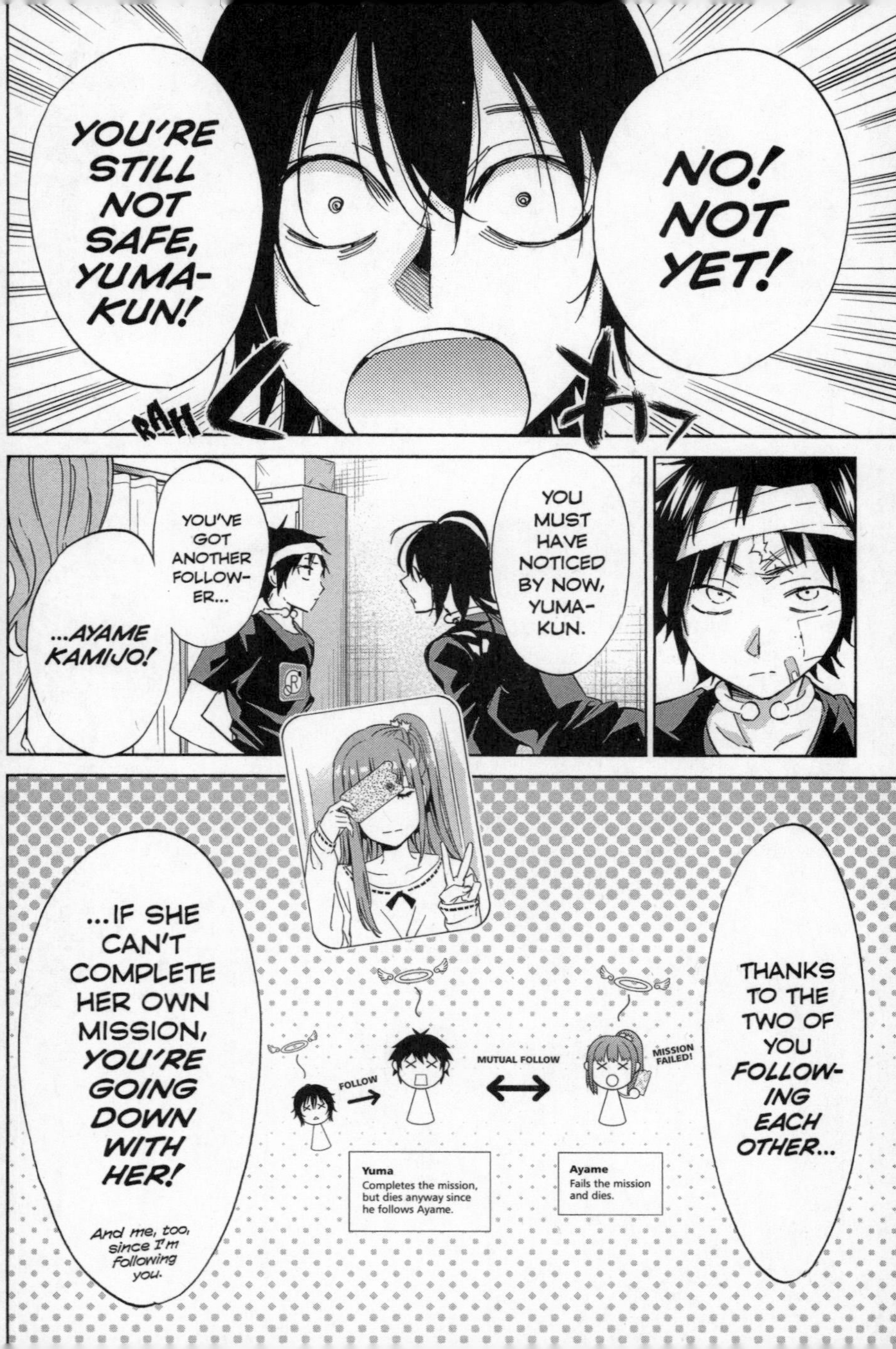
NO! NOT YET!
YOU'RE STILL NOT SAFE, YUMA-KUN!
RAH
YOU MUST HAVE NOTICED BY NOW, YUMA-KUN.
YOU'VE GOT ANOTHER FOLLOW-ER...
...AYAME KAMIJO!
THANKS TO THE TWO OF YOU FOLLOWING EACH OTHER...
MUTUAL FOLLOW
MISSION FAILED!
FOLLOW
Ayame
Fails the mission and dies.
Yuma
Completes the mission, but dies anyway since he follows Ayame.
...IF SHE CAN'T COMPLETE HER OWN MISSION, YOU'RE GOING DOWN WITH HER!
And me, too, since I'm following you.

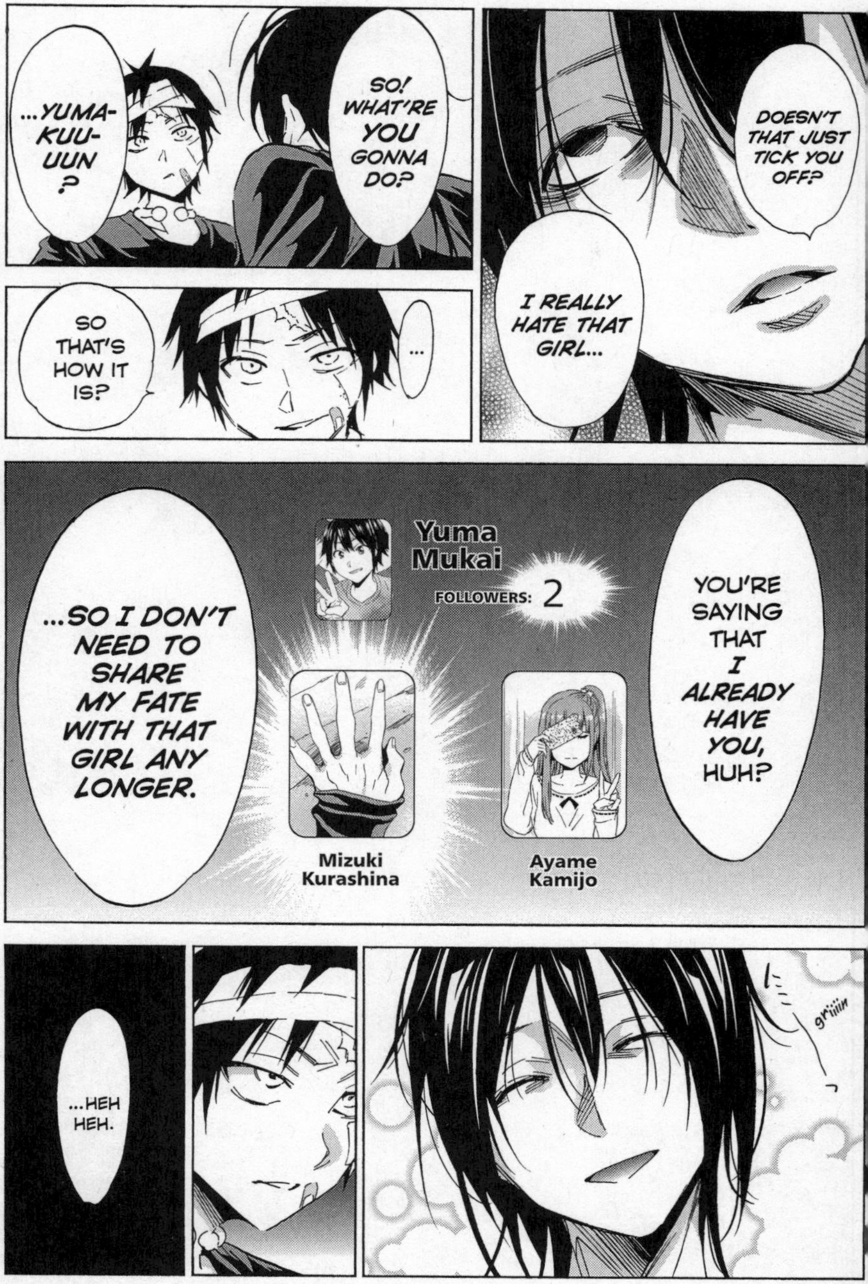
DOESN'T THAT JUST TICK YOU OFF?
I REALLY HATE THAT GIRL...
SO! WHAT'RE YOU GONNA DO?
...YUMA-KUUUUN?
...
SO THAT'S HOW IT IS?
YOU'RE SAYING THAT I ALREADY HAVE YOU, HUH?
Yuma Mukai
FOLLOWERS: 2
Ayame Kamijo
Mizuki Kurashina
...SO I DON'T NEED TO SHARE MY FATE WITH THAT GIRL ANY LONGER.
griiiin
...HEH HEH.

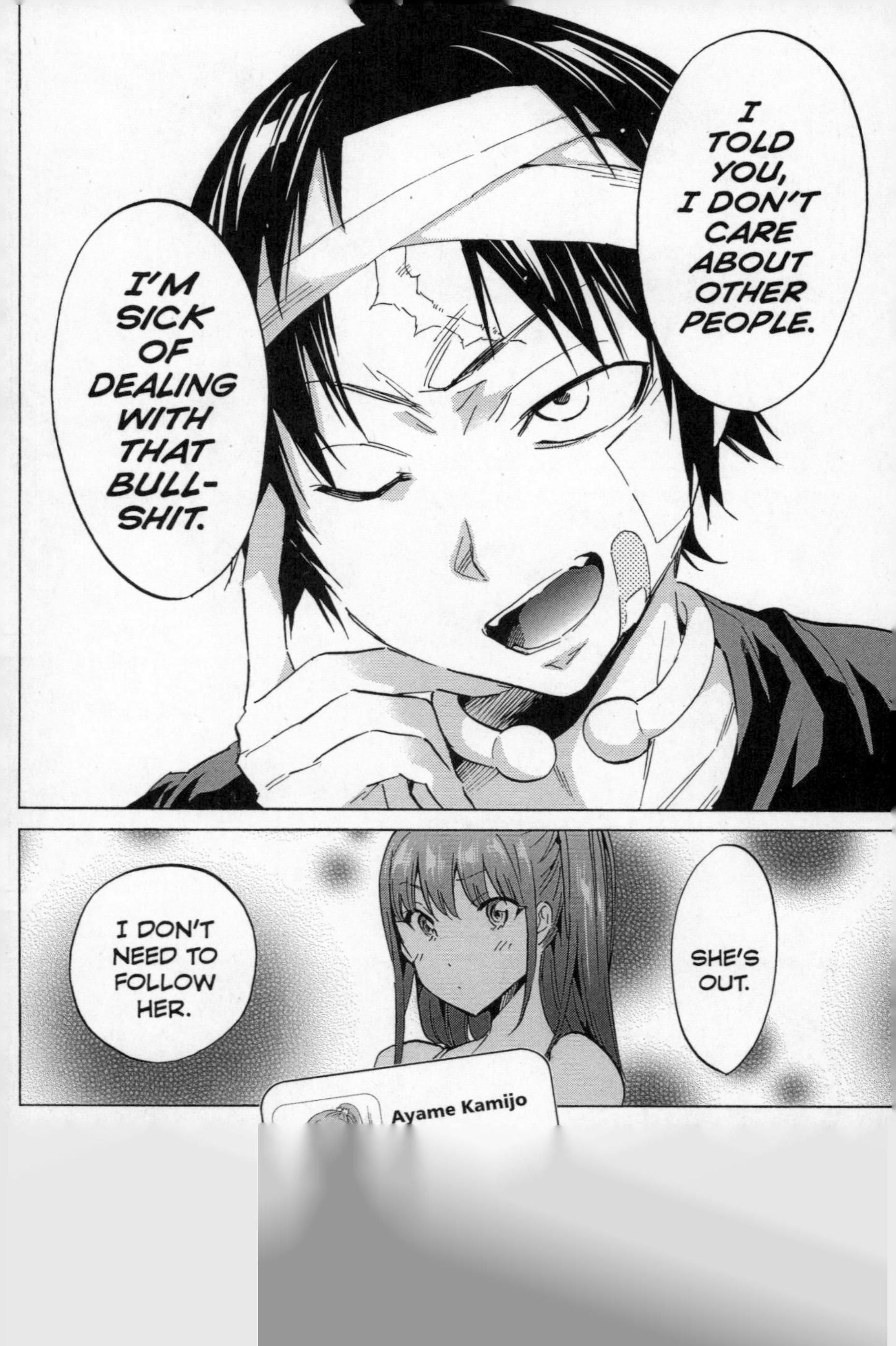
I TOLD YOU, I DON'T CARE ABOUT OTHER PEOPLE.
I'M SICK OF DEALING WITH THAT BULL-SHIT.
SHE'S OUT.
I DON'T NEED TO FOLLOW HER.
Ayame Kamijo

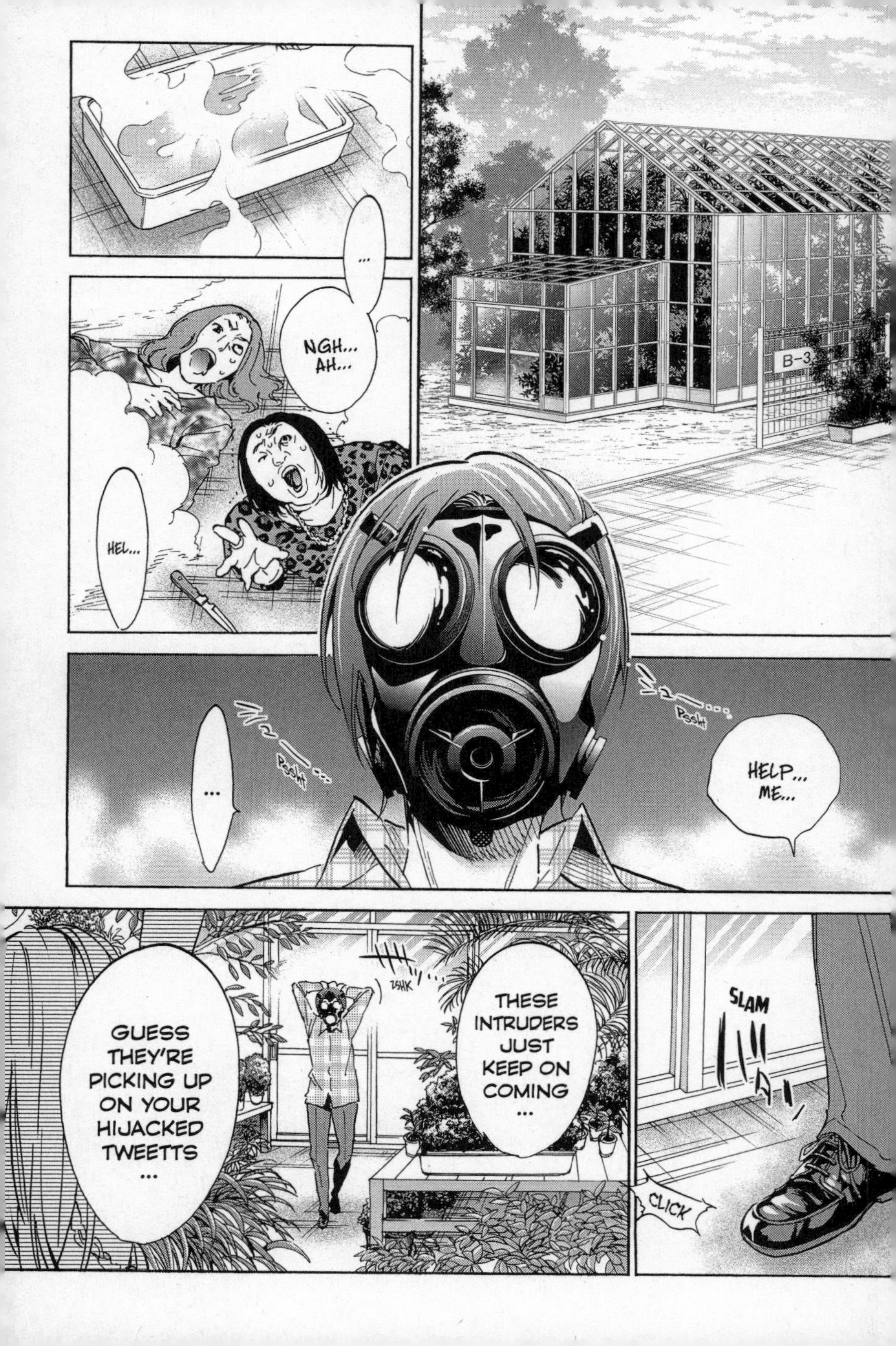

B-3
...
NGH... AH...
HEL...
Pssht
HELP... ME...
Pssht
...
SLAM
CLICK
ZSHK
THESE INTRUDERS JUST KEEP ON COMING ...
GUESS THEY'RE PICKING UP ON YOUR HIJACKED TWEETTS ...

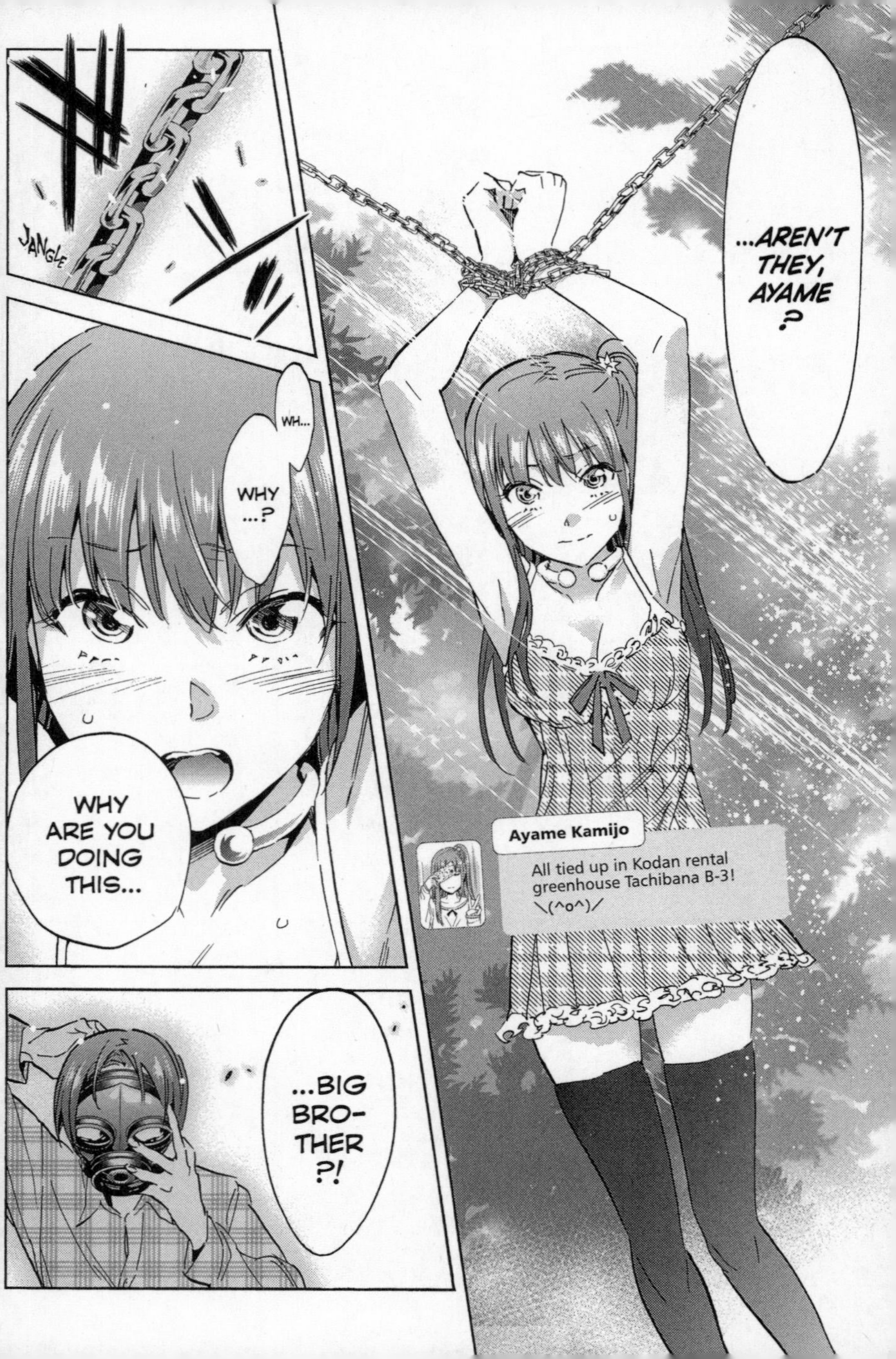
...AREN'T THEY, AYAME?
Ayame Kamijo
All tied up in Kodan rental greenhouse Tachibana B-3! \(^o^)/
JANGLE
WH...
WHY...?
WHY ARE YOU DOING THIS...
...BIG BROTHER?!

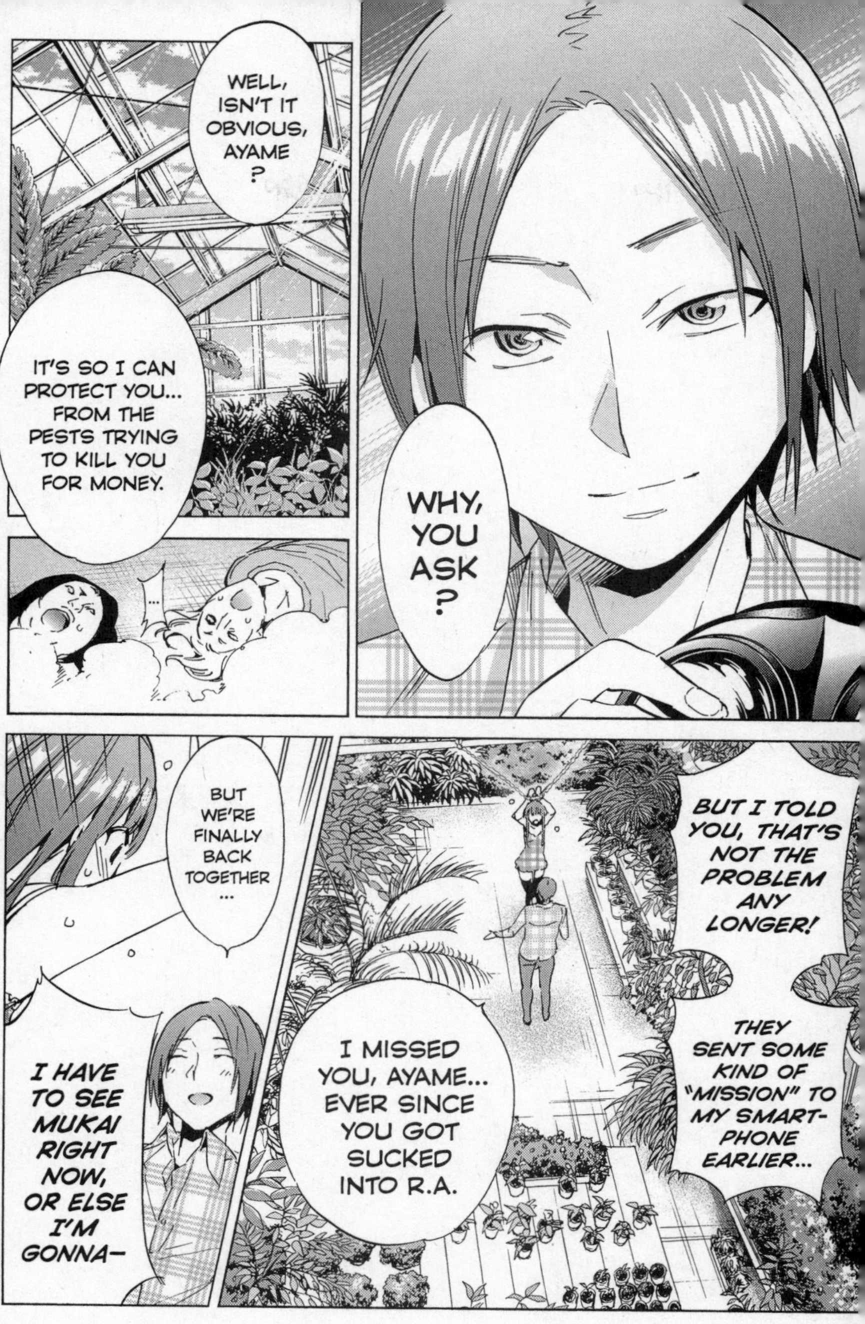
WHY, YOU ASK?
WELL, ISN'T IT OBVIOUS, AYAME?
IT'S SO I CAN PROTECT YOU... FROM THE PESTS TRYING TO KILL YOU FOR MONEY.
...
BUT I TOLD YOU, THAT'S NOT THE PROBLEM ANY LONGER!
THEY SENT SOME KIND OF "MISSION" TO MY SMART-PHONE EARLIER...
I MISSED YOU, AYAME... EVER SINCE YOU GOT SUCKED INTO R.A.
BUT WE'RE FINALLY BACK TOGETHER...
I HAVE TO SEE MUKAI RIGHT NOW, OR ELSE I'M GONNA–

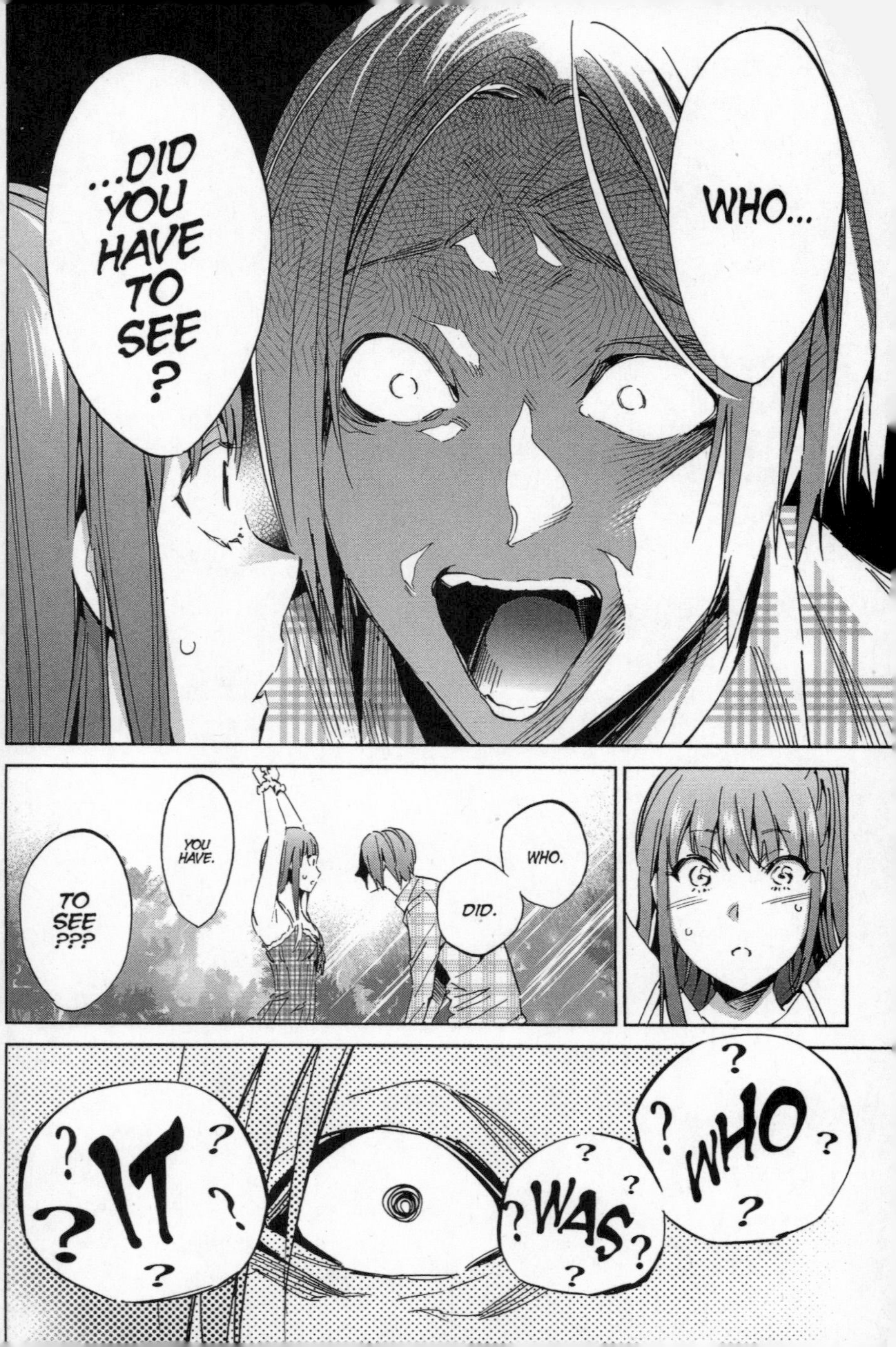
WHO...
...DID YOU HAVE TO SEE?
WHO.
DID.
YOU HAVE.
TO SEE???
WHO
WAS
IT

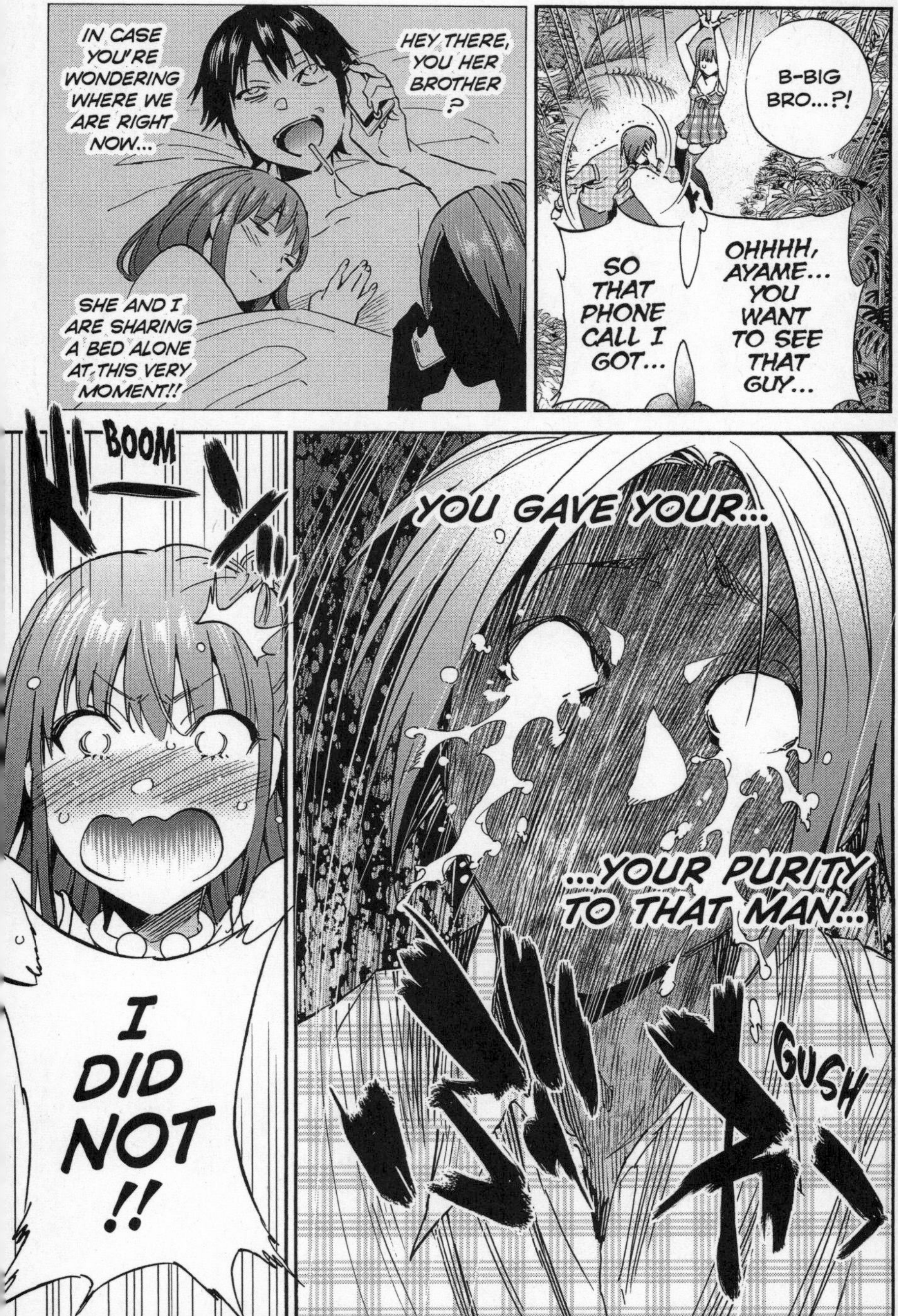
B-BIG BRO...?!
OHHHH, AYAME... YOU WANT TO SEE THAT GUY...
SO THAT PHONE CALL I GOT...
HEY THERE, YOU HER BROTHER?
IN CASE YOU'RE WONDERING WHERE WE ARE RIGHT NOW...
SHE AND I ARE SHARING A BED ALONE AT THIS VERY MOMENT!!
YOU GAVE YOUR...
...YOUR PURITY TO THAT MAN...
GUSH
BOOM
I DID NOT!!

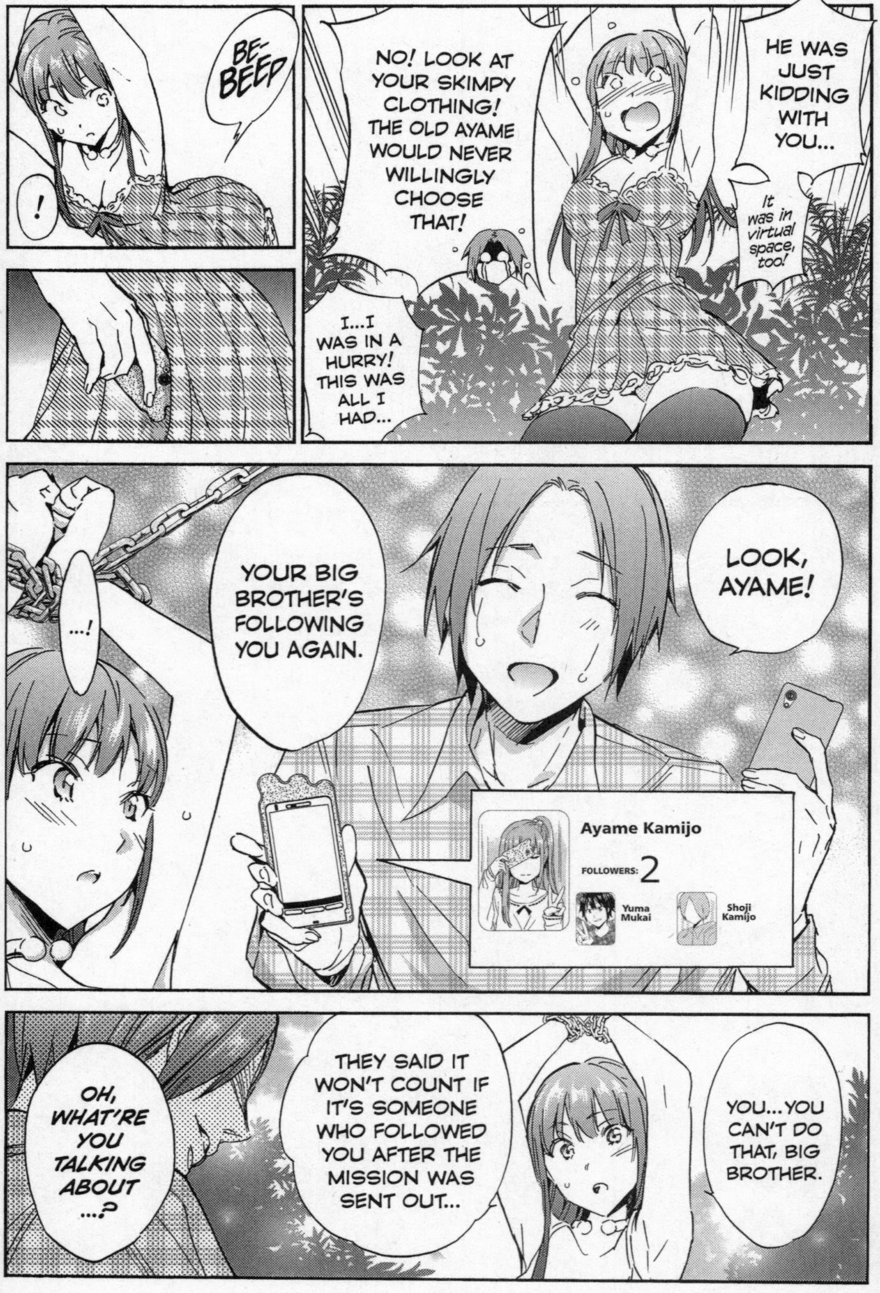
HE WAS JUST KIDDING WITH YOU...
It was in virtual space, too!
NO! LOOK AT YOUR SKIMPY CLOTHING! THE OLD AYAME WOULD NEVER WILLINGLY CHOOSE THAT!
I...I WAS IN A HURRY! THIS WAS ALL I HAD...
BE-BEEP
!
LOOK, AYAME!
YOUR BIG BROTHER'S FOLLOWING YOU AGAIN.
...!
Ayame Kamijo
FOLLOWERS: 2
Yuma Mukai
Shoji Kamijo
YOU...YOU CAN'T DO THAT, BIG BROTHER.
THEY SAID IT WON'T COUNT IF IT'S SOMEONE WHO FOLLOWED YOU AFTER THE MISSION WAS SENT OUT...
OH, WHAT'RE YOU TALKING ABOUT ...?

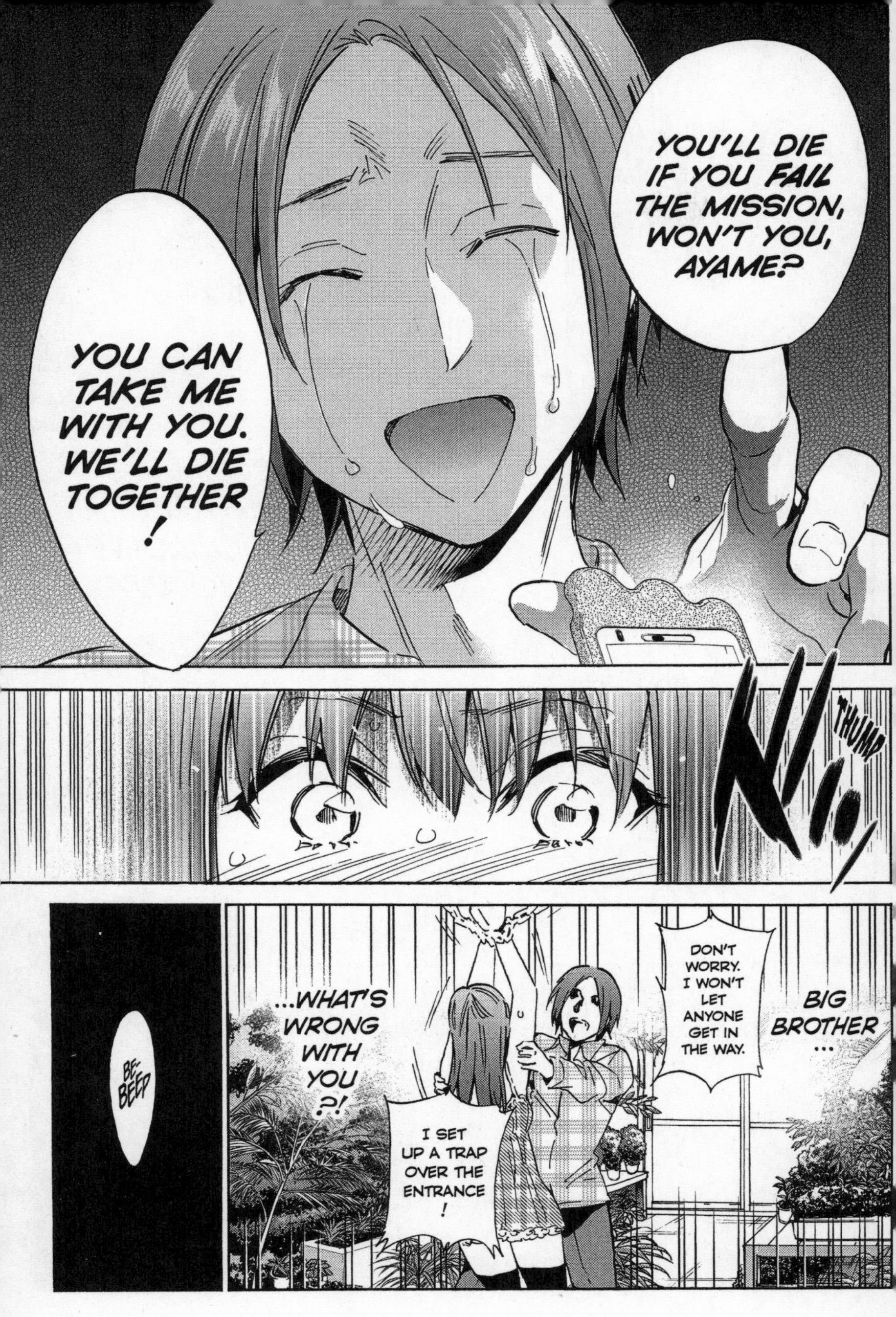

YOU'LL DIE IF YOU FAIL THE MISSION, WON'T YOU, AYAME?
YOU CAN TAKE ME WITH YOU. WE'LL DIE TOGETHER!
THUMP
BIG BROTHER...
DON'T WORRY. I WON'T LET ANYONE GET IN THE WAY.
...WHAT'S WRONG WITH YOU?!
I SET UP A TRAP OVER THE ENTRANCE!
BE-BEEP

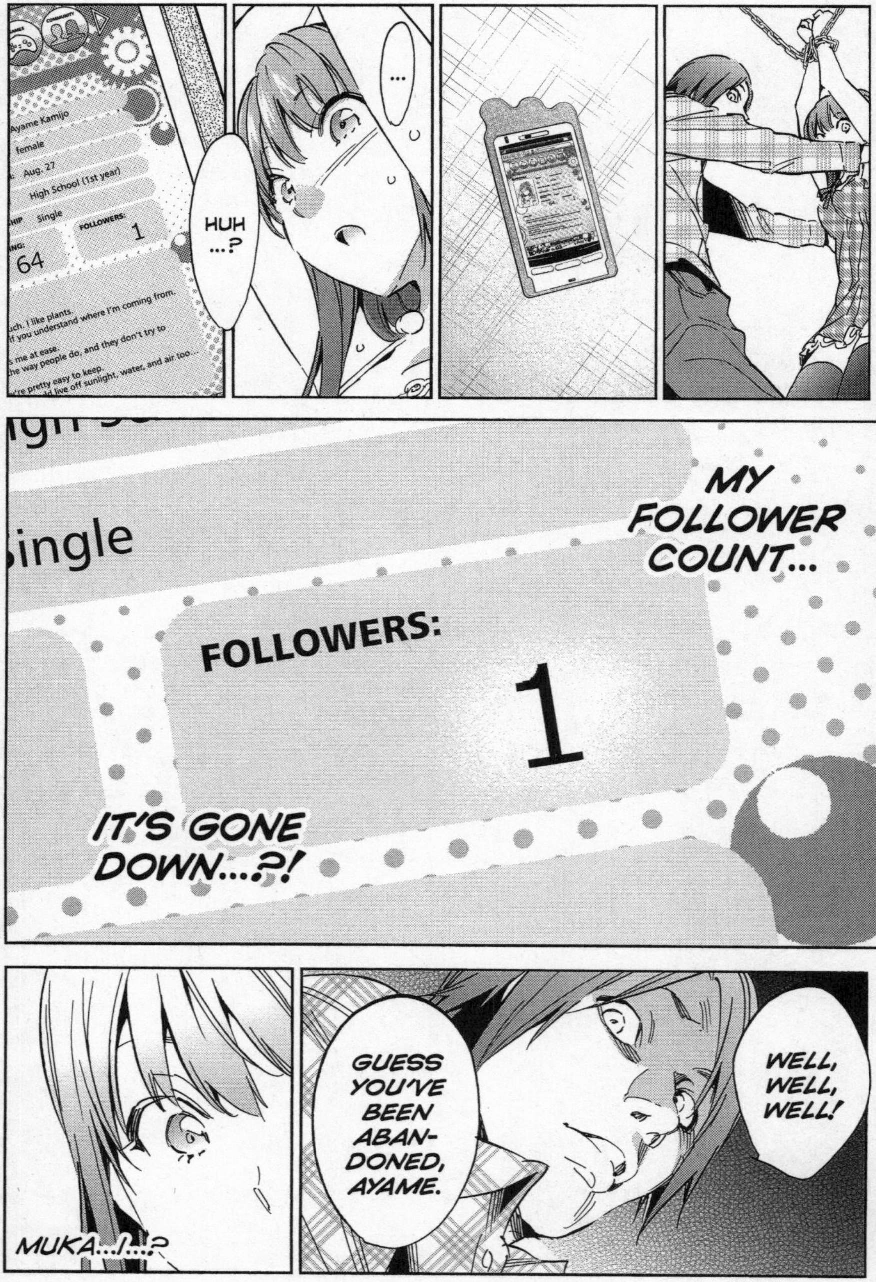

…
HUH …?
Ayame Kamijo
female
Aug. 27
High School (1st year)
Single
FOLLOWERS:
1
64
I like plants.
if you understand where I'm coming from.
s me at ease.
the way people do, and they don't try to
re pretty easy to keep.
ld live off sunlight, water, and air too…
MY FOLLOWER COUNT…
Single
FOLLOWERS:
1
IT'S GONE DOWN…?!
WELL, WELL, WELL!
GUESS YOU'VE BEEN ABAN-DONED, AYAME.
MUKA…I…?

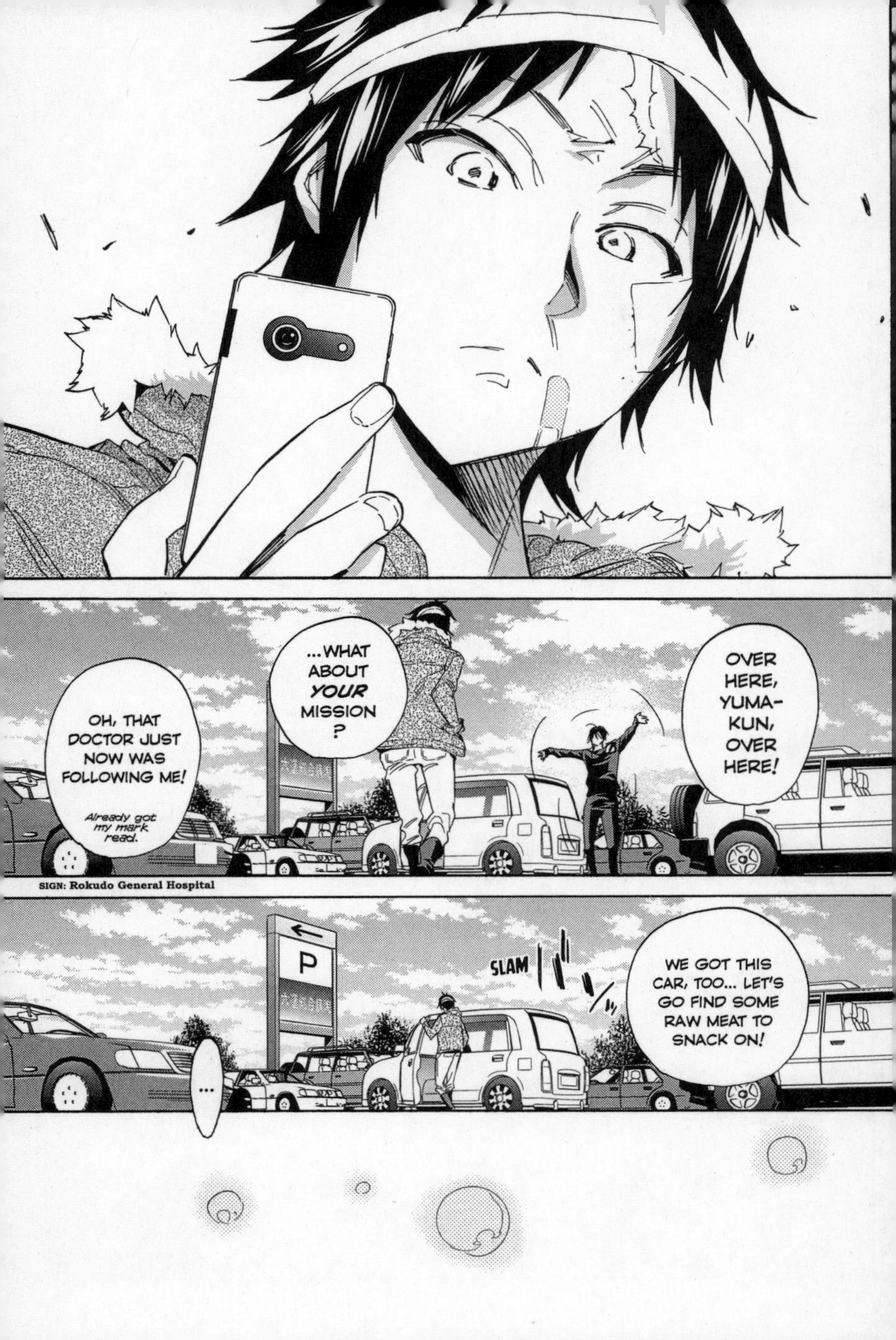
OVER HERE, YUMA-KUN, OVER HERE!
...WHAT ABOUT *YOUR* MISSION?
OH, THAT DOCTOR JUST NOW WAS FOLLOWING ME!
Already got my mark read.
WE GOT THIS CAR, TOO... LET'S GO FIND SOME RAW MEAT TO SNACK ON!
SLAM
P
...

SIGN: Rokudo General Hospital

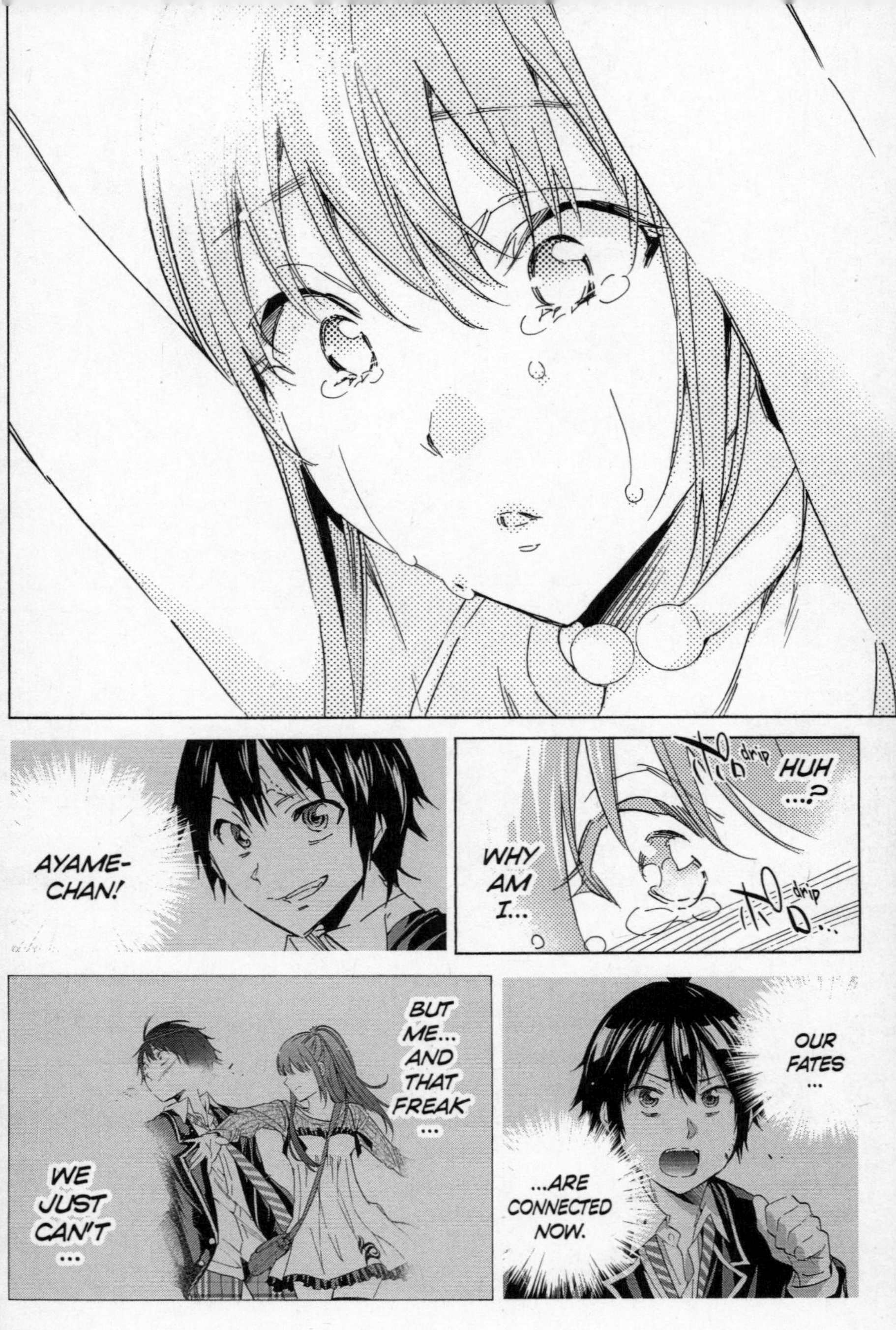
drip
HUH ...?
WHY AM I...
drip
AYAME-CHAN!
OUR FATES ...
...ARE CONNECTED NOW.
BUT ME... AND THAT FREAK ...
WE JUST CAN'T ...

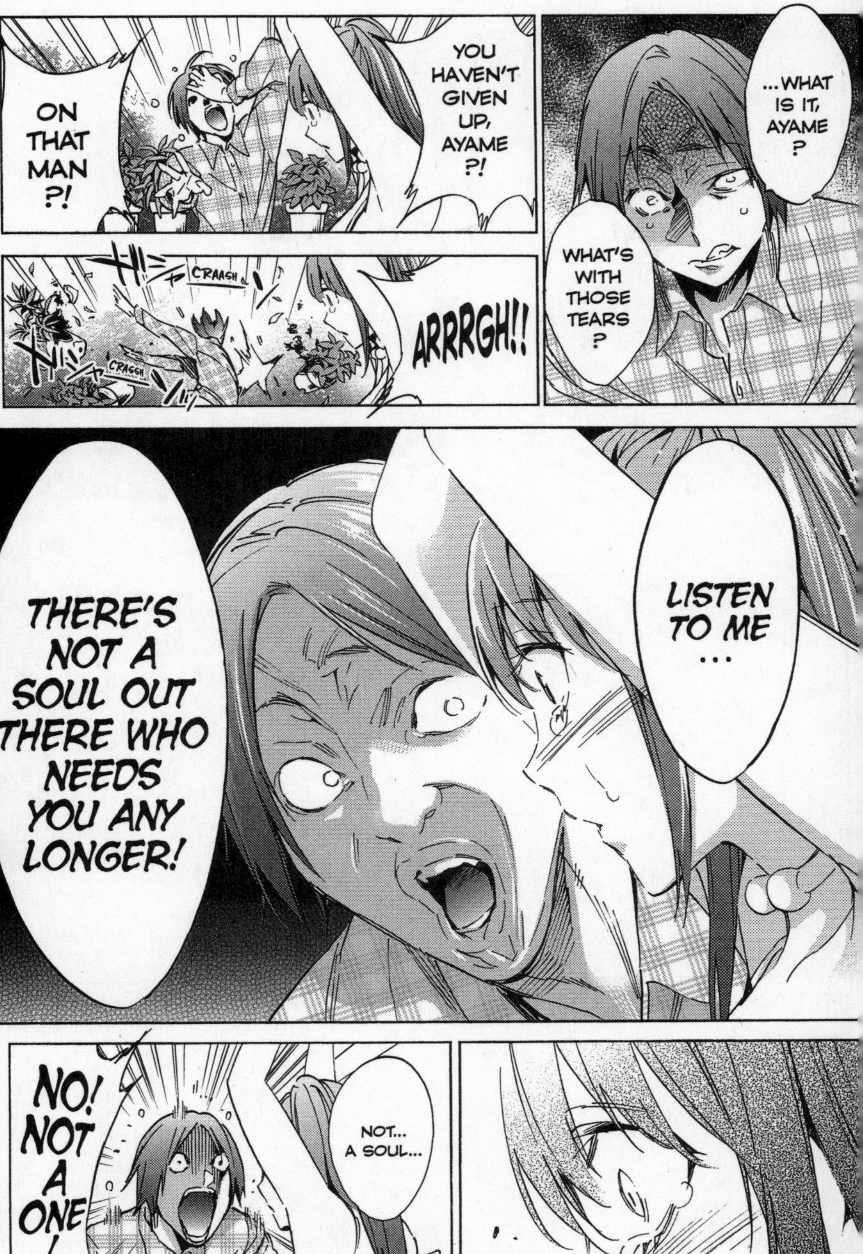
...WHAT IS IT, AYAME?
WHAT'S WITH THOSE TEARS?
YOU HAVEN'T GIVEN UP, AYAME?!
ON THAT MAN?!
CRAASH
ARRRGH!!
CRASSH
LISTEN TO ME...
THERE'S NOT A SOUL OUT THERE WHO NEEDS YOU ANY LONGER!
NOT... A SOUL...
NO! NOT A ONE!

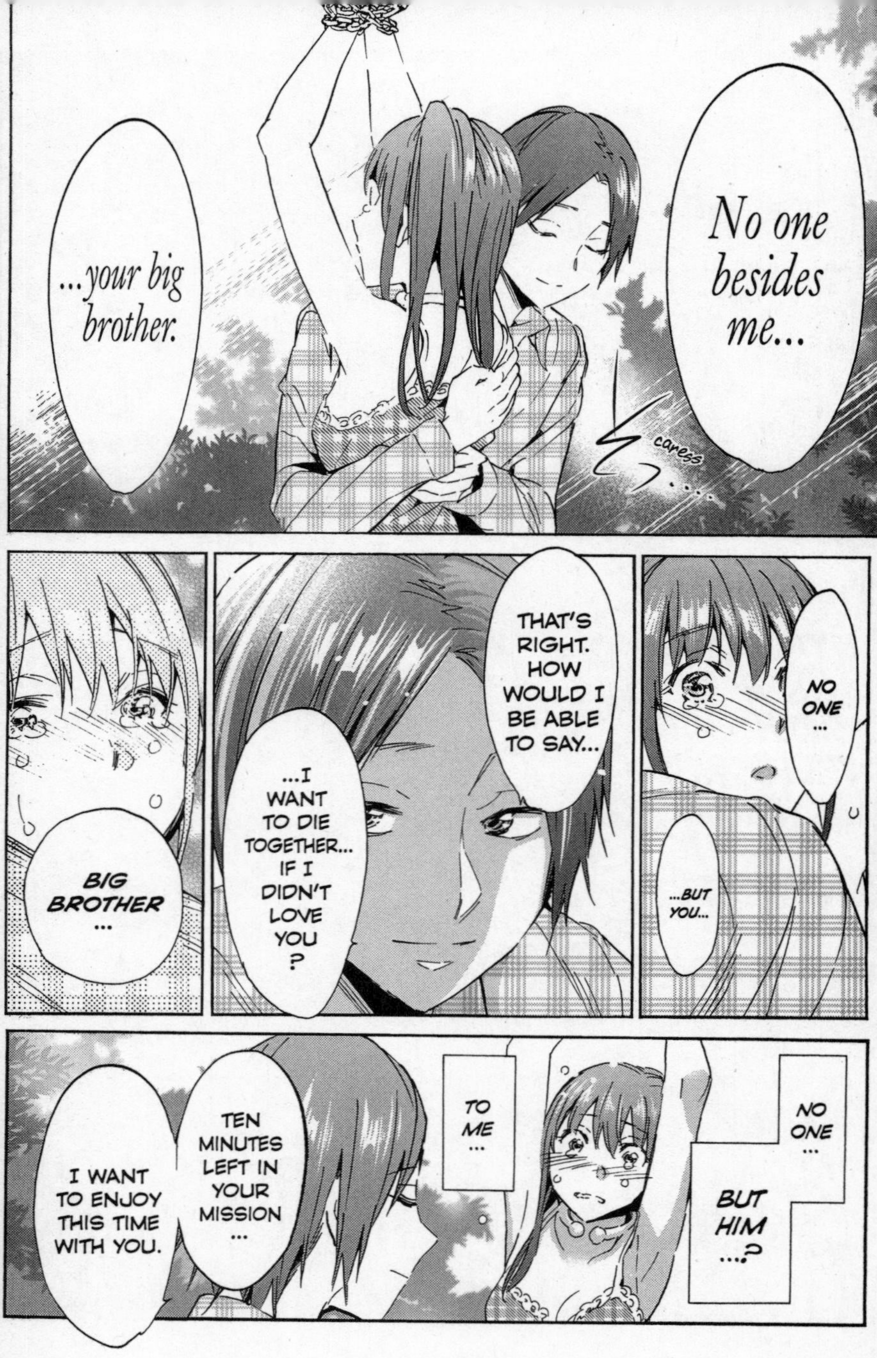
No one besides me...
caress
...your big brother.
NO ONE ...
...BUT YOU...
THAT'S RIGHT. HOW WOULD I BE ABLE TO SAY...
...I WANT TO DIE TOGETHER... IF I DIDN'T LOVE YOU ?
BIG BROTHER ...
NO ONE ...
BUT HIM ...?
TO ME ...
TEN MINUTES LEFT IN YOUR MISSION ...
I WANT TO ENJOY THIS TIME WITH YOU.

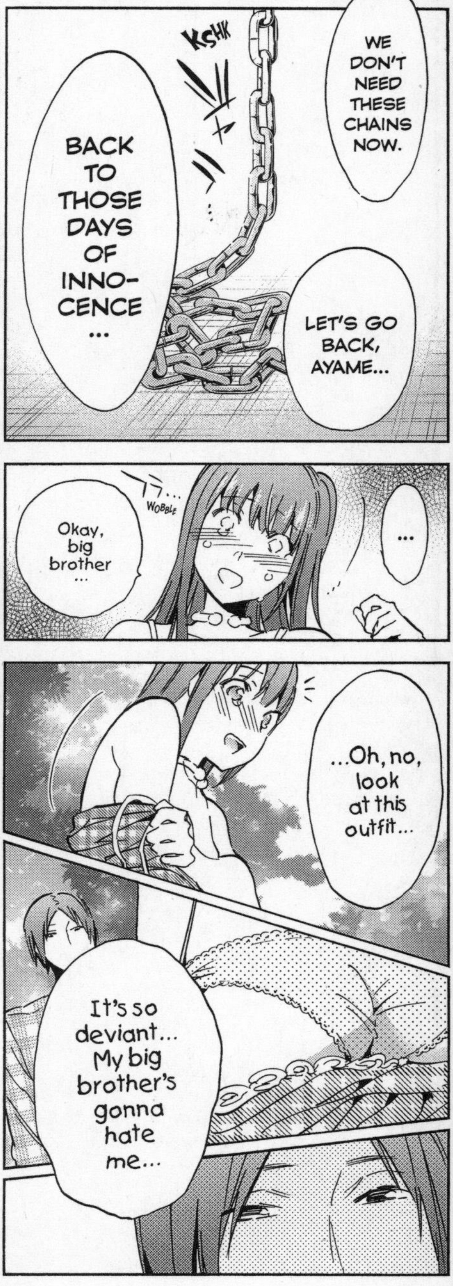
WE DON'T NEED THESE CHAINS NOW.
KSHK
LET'S GO BACK, AYAME...
BACK TO THOSE DAYS OF INNO-CENCE ...
...
WOBBLE
Okay, big brother ...
...Oh, no, look at this outfit...
It's so deviant... My big brother's gonna hate me...
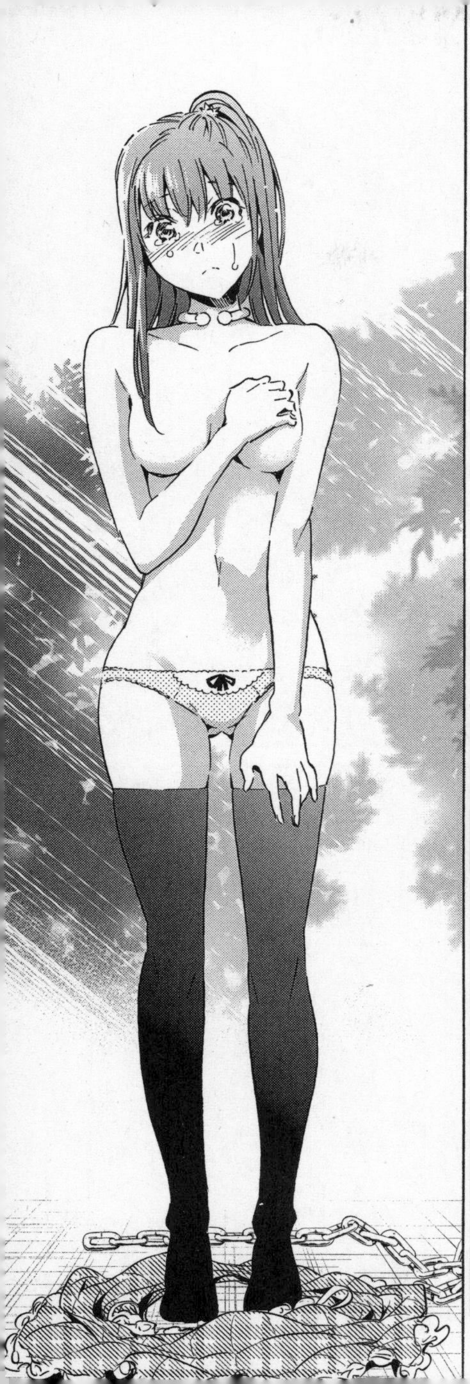

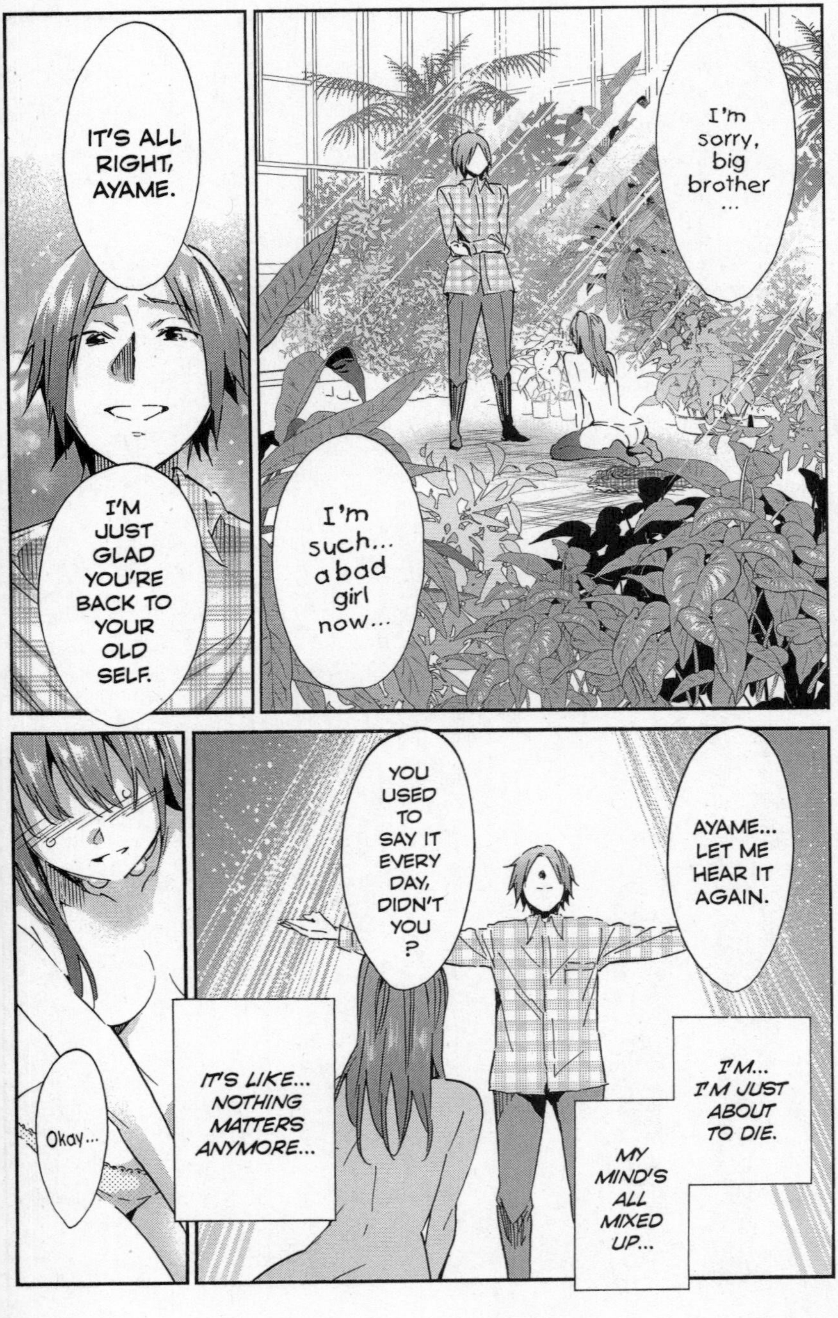
I'm sorry, big brother...
I'm such... a bad girl now...
IT'S ALL RIGHT, AYAME.
I'M JUST GLAD YOU'RE BACK TO YOUR OLD SELF.
AYAME... LET ME HEAR IT AGAIN.
YOU USED TO SAY IT EVERY DAY, DIDN'T YOU?
I'M... I'M JUST ABOUT TO DIE.
MY MIND'S ALL MIXED UP...
IT'S LIKE... NOTHING MATTERS ANYMORE...
Okay...

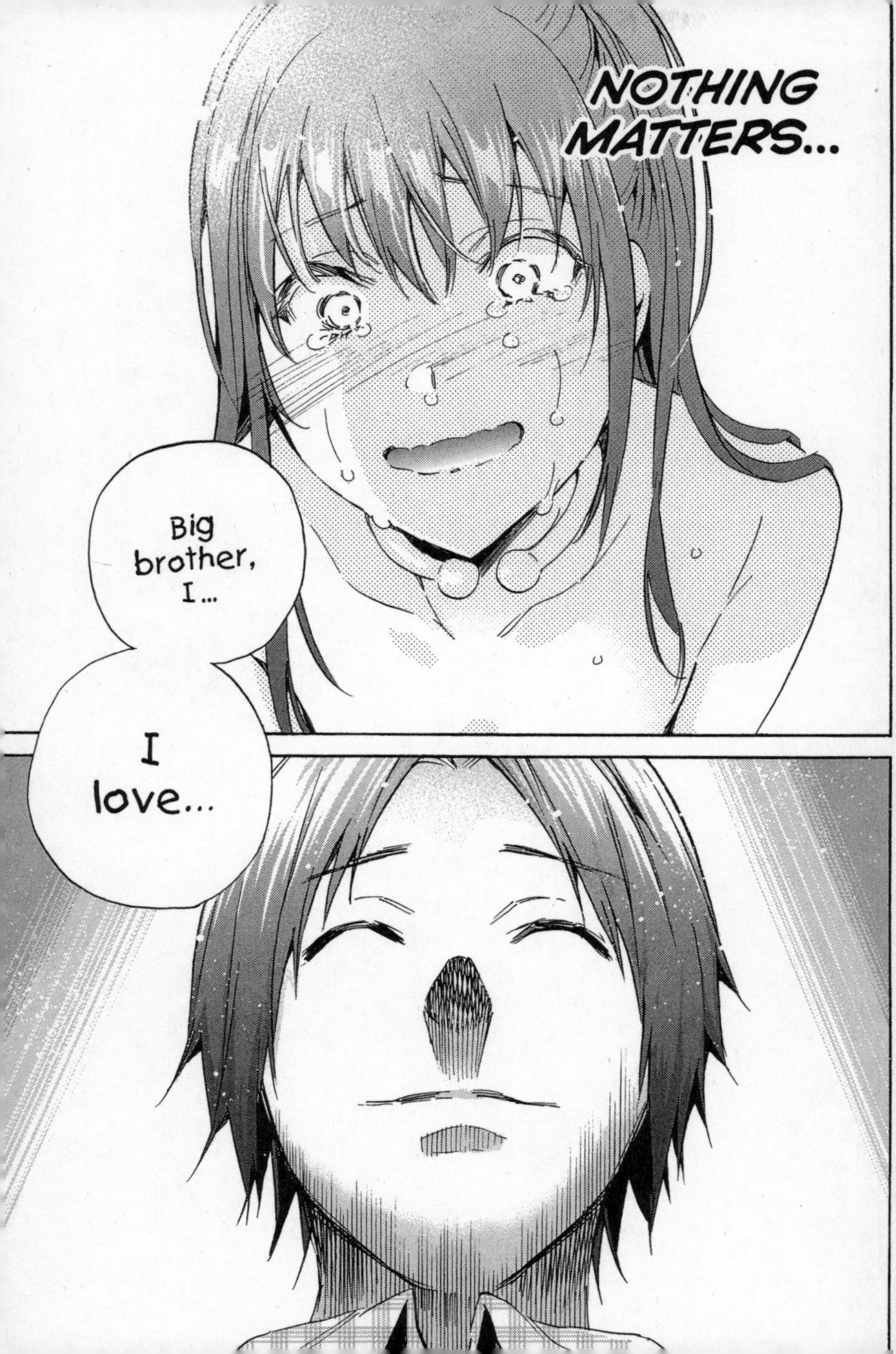
NOTHING MATTERS...
Big brother, I...
I love...

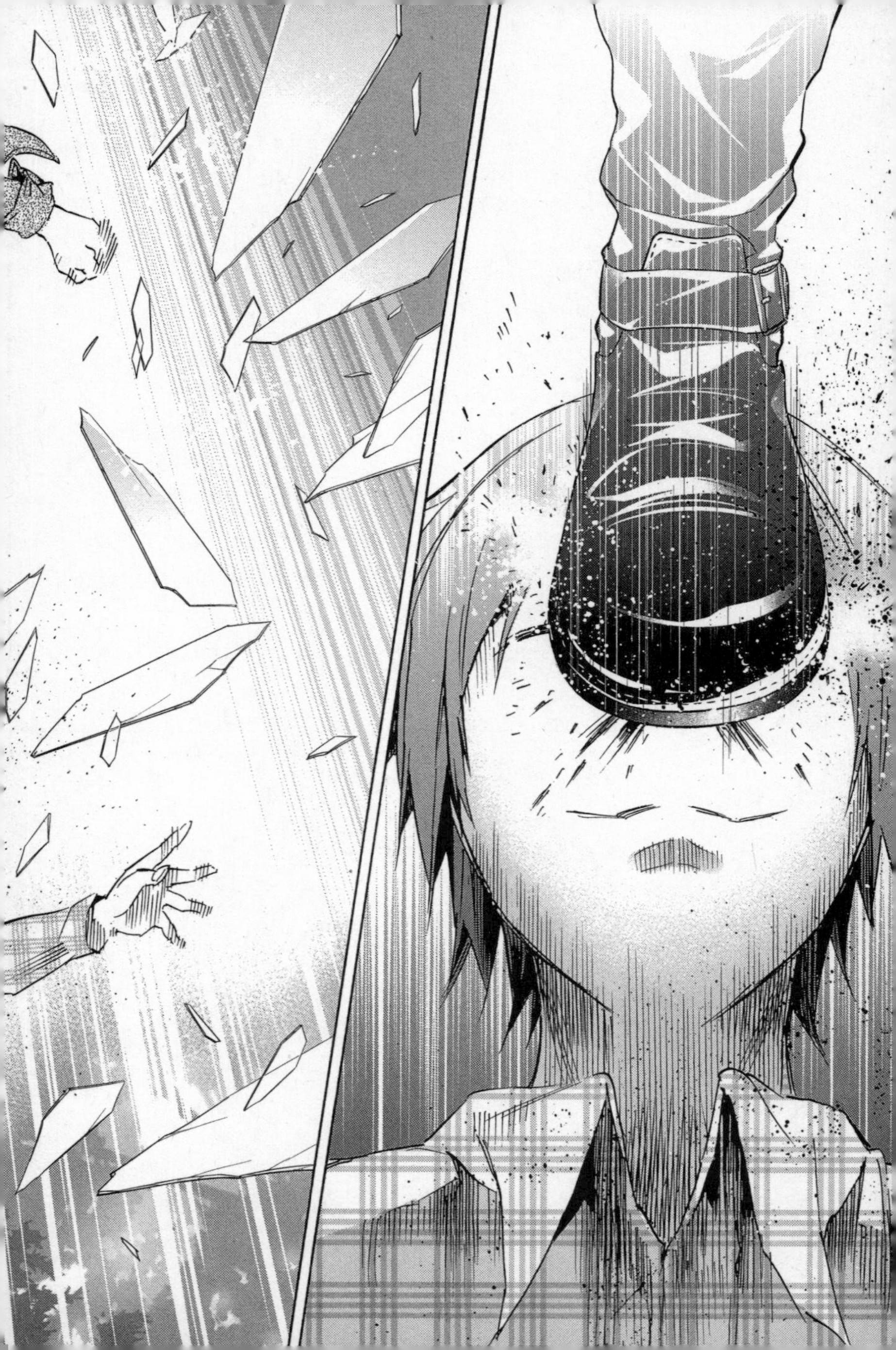

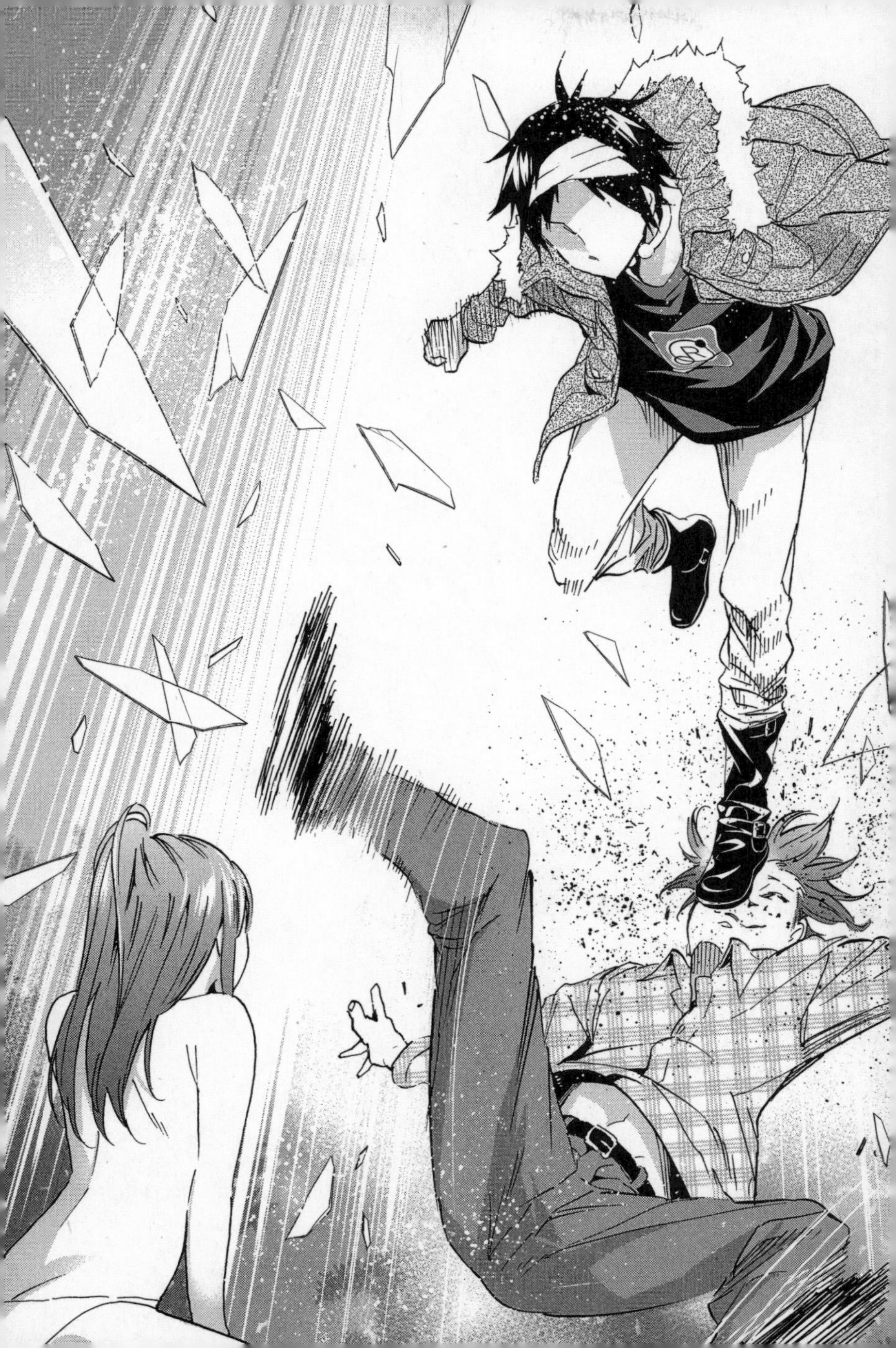

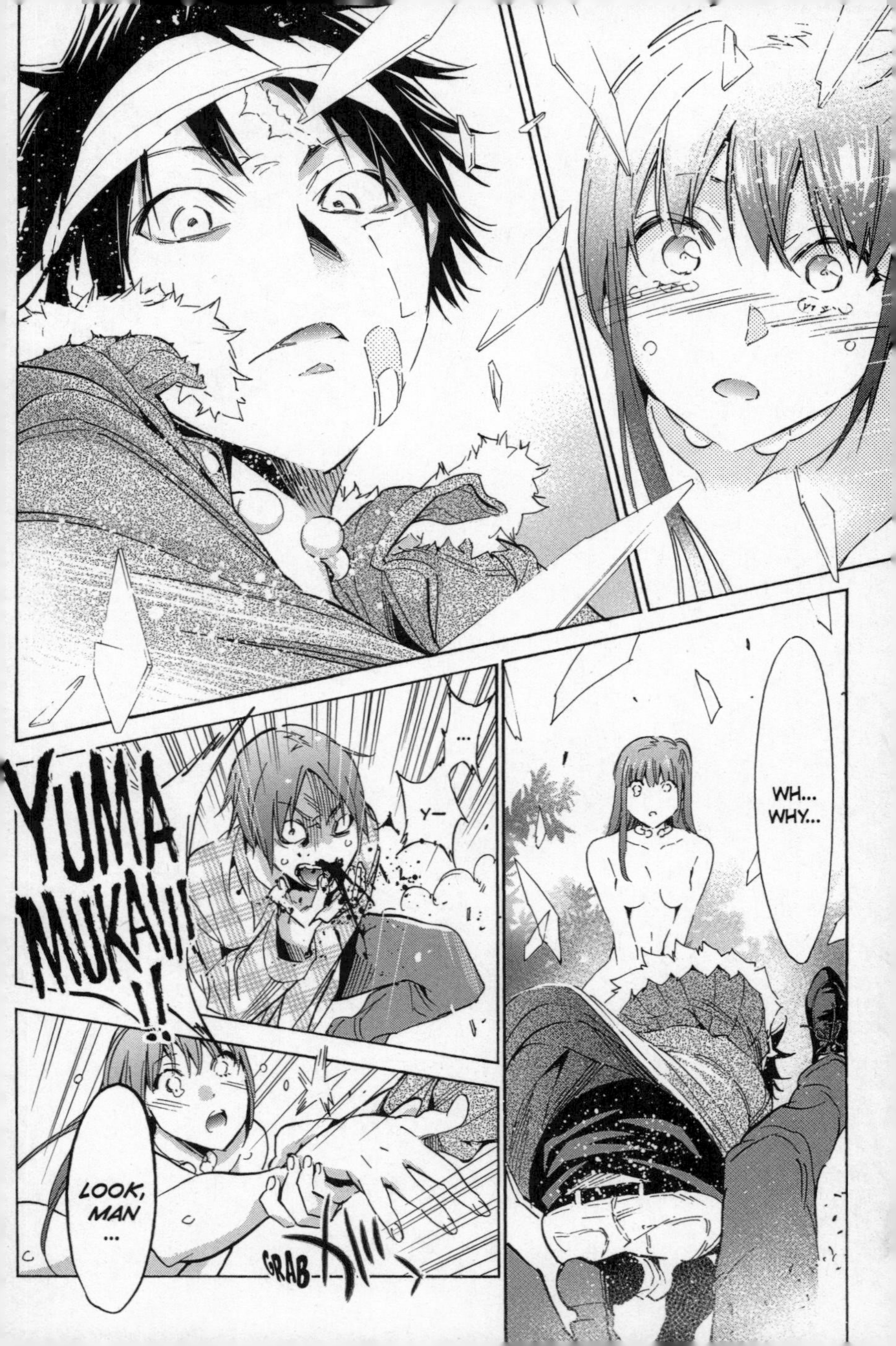
WH... WHY...
...
Y—
YUMA MUKAI!! !!
LOOK, MAN ...
GRAB

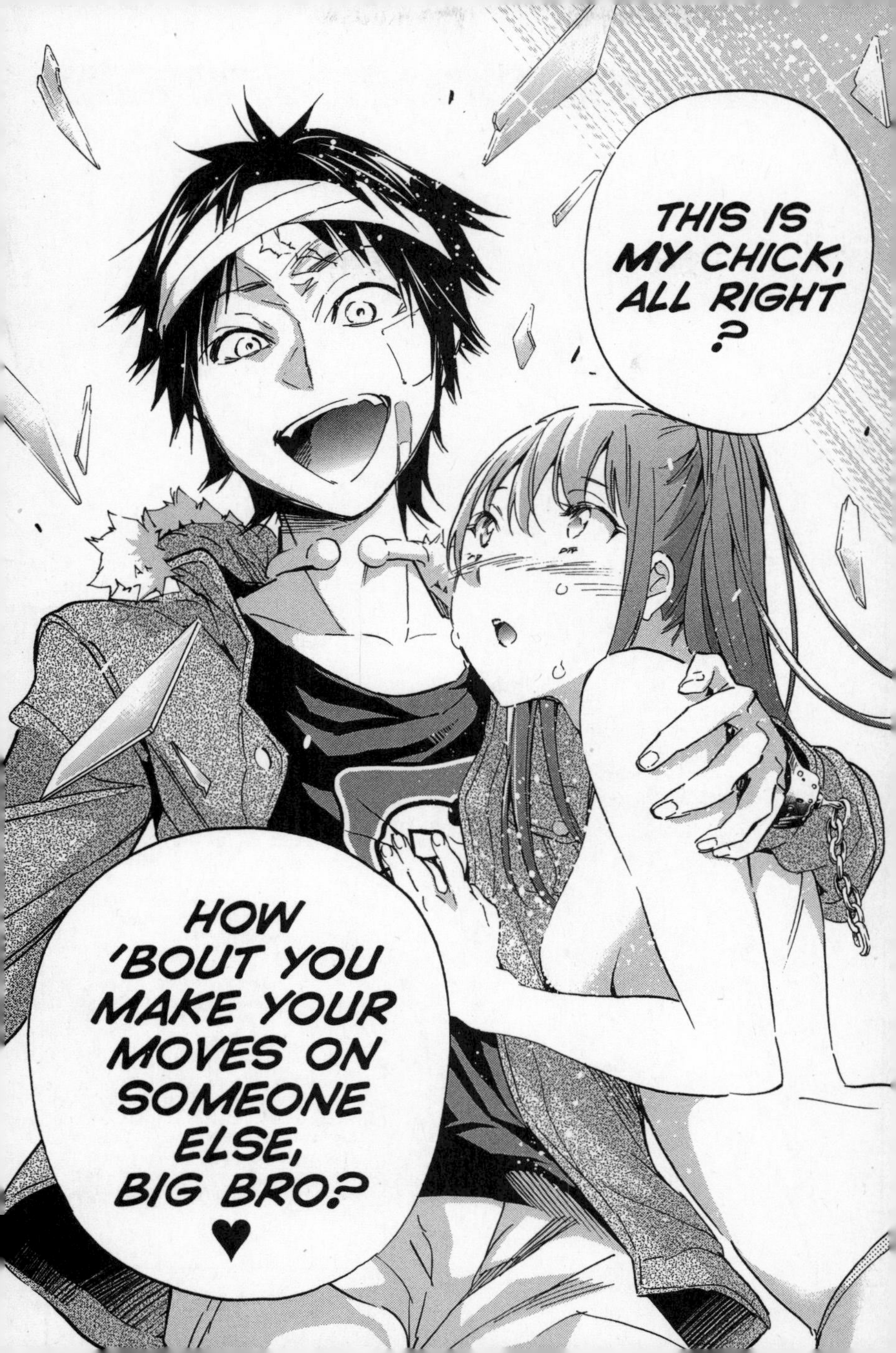
THIS IS MY CHICK, ALL RIGHT ?
HOW 'BOUT YOU MAKE YOUR MOVES ON SOMEONE ELSE, BIG BRO? ♥

CHARACTER

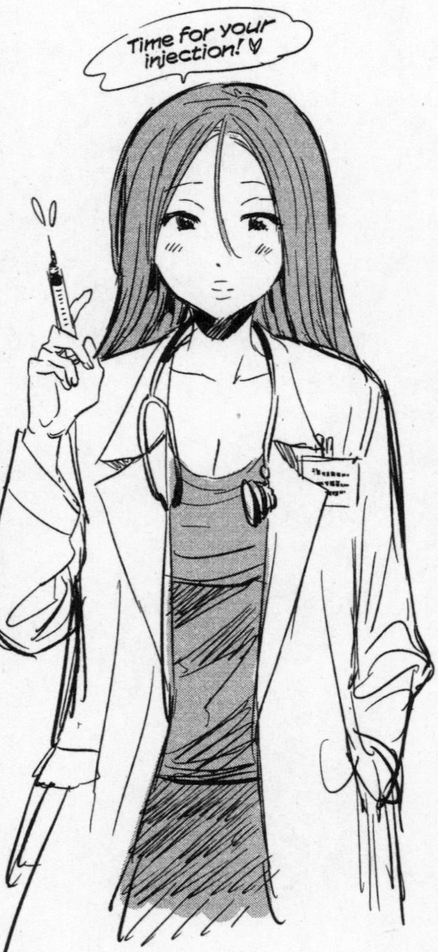
Time for your injection! ♡

Follower of Mizuki Kurashina

Dr. Tamae Hanada (30)

After being dumped by her true love (a musician younger than her), Tamae resolved to commit suicide. The drive to kill herself eventually led her to the Black Aquarium, the suicide website run by Mizuki. But on the very day she chose as her last, she caught sight of Mizuki—who stopped over to "help out"—and immediately fell in love with him, making all of her suicidal thoughts vanish.

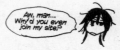

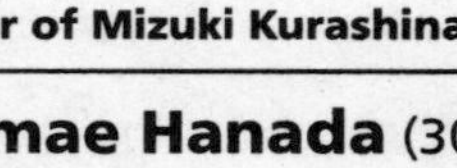
Aw, man... Why'd you even join my site?

Ever since, she has practically worshipped the ground Mizuki walks on. Her love outclasses even her sense of ethics, enabling her to steal medicine and supplies from her hospital to provide to him. She has a particular gift for intravenous injections.

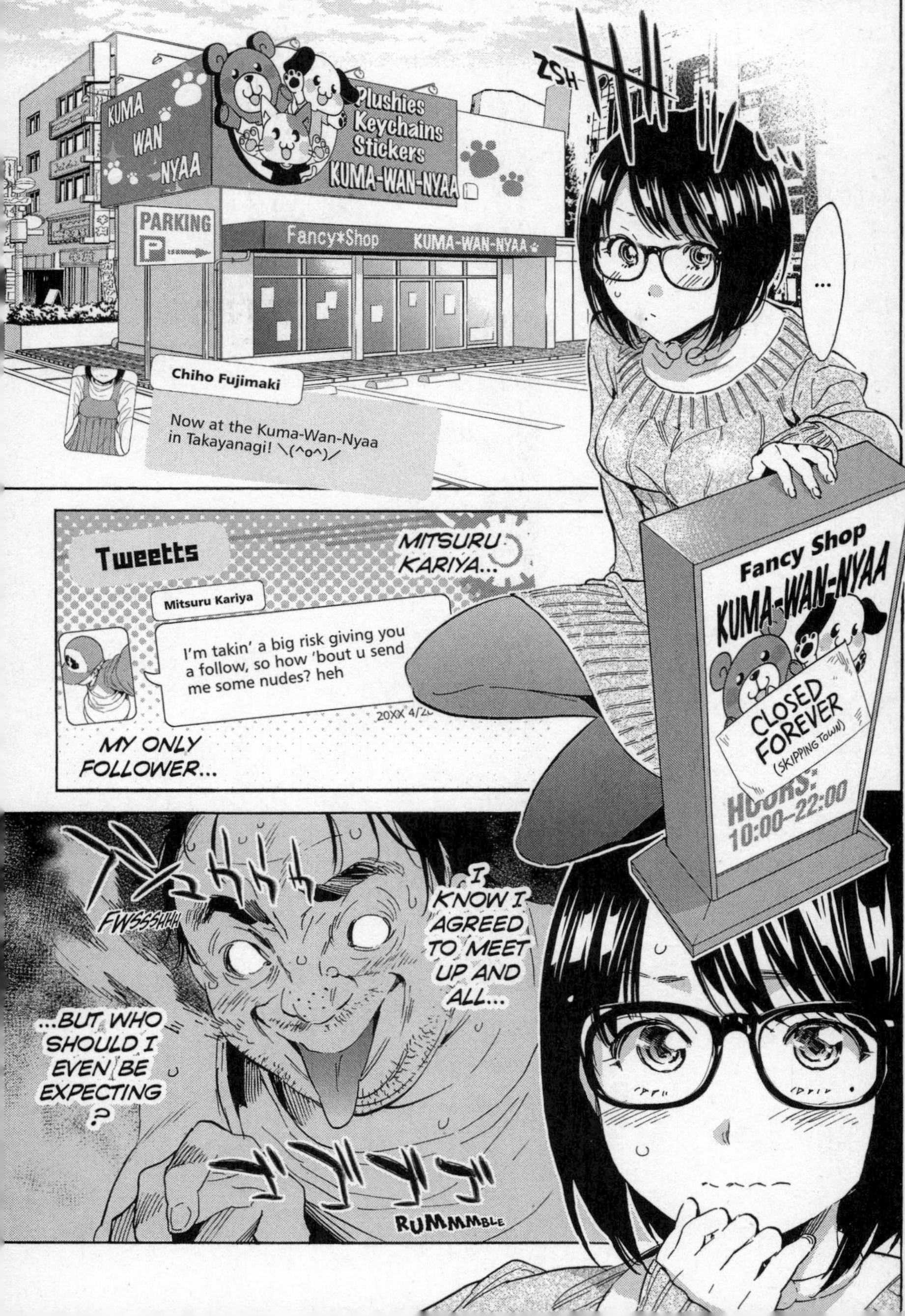
ZSH
...
Fancy Shop
KUMA-WAN-NYAA
CLOSED FOREVER
(SKIPPING TOWN)
HOURS:
10:00–22:00
KUMA
WAN
NYAA
Plushies
Keychains
Stickers
KUMA-WAN-NYAA
PARKING
P
Fancy*Shop
KUMA-WAN-NYAA
Chiho Fujimaki
Now at the Kuma-Wan-Nyaa in Takayanagi! \(^o^)/
MITSURU KARIYA...
Tweetts
Mitsuru Kariya
I'm takin' a big risk giving you a follow, so how 'bout u send me some nudes? heh
MY ONLY FOLLOWER...
I KNOW I AGREED TO MEET UP AND ALL...
FWSSSHHH
...BUT WHO SHOULD I EVEN BE EXPECTING?
RUMMMBLE

ACCOUNT 38 SQUEEKEK.com

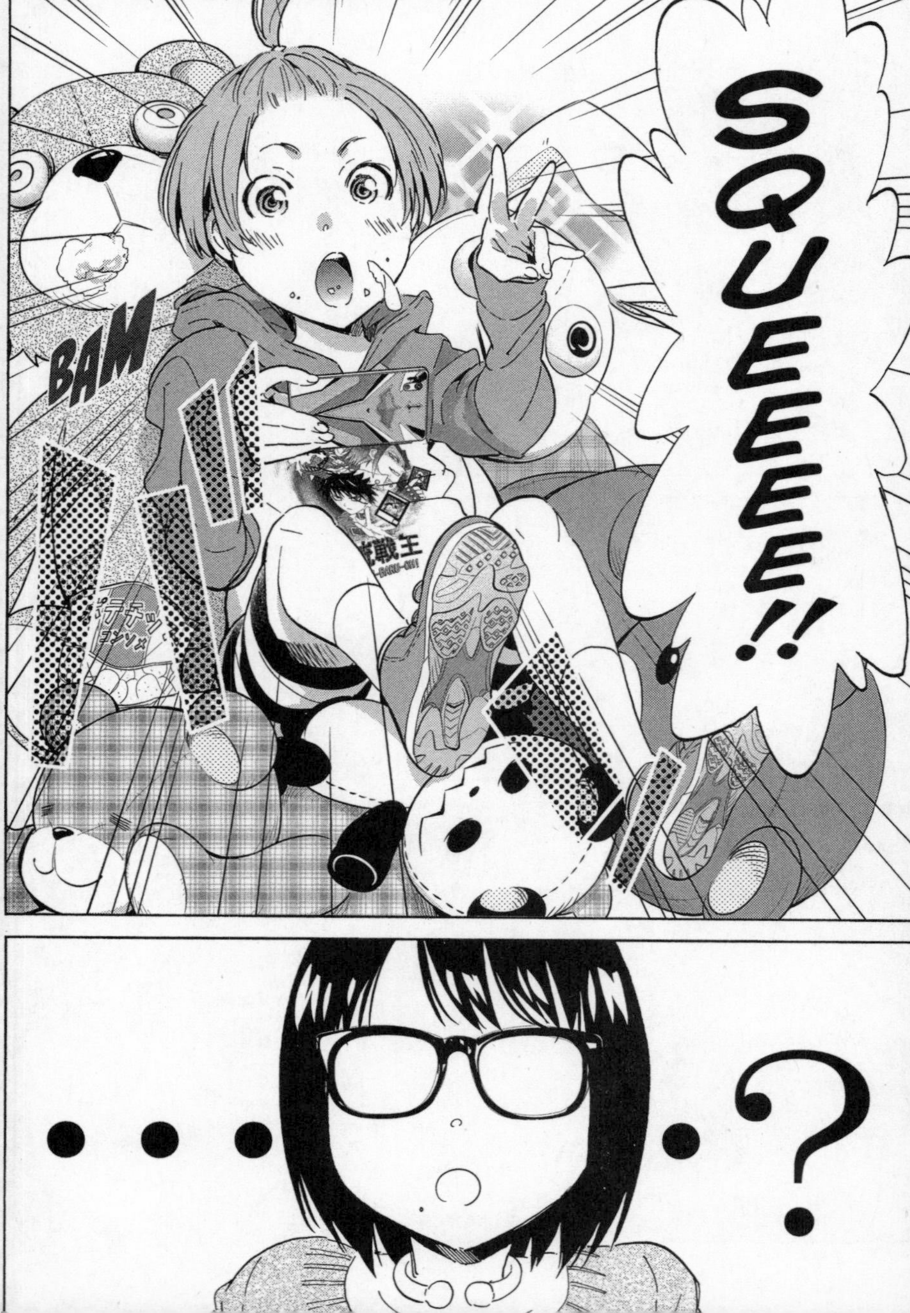
SQUEEEEE!!
BAM
...?

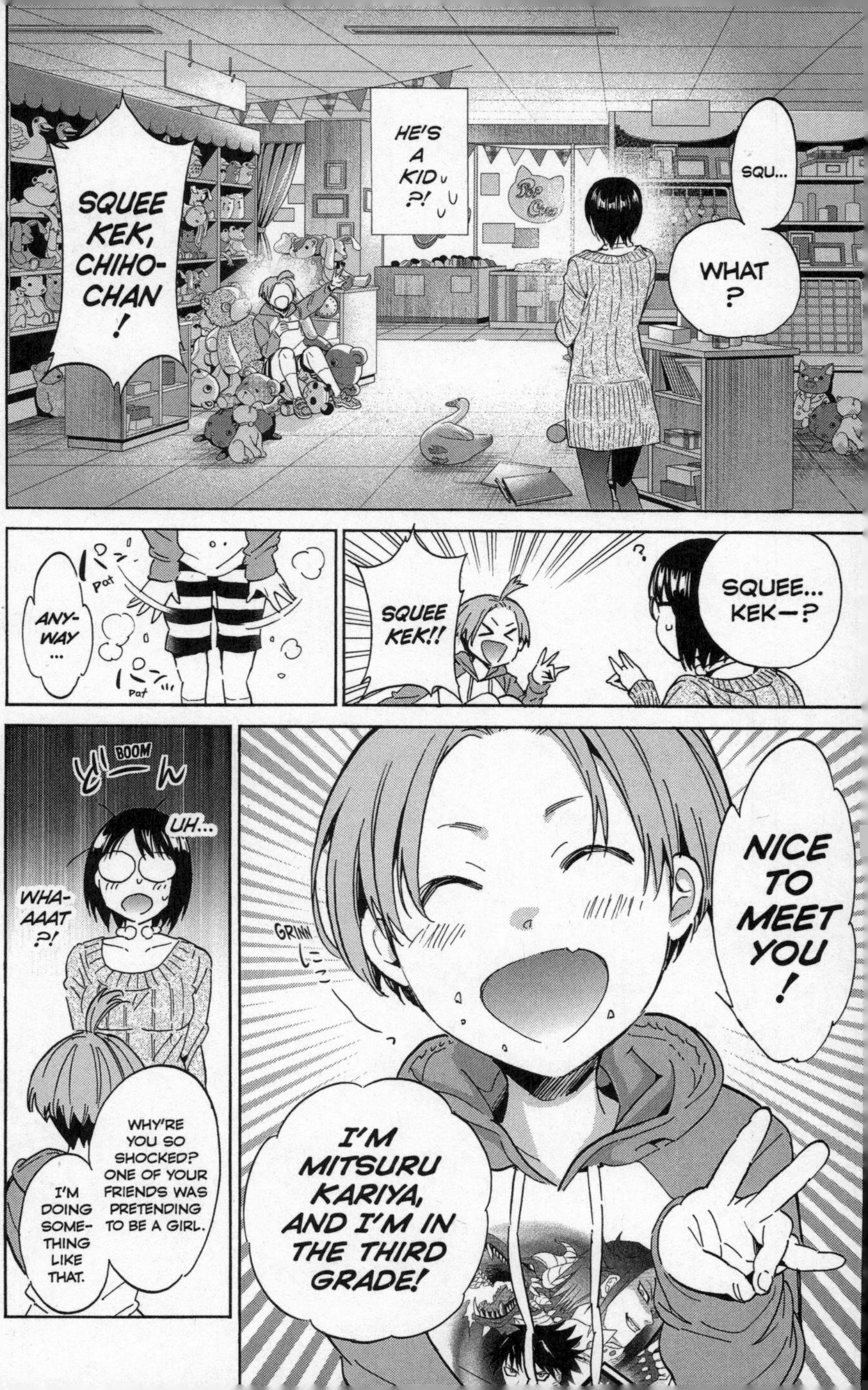
SQU... WHAT?
HE'S A KID?!
SQUEE KEK, CHIHO-CHAN!
SQUEE... KEK—?
SQUEE KEK!!
Pat
ANY-WAY...
Pat
NICE TO MEET YOU!
GRINN
I'M MITSURU KARIYA, AND I'M IN THE THIRD GRADE!
BOOM
UH...
WHA-AAAT?!
WHY'RE YOU SO SHOCKED? ONE OF YOUR FRIENDS WAS PRETENDING TO BE A GIRL.
I'M DOING SOME-THING LIKE THAT.

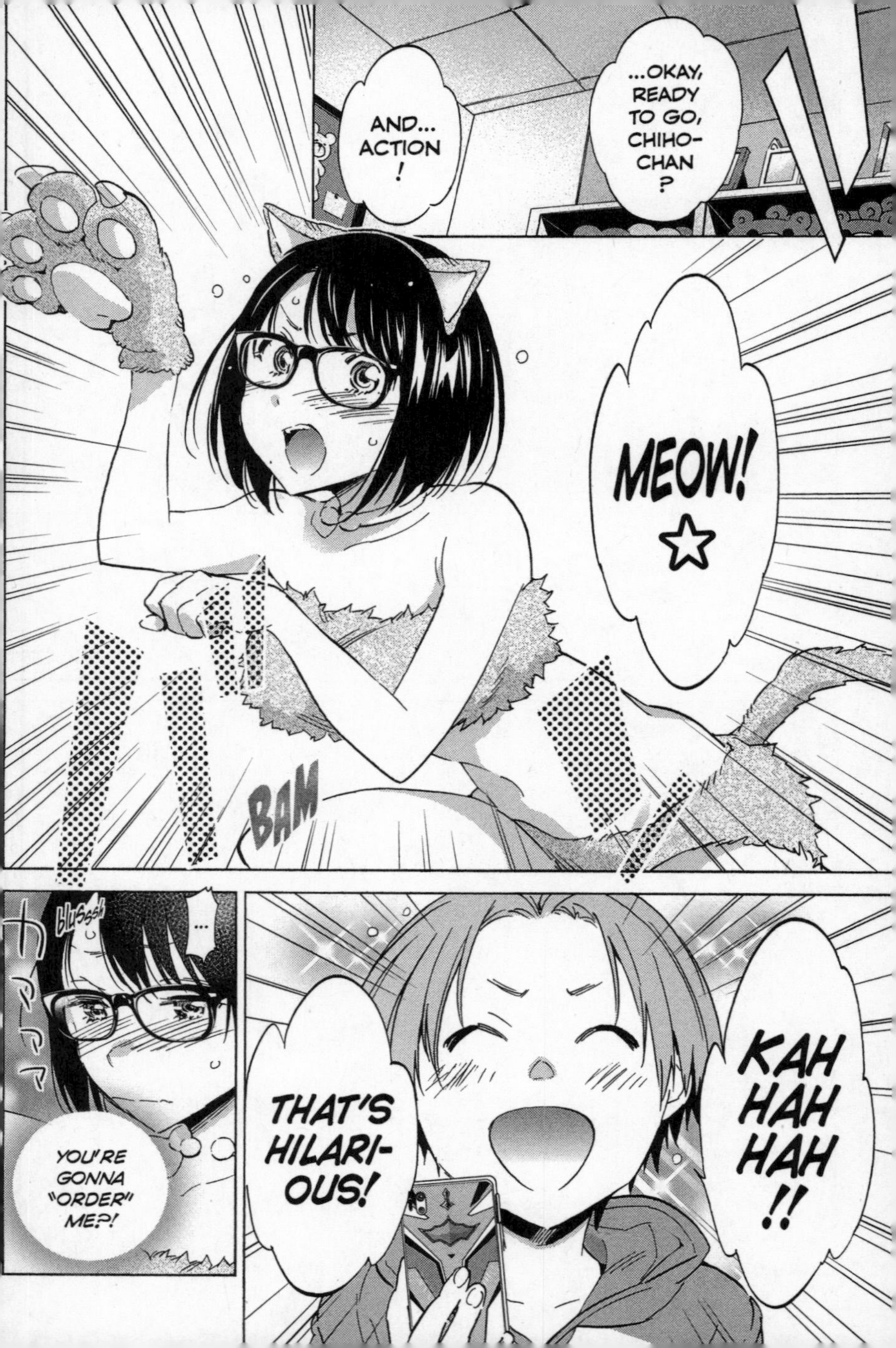
...OKAY, READY TO GO, CHIHO-CHAN?
AND... ACTION!
MEOW! ☆
BAM
KAH HAH HAH!!
THAT'S HILARI-OUS!
bluSssh
...
YOU'RE GONNA "ORDER" ME?!

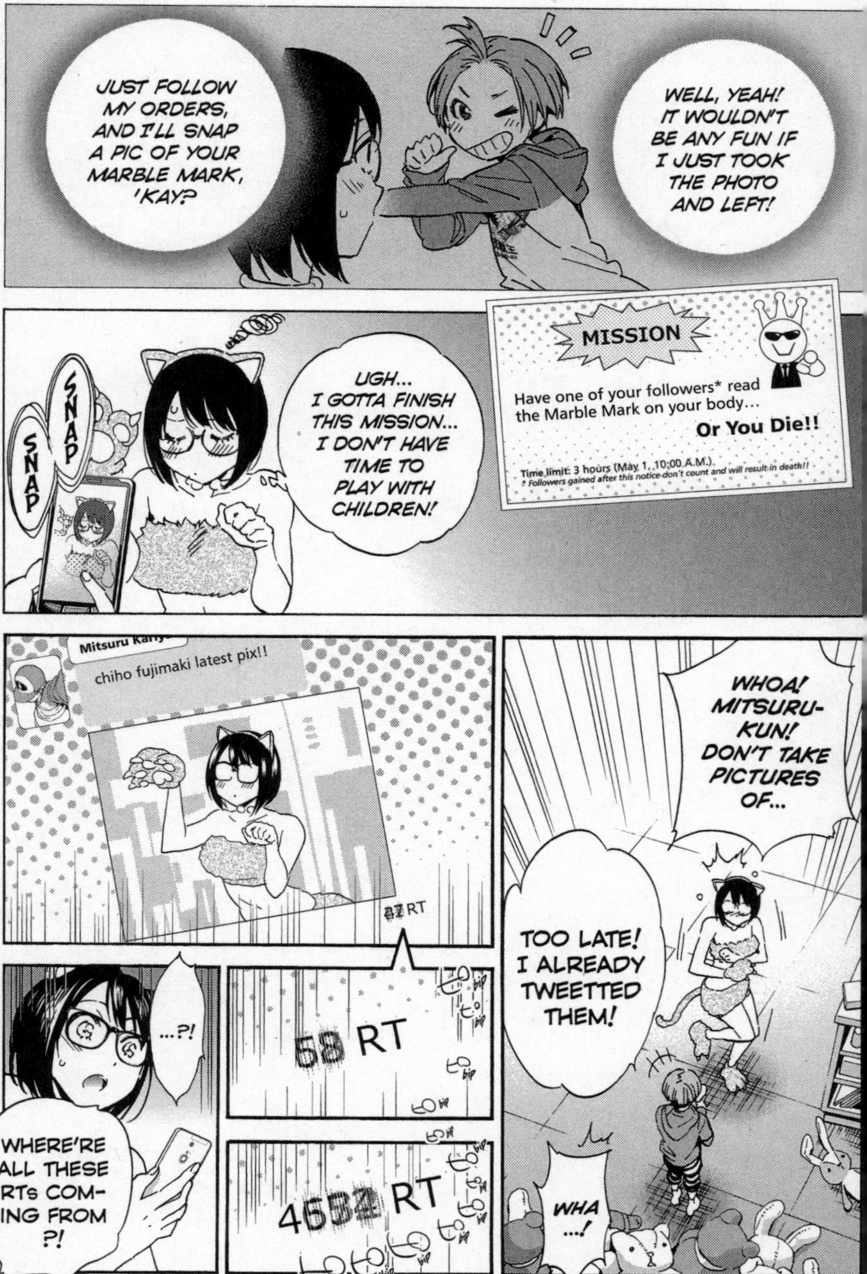
WELL, YEAH! IT WOULDN'T BE ANY FUN IF I JUST TOOK THE PHOTO AND LEFT!
JUST FOLLOW MY ORDERS, AND I'LL SNAP A PIC OF YOUR MARBLE MARK, 'KAY?
MISSION
Have one of your followers* read the Marble Mark on your body...
Or You Die!!
Time limit: 3 hours (May 1, 10:00 A.M.)
* Followers gained after this notice don't count and will result in death!!
UGH... I GOTTA FINISH THIS MISSION... I DON'T HAVE TIME TO PLAY WITH CHILDREN!
SNAP
SNAP
WHOA! MITSURU-KUN! DON'T TAKE PICTURES OF...
TOO LATE! I ALREADY TWEETTED THEM!
WHA...!
chiho fujimaki latest pix!!
RT
bip bip
58 RT
bip bip
bip bip bip bip bip bip
RT
...?!
WHERE'RE ALL THESE RTs COMING FROM?!

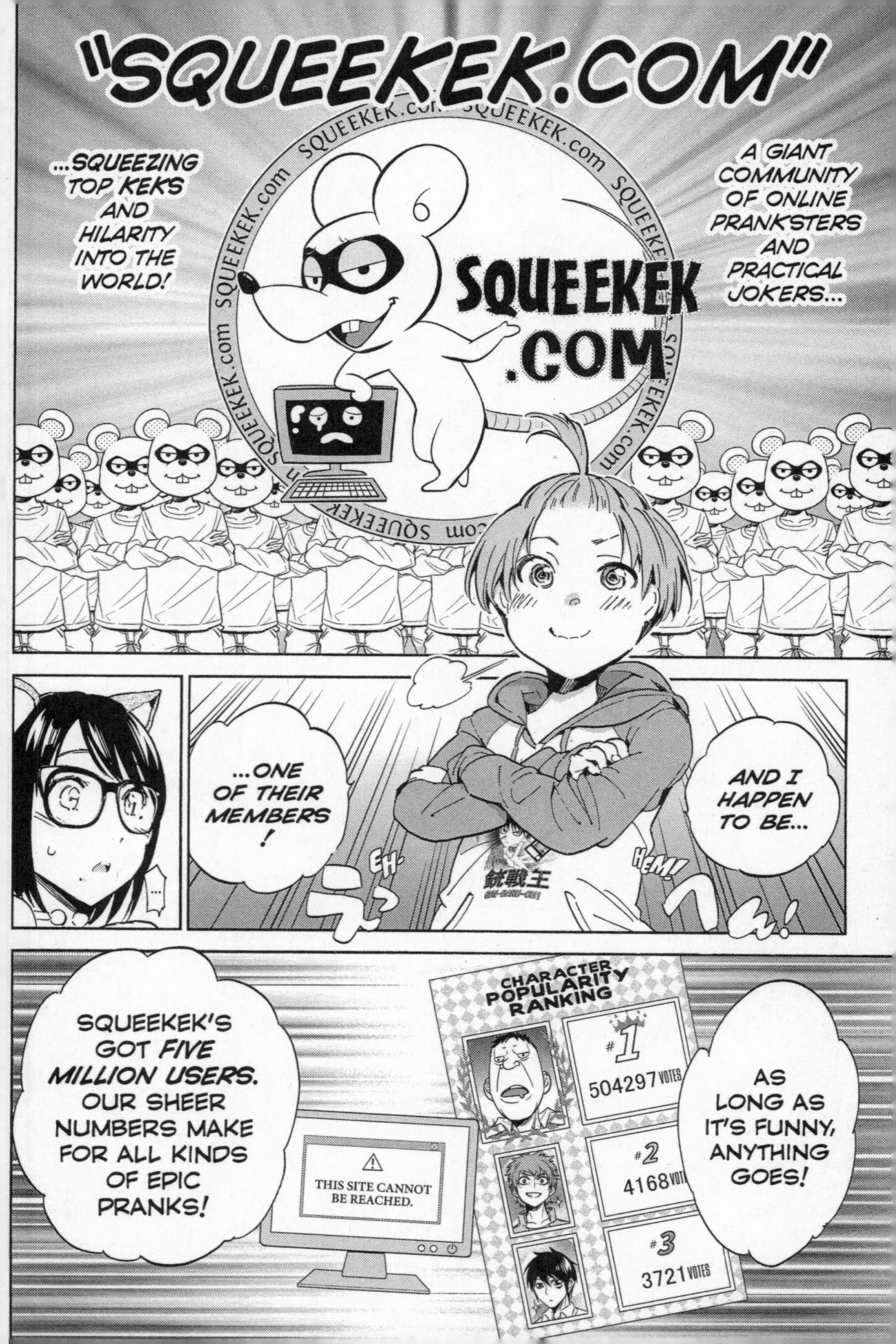
"SQUEEKEK.COM"
A GIANT COMMUNITY OF ONLINE PRANKSTERS AND PRACTICAL JOKERS...
SQUEEKEK .COM
...SQUEEZING TOP KEKS AND HILARITY INTO THE WORLD!
AND I HAPPEN TO BE...
HEM!
...ONE OF THEIR MEMBERS!
EH-
...
AS LONG AS IT'S FUNNY, ANYTHING GOES!
CHARACTER POPULARITY RANKING
#1 504297 VOTES
#2 4168
#3 3721 VOTES
THIS SITE CANNOT BE REACHED.
SQUEEKEK'S GOT FIVE MILLION USERS. OUR SHEER NUMBERS MAKE FOR ALL KINDS OF EPIC PRANKS!

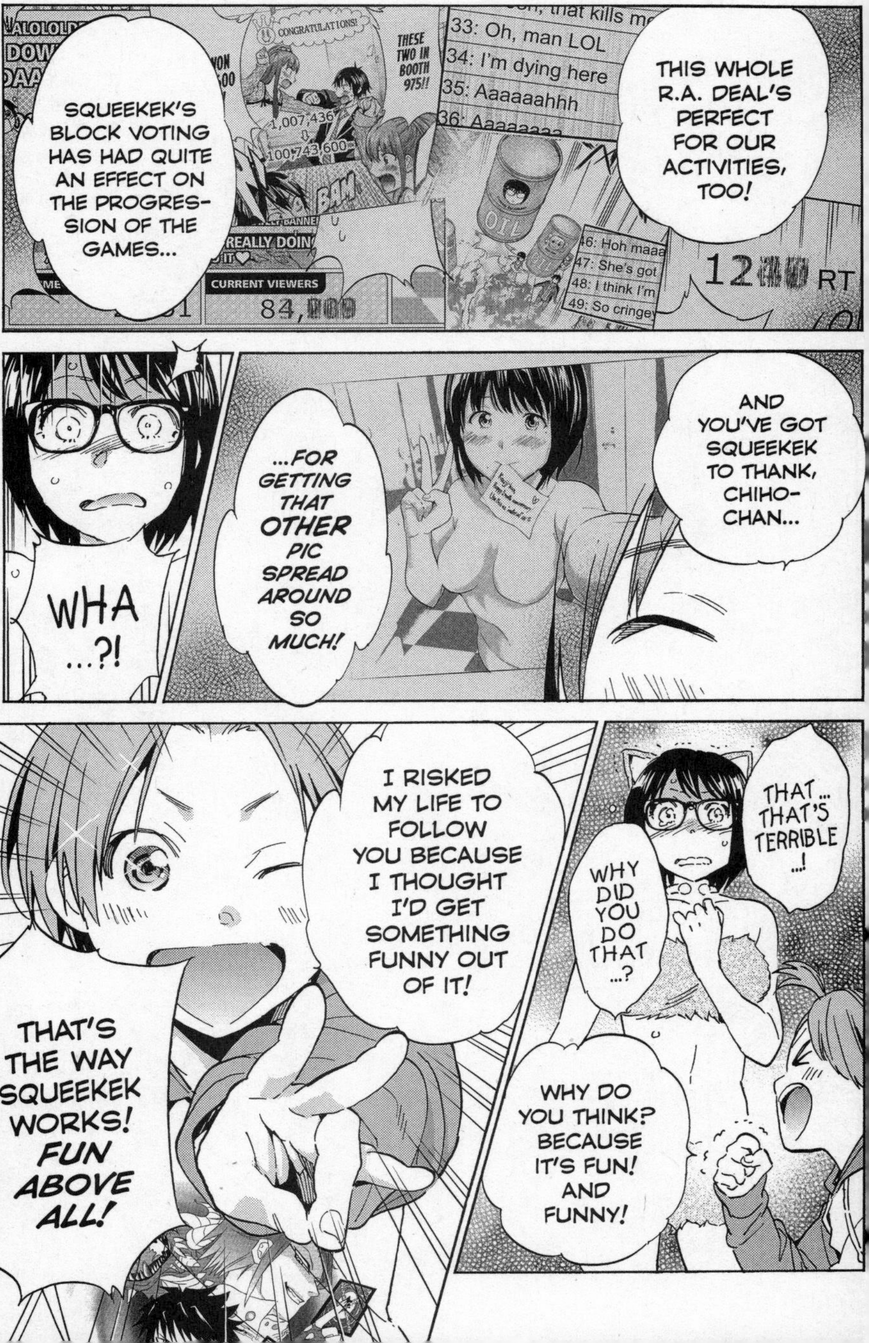
CONGRATULATIONS!
THESE TWO IN BOOTH 975!!
33: Oh, man LOL
34: I'm dying here
35: Aaaaaahhh
CURRENT VIEWERS
THIS WHOLE R.A. DEAL'S PERFECT FOR OUR ACTIVITIES, TOO!
SQUEEKEK'S BLOCK VOTING HAS HAD QUITE AN EFFECT ON THE PROGRESSION OF THE GAMES...
AND YOU'VE GOT SQUEEKEK TO THANK, CHIHO-CHAN...
...FOR GETTING THAT OTHER PIC SPREAD AROUND SO MUCH!
WHA ...?!
THAT... THAT'S TERRIBLE ...!
WHY DID YOU DO THAT ...?
WHY DO YOU THINK? BECAUSE IT'S FUN! AND FUNNY!
I RISKED MY LIFE TO FOLLOW YOU BECAUSE I THOUGHT I'D GET SOMETHING FUNNY OUT OF IT!
THAT'S THE WAY SQUEEKEK WORKS! FUN ABOVE ALL!

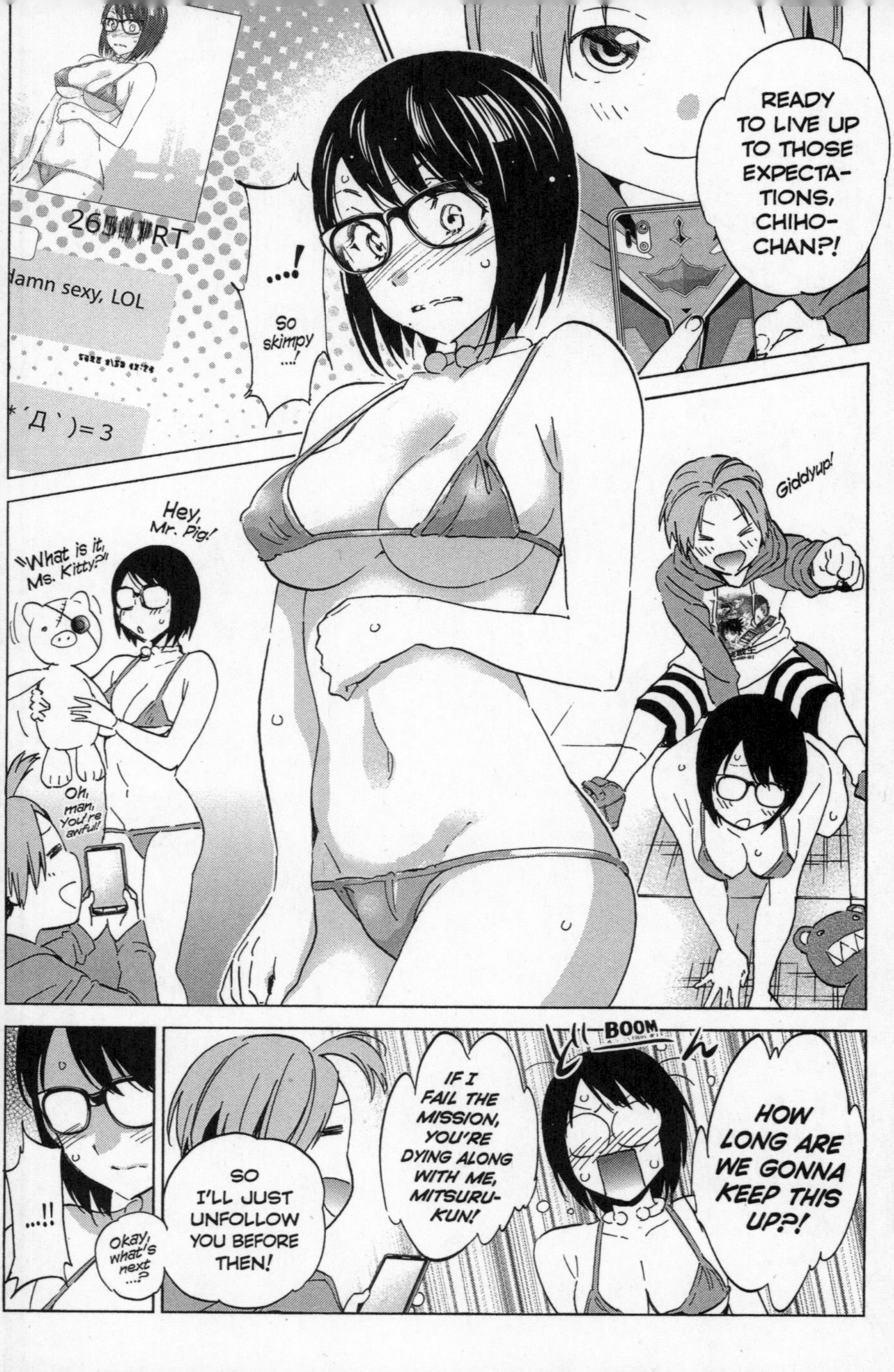
READY TO LIVE UP TO THOSE EXPECTATIONS, CHIHO-CHAN?!
265[redacted]RT
damn sexy, LOL
*´Д`)=3
...!
So skimpy ...!
Giddyup!
Hey, Mr. Pig!
"What is it, Ms. Kitty?"
Oh, man, you're awful!
HOW LONG ARE WE GONNA KEEP THIS UP?!
BOOM
IF I FAIL THE MISSION, YOU'RE DYING ALONG WITH ME, MITSURU-KUN!
SO I'LL JUST UNFOLLOW YOU BEFORE THEN!
Okay, what's next ...?
...!!

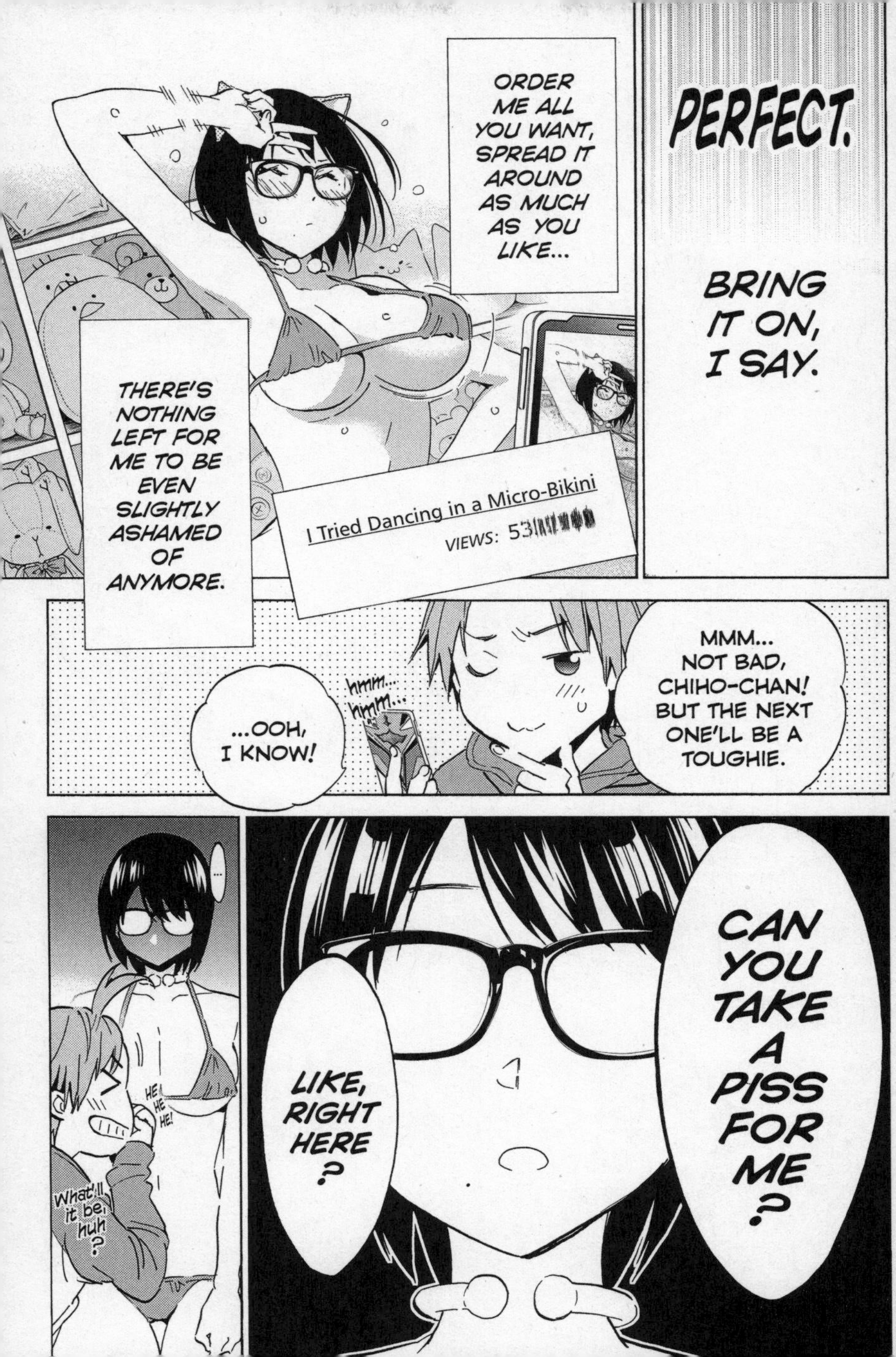
PERFECT.
BRING IT ON, I SAY.
ORDER ME ALL YOU WANT, SPREAD IT AROUND AS MUCH AS YOU LIKE...
THERE'S NOTHING LEFT FOR ME TO BE EVEN SLIGHTLY ASHAMED OF ANYMORE.
I Tried Dancing in a Micro-Bikini
VIEWS: 53
MMM... NOT BAD, CHIHO-CHAN! BUT THE NEXT ONE'LL BE A TOUGHIE.
hmm... hmm...
...OOH, I KNOW!
CAN YOU TAKE A PISS FOR ME?
LIKE, RIGHT HERE?
...
HE HE HE!
What'll it be, huh?

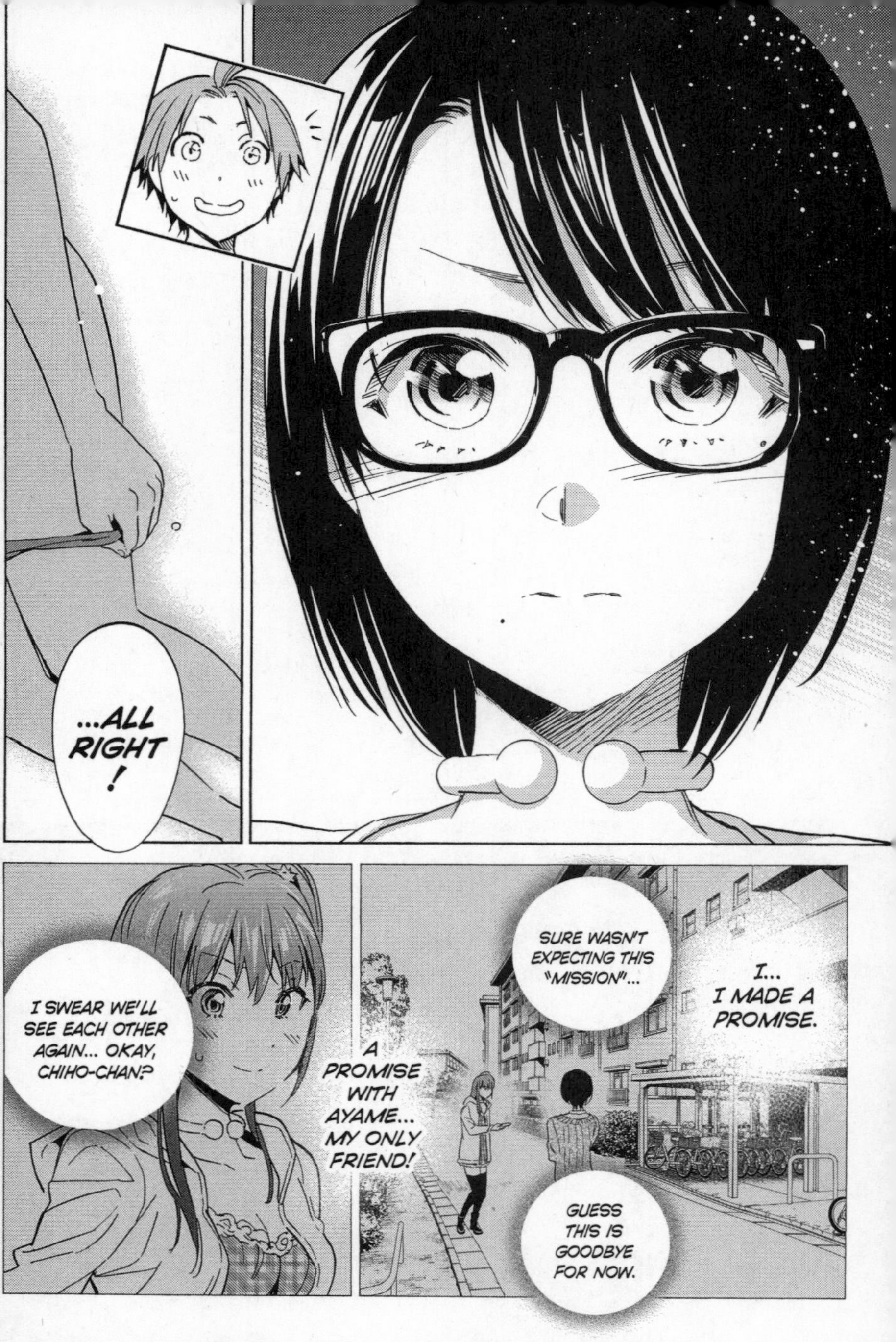
...ALL RIGHT!
SURE WASN'T EXPECTING THIS "MISSION"...
GUESS THIS IS GOODBYE FOR NOW.
I... I MADE A PROMISE.
A PROMISE WITH AYAME... MY ONLY FRIEND!
I SWEAR WE'LL SEE EACH OTHER AGAIN... OKAY, CHIHO-CHAN?

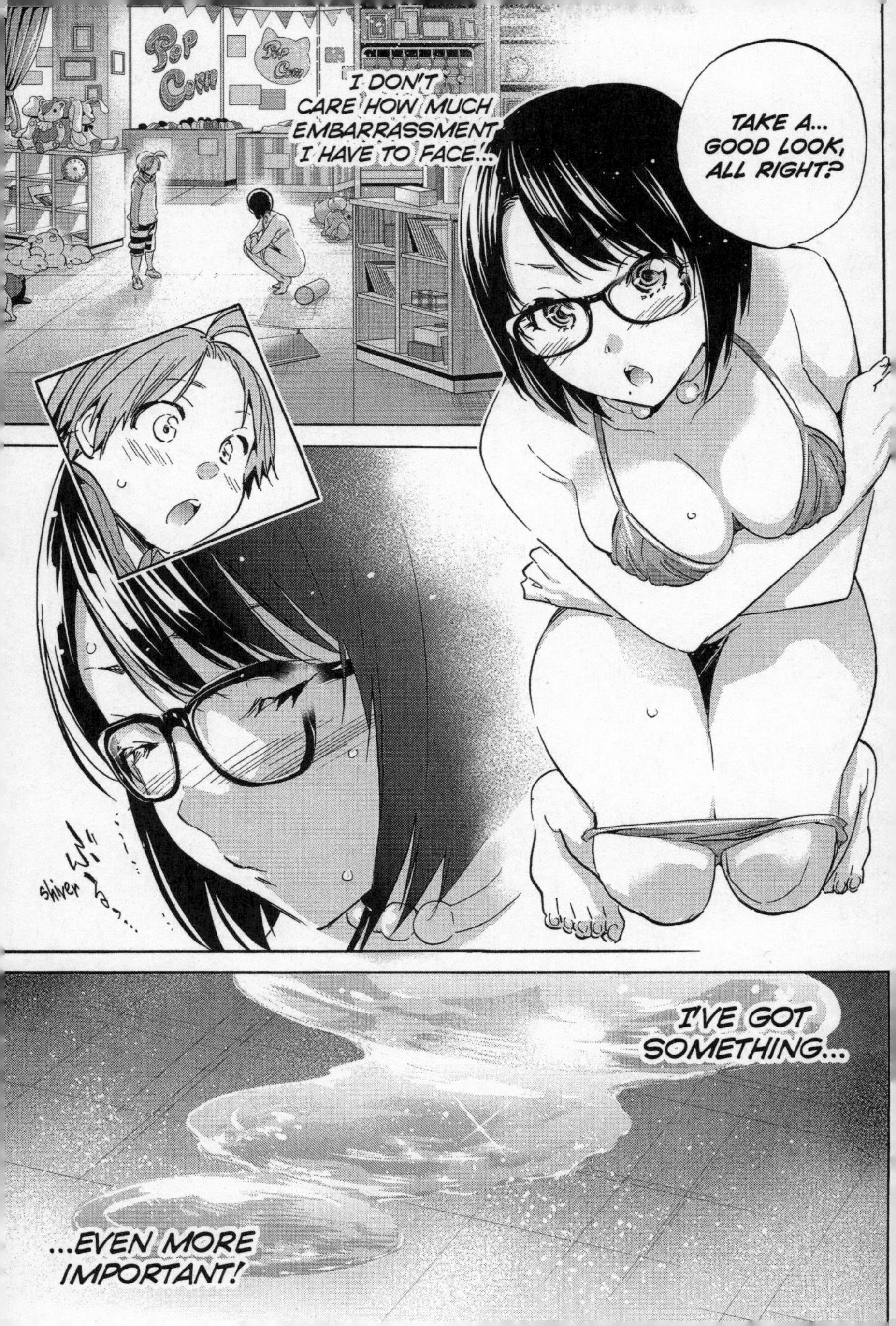

TAKE A... GOOD LOOK, ALL RIGHT?
I DON'T CARE HOW MUCH EMBARRASSMENT I HAVE TO FACE...
Pop Corn
shiver
I'VE GOT SOMETHING...
...EVEN MORE IMPORTANT!

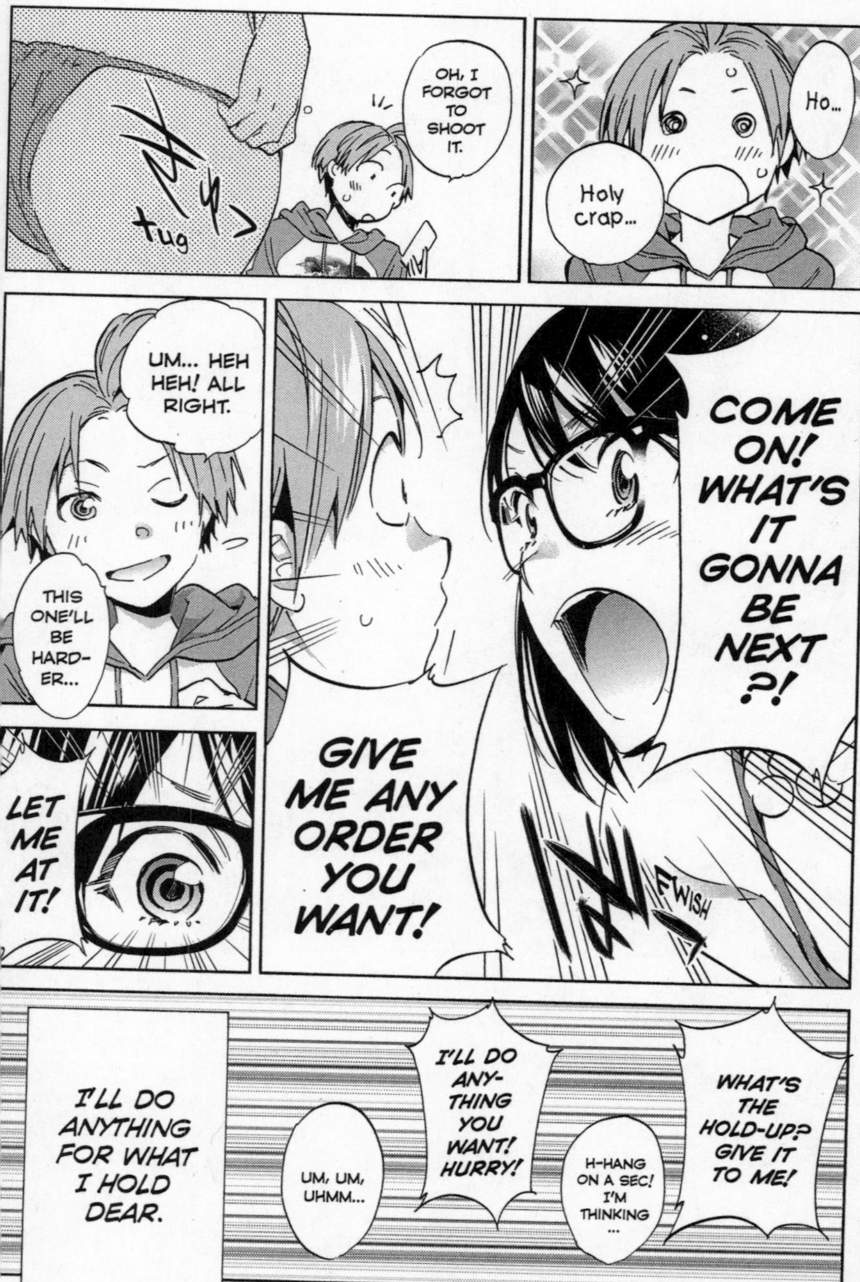
Ho...
Holy crap...
OH, I FORGOT TO SHOOT IT.
tug
COME ON! WHAT'S IT GONNA BE NEXT?!
GIVE ME ANY ORDER YOU WANT!
FWISH
UM... HEH HEH! ALL RIGHT.
THIS ONE'LL BE HARDER...
LET ME AT IT!
WHAT'S THE HOLD-UP? GIVE IT TO ME!
H-HANG ON A SEC! I'M THINKING ...
I'LL DO ANYTHING YOU WANT! HURRY!
UM, UM, UHMM...
I'LL DO ANYTHING FOR WHAT I HOLD DEAR.

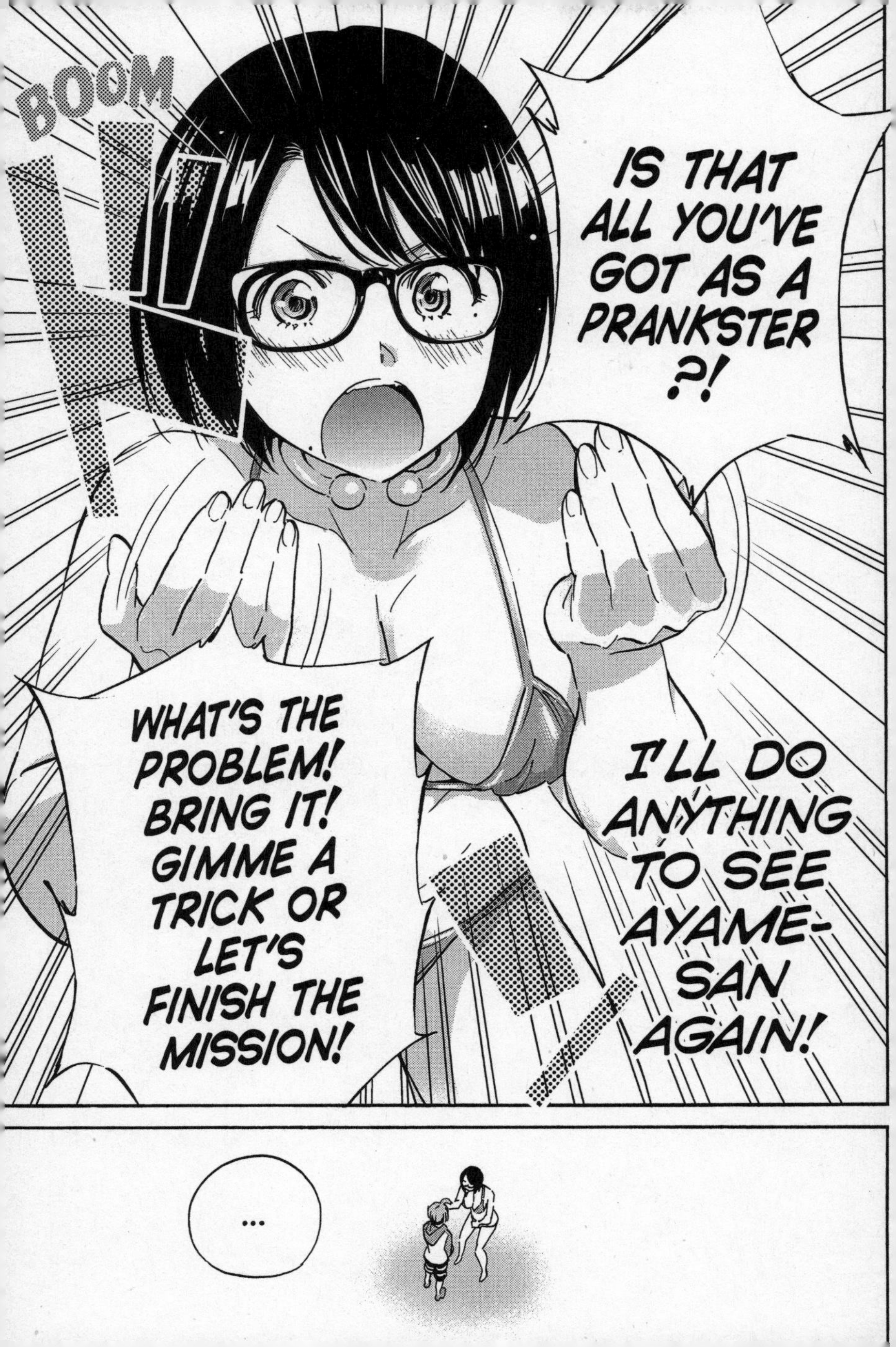
IS THAT ALL YOU'VE GOT AS A PRANKSTER ?!
BOOM
I'LL DO ANYTHING TO SEE AYAME-SAN AGAIN!
WHAT'S THE PROBLEM! BRING IT! GIMME A TRICK OR LET'S FINISH THE MISSION!
...

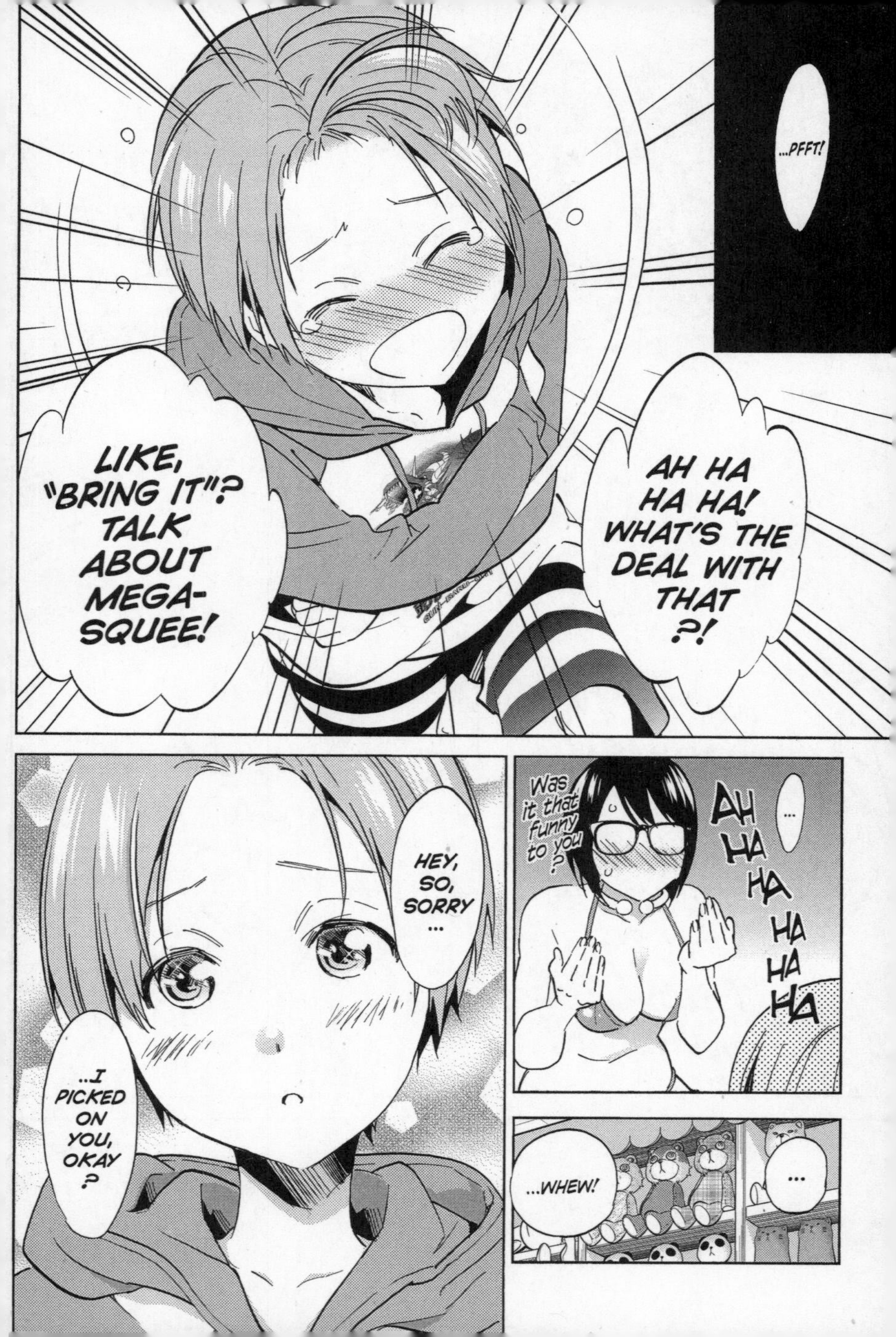
...PFFT!
AH HA HA HA! WHAT'S THE DEAL WITH THAT ?!
LIKE, "BRING IT"? TALK ABOUT MEGA-SQUEE!
...
AH HA HA HA HA HA
Was it that funny to you ?
...
...WHEW!
HEY, SO, SORRY ...
...I PICKED ON YOU, OKAY ?

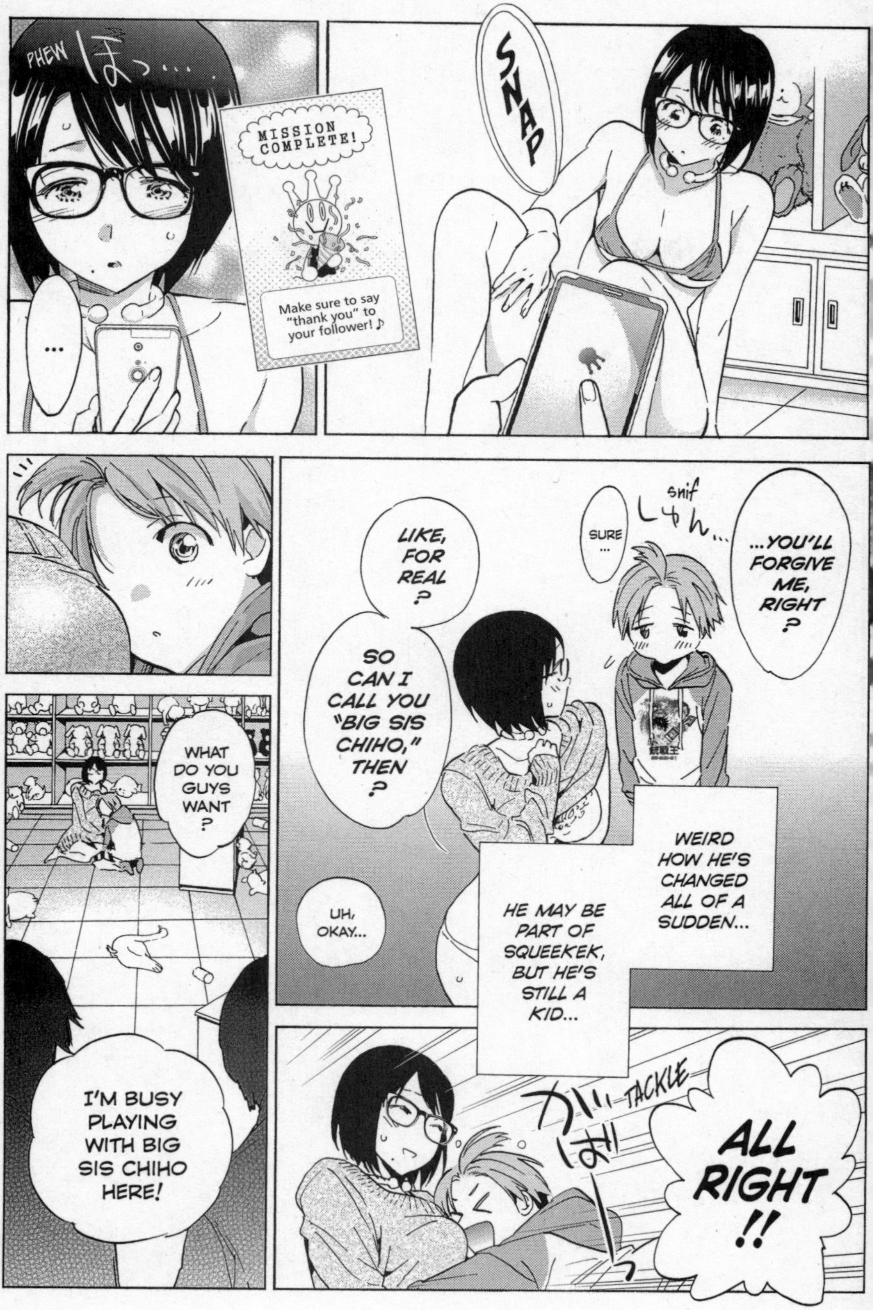
SNAP
PHEW ほっ...
MISSION COMPLETE!
Make sure to say "thank you" to your follower! ♪
...
...YOU'LL FORGIVE ME, RIGHT?
snif しゅん...
SURE...
LIKE, FOR REAL?
SO CAN I CALL YOU "BIG SIS CHIHO," THEN?
WEIRD HOW HE'S CHANGED ALL OF A SUDDEN...
HE MAY BE PART OF SQUEEKEK, BUT HE'S STILL A KID...
UH, OKAY...
ALL RIGHT!!
TACKLE がばーっ
WHAT DO YOU GUYS WANT?
I'M BUSY PLAYING WITH BIG SIS CHIHO HERE!

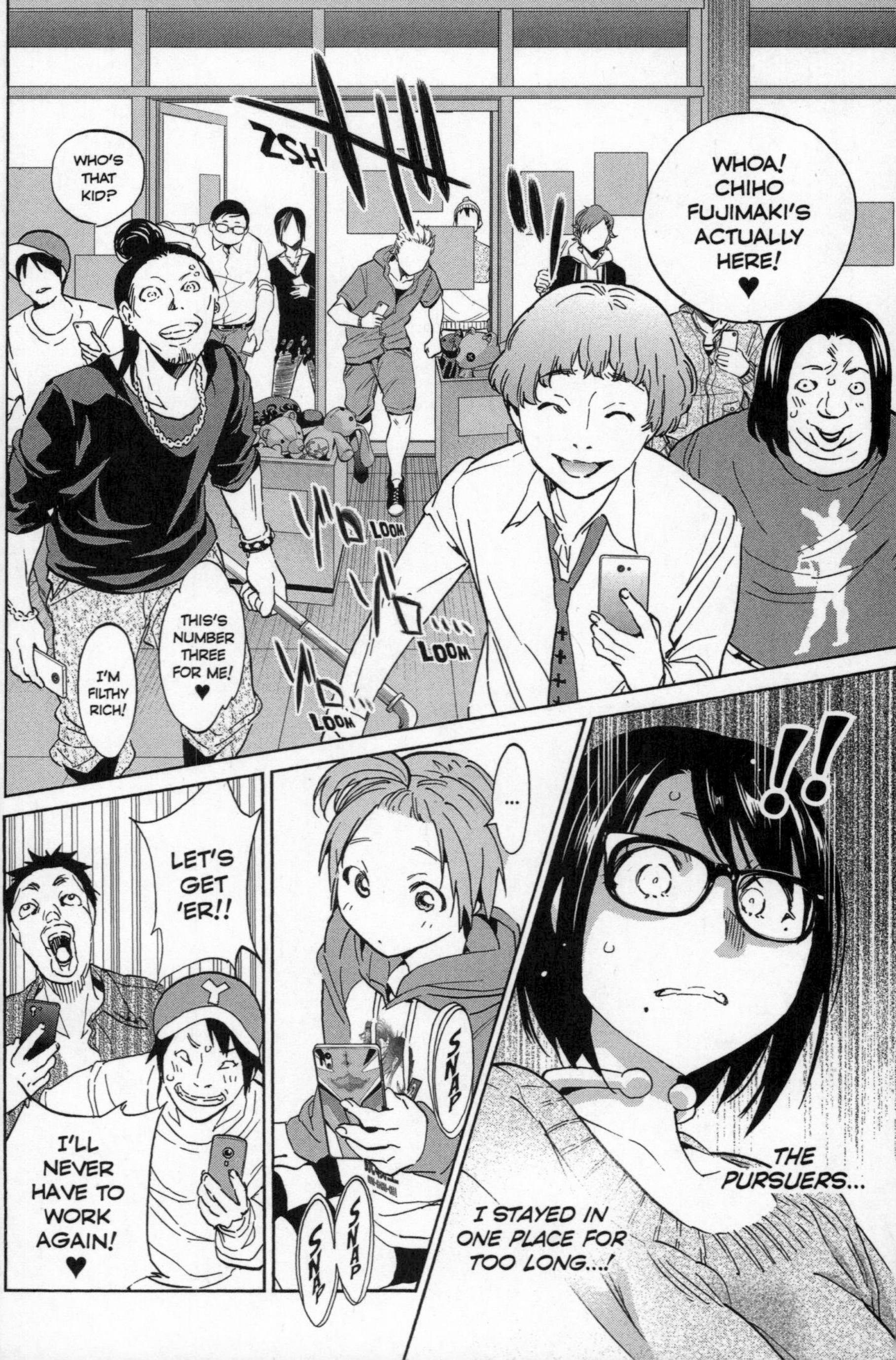
WHOA! CHIHO FUJIMAKI'S ACTUALLY HERE! ♥
ZSH
WHO'S THAT KID?
LOOM
LOOM
LOOM
THIS'S NUMBER THREE FOR ME! ♥
I'M FILTHY RICH!
!!
THE PURSUERS...
I STAYED IN ONE PLACE FOR TOO LONG...!
...
SNAP
SNAP
SNAP
LET'S GET 'ER!!
I'LL NEVER HAVE TO WORK AGAIN! ♥

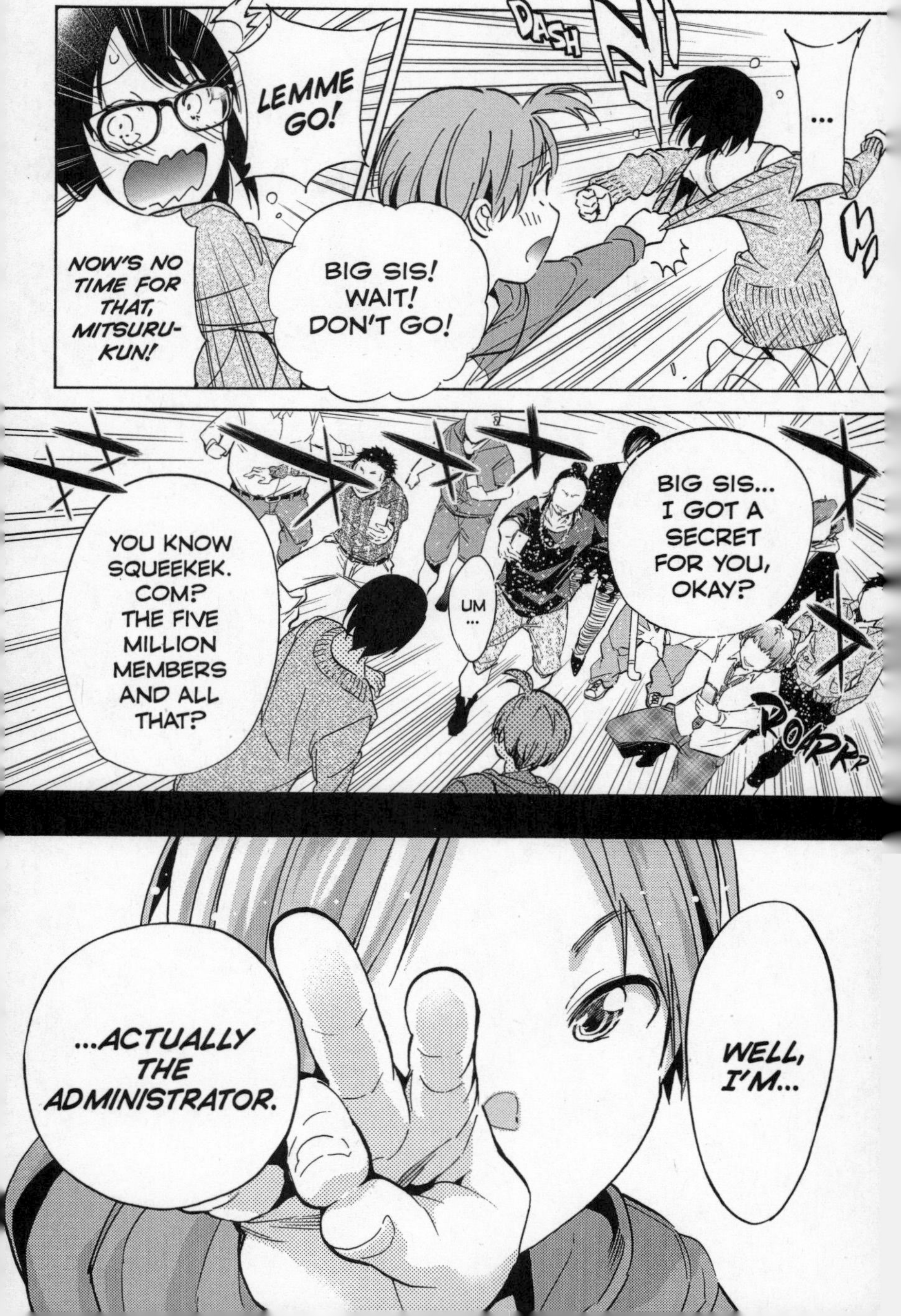
DASH
...
LEMME GO!
BIG SIS! WAIT! DON'T GO!
NOW'S NO TIME FOR THAT, MITSURU-KUN!
BIG SIS... I GOT A SECRET FOR YOU, OKAY?
UM ...
YOU KNOW SQUEEKEK.COM? THE FIVE MILLION MEMBERS AND ALL THAT?
WELL, I'M...
...ACTUALLY THE ADMINISTRATOR.

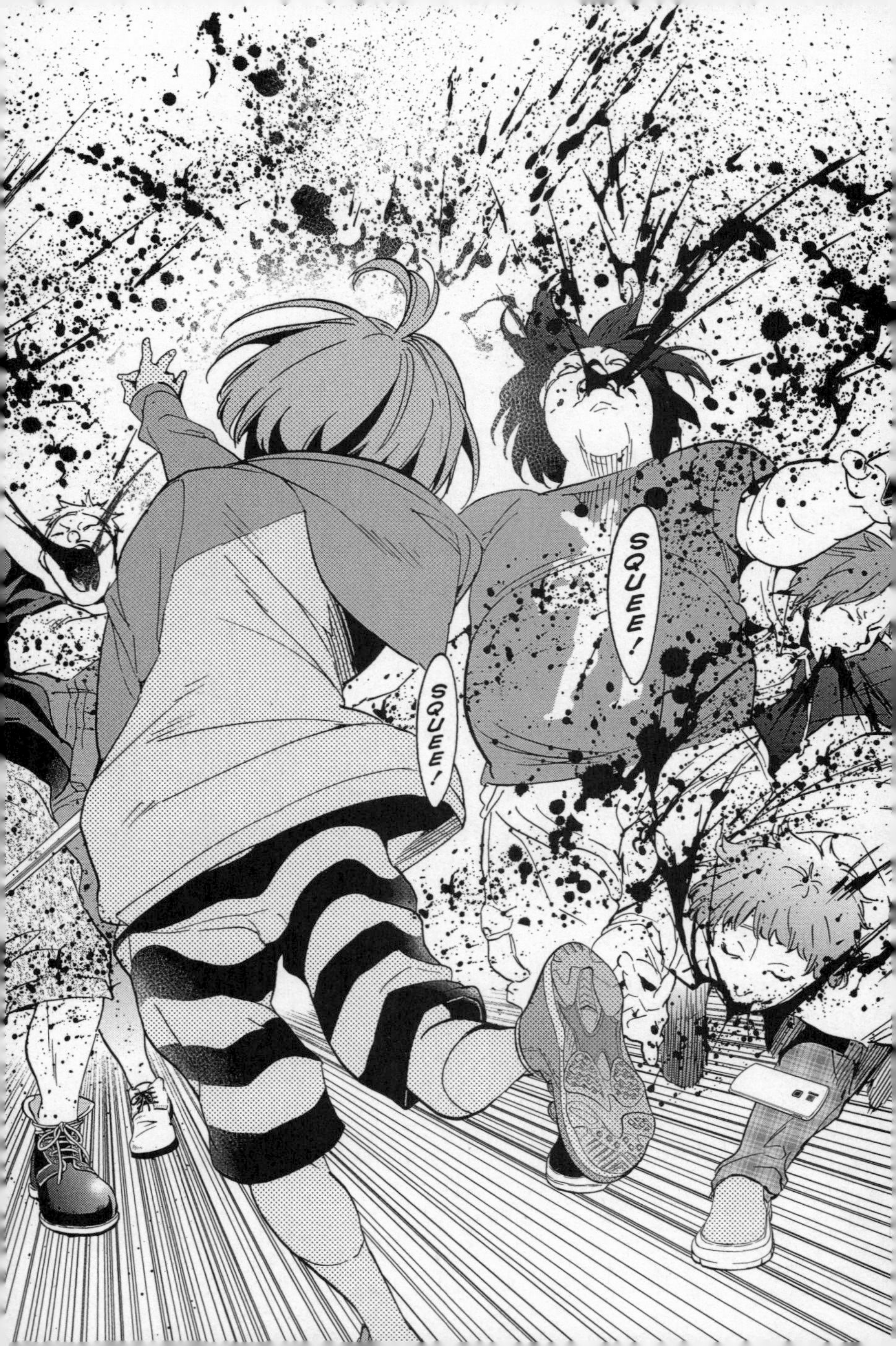
SQUEE!
SQUEE!

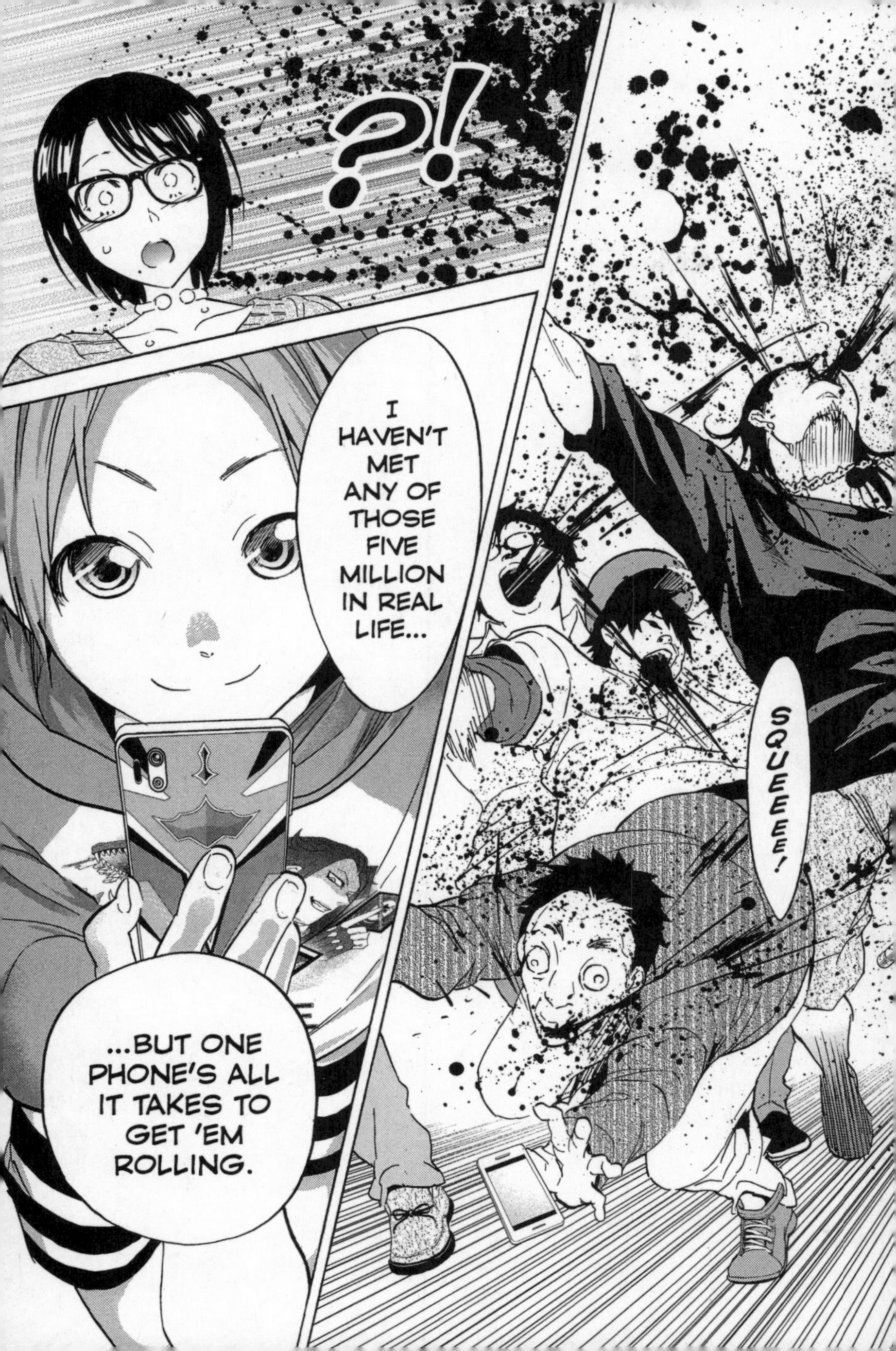
SQUEEEE!
?!
I HAVEN'T MET ANY OF THOSE FIVE MILLION IN REAL LIFE...
...BUT ONE PHONE'S ALL IT TAKES TO GET 'EM ROLLING.

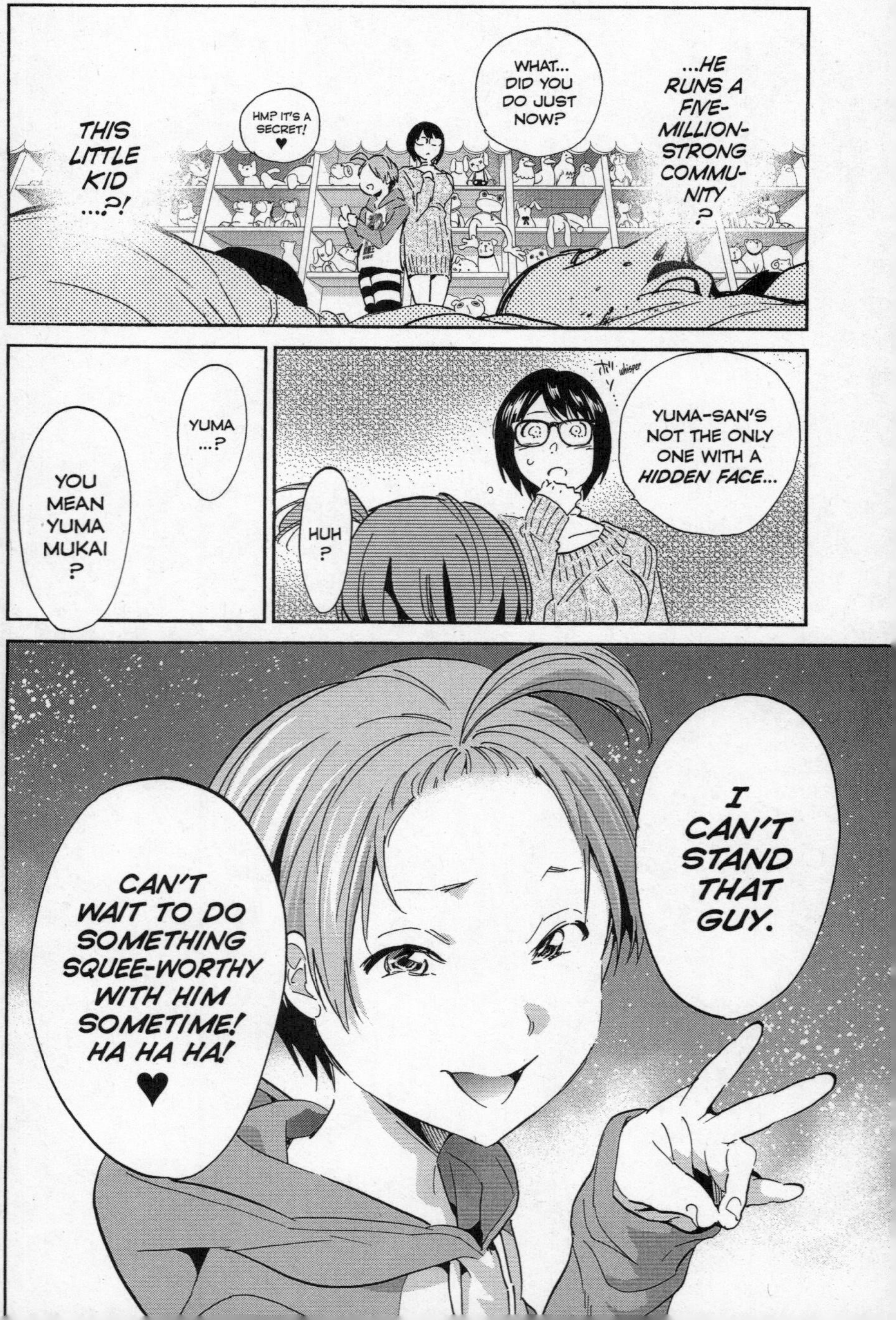
...HE RUNS A FIVE-MILLION-STRONG COMMUNITY?
WHAT... DID YOU DO JUST NOW?
HM? IT'S A SECRET! ♥
THIS LITTLE KID ...?!
whisper
YUMA-SAN'S NOT THE ONLY ONE WITH A *HIDDEN FACE*...
HUH?
YUMA ...?
YOU MEAN YUMA MUKAI?
I CAN'T STAND THAT GUY.
CAN'T WAIT TO DO SOMETHING SQUEE-WORTHY WITH HIM SOMETIME! HA HA HA! ♥

ACCOUNT 37 Epilogue

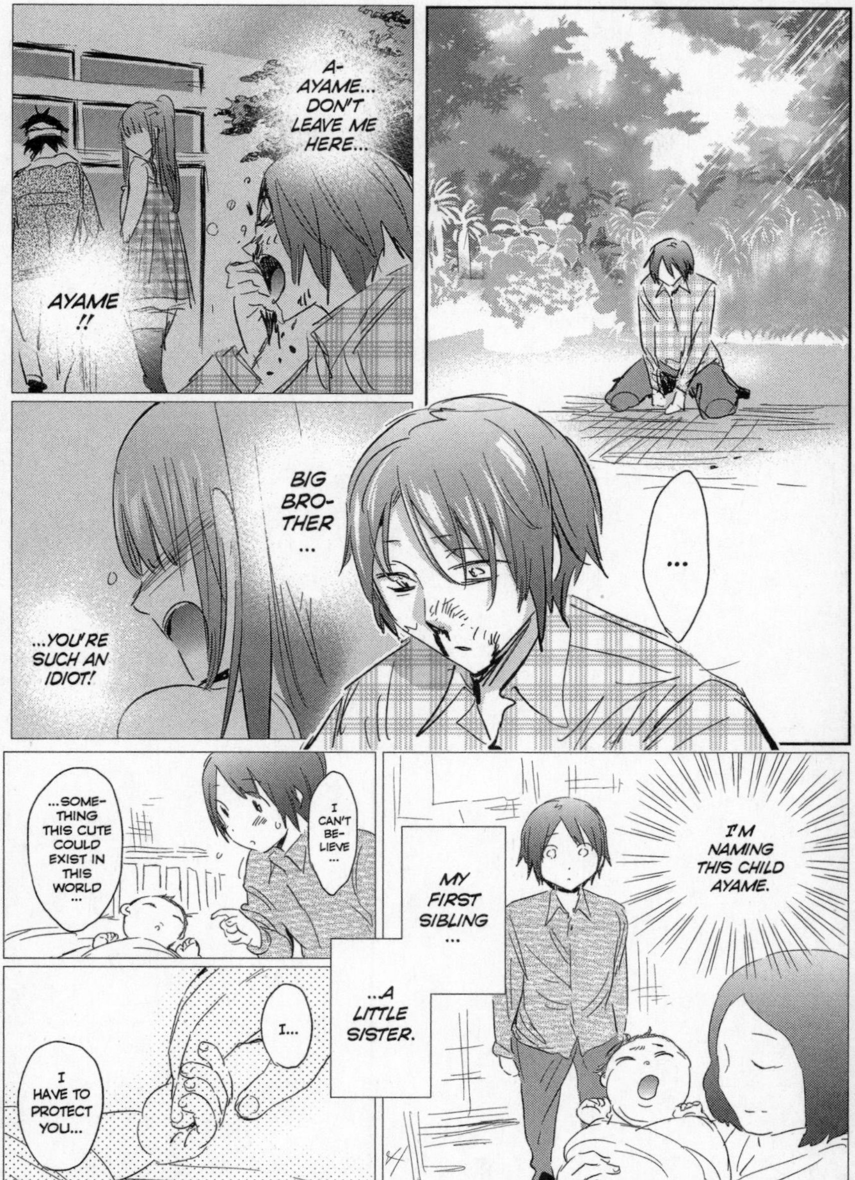
A-AYAME... DON'T LEAVE ME HERE...
AYAME!!
...
BIG BROTHER...
...YOU'RE SUCH AN IDIOT!
I'M NAMING THIS CHILD AYAME.
MY FIRST SIBLING...
...A LITTLE SISTER.
I CAN'T BELIEVE...
...SOMETHING THIS CUTE COULD EXIST IN THIS WORLD...
I...
I HAVE TO PROTECT YOU...

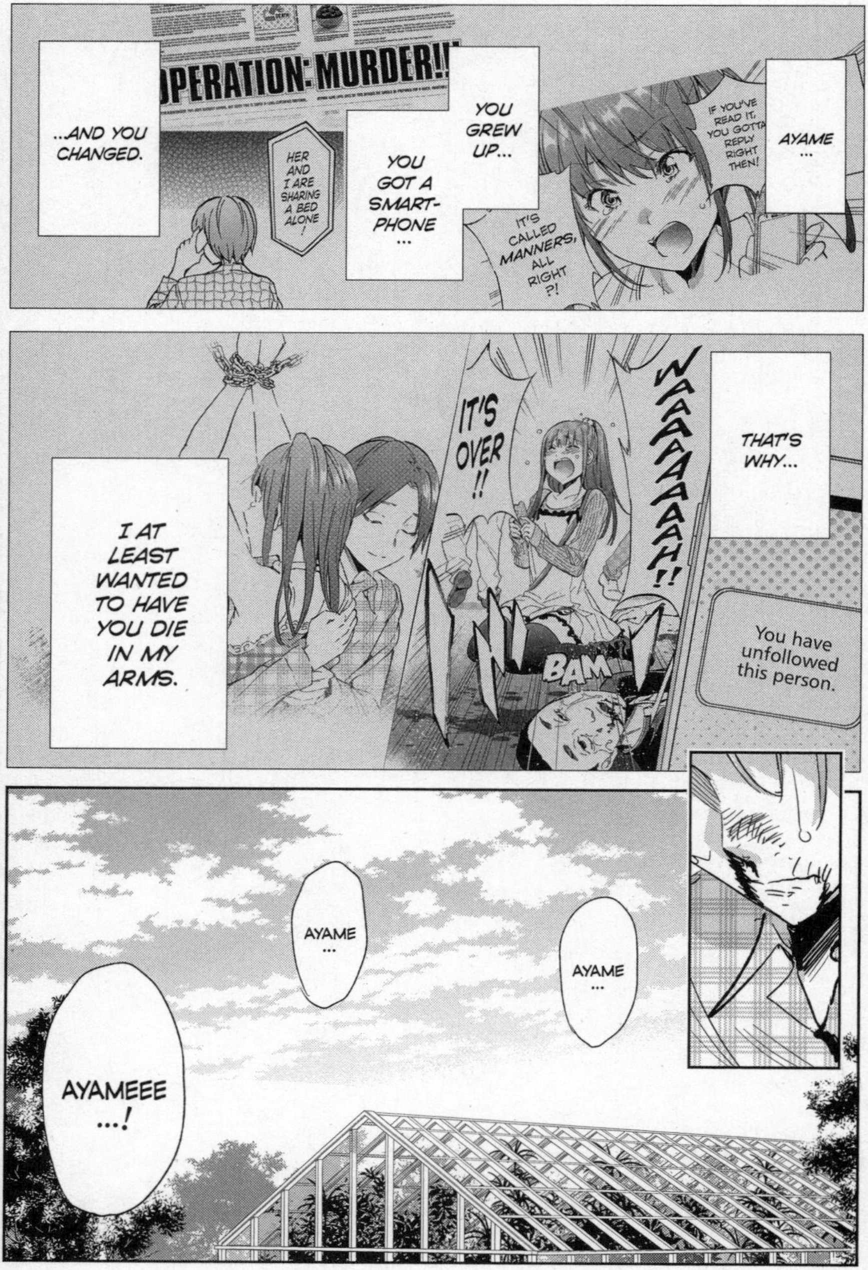
AYAME ...
IF YOU'VE READ IT, YOU GOTTA REPLY RIGHT THEN!
IT'S CALLED MANNERS, ALL RIGHT?!
YOU GREW UP...
YOU GOT A SMART-PHONE ...
OPERATION: MURDER!!
HER AND I ARE SHARING A BED ALONE!
...AND YOU CHANGED.
THAT'S WHY...
You have unfollowed this person.
WAAAAAAAAAH!!
IT'S OVER!!
BAM
I AT LEAST WANTED TO HAVE YOU DIE IN MY ARMS.
AYAME ...
AYAME ...
AYAMEEE ...!

ACCOUNT 39 Missing...

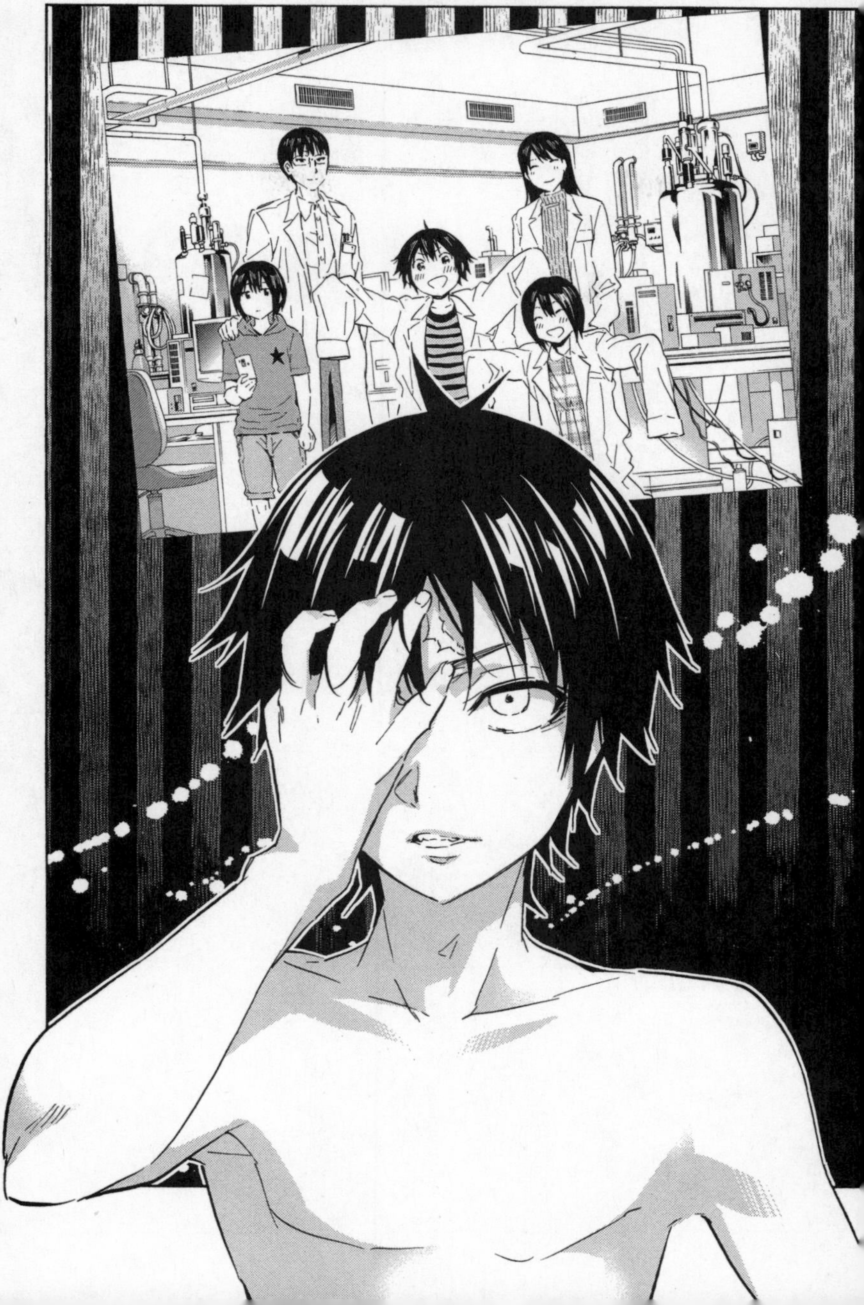

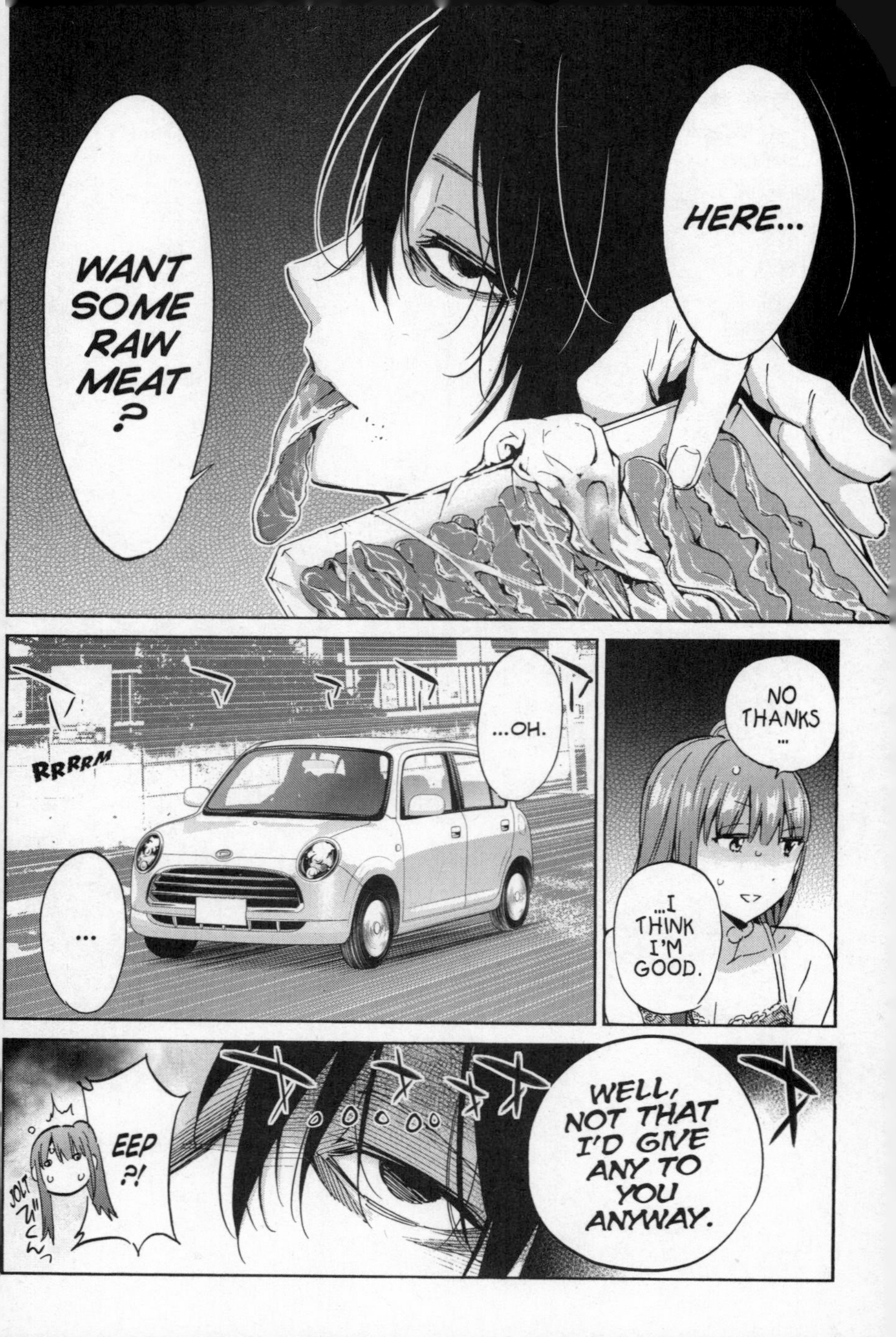
HERE...
WANT SOME RAW MEAT?
NO THANKS...
...I THINK I'M GOOD.
...OH.
RRRRM
...
WELL, NOT THAT I'D GIVE ANY TO YOU ANYWAY.
EEP?!
JOLT

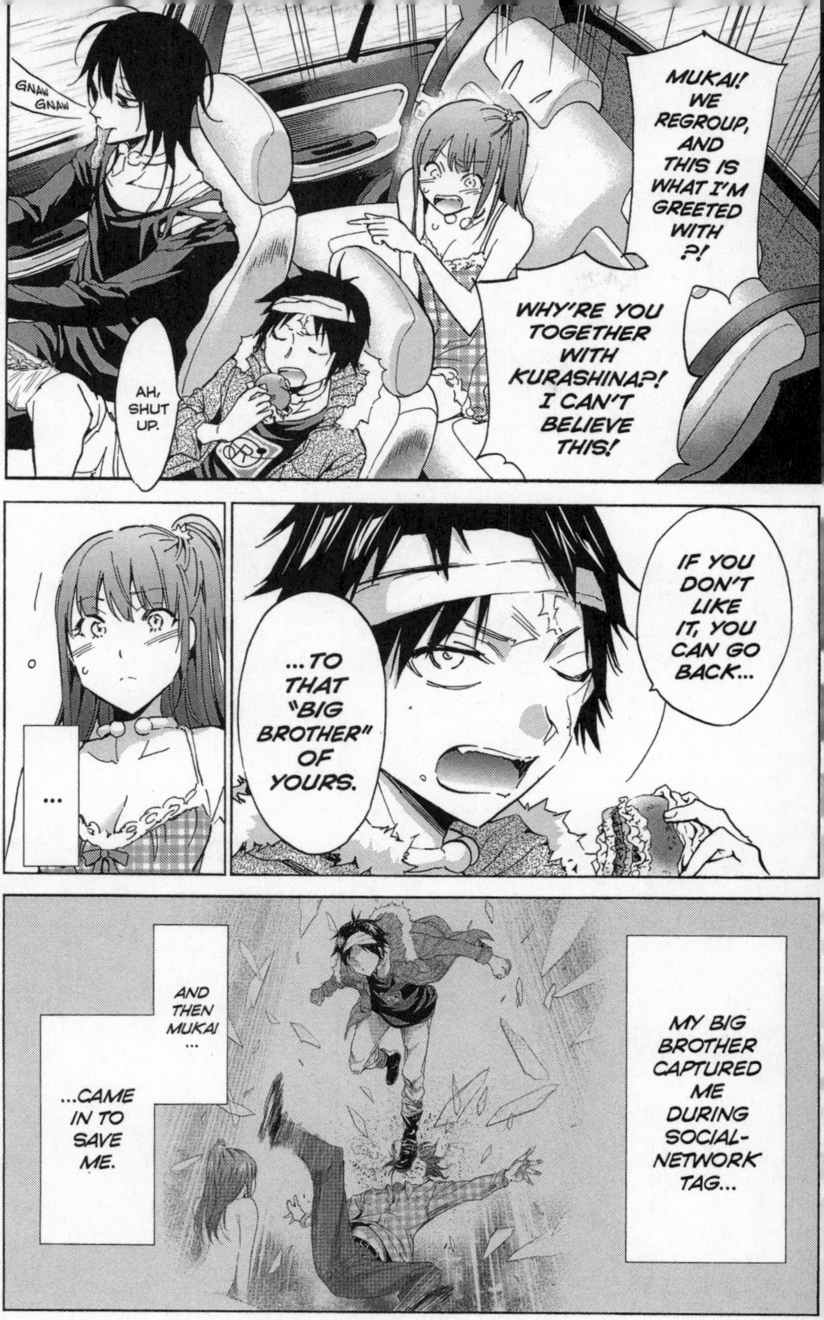
MUKAI! WE REGROUP, AND THIS IS WHAT I'M GREETED WITH ?!
WHY'RE YOU TOGETHER WITH KURASHINA?! I CAN'T BELIEVE THIS!
GNAW GNAW
AH, SHUT UP.
IF YOU DON'T LIKE IT, YOU CAN GO BACK...
...TO THAT "BIG BROTHER" OF YOURS.
...
MY BIG BROTHER CAPTURED ME DURING SOCIAL-NETWORK TAG...
AND THEN MUKAI ...
...CAME IN TO SAVE ME.

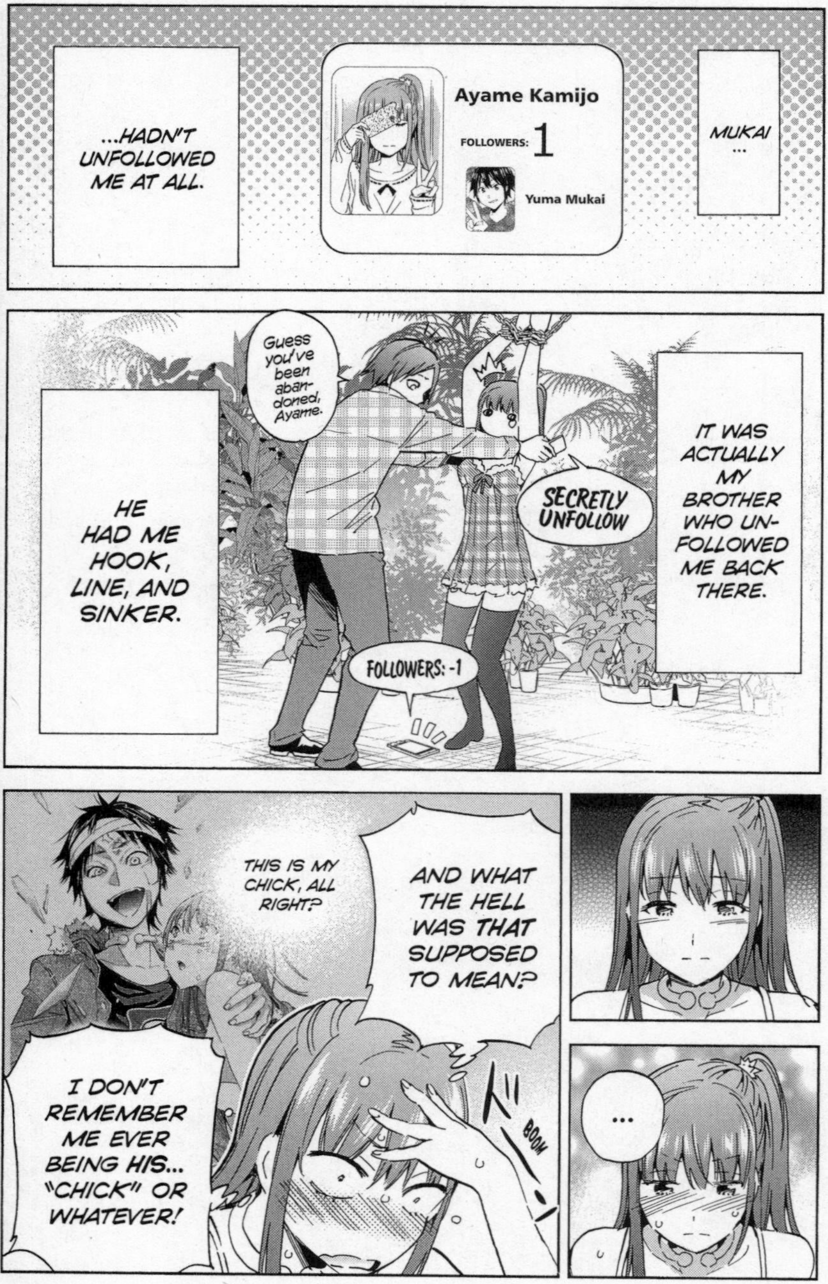
MUKAI ...
Ayame Kamijo
FOLLOWERS: 1
Yuma Mukai
...HADN'T UNFOLLOWED ME AT ALL.
IT WAS ACTUALLY MY BROTHER WHO UN-FOLLOWED ME BACK THERE.
Guess you've been aban-doned, Ayame.
SECRETLY UNFOLLOW
FOLLOWERS: -1
HE HAD ME HOOK, LINE, AND SINKER.
...
AND WHAT THE HELL WAS THAT SUPPOSED TO MEAN?
THIS IS MY CHICK, ALL RIGHT?
BOOM
I DON'T REMEMBER ME EVER BEING HIS... "CHICK" OR WHATEVER!

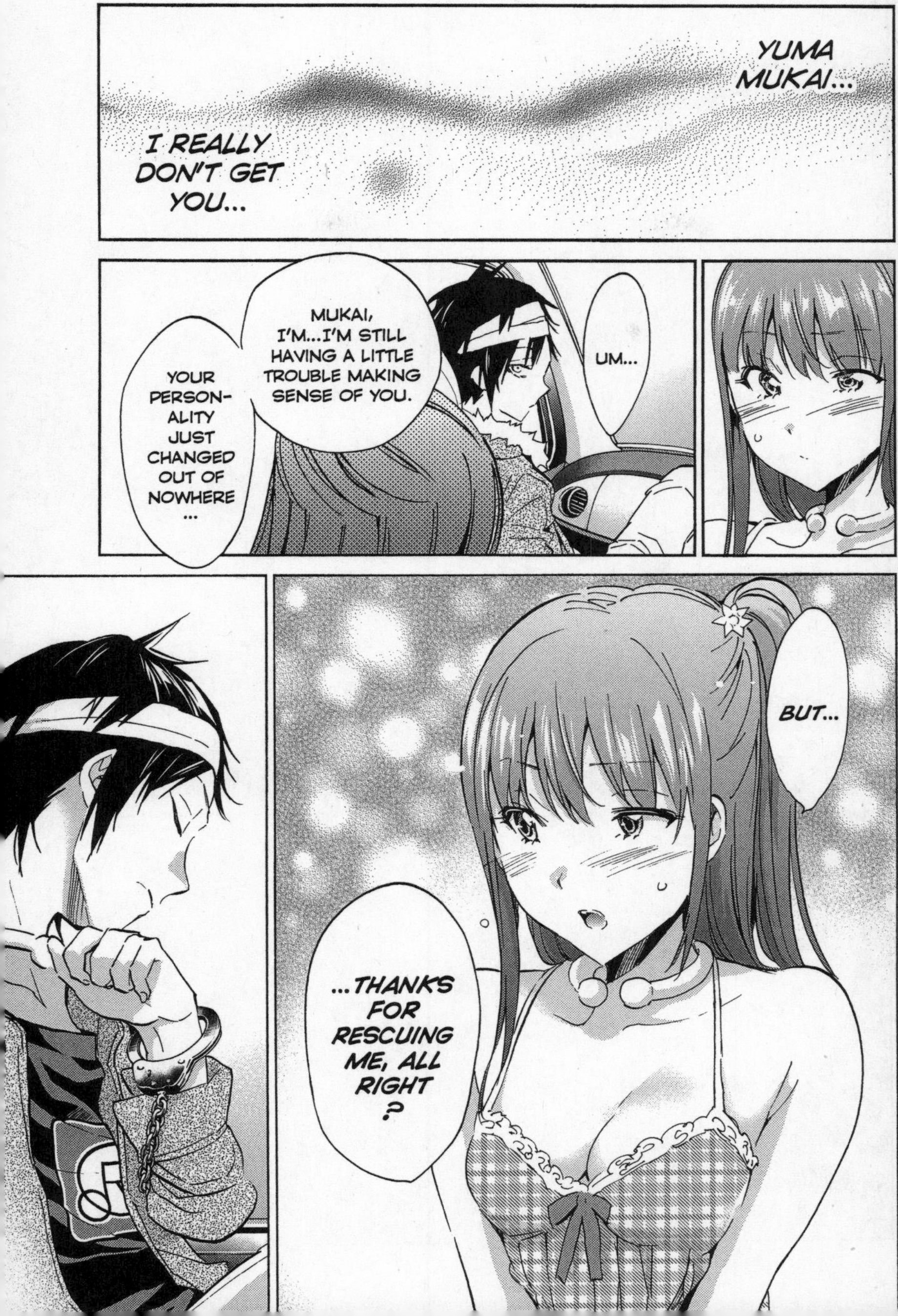
YUMA MUKAI...
I REALLY DON'T GET YOU...
UM...
MUKAI, I'M...I'M STILL HAVING A LITTLE TROUBLE MAKING SENSE OF YOU.
YOUR PERSON-ALITY JUST CHANGED OUT OF NOWHERE...
BUT...
...THANKS FOR RESCUING ME, ALL RIGHT?

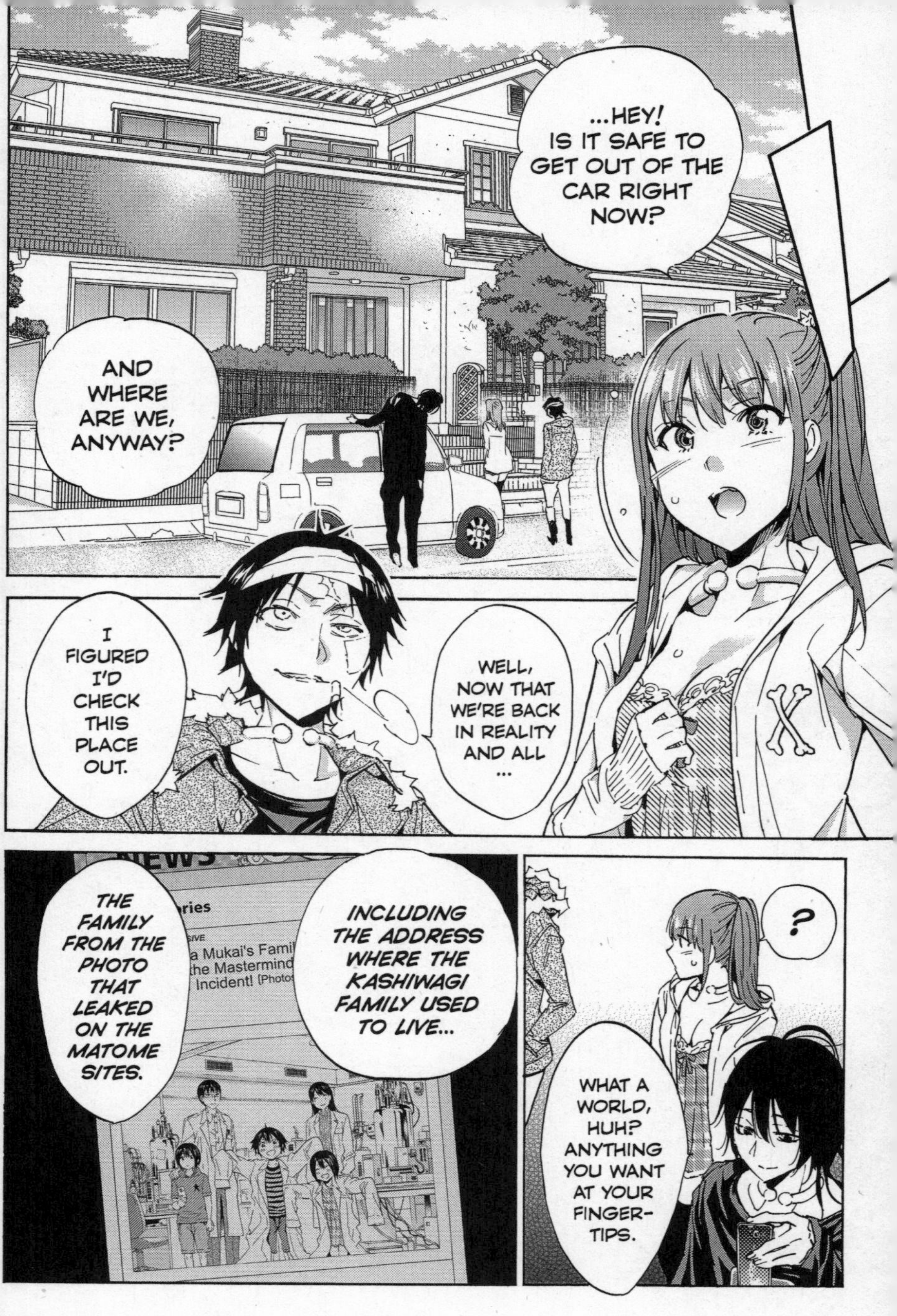
...HEY! IS IT SAFE TO GET OUT OF THE CAR RIGHT NOW?
AND WHERE ARE WE, ANYWAY?
WELL, NOW THAT WE'RE BACK IN REALITY AND ALL ...
I FIGURED I'D CHECK THIS PLACE OUT.
?
WHAT A WORLD, HUH? ANYTHING YOU WANT AT YOUR FINGER-TIPS.
INCLUDING THE ADDRESS WHERE THE KASHIWAGI FAMILY USED TO LIVE...
THE FAMILY FROM THE PHOTO THAT LEAKED ON THE MATOME SITES.

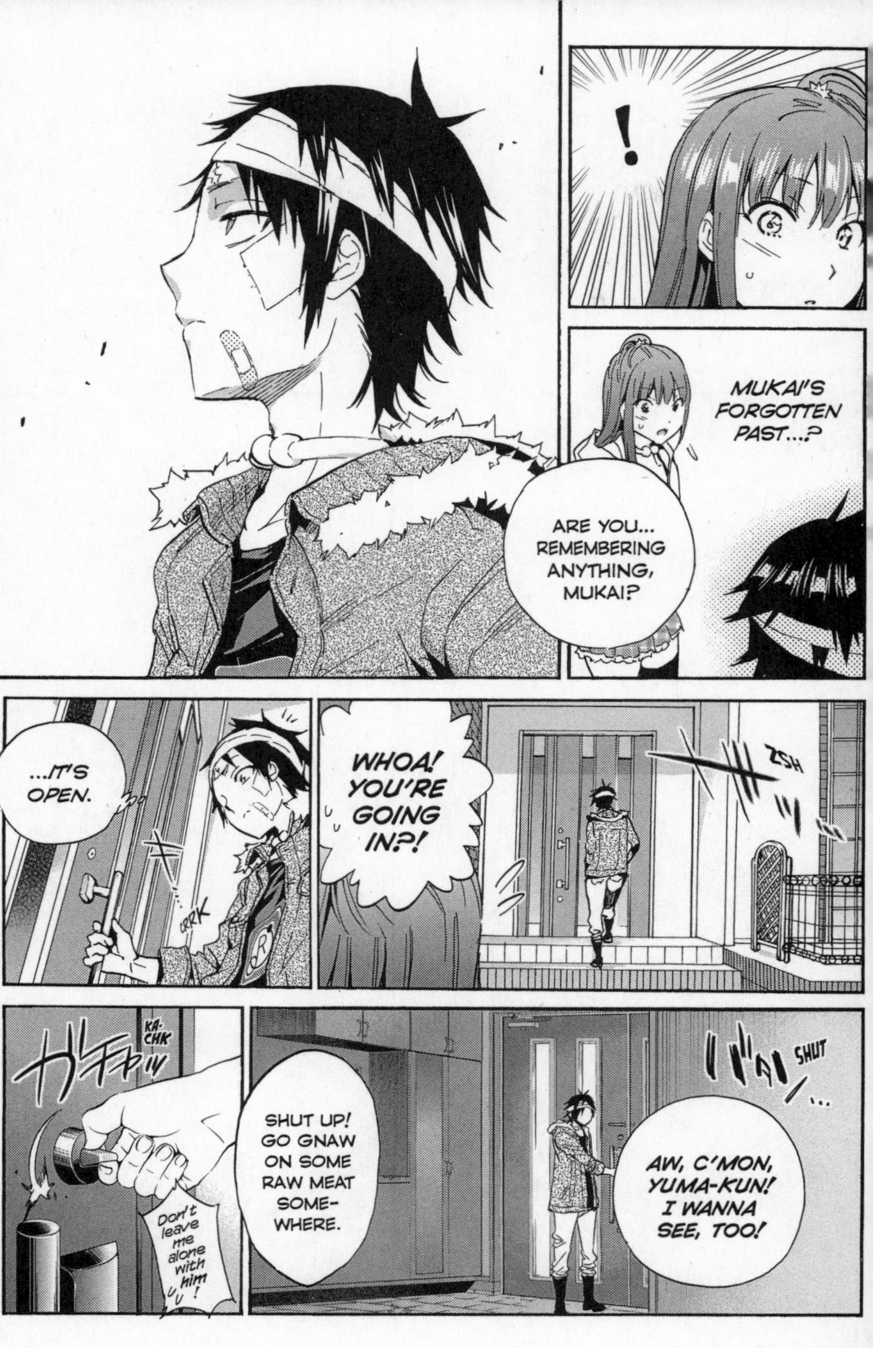
!
MUKAI'S FORGOTTEN PAST...?
ARE YOU... REMEMBERING ANYTHING, MUKAI?
ZSH
WHOA! YOU'RE GOING IN?!
...IT'S OPEN.
CRRK
SHUT
AW, C'MON, YUMA-KUN! I WANNA SEE, TOO!
SHUT UP! GO GNAW ON SOME RAW MEAT SOME-WHERE.
KA-CHK
Don't leave me alone with him!

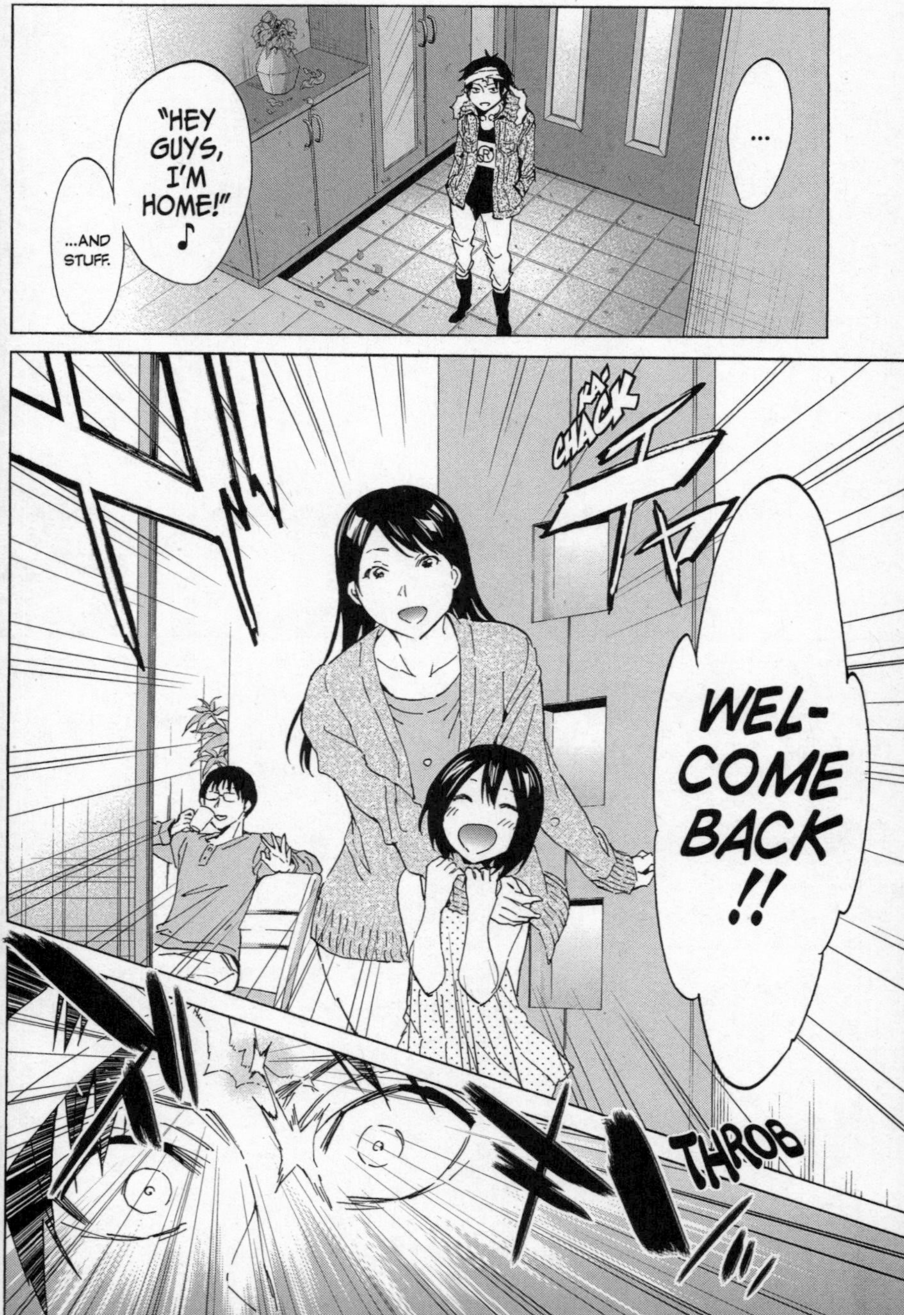
...
"HEY GUYS, I'M HOME!" ♪
...AND STUFF.
KA-CHACK
WEL-COME BACK!!
THROB

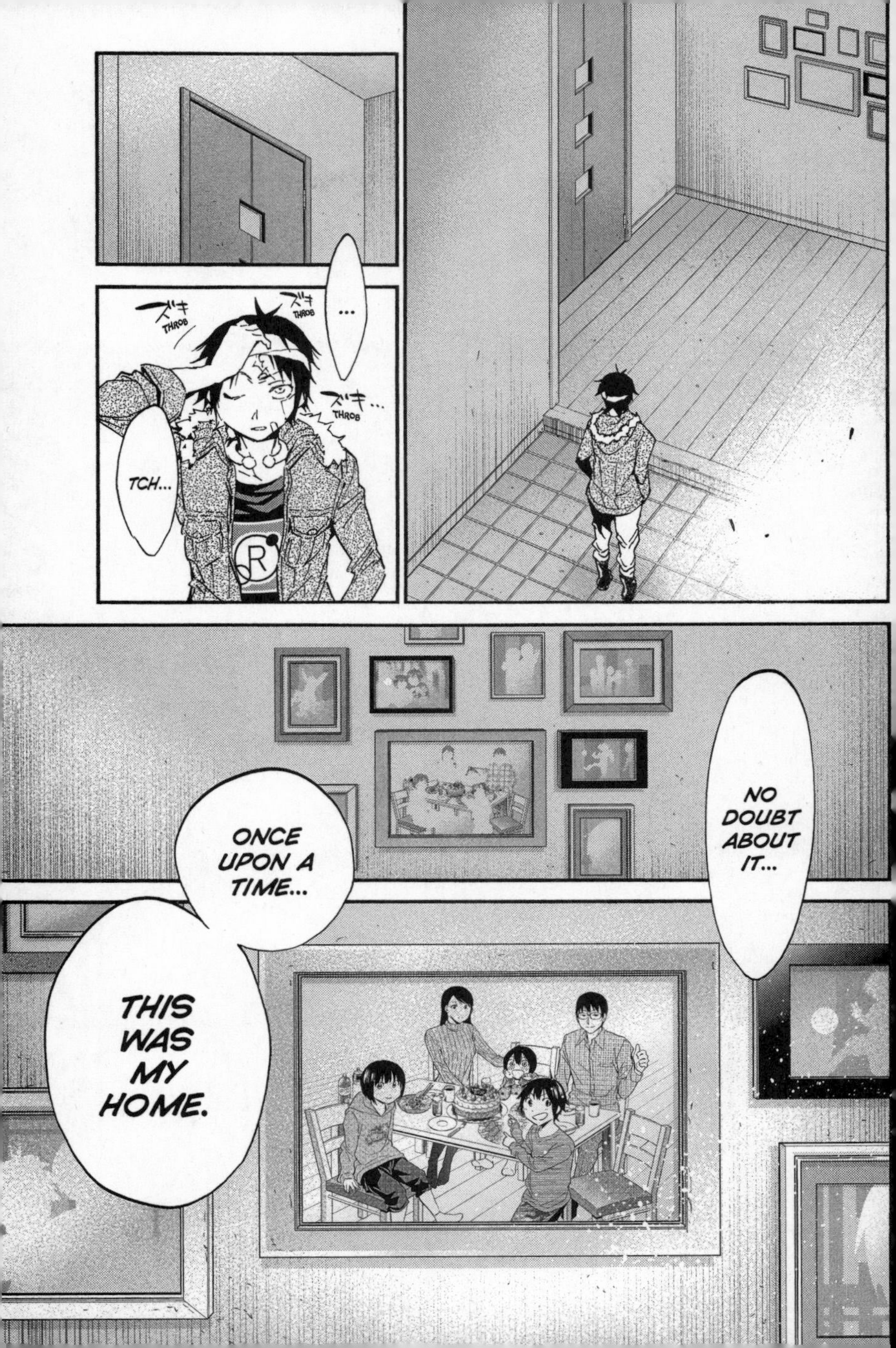
...
ズキ THROB
ズキ THROB
ズキ... THROB
TCH...
NO DOUBT ABOUT IT...
ONCE UPON A TIME...
THIS WAS MY HOME.

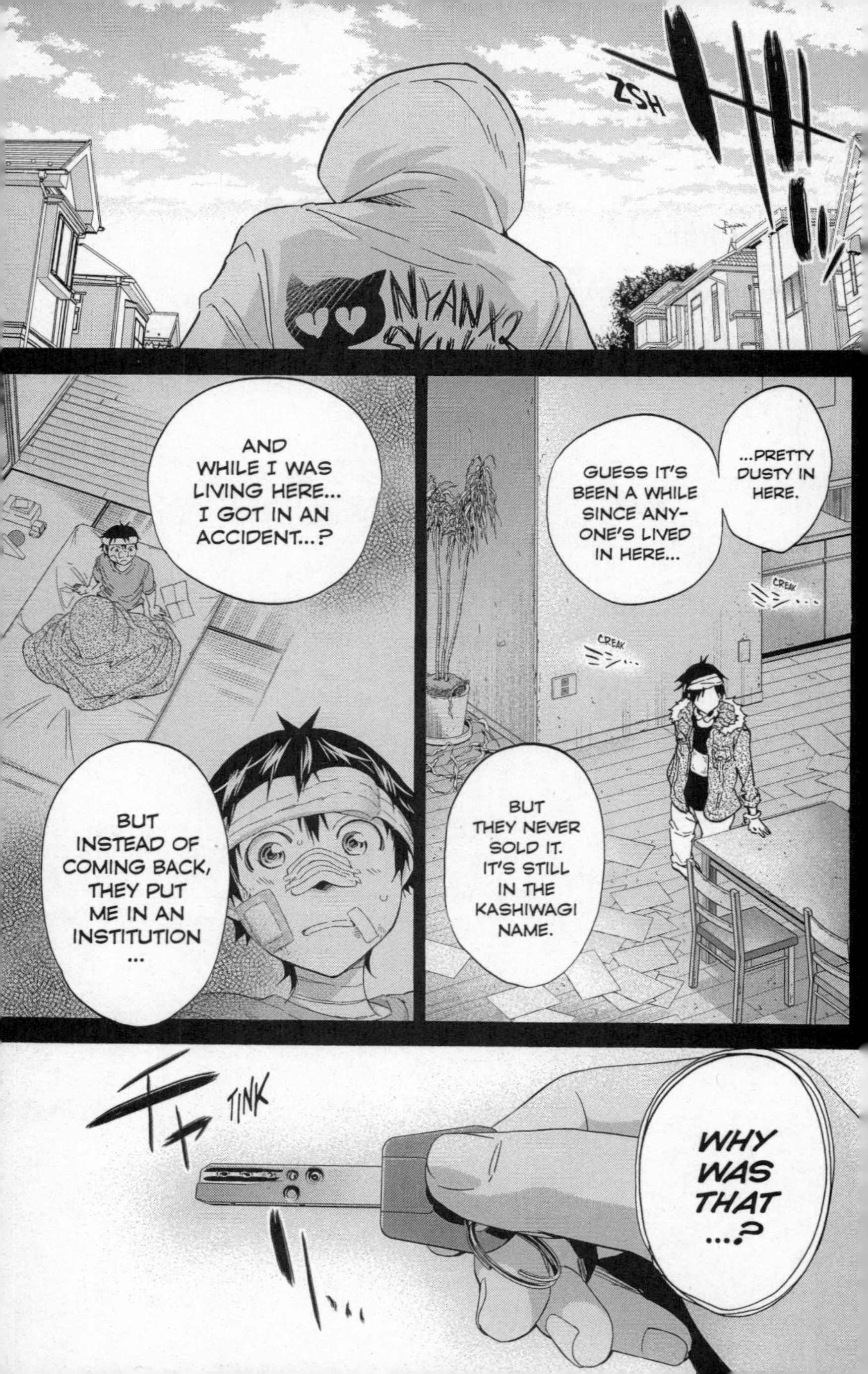
ZSH
...PRETTY DUSTY IN HERE.
GUESS IT'S BEEN A WHILE SINCE ANY-ONE'S LIVED IN HERE...
CREAK
CREAK
BUT THEY NEVER SOLD IT. IT'S STILL IN THE KASHIWAGI NAME.
AND WHILE I WAS LIVING HERE... I GOT IN AN ACCIDENT...?
BUT INSTEAD OF COMING BACK, THEY PUT ME IN AN INSTITUTION ...
TINK
WHY WAS THAT ...?

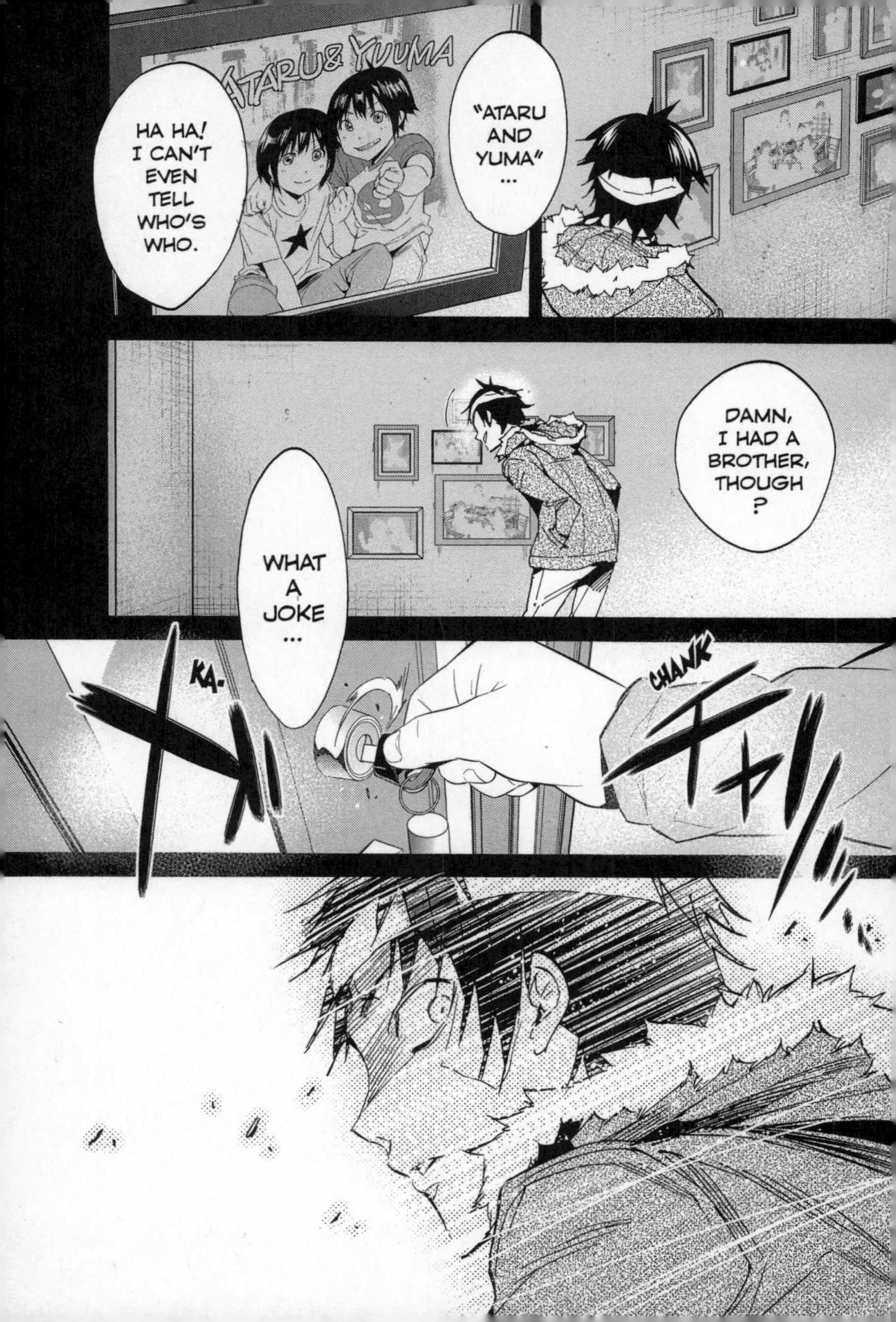
"ATARU AND YUMA" ...
ATARU& YUUMA
HA HA! I CAN'T EVEN TELL WHO'S WHO.
DAMN, I HAD A BROTHER, THOUGH?
WHAT A JOKE ...
KA-
CHANK

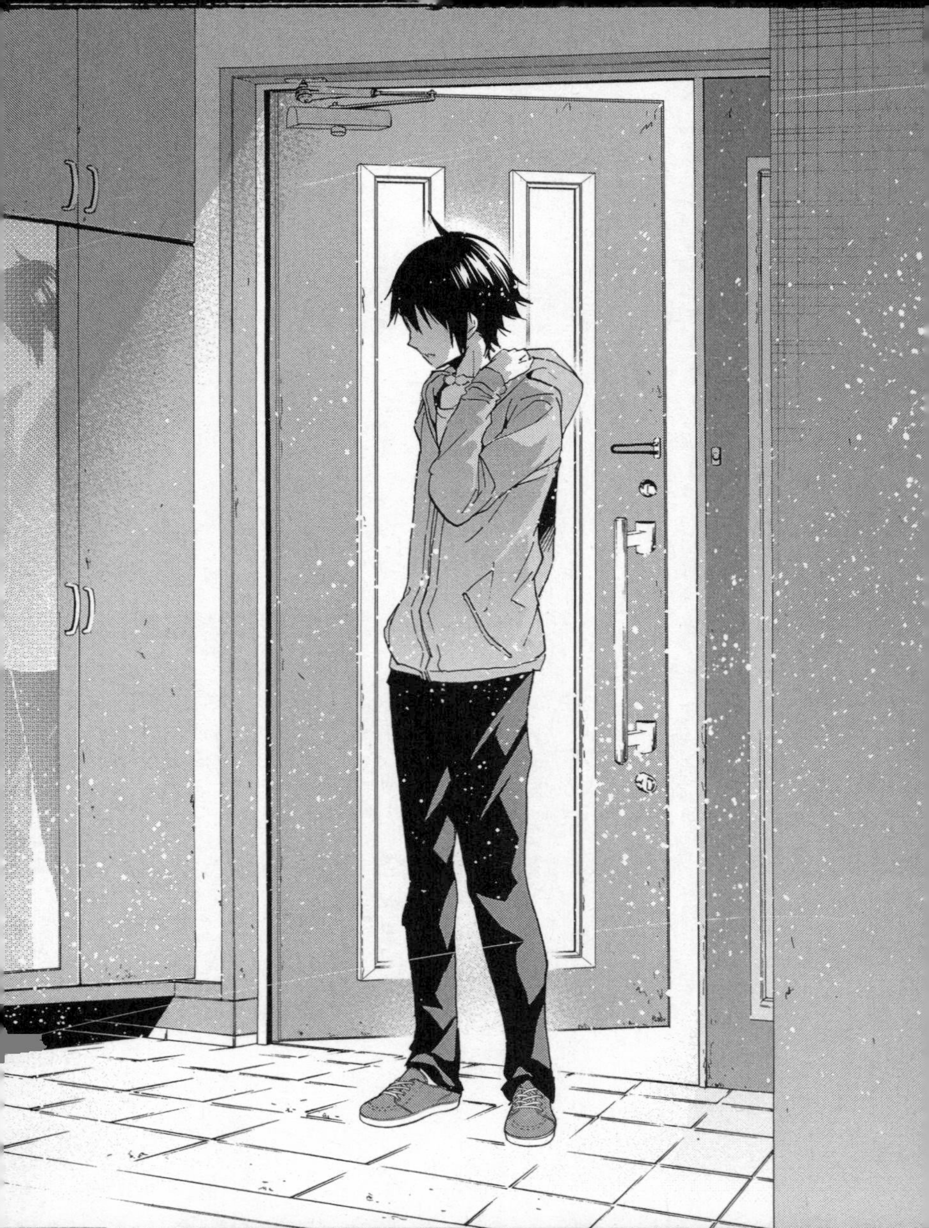

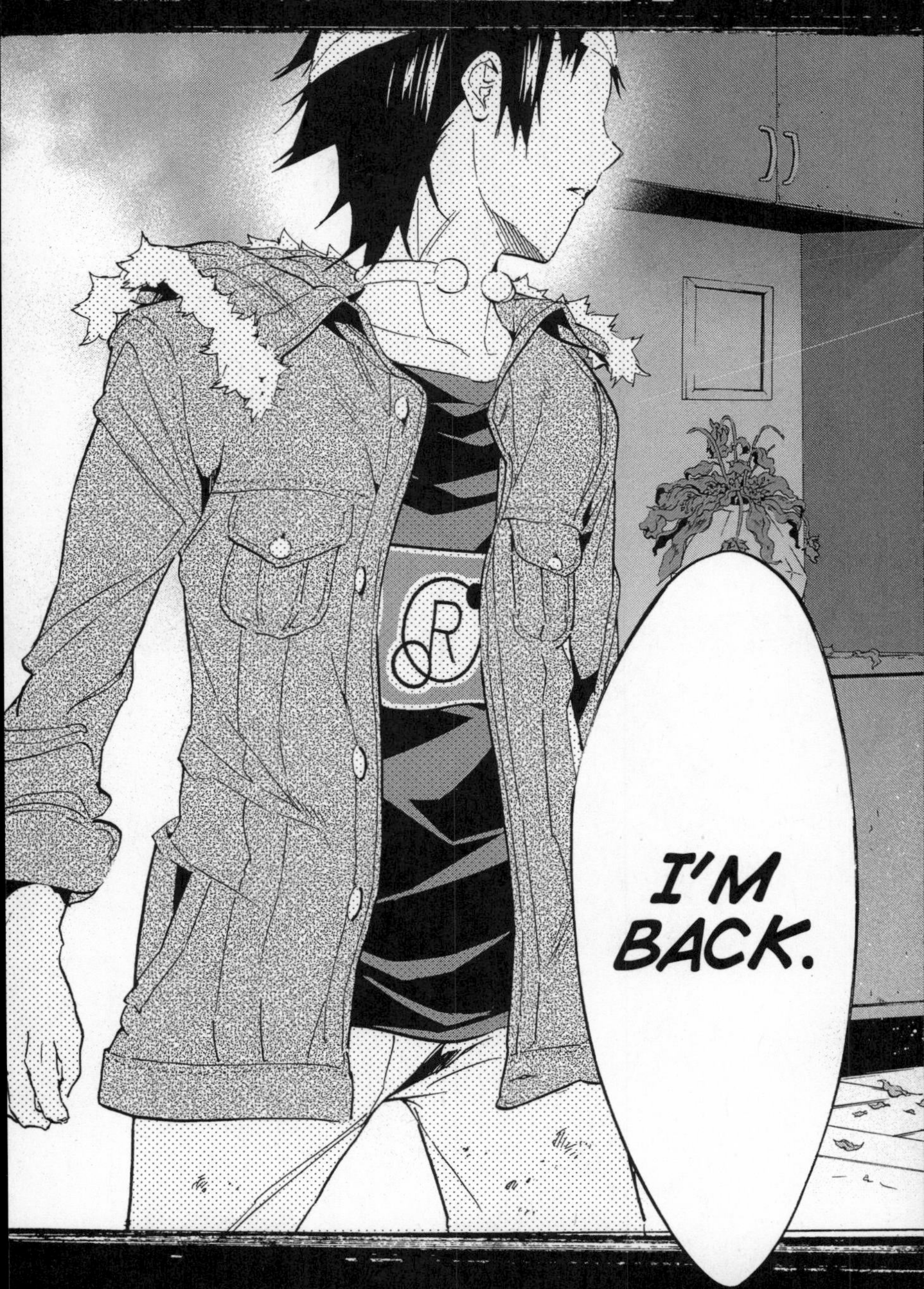
I'M BACK.

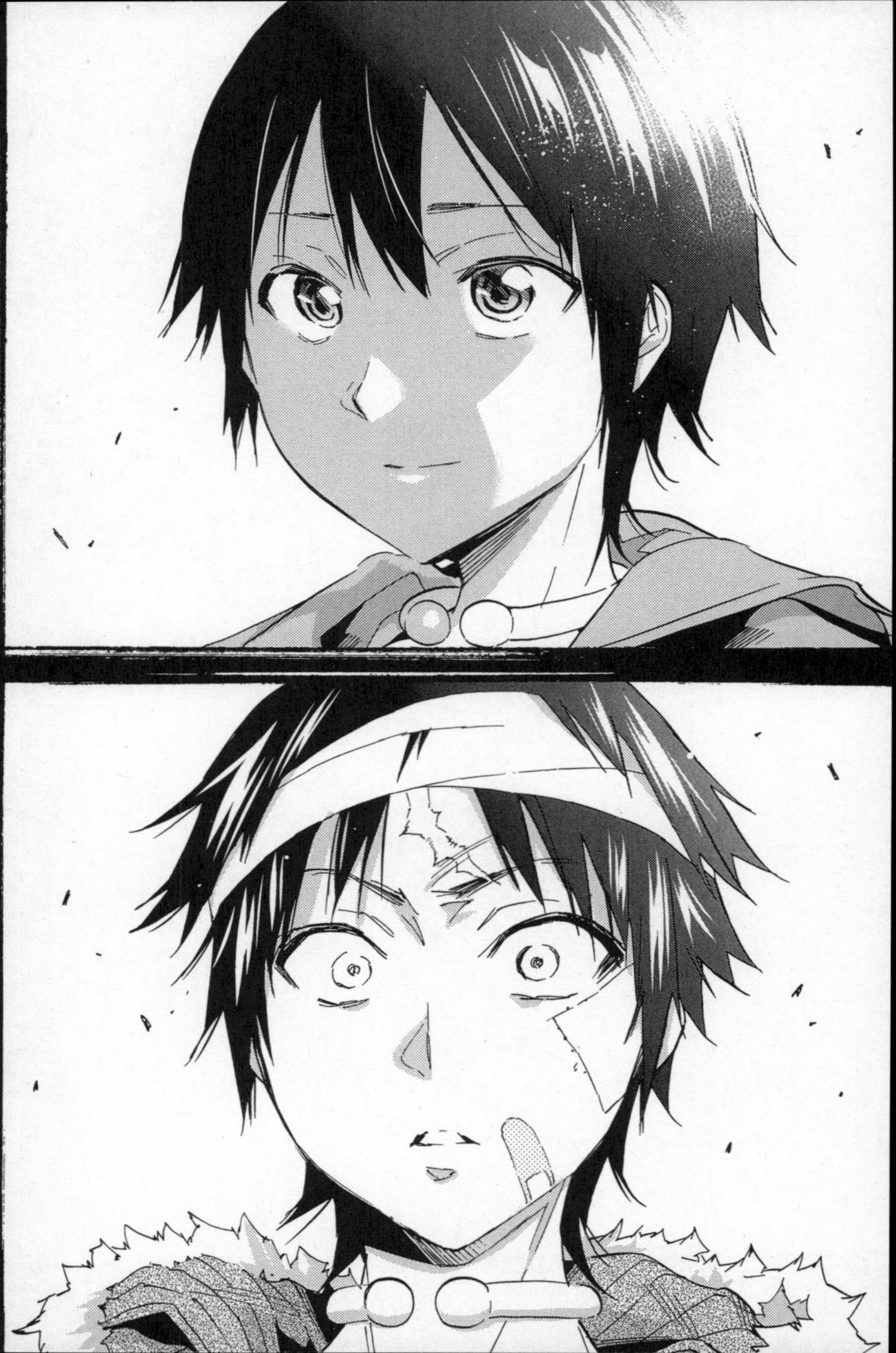

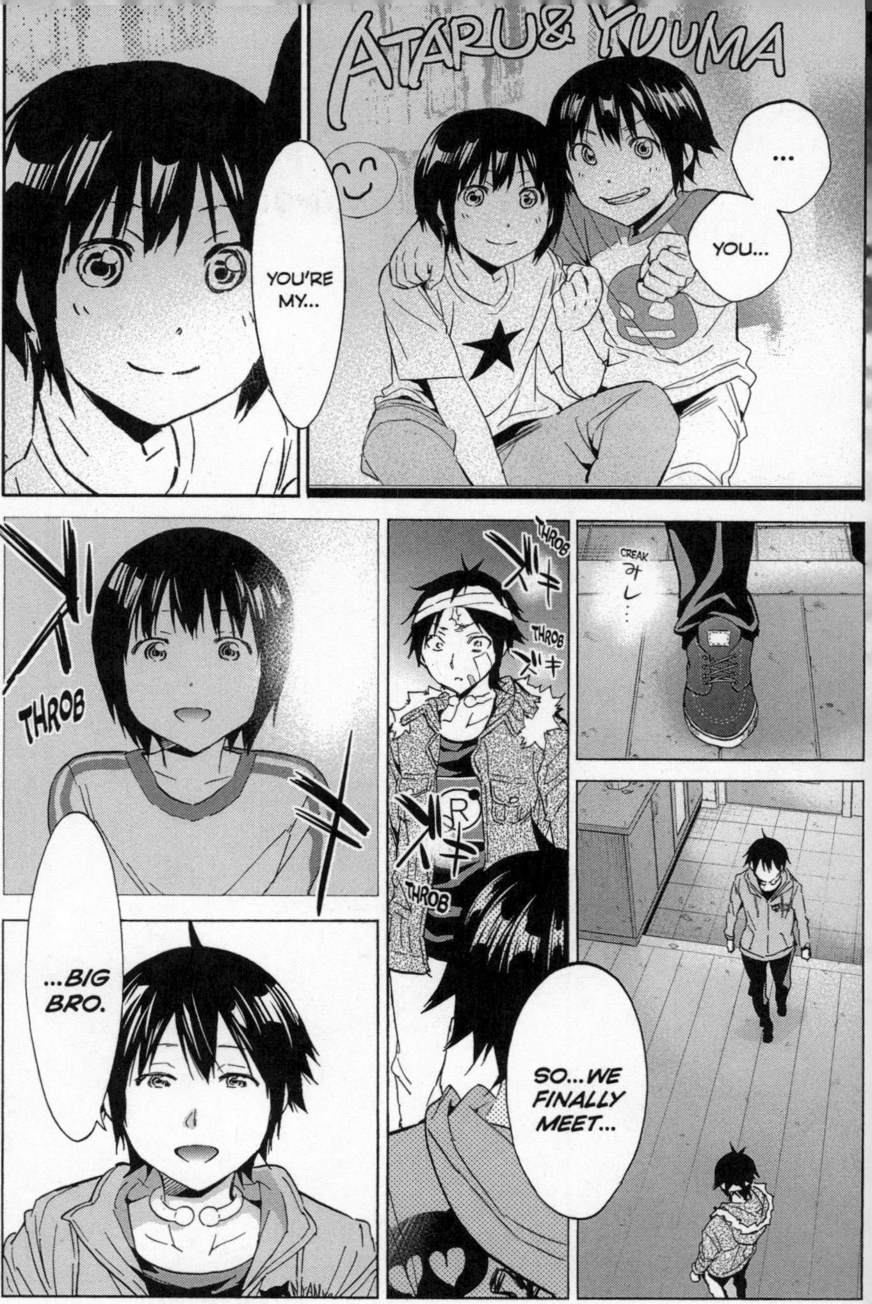
ATARU& YUUMA
...
YOU...
YOU'RE MY...
CREAK
みし…
THROB
THROB
THROB
SO...WE FINALLY MEET...
THROB
...BIG BRO.

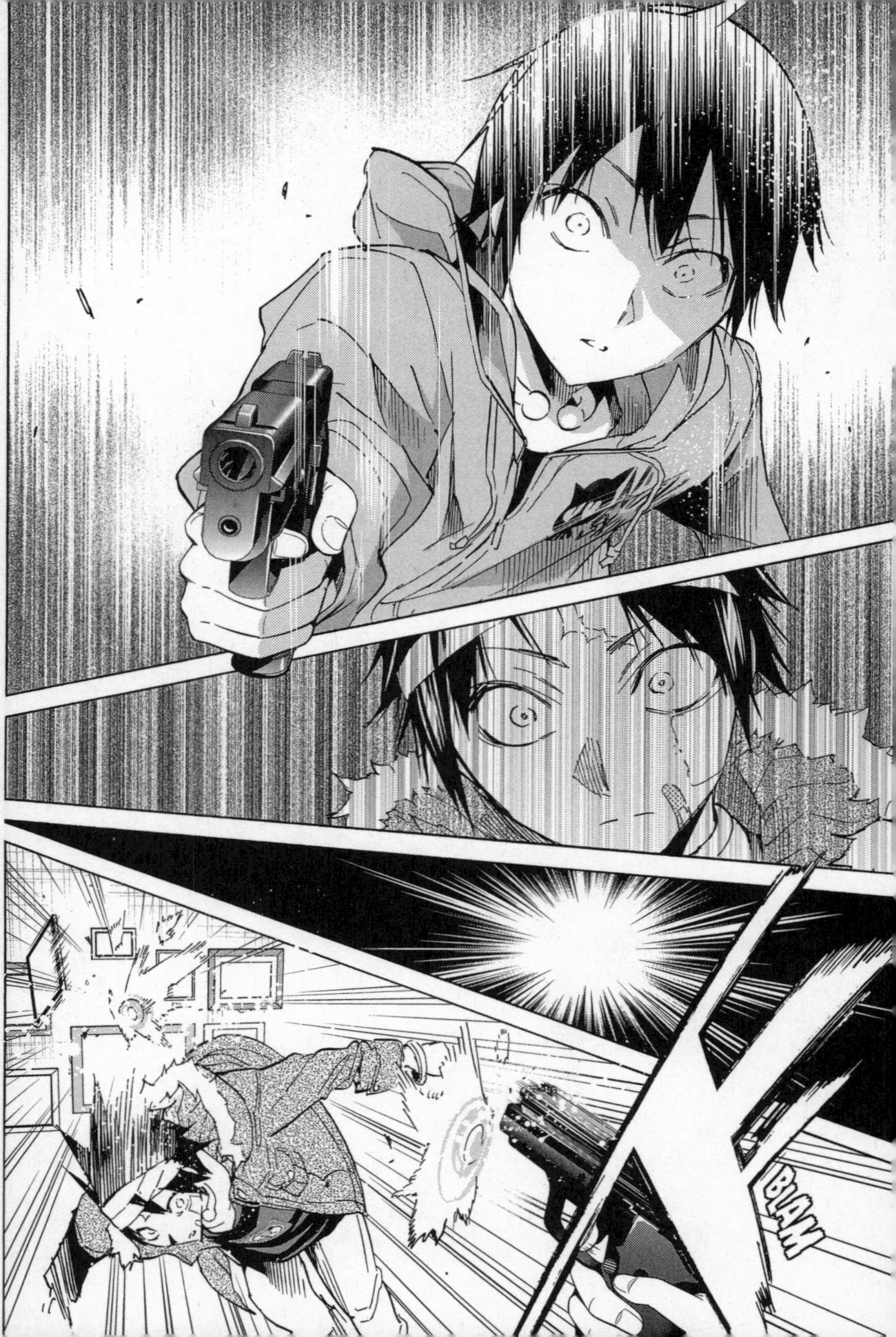
BLAM

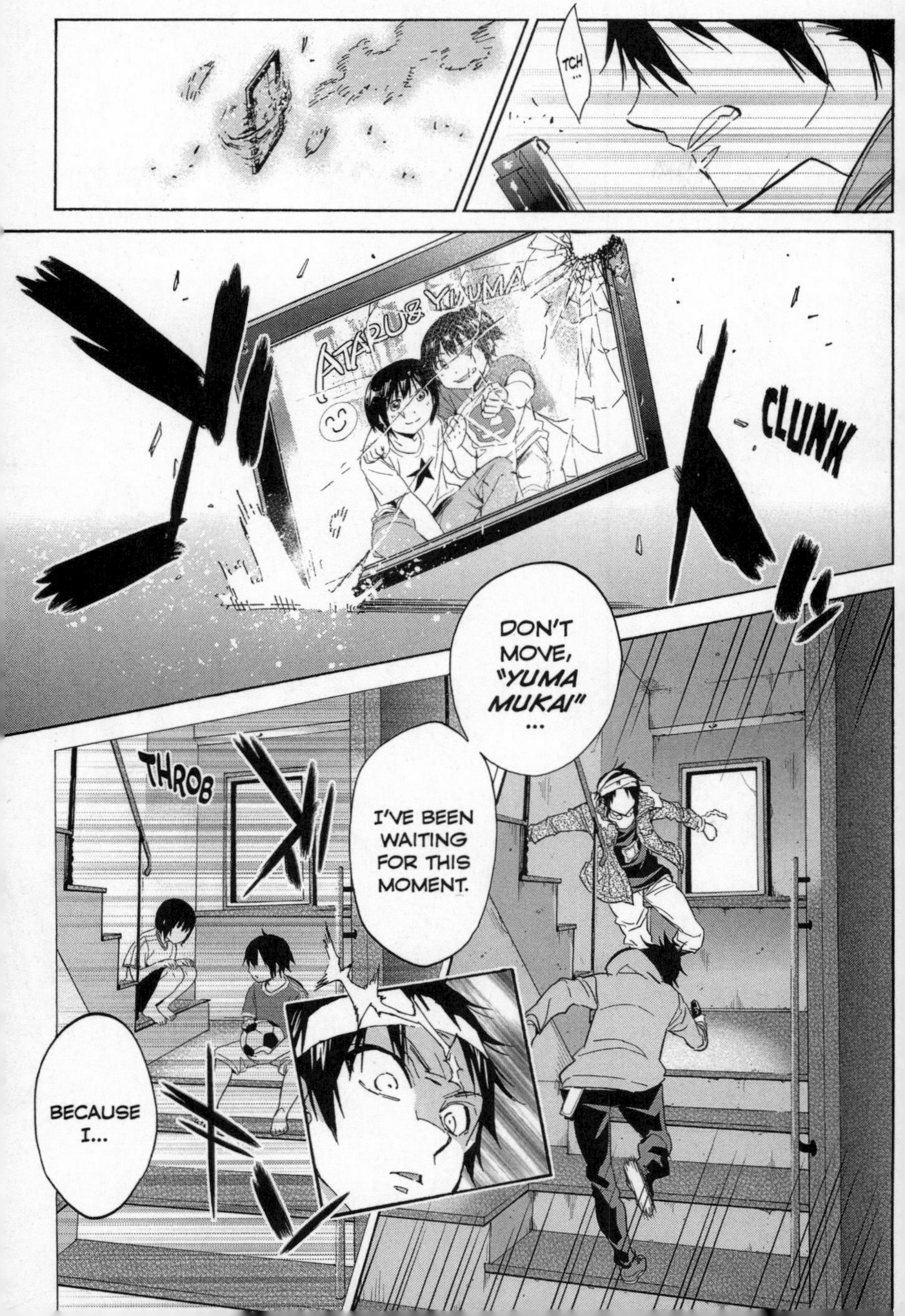
TCH...
CLUNK
DON'T MOVE, "YUMA MUKAI"...
I'VE BEEN WAITING FOR THIS MOMENT.
THROB
BECAUSE I...

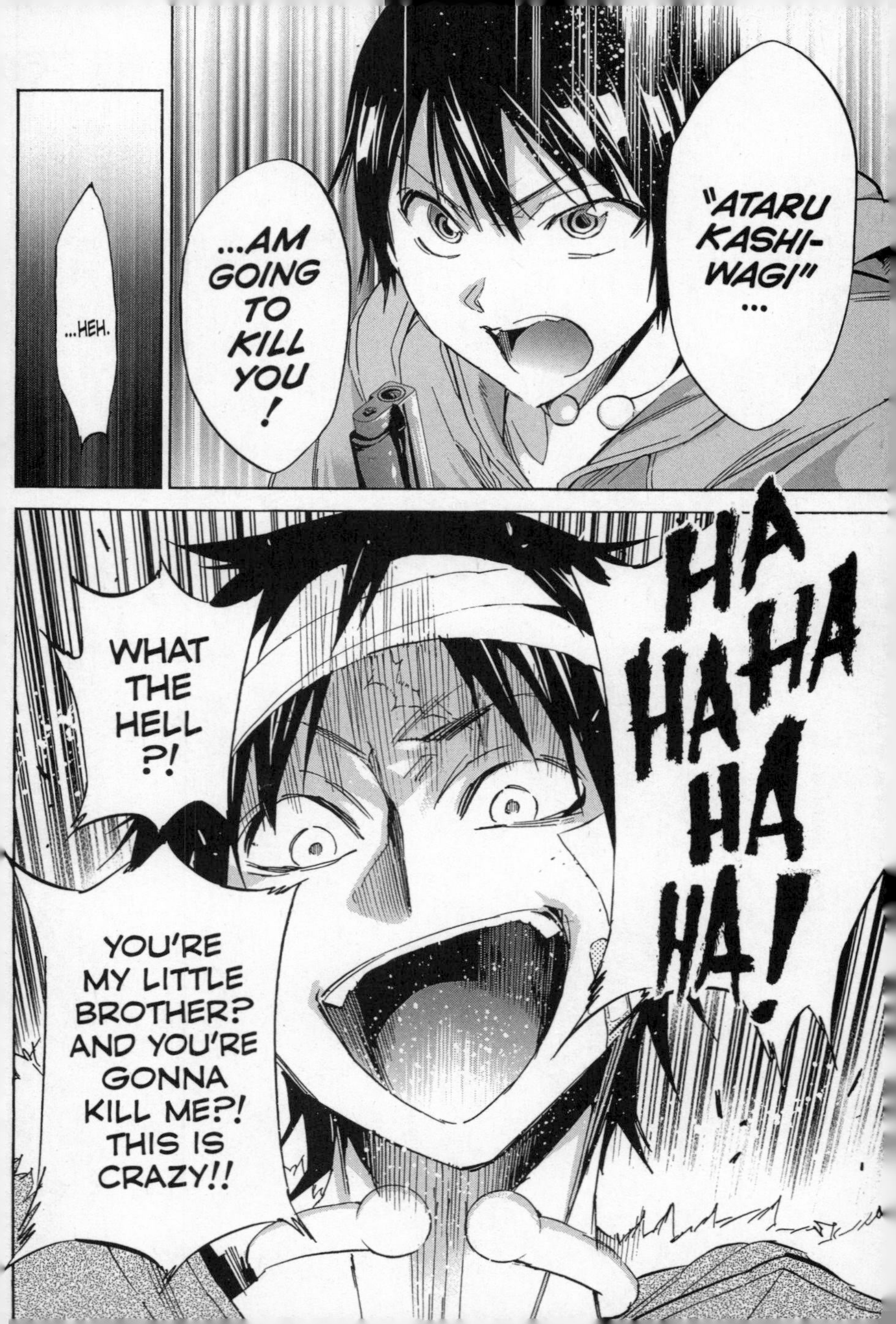
"ATARU KASHIWAGI"...
...AM GOING TO KILL YOU!
...HEH.
HA HA HA HA HA HA HA HA!
WHAT THE HELL?!
YOU'RE MY LITTLE BROTHER? AND YOU'RE GONNA KILL ME?! THIS IS CRAZY!!

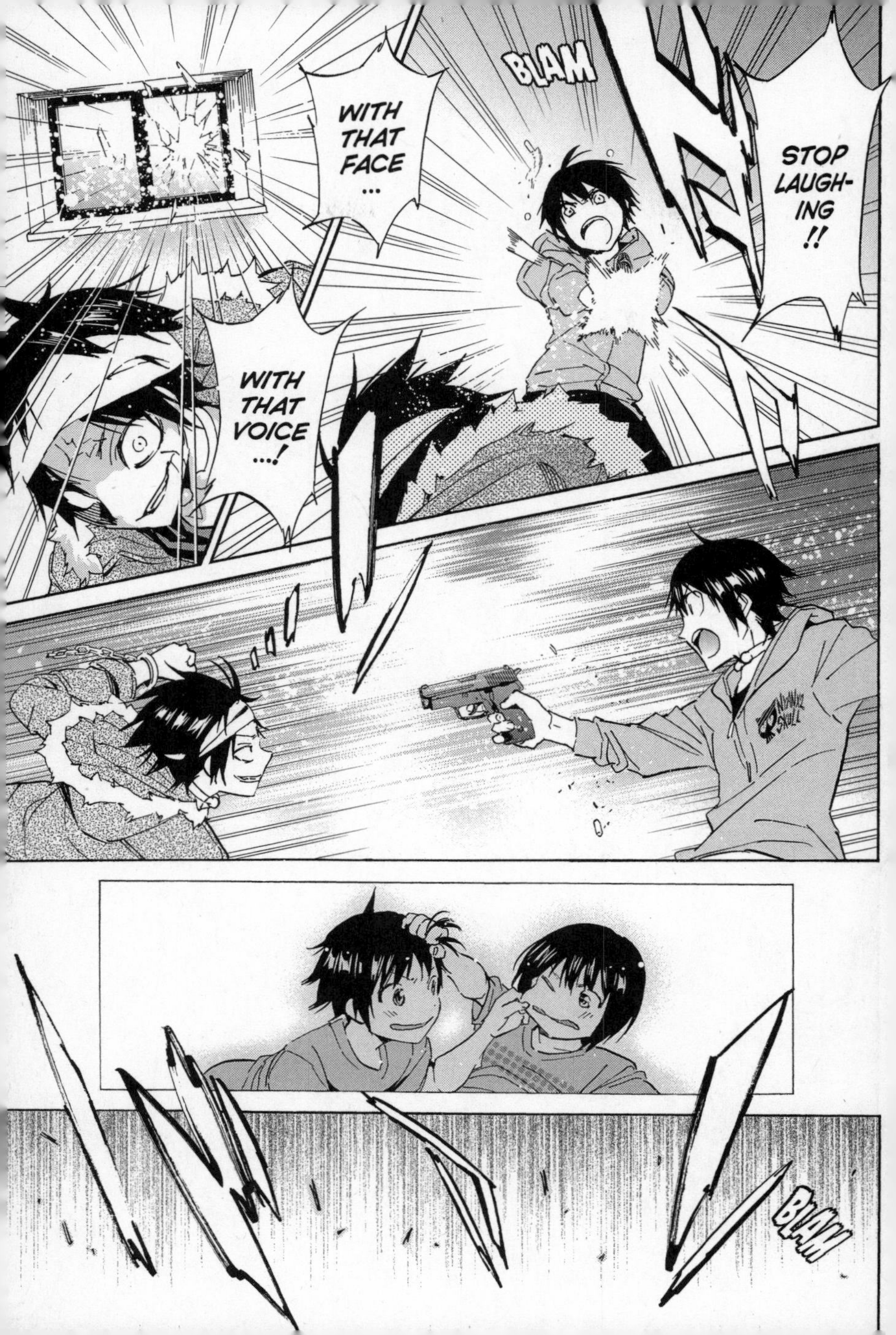
BLAM
STOP LAUGH-ING!!
WITH THAT FACE...
WITH THAT VOICE...!
BLAM

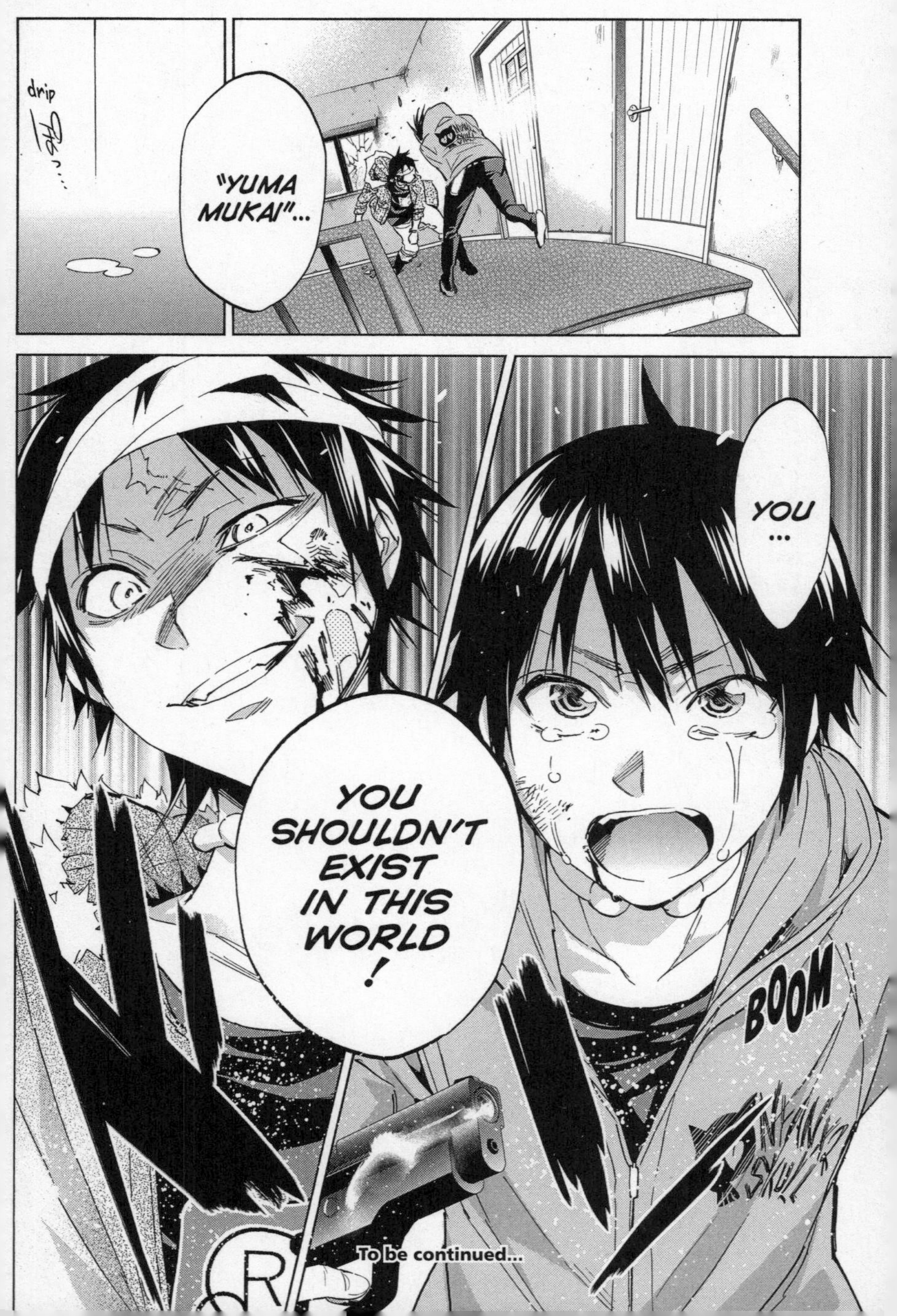
"YUMA MUKAI"...
drip
YOU ...
YOU SHOULDN'T EXIST IN THIS WORLD!
BOOM
To be continued...

Meanwhile, back in the car with Mizuki and Ayame...

...
ゴオオオオ
VROOM
...
...
We're seriously buying more meat!?
...
IS RAW MEAT REALLY THAT APPETIZING?
...UH-HUH.
...OH.
...
DO YOU EAT YAKINIKU OR ANYTHING?
IF IT'S COOKED, I PUKE IT ALL UP...
...OH.
ゴオオオオオ
VROOM
...

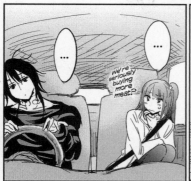

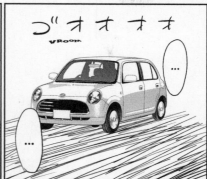

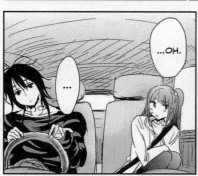

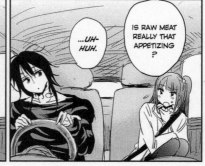

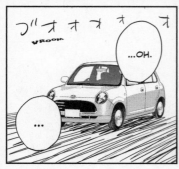

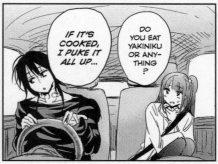

Blehh

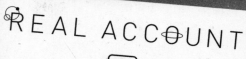

REAL ACCOUNT

Shizumu Watanabe   **Okushou**

STAFF
Shotaro Kunimoto
Iyo Mori
Minato Fuma
Nyan-Nyan Okeishi
Mio Otsuka

HELP STAFF
Yushi Takayama

EDITORS
Kazuhiko Otoguro
Sho Igarashi
Hideki Morooka
(Japanese GN)

JAPANESE COVER DESIGN
Tadashi Hisamochi
(HIVE)

Artist:
Shizumu Watanabe
Twitter account: @shizumukun
The game that kicks off this volume is
a departure from before. It's all about
running, running, and more running!
I'm drawing this in the hope that it
develops into something that can go
in all kinds of directions and be fun in
lots of different ways. Hope you'll join
me for the ride!

Author:
Okushou
Twitter account: @okushou
We live in an era where even grade-
schoolers have Twitter accounts and
personal blogs. Thinking about that,
who do you think's the youngest
Twitter user out there? Maybe five or
six years old? You think he's tweeting
"Snacktime!" or something?

Derp Marbles behind
Close-up
Someone holding Mask
With movement

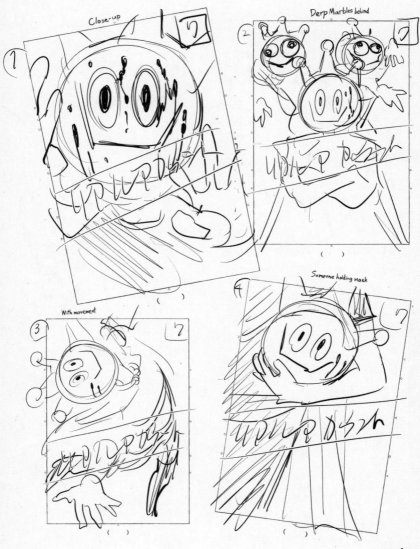

Four sketches for the Volume 7 cover. Sketch 1 was accepted. Marble-kun makes his cover debut out of nowhere.

渡辺静

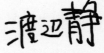

-Shizumu Watanabe

Since this was first released in January...

MARBLE FUKUWARAI

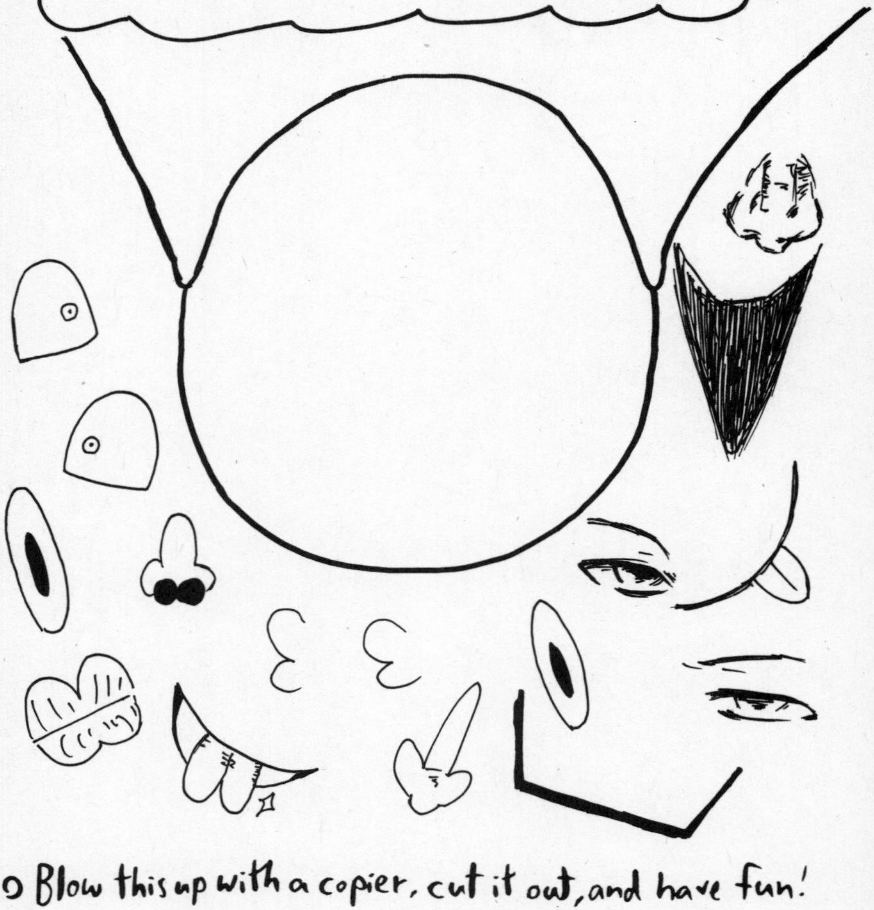

○ Blow this up with a copier, cut it out, and have fun!

※ This is definitely not me getting lazy this volume. By: Okushou

Translation Notes

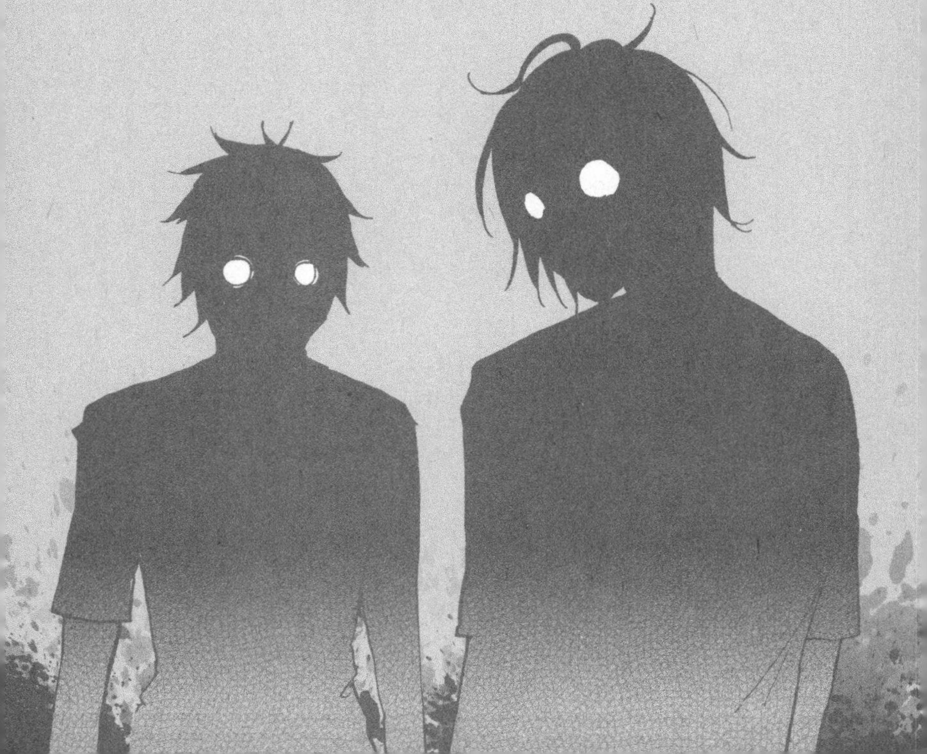

PAGE 34

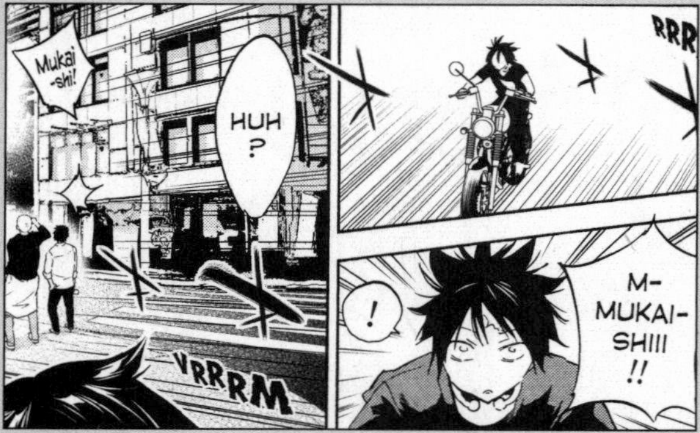
RRR
!
M-MUKAI-SHIII !!
Mukai -shi!
HUH ?
VRRRM

-SHI

-Shi is a Japanese honorific (like -san, -kun, and -chan) added to the end of a person's name to express respect. This honorific is typically used for men, but it is not strictly limited by gender.

PAGE 62

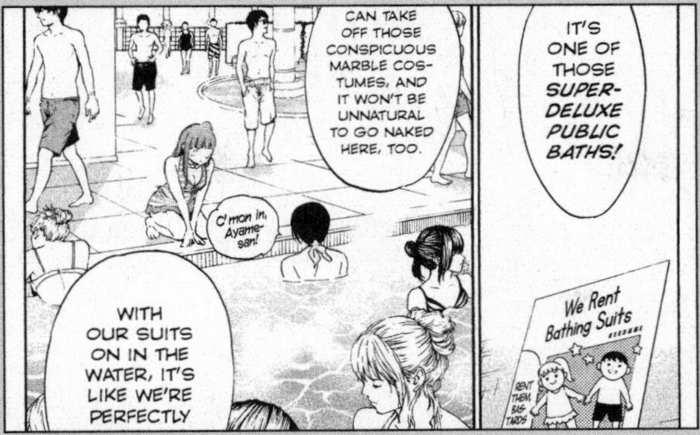

IT'S ONE OF THOSE SUPER-DELUXE PUBLIC BATHS!
We Rent Bathing Suits
RENT THEM, BAS-TARDS
CAN TAKE OFF THOSE CONSPICUOUS MARBLE COS-TUMES, AND IT WON'T BE UNNATURAL TO GO NAKED HERE, TOO.
C'mon in, Ayame-san!
WITH OUR SUITS ON IN THE WATER, IT'S LIKE WE'RE PERFECTLY

SUPER-DELUXE PUBLIC BATHS

Public bathing is a key part of Japanese culture, and so there are various venues for public bathing available in Japan. Besides *onsen* (hot springs), which most anime/manga fans may already be familiar with, the most common and accessible form of public bathing is the *sento. Sento* are basic indoor bathing facilities. They usually include no frills—just an entrance/reception area, changing room, and the baths themselves. But around the mid-80s, deluxe facilities called *suupaa sento* started to pop up across Japan. Some of the main differences are the inclusion of separate areas for food or primping, different types of baths like Jacuzzis, and having locations that are usually along highways or more on the outskirts of a neighborhood or town.

PAGE 100

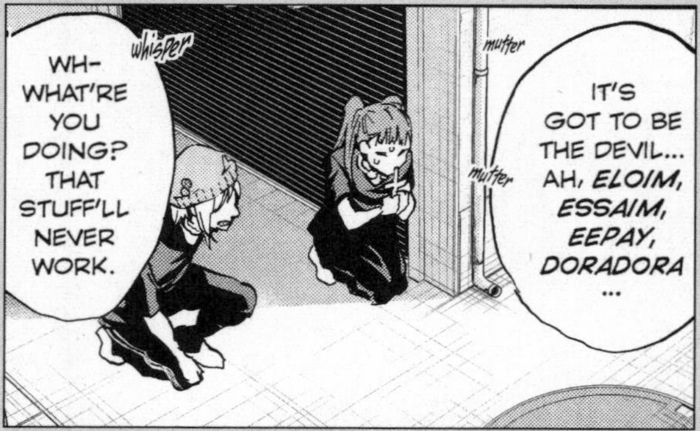
WH- WHAT'RE YOU DOING? THAT STUFF'LL NEVER WORK.
whisper
mutter
mutter
IT'S GOT TO BE THE DEVIL... AH, *ELOIM, ESSAIM, EEPAY, DORADORA* ...

ELOIM, ESSAIM, EEPAY, DORADORA

Most of what she incants is nonsense, but the "Eloim, Essaim" bit is from the Black Pullet, an 18th-century French book that purports to teach the reader assorted occult magic practices. The phrase gained a presence in Japanese pop culture because the main character of the classic Shigeru Mizuki horror manga *Akuma-kun* intoned it in front of a magic pentacle in order to summon devils to do his bidding. The second half of her incantation are names for hands in mahjong. *Eepay* is the Japanese name for a double run or pure double chow, and *doradora* is when two dora tiles increase the han value by two. These were included in the spell because it has been often noted that the names for many moves and hands in mahjong sound like incantations to Japanese ears.

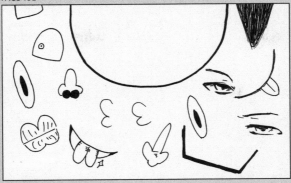

FUKUWARAI

Fukuwarai, a game traditionally played around New Years in Japan, has the same basic concept as Pin the Tail on the Donkey. Blindfolded players are tasked with putting facial parts on a blank face, then everyone laughs at the zany results.

INUYASHIKI

A superhero like none you've ever seen, from the creator of "Gantz"!

Ichiro Inuyashiki is down on his luck. He looks much older than his 58 years, his children despise him, and his wife thinks he's a useless coward. So when he's diagnosed with stomach cancer and given three months to live, it seems the only one who'll miss him is his dog.

Then a blinding light fills the sky, and the old man is killed... only to wake up later in a body he almost recognizes as his own. Can it be that Ichiro Inuyashiki is no longer human?

comes in extra-large editions with color pages!

Maria
THE VIRGIN WITCH

PURITY AND POWER

As a war to determine the rightful ruler of medieval France ravages the land, the witch Maria decides she will not stand idly by as men kill each other in the name of God and glory. Using her powerful magic, she summons various beasts and demons —even going as far as using a succubus to seduce soldiers into submission under the veil of night— all to stop the needless slaughter. However, after the Archangel Michael puts an end to her meddling, he curses her to lose her powers if she ever gives up her virginity. Will she forgo the forbidden fruit of adulthood in order to bring an end to the merciless machine of war? Available now in print and digitally!

Japan's most powerful spirit medium delves into the ghost world's greatest mysteries!

Story by Kyo Shirodaira, famed author of mystery fiction and creator of *Spiral*, *Blast of Tempest*, and *The Record of a Fallen Vampire*.

Both touched by spirits called yôkai, Kotoko and Kurô have gained unique superhuman powers. But to gain her powers Kotoko has given up an eye and a leg, and Kurô's personal life is in shambles. So when Kotoko suggests they team up to deal with renegades from the spirit world, Kurô doesn't have many other choices, but Kotoko might just have a few ulterior motives...

IN/SPECTRE

STORY BY KYO SHIRODAIRA
ART BY CHASHIBA KATASE

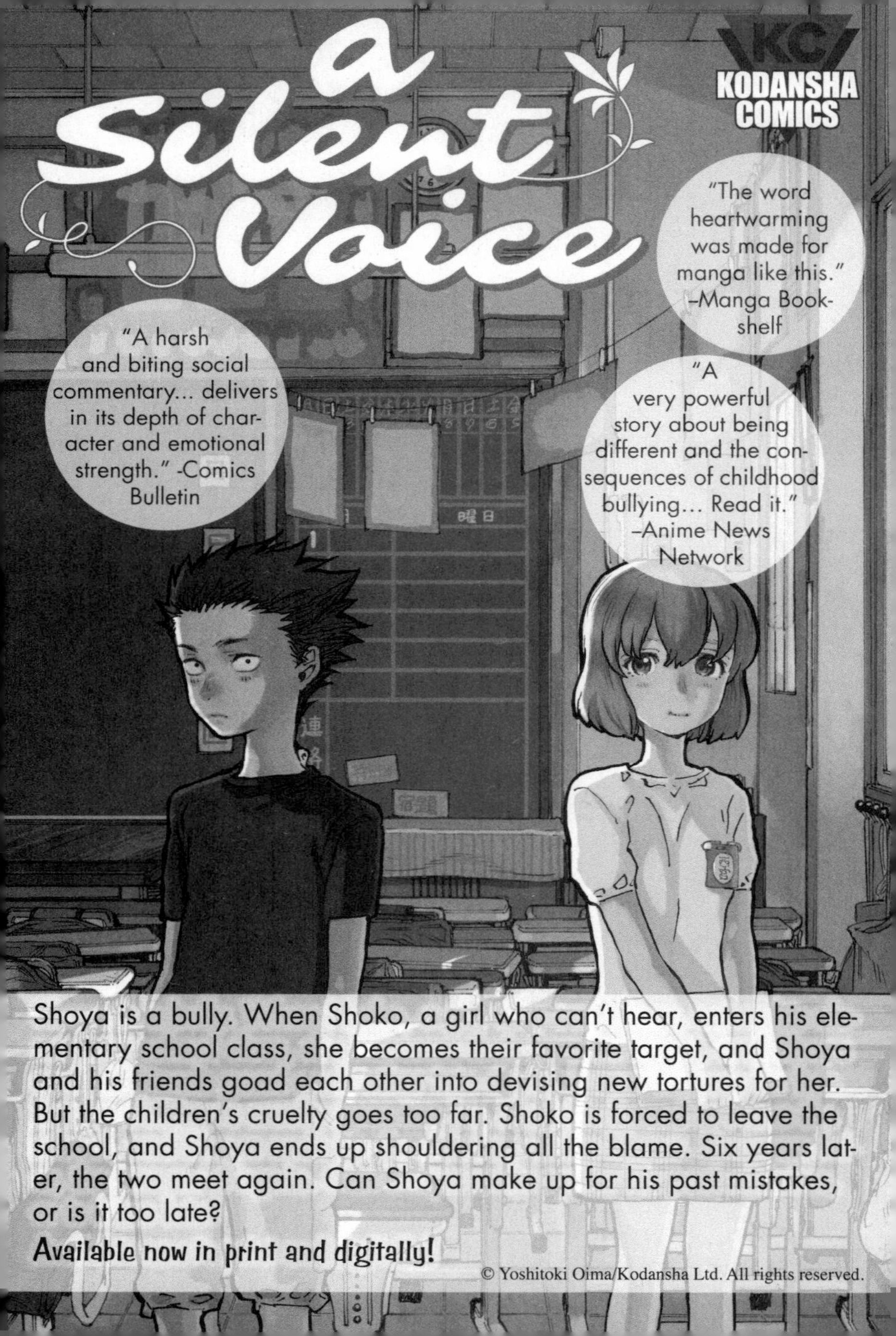
KC
KODANSHA COMICS
a Silent Voice
"The word heartwarming was made for manga like this." –Manga Bookshelf
"A harsh and biting social commentary... delivers in its depth of character and emotional strength." -Comics Bulletin
"A very powerful story about being different and the consequences of childhood bullying... Read it." –Anime News Network
Shoya is a bully. When Shoko, a girl who can't hear, enters his elementary school class, she becomes their favorite target, and Shoya and his friends goad each other into devising new tortures for her. But the children's cruelty goes too far. Shoko is forced to leave the school, and Shoya ends up shouldering all the blame. Six years later, the two meet again. Can Shoya make up for his past mistakes, or is it too late?
Available now in print and digitally!
© Yoshitoki Oima/Kodansha Ltd. All rights reserved.

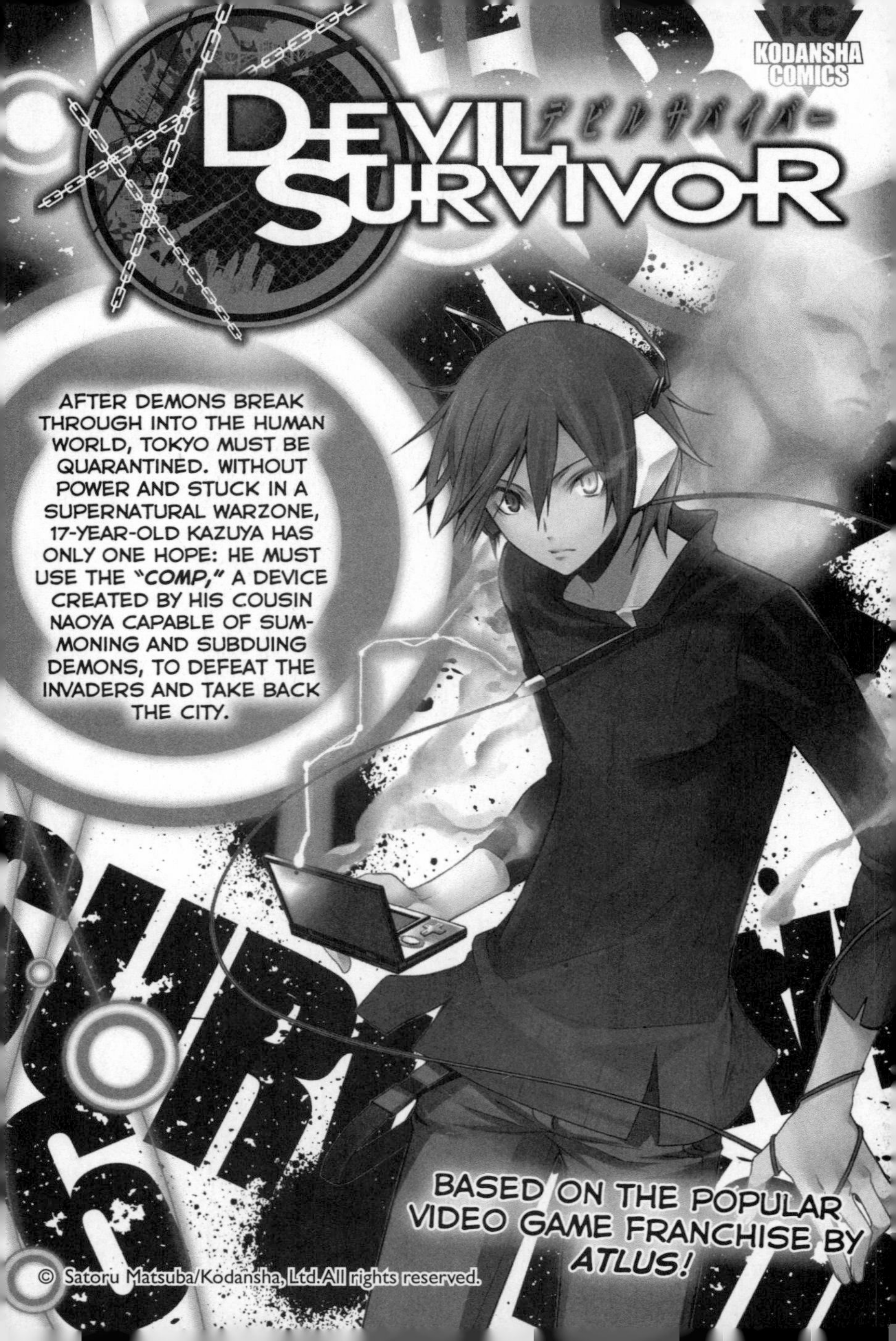
KC
KODANSHA COMICS
DEVIL SURVIVOR
デビルサバイバー
AFTER DEMONS BREAK THROUGH INTO THE HUMAN WORLD, TOKYO MUST BE QUARANTINED. WITHOUT POWER AND STUCK IN A SUPERNATURAL WARZONE, 17-YEAR-OLD KAZUYA HAS ONLY ONE HOPE: HE MUST USE THE "COMP," A DEVICE CREATED BY HIS COUSIN NAOYA CAPABLE OF SUMMONING AND SUBDUING DEMONS, TO DEFEAT THE INVADERS AND TAKE BACK THE CITY.
BASED ON THE POPULAR VIDEO GAME FRANCHISE BY ATLUS!
© Satoru Matsuba/Kodansha, Ltd. All rights reserved.

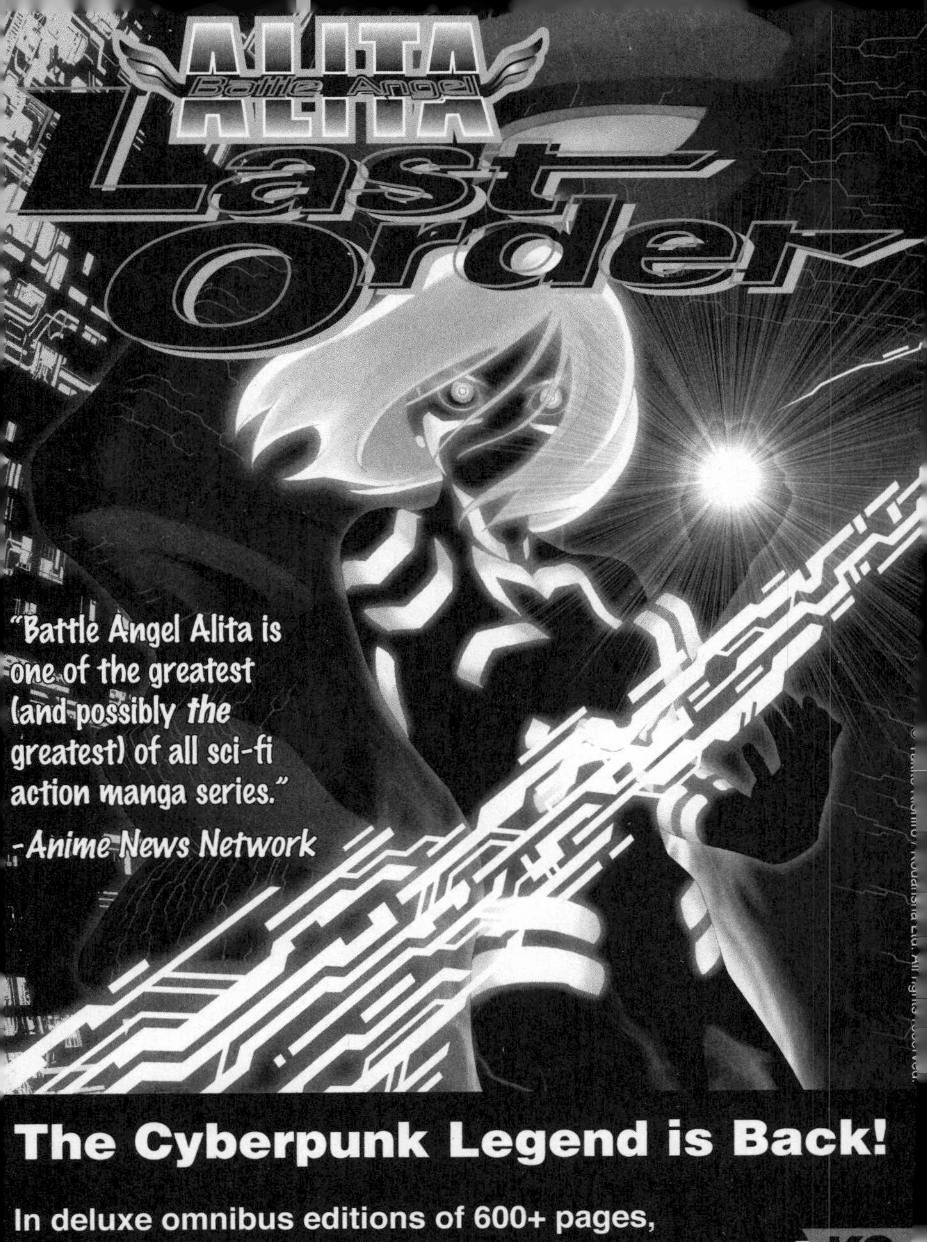
ALITA Battle Angel ALITA
Last Order
"Battle Angel Alita is one of the greatest (and possibly *the* greatest) of all sci-fi action manga series."
-Anime News Network
Kodansha Ltd. All rights reserved.
The Cyberpunk Legend is Back!
In deluxe omnibus editions of 600+ pages, including ALL-NEW original stories by Alita creator Yukito Kishiro!

New action series from Hiroyuki Takei, creator of the classic shonen franchise Shaman King!

In medieval Japan, a bell hanging on the collar is a sign that a cat has a master. Norachiyo's bell hangs from his katana sheath, but he is nonetheless a stray — a ronin. This one-eyed cat samurai travels across a dishonest world, cutting through pretense and deception with his blade.

Nekogahara

STRAY CAT SAMURAI

By
Hiroyuki Takei

H A P P I N E S S

——ハピネス——

By **Shuzo Oshimi**

From the creator of *The Flowers of Evil*

Nothing interesting is happening in Makoto Ozaki's first year of high school. HIs life is a series of quiet humiliations: low-grade bullies, unreliable friends, and the constant frustration of his adolescent lust. But one night, a pale, thin girl knocks him to the ground in an alley and offers him a choice.

Now everything is different. Daylight is searingly bright. Food tastes awful. And worse than anything is the terrible, consuming thirst...

Praise for Shuzo Oshimi's *The Flowers of Evil*

"A shockingly readable story that vividly—one might even say queasily—evokes the fear and confusion of discovering one's own sexuality. Recommended." —The Manga Critic

"A page-turning tale of sordid middle school blackmail." —Otaku USA Magazine

"A stunning new horror manga." —Third Eye Comics

KC

**KODANSHA
COMICS**

A Kodansha Comics Trade Paperback Original.

Published in the United States by Kodansha Comics, an imprint of Kodansha USA Publishing, LLC, New York.

Publication rights for this English edition arranged through Kodansha Ltd., Tokyo.

First published in Japan in 2016 by Kodansha Ltd., Tokyo, as *Real Account* volume 7.

ISBN 978-1-63236-440-1

Printed in the United States of America.

www.kodanshacomics.com

9 8 7 6 5 4 3 2 1

Translation: Kevin Gifford
Lettering: Evan Hayden
Editing: Ajani Oloye
Kodansha Comics edition cover design: Phil Balsman